Rowland Williams, Ellen Cotesworth Williams

The Hebrew Prophets Translated Afresh from the Original

With regard to the Anglican version, and with illustrations for English readers

Rowland Williams, Ellen Cotesworth Williams

The Hebrew Prophets Translated Afresh from the Original
With regard to the Anglican version, and with illustrations for English readers

ISBN/EAN: 9783337037635

Printed in Europe, USA, Canada, Australia, Japan

Cover: Foto ©Lupo / pixelio.de

More available books at **www.hansebooks.com**

THE

HEBREW PROPHETS,

TRANSLATED AFRESH FROM THE ORIGINAL,

WITH REGARD TO THE ANGLICAN VERSION,

AND WITH

ILLUSTRATIONS FOR ENGLISH READERS.

BY THE LATE
ROWLAND WILLIAMS, D.D.
VICAR OF BROAD-CHALKE, WILTS,
SOME TIME FELLOW AND TUTOR OF KING'S COLLEGE, CAMBRIDGE.

VOL. II.

WILLIAMS AND NORGATE:
14, HENRIETTA STREET, COVENT GARDEN, LONDON;
AND 20, SOUTH FREDERICK STREET, EDINBURGH.

1871.

THE

HEBREW PROPHETS.*

THAT IS

THE PREACHERS OF RIGHTEOUSNESS,

AFTER THE ORDER OF THE ANCIENT SCRIPTURE,

WITH THE COMMON VERSION REVISED,

AND THEIR MEANING TRULY EXPLAINED, WITH THE HELP OF

HISTORY AND THE CONTEXT.

BY

ROWLAND WILLIAMS, D.D.

Sacrifice and offering thou didst not desire: mine ears hast thou opened: burnt offering and sin offering hast thou not required. Then said I, Lo, I come: in the volume of the book it is written of me, I delight to do thy will, O my GOD: yea, thy law is within my heart. I have preached righteousness in the great congregation: lo, I have not refrained my lips, O LORD, thou knowest.—*Ps.* xl. 6—10.

QUOD DIE MEO NATALI AUGUST. XVI. MDCCCLVIII. INCEPTUM
ÆTERNUS SOSPITATOR DEUS O. M.
PRO INFINITA SUA GRATIA ET FIDE FELIX FAUSTUMQUE FAXIT
ET IN TOTAM VERITATEM FELICITER PERDUCAT
IN HONOREM NOMINIS ÆTERNI
ET HOMINUM CÆCORUM ILLUMINATIONEM.
AMEN.

---

* Title page found on original MS.

TABLE OF CONTENTS.

	PAGE.
INTRODUCTION TO HABAKKUK	1
VERSION OF HABBAKKUK	21
INTRODUCTION TO ZEPHANIAH	34
VERSION OF ZEPHANIAH	41
INTRODUCTION TO JEREMIAH	54
VERSION OF JEREMIAH	76
VERSION OF EZEKIEL	330
VERSION OF ISAIAH LII. 13—LIII.	341

ERRATA.

Page 11, line 22, *for* denies, *read* devises.
,, 37, line 30, *for* ii. 13, *read* ii. 11.
,, 37, line 32, *for* Isa. xiii., *read* xii.
,, 57, insert as note at beginning of last paragraph, "References to chapters throughout this Introduction are to those of the A.V."
,, 107, note 76, *for* Matt. xx. *read* xxiv.
,, 120, com. line 2, *for* lvii., *read* lviii.
,, 148, note 160, *omit* full stop after " have read," and connect sentences.
,, 161, note 186, *for* desirable, *read* derivable.
,, 185, note 229, *for* 25, *read* 26.
,, 196, note 263, *for* xiv., *read* xxiv.

PREFACE.

IMMEDIATELY after Dr. Williams' death, a hope was expressed in many quarters that what remained in MS. of his Hebrew Prophets might be given to the world with as little delay as possible. In compliance with this desire the present volume is now published, amid mingled emotions of thankfulness and sadness—thankfulness that so much has been left, and that I have been permitted to watch over its publication—sadness that there is no more, and that the master hand has been wanting for its correction. Thus I suppose it must ever be with the editing of a posthumous work, especially when, as in the present case, it is an unfinished work upon which death has set his seal. Those who have been engaged in a like task will know well the sacred feeling with which, under such circumstances, the MS. is first taken up—with what loving eagerness the pages are turned—the breathless longing that the end may not yet be reached—the disappointment when we find that much we hoped for is missing—the desire that others should benefit, (and yet) the grudging jealousy with which it is spared to the printer's hand—all this, no doubt, has been experienced by others, and need not be dwelt on here.

On first looking at the MS. of the second volume, the title on its back, "The Hebrew Prophets during the Babylonian and Persian Empires," gave hopes that the work had been more nearly completed; but on closer inspection it was found that it did not extend much, if at all beyond the former of these periods, and that with the post-Babylonian Prophets, we also miss the summary at the conclusion, which would probably have surveyed the ground gone over, and touched on those religious topics which the criticism and commentary had thrown light upon.

The volume includes the Prophets Habakkuk, Zephaniah, and Jeremiah, with their several Introductions, but stops short with the beginning of the 4th chapter of Ezekiel, the Introduction to which book is wanting.

The period traced (if we except a chapter of Habakkuk, as possibly of an earlier date, the closing verses of Zephaniah, and some passages and chapters of Jeremiah, supposed to be the work of a later hand, and relegated at earliest to the time of Cyrus) is of about sixty years, from about B.C. 647—B.C. 586-5. The title on the MS. of the volume is however retained as showing what had been the Author's plan, and a title page found at the beginning of the Note Book of the entire work, with the date of its commencement, is added.

A translation of Isa. liii.* found in the same Note Book, though not properly in order here, is subjoined as a fragment, being all that there is of the second Isaiah—some idea of what would have been the line of argument pursued as regards this Prophet may be found by referring to the Introduction to Isaiah, together with the notes on chapters xii. (A. V. xiii.) xxix. xxx. (A. V. xxxiv. xxxv.) in Vol. I.

The MS. has been scrupulously followed and necessary corrections (which have been but few) alone made. References have been added as intended to the A. V. for the

---

* See a sermon on this chapter, entitled *The Prophetic Christ*, in Broadchalke Sermon Essays.

benefit of the English reader, and a Table of the LXX. chapters of Jer. has also been annexed. With these exceptions it has been thought best to publish the MS. as it stood. If some sentences lack the final polish which the Author himself might have given them, the book has at least the advantage of bearing the impress of his own spirit without suffering from the diluting effect of editor's gloss.

I desire here to express my deep gratitude to the Rev. W. W. Harvey, who, in memory of Eton and King's College days, and in token of friendship and sincere regard, wrote at once on Dr. Williams' death to the executors offering his services as regarded any literary remains having a bearing on Hebrew literature, and who subsequently made himself responsible for the revision of the Hebrew, Latin, and Greek of the present volume, and has besides given many useful hints while the work has been going through the press. The value of his assistance has been much enhanced to me by the knowledge of the motives which actuated it.

With the same feeling of grateful thanks I would also add, that to (Dr. Williams' much valued friend) Dr. Muir, for his munificent contribution, and to the publishers, Messrs. Williams and Norgate, for the liberal terms proposed by them, I am in great measure indebted for being enabled to carry out my wish of publishing the work without more delay, at a time when I think it possesses a special interest, as bearing on the elucidation of a part of the Scriptures now in progress of revision.

For those we love, from whom death parts us, our heart's fond desire is, that their labours may continue to exercise an abiding and ever deepening influence on the minds of men—and it is not without a mournful satisfaction that as the anniversary of the day which took him from us comes round, I give a fresh volume of my husband's Hebrew Prophets to the world, thankful that on the subject considered by himself peculiarly his own, some writings remain to us, which may be regarded as especially stamped with his genius, and in which

"He being dead yet speaketh."

ELLEN WILLIAMS.

Jan. 18, 1871.

PART II.

THE HEBREW PROPHETS

DURING THE

BABYLONIAN AND PERSIAN EMPIRES.

INTRODUCTION TO HABAKKUK.

THE books of Habakkuk and Zephaniah seem too nearly contemporaneous to require change in their arrangement. We know of Habakkuk, neither his father nor his mother, nor his birthplace, nor whether he had wife or child, nor where he died, or was buried, nor whether his name means *Amabilis Domini*, the Lord's beloved, or *Contestatio*, protestation, from the vehemence of his remonstrance. He may, as the Alexandrine title in the Greek or Apocryphal book of Daniel represents, have been the son of Jesus, of the tribe of Levi. He may, according to the later and fabulous biography of Pseudo-Epiphanius, have been of the tribe of Simeon. His remains can hardly, according to Sozomen, vii. 29, have been discovered in the reign of Theodosius at Keilah; for the story of a dream of Bishop Zeben of Eleutheropolis, and the connexion in which the good chronicler relates it, as if the public estimate of episcopal virtues required to be fortified by miracles, brand the story as fabulous. We must reject as less mendacious, but equally anile, the Rabbinical dream which connects the name in the sense of embrace, with the miraculous conception of the Shunamite's child, II Kings iv. 16. A mystical meaning, as of a wrestler with God, is far more probable. St. Jerome, who so often, by supplying us with the materials on which his own judgment proceeded, enables us to discriminate the boundaries of history and fable, may so serve us here: "That Habakkuk lived (he says), during the cap-
"tivity of Judah, you may learn from Daniel, to whom
"Habakkuk was sent with a dinner in the den of lions;
"although this story is not found in the Hebrew; whether

"then any one receives the story as scripture or not, it "equally makes for us; for if he receives it, the prophet's "book is subsequent to that event, or if not, the author "writes predictively what he knows will come." *Proem. in* H. The reasoning of the second alternative is truly Patristic: for how does it follow, because an apocryphal account be rejected, that a person mentioned in it lived at a different time? or that he lived earlier? The more logical conclusion is, that the Prophet's age must be deduced from his own book, and in default of evidence to the contrary, his description of things as present suggests contemporaneousness.

If we turn from fables to the man of God, we hear in his book a voice of one crying in a wilderness of wrongdoings; the less followed by the greater as a judgment, the greater mysteriously needing faith or expostulation. Whether the death of Josiah, and the Egyptian supremacy, which after the brief reign of Jehoahaz set up Jehoiakim, had engendered domestic misrule (for such is a natural inference from the opening verses), or whether, as rather seems, Nebuchadnezzar was already on the scene, tracking his path by transport of populations and erection of new cities with forced labour, the silence of Heaven amidst spoiling and violence on earth provoked the prophet to plead aloud with Providence. He is not like Nahum, one who lifts up his parable over a fallen city, nor like Isaiah, a challenger of opposite counsels and invading armies; but more like Jeremiah, perplexed, yet not cast down by the tyranny of an irresistible conqueror, he turns now to God for explanation or redress, and now to man with assurance that the vision of redress will be fulfilled, if we wait in faithfulness on Him who is faithful. Thus he is more Prophet than Poet, though his poetry has whatever the Hebrew mind could conceive of sublimity. We have seen in the eighteenth chapter of our Isaiah (A. V. xxi. 6,) the foreboding heart of the Prophet symbolically represented as a watchman, who, gazing on a mirror, or (more naturally) from a tower, discerns signs as of a twin host approaching; then he divines, Fallen, fallen is Babylon. So Habakkuk discerns the eternal Arbiter of the world's destiny raising up that bitter and hasty nation the Chaldæans, who, though of extreme antiquity, (Vol. I. p. 304) stamped a new impress of dominion on Semitic Asia for the seventy years intervening between Cyaxares, the great Median king, and Cyrus, the still greater Persian; the Prophet then asks, For how long shall be the calamity? and the vision which the Divine faithfulness suggests to him in reply, is one of the vanquished nations taking up a parable against their oppressor, as in Isaiah, xii. 25 (A. V. xiv. 4); for since God abides in his eternal sanctuary, whatever idolatrous tyranny opposes itself to Him must come to an end, ii. 12. (A. V. ii. 20.)

So far, two chapters are clear. Whether the third chapter is a poetical strengthening of the prophet's faith, by reverting in thought to the ancient deliverances of Israel in Egypt and the field of Zoan, I leave undecided, out of deference to good critics who think so. My unassisted judgment would lay more stress upon the title with which the third chapter commences; a title certainly of older form than the one prefixed to the first. I could not find in such affinity of sentiment as links the concluding poem to the preceding remonstrance any such connexion of thought as implies necessarily identity of origin, but rather enough to account for the association of pieces originally distinct; while the verbal colour of style is certainly more poetical in the last piece, if not as it would seem to me, altogether more archaic. Hence I would suggest for consideration, whether this poem were not the original Habakkuk, and whether it may be older by some centuries than the age of Nebuchadnezzar. A farther question would be, whether the vivid poetical figures of this very piece did not pass in a prosaic sense into some of the national chronicles. If we suppose this might be so, it would not destroy the strong personality of the author of our first and second chapters, but separate his work of pleading with God from that of poetical celebration which accompanies it. However that may be, the Poem is evidently adapted to music, and has all the characteristics of a Psalm. It is not so inconsistent with that Pindaric notion of inspiration as a furor, which prevailed in the latter half of the eighteenth century, as most of the Prophetic writings, in their life-like pertinence to realities, are. The difficulty of its interpretation is so great, that as many differences between good critics occur in it as in a dozen ordinary chapters.

If it were not for Josephus, and some fragments of Berossus preserved by him (J. A. x. 6, and C. Apion, i. 19, 20) we should find beyond the Biblican Canon little answering to the vast impression of tyranny and renown which we associate with Nebuchadnezzar. That he conquered Necho in the battle of Carchemish, had a Median queen, was a great builder, a devout worshipper of deities, and that he died in the forty-third year of his reign, seem to be the earlier statements; that he extended his conquests to Spain, and foretold before his death the coming destruction of his city, are somewhat later traditions. The native annalist by making him a builder, and transferring to him the fame of some erections which the Greeks ascribed to Semiramis,[1] eminently illustrates our

---

[1] Jos. J. A. x. 6. C. Apion, i. 19, 20. Euseb. *Præp. Ev.* ix. 41. Strabo, xv. p. 687, seemingly from Megasthenes, or hearsay. Jahn, *H. C.* vi.

second chapter. Habakkuk's description of the Chaldæan progress is that of a spectator; his vision of its ultimate check is what faith inspires; the taunting tone, characteristic of the Hebrew mind, is imagined as running in the future along a line of nations re-arisen.

Those critics who conceive of the earlier Prophets as more original than the later, represent Habakkuk as living about the division of epochs, and as stamped by the creative freshness which marks the youth of poetry, such as distinguishes for instance Lucretius from Virgil, and Æschylus from Sophocles. We may indeed suspect that the earlier writers are the less scrupulous in borrowing, though they seem original, because their models have perished, or the range of ideas in which they moved is farthest from our own. Aristotle said truly, it is likely there were many poets before Homer. Yet the criticism is so far just that our Prophet's thoughts govern or create his words, and are not introduced for their sake. He has the earnest freedom from conventionalism, which belongs to one face to face with his Maker. Hence it was given him to strike clearly the key-note of the New Testament, the source of courage and strength for all ages yet to come, '*The righteous shall live by his faithfulness.*' That voice, sounding to us across a waste of war and disaster, loses none of its power from the obscurity which surrounds all else belonging to its author. Many, before the principle was thus enunciated, had lived by it, and many since who had never heard it taught; but this special expression of it is consecrated for us by the sanction which it transferred from the Old Testament to the New, and by the experience of many generations.

⁎ Some remarks on ecclesiastical developments of the principle of faith may be here pardoned to the clergyman, if hardly needed from the expositor.

When our Anglican Reformers surveyed the field of Scholastic Theology, seeking a formula which should express their horror of the sale of Indulgences and kindred enormities, none seemed to them so appropriate as that of Justification by Faith alone. This had already been employed by St. Paul against the bondage of Mosaic ritualists, Romans iv. 11, and by St. Augustine against what seemed the self-dependent morality of Pelagianism. It expressed both the idea that our salvation is a thing of heart and conscience, Galatians v. 6, instead of external conformity or ecclesiastical privilege, Luke iii. 8; John iii. 6—16; and also that it is not our achievement, but the gift of God. Yet it might well, in ecclesiastical hands, leave untouched the idea that faith finds its legitimate expression in appointed rites, as St. Austin calls Baptism the sacrament of faith; and it was always by sober thinkers combined with the requirement of correspondent life. Good deeds, which our Homily distinguishes from works of church adornment, were considered tests of faith's reality; good fruits of a good tree; or by some, as conditions of the efficacy of faith; nay, even as the criteria of a man's destiny, though criteria such as required faith for a preliminary.

However precious the principle of faith were for its own sake, as it had been the strength of devotional minds ever, the connection of thought in which our Reformers considered it gave a one-sided tone to their statements. For, since it was as a negation of merit that the principle most availed them as a weapon against supererogation or ceremonial, so they confined its justifying office to this aspect; while they admitted charity, holiness, humility, rectitude of word and deed, to accompany it in effect, they excluded such effects from share in the process of justifying man, or rendering him acceptable to God. They adopted fully St. Augustine's principle, *Bona opera sequuntur justificatum, non præcedunt justificandum*, Hom. xvi. 1. This was Hooker's well-weighed sentence with the whole case before him, Sermon ii. Passages of larger sound abound in the Liturgy, and may be inferentially extracted from the Homilies ; but such was the main doctrine of the Reformation in the consciousness of those who settled our Church. Be holy, they said, but plead not your holiness. We work not for life, or towards life, but out of a life first given us. The repentance which God requires, He enables you to feel. The love which perfects your faith comes of your having first been loved. Your need moved the Divine compassion, not your fitness. Give to God the glory, and believe that to have been His end from the beginning, which you see attained. Whatever He is now doing, He always intended to do. He saves by a grace unmerited; His purpose cannot have been less than eternal.

As we cannot do justice to this system, as a matter of ecclesiastical terminology, without remembering the abuses against which it was levelled, nor reconcile it with ethical requirements, unless we observe the wholesome effects which by means of love and gratitude it produces upon men's life, so neither can we allow it standing-ground in the deep waters of scientific or dogmatical theology, unless we combine the 17th of our Articles with the 11th, and bear in mind that our Reformers as little separated the work, as the person, of the Spirit from the Son. It was an actual righteousness which they conceived Divinely given, though they fastened men's glance on the giver, not on the receiver. As Justification in its technical sense, *i.e.* the Forgiveness of sins (*Hom.* iii. and iv.) seemed to them God's act, but incomplete or transient without the Holy Spirit teaching us to trust and obey, so a barren imputation of merit, or a fiction of its transfer, was as far from their mind, if not from their phraseology, as from those of Archbishop Whately and Dr. Newman.

But if, on the devotional side, all tender and emotional kind of experience confirms the wisdom of looking to the Giver instead of founding a claim upon the gift; and if in respect of dialectics, whether impregnable or not, our Reformers' scheme of salvation will bear favourable comparison with those of earlier Councils and Fathers, its very logical harmony had a danger. It is one thing to ascribe all good to God, or to believe humbly that the worlds of Nature and Grace are pervaded by a Divine causation: it is another thing to take our stand at an ideal commencement, and with frail human vision to gaze down the long abyss of intertangled actions, motives, organization, education, circumstance, retribution, and often ruin apparently irretrievable. The very light blinds by its excess. The knowledge kills. The mere blank becomes instinct with awful possibilities. Things are fruitful. Man's personality fades into a result, becomes intertwined as a link. What then is our righteousness; where is that of God? If no system will bear to be carried out, why have a system? Yet, if Christianity throws light on our destiny, how can it be deaf to the question of questions, the hinge of our weal or woe? *What is that to thee? follow thou me*, may be said to a disciple in presence of the Saviour; but not by ecclesiastics who introduce questions inwoven in the fabric of their doctrine. Exclude logic, wisely, if you will; but do not impose a paralogism.

It was natural that attempts, for the most part of fruitless ingenuity, should be made to dissever the Protestant doctrine (though it had also been held by Augustinians and Dominicans) from its predestinarian consequences. Thus Augustine with little reason was represented as stopping short of Calvin. The root of the matter was sometimes omitted, by embracing his system with the exception of its distinguishing decree. Men were bidden to believe, that the Divine decree, while inscrutable to man, has just reasons; though the only reason which could make it just, and yet preserve the anti-papal or solifidian aspect of justification, by finding ground in some human element of act or acceptance, was expressly excluded.

With some faith was said to justify, but already pregnant with good works. With others it was a lively faith, but not saving in respect of its life, or faith perfected in charity, but not saving in respect of its charity; *fides quæ viva*, but not *quâ viva est*. Whatever made the justifying act, or the ground of that act, human and not Divine, except so far as Humanity merited it in Christ, was alien to our Reformers' idea. Still the moral instincts of man, even animated by a zeal for the Divine honour, sought for some ground of the sinner's final condemnation; therefore something, which by absence, if by nothing more positive, might associate fitness with mercy to the saved. Was it acceptance of Christ: this was less guilty than rejection. Was it wretchedness conscious of itself, and crying in the darkness; it was congruous with the Divine mercy to shed light on this dark struggle. Hence merit of congruity, so alien in its scholastic form to our Protestant instincts, had a root in the fitness of things, nay, even in a humble and passionate zeal for God's honour. Again, if God has appointed by his Son, or brought about by his providence, modes of accepting his grace, which are embodied in sacramental acts, or expressed in prayer, He cannot mock us with them, as with idle formalities. Where can the act of Justification be more fitly placed in thought, than contemporaneously with our acceptance of Christ by baptism? or how can the state, impaired, if not forfeited by sin, be more certainly renewed, than by a repentance and fresh dedication of ourselves, in connexion with our remembrance of Christ's death, and our acceptance in thought and act of the symbols of his passion? We call it our remembrance, but if God's sacrifices are spiritual, what less do we in remembering, than shew forth the Lord's death, in the form most acceptable to Heaven, renewing its oblation, without renewing its pain? Hence moral and ecclesiastical considerations combined in rendering it inevitable for the Church to drift from that stronger mind of the Reformers, which gave their presentation of Faith in the 11th and 17th Articles an aspect not destitute of relative truth, and never likely to lose polemical value, but not so exhaustive of Catholicity as to satisfy all the demands of systematic theology. Twice in little more than three centuries, the tendency thus engendered by incompleteness has fermented until it became dominant; both times it found its basis of support in our liturgical or sacramental offices, and its confirmation in Patristic or Scholastic theology. The first period of transformation reached its acme in the writings of Jeremy Taylor, whose eloquence should not blind us to his wisdom, and who would have been the last to think of contradicting his Church factiously, but whose system is a development from the Homilies, in almost a sense of opposition. Even Burnet, whose intentions were strongly Protestant, yet by making faith a complex term which might include the Christian religion, opened the way to an inclusion of the requirements of morality amongst the grounds of our acceptance; and so needed, as much as the Caroline Divines, a reading of the 11th Article which would lessen its point against Rome. Somewhat less open to a similar remark is the system of reasonable sound which represents all men as rendered salvable, or potentially justified, by faith, that is, by God's mere grace manifested to us in Christ; but distinguishes the actually saved by their use of privileges granted to them. Their system is embarrassed by its adoption of the idea of merit in the classical and old ecclesiastical sense, while yet it rejects the term in deference to Protestant associations with it of the right of claim. The last word of the Anglican re-action in favour of responsibility or symmetry, before the tide of Methodism swept it away, was best spoken by Waterland. He was deficient in critical knowledge, and narrow in sympathy; but his admirable balance of mind enabled him to bring into just relief all the points of a complex system. Even his history of the Athanasian Creed has a candid bigotry.

Those phases of doctrine which, as merely ethical, or more mystically spiritual, represents salvation under the form of soundness or spiritual health, are not here dwelt upon, because they appear seldom widely held, and whatever truth they contain is more tangibly presented under figures of general apprehension. For the most part they require faith more as an instrument, and less as a condition. They happily avoid the coarser notions of a bargain or a compact, and dwell more on communion with God.

Throughout changes of controversy men bent chiefly on practical life, especially clergymen, have been inclined to acquiesce in some Melanchthonian compromise, which yet was unable to satisfy minds impelled by duty, or by dialectical impulses, to seek harmony in their convictions. In the long run, the stronger, more consistent, Predestinarianism proved better able to support religious life, than the feebler kind which limited itself to the attractive features; for the one, being in earnest, had the strength of symmetry and reality;

the other, half-conscious of internal untenableness, became the form, without the power.

It is difficult to abstract, though useful to distinguish, our modes of apprehending Divine action from the principle which is the salt of them all. We may hope that fragments, though held as systems, have not been without providential reason for existence, whether a truth revived, or one adapted to recipients of different orders of mind. The direct vision, as of Revelation, in which logical distinctions fade, seems from the history of the higher Mysticism, to have something evanescent, as if it were a sentiment too delicate for our air.

The later analogies of the Reformation and of the Caroline period seem hardly in all respects equal to their prototypes. Methodism in its branches had fresh life and vision, but not the learning, measure, and comparative consistency of Cranmer. It is no exaggeration to say, that disclaiming merit has been substituted for the large field of Christian requirement; hence the idea of moral probation, except where conscience, truer than her teachers, supplied it, has become faint; doctrines, consisting much of dislocated texts, becoming Shibboleths, or opiates, have fed that weakness of all churches and all creeds which denies formalism as a refuge from responsibility. Here, too, the stronger, ruder, forms have retained more primitive vitality than the developments softened by culture. The School of re-action, starting from the Tracts for the Times, attempted to restore symmetry to Theology, but failed, chiefly from the materialistic tinge, which a real, if not conscious, affinity to Rome gave to its conceptions of doctrine. It began with a reverence and gentleness, which soon faded. Its habit of quoting authorities indiscriminately became literary irrelevancy, if not disingenuousness. The "Lectures on Justification" had not the precision of Bull, but exhibited a Hermeneutical sophistry, which he would have disdained. The School's notions of sacrifice fell in spirituality short of Waterland. Baptismal grace was carnalised. The sign, water, was raised into the instrument, in defiance of our Catechism. Blood, the sign of the propitiatory virtue of the Death of Christ, was with more countenance from loose language, with equal contradiction to

Scripture (Heb. ix. 22, 23; x. 9), identified with the Atonement. The symbols of faith were confounded with its objects. Faith itself, which others had transformed from an ennobling trust in God (Homily iv. 1, 2, 3), into egotistic confidence or vicariousness (Nelson's *Life of Bull*, Al. Knox's *Essays*, Whately's *Difficulties of St. Paul*, Penrose *on the Atonement*) was by this school, in a manner ill-harmonizing with its religious side, changed into literary belief, and this directed to constructions doubtful, or frequently refuted, sometimes to interpolations, or documents[2] forged. The question became, not how much of the inheritance of our church could in affectionate loyalty be maintained, without violating veracity or charity, but how a system could be strengthened by suppression of whatever opposed it. We need not ask here the effect of Druidical stoles and copes, or crosiers and processions, on priestly minds, fancying themselves separated from the congregation (1 Pet. v. 3); but where was the faith by which the righteous lives? No school oftener suggested the question, "When the Son of Man cometh, shall He find faith "upon earth?"

It was natural, and it became from exaggerations necessary for the world at length to question the principle of Faith. Is its essential principle confidence? then its value in life is evident, but do we not desiderate in it an element fit to be the turning-point of Divine approval? We see it mislead as often as save; sometimes it renders injurious. Wise teachers prefer the diffident child. Again, is its essence belief? the dogmatical schools tell us so; but do they mean belief upon evidence, or against evidence? The first is too natural for praise, the second would be blameable; as without evidence it could be but neutral. Would it not be wiser to shew ground for belief, instead of bribing the understanding by a premium on an artificial virtue? Have not history, literature, all the sciences, suffered from biassing bodies of men to preconcep-

---

[2] Comp. Julius Hare, *Victory of Faith, Mission of Comforter, Vindication of Luther,* Neander's *Planting of Christianity,* Bunsen's *Hippolytus and his times,* 1st edition, Isaac Taylor's *Ancient Christianity,* Dr. Arnold's *Sermons,* and his Polemical Works, Dr. Pusey's *Lectures on Daniel,* and his various Tracts.

tions? Even integrity suffers. Those who compare the Greek and the Turk, find a higher veracity in the one who makes rectitude the starting-point, than in the votary of opinion. Amongst Christians, has not charity a claim to be a better criterion of character than belief? Again, if Faith borrows its excellence from Christ, as introducing from him a higher standard than that of unaided humanity, what was it before Christ came? What is it with those who never hear of him? with extinct generations, distant nations, the majority of the human race? What was it with the Prophet Habakkuk? Especially if creeds involve views of chronology, national pre-eminence, standards, or precedents cruel or licentious, policies rude, canons of literature, proved amidst assumptions of infallibility erroneous, or maintained by warping discussion and suppression of evidence, what a foundation is this for religion, that men should believe what the natural causes of belief contravene? Is God then pleased with error? nay, even with truth sophistically controversial? and not rather with heart, conscience, life?

Such questions are asked respecting the selection of faith as a justifying principle, and find sufficient echo in general observation to deserve the best answer we can give. Setting aside distortions, why do we live by faith?

If we approach the subject speculatively, we should expect that whatever cardinally commends us to God will be a spiritual principle. It cannot be mere action; for right must have its root in thought; action, traversed by circumstance and ill-obeying intention, is an imperfect clue to character. If it begin as a spiritual process with feeling, it cannot terminate in the region of feeling; for the great Being to whom Nature and Reason point gives abundant signs of intelligence as ordering His own processes, and requires of us, under severe penalties of miscarriage, that our feelings shall have guidance and discipline. Love, ill-directed, is but ruin, Hope, without reason, a blinding dream. If we ask, what principle starting in awe or dim feeling, but soon strengthening itself by inference and experience, most points our mind to an unseen standard, which though we err in reaching it is not warped by our error, and though independent of our affections gives the holiest guidance to them all, we find something answering to the term faith. In morals, it is belief in the reality of right and wrong, or the affirmation of an ideal standard, not alterable by our will. In cosmical speculation it is the belief in an Eternal Mind. Those who come to God must first believe that He is, and that He is a rewarder of them that diligently seek Him. In practice it is the subordination of profit or pleasure to duty, the postponement of gratification to a nobler end, or a more rightful time; often the sacrifice of ourself to our parents, friends, country. As regards life beyond the grave, it seems an instinct, or an aspiration, grounded on the nature of God, and on the communion with Him of our own minds. In all things faith seems the opposite of materialism, though materialising symbols aid its less imaginative forms. I would not say without it rectitude cannot be, but it is rectitude's greatest ally. It is to God what integrity is to Man. Such a principle being life's mainstay, and leading beyond life, may well commend us primarily to God. Not that He in His goodness need treat us unjustly, even if we are without it, but through it He gives us the blessing of drawing nigh to Him.

Certainly, instances of past faith feed our own. The voices of many witnesses swell. Love is contagious, and love, as well as reason, enters into faith. I do not find that God has so left himself without witness[3] in any age or clime that written records should be our only foundation. Nor yet are past witnesses to faith incapacitated for testimony by a thousand errors, since even we, who err, testify truly. In History Divines wish belief to be faith, yet feel it is not true faith. Surely they would better distinguish things so different. Testimony, when strong, enforces belief; when weak, invites credulity; neither of these is faith, unless a moral or spiritual affirmation supervene. Faith removes mountains, not Belief. Faith made an apostle cry out *Wretched Man that I am!* not mere confidence. That Cæsar visited Britain, was owned by his enemies; that he

---

[3] Homo fide, spe, et caritate subnixus, eaque inconcusse retinens, non indiget Scripturis, nisi ad alios instruendos. Itaque multi per hæc tria etiam in solitudine sine codicibus vivunt. Unde in illis arbitror jam impletum quod dictum est. 1 Cor. xiii. 8. Augustin. Doct. Christ. I. xxxix.

conquered the Britons is affirmed by himself; our belief in either assertion is not faith; though if, as Cæsar's friends, we accepted the weaker for his sake, that would be an act of faith. Association connects with faith its exemplifications, the reality of which yet must be verified by the instruments of belief. Divine authority for belief is not command, but reason, or adequate motive, as when men are drawn by love or swayed by testimony.

Whether Holy Scripture is in itself, and as such, a primary object of the Christian's faith, is not agreed. But if men would notice the variety of its subject-matter, the revocation of some of its precepts, the limitations of its writers, or the contradictions which arise from forced harmonies, and if they would go on to distinguish the directness of Divine action from the instrumentality of ecclesiastical records and systems, we have abundant materials for a conclusion. It may be a Providential record, an instrument of conscience, an ecclesiastical assemblage of sacred instances, and yet the innermost life may be but identical with our own, and neither of them depend upon literary accidents. When one of the worst of Gentile tyrants was dying, he would save his wife from revenge by sending her to her friends. She answered that she had not married him for his splendour, to leave him in his downfall, but to be faithful to him to the end. This poor Heathen's affection was as holy before God, as our matrimonial vow for better, for worse; though the life of Agathocles cannot be as sacred to us as our Bible or Prayer-book.

Christ is our object of faith, because he sums up the conscience of Nature and Scripture, shewing us in himself what God is, what Man ought to be. The Divine likeness is in Him exhibited bodily, and the idea at which Faith aims is fulfilled. Yet Christ propounds himself as a Mediator, not such as Moses, keeping men afar, but by community of a better nature joining in one. He is not jealous, if any can otherwise learn God; so He has not bid us curse the Heathen world; yet those who hearing of Him reject his way are likely to miss his truth, and not share his life. Still He is not the Goal, but the Way. His manifestation is for the Father's sake, and not the Father's existence for Him. His sacrifice is perfect, and its excellence flows into ours, so that we offer ourselves acceptably; yet his obedience was dearer to God than his pain; his life had his blood but for a precious symbol; his spirit must perfect what his death began; He is not a substitute for any who will not share in Him actually and truly. The Gospel is not vicariousness, but participation; and not mere forgiveness, but also holiness. We cannot plead the gifts as our own merits, but we must accept all of them, and accept them truly, if the Giver is to profit us. Christ would redeem all, but calling Him Redeemer is nothing, unless we are redeemed from evil. The things we see on earth as holiness or obedience are in Heaven acceptance. Christ's merits are truly his earnings, or all that He brings about. Our regeneration, repentance, perseverance, come of his merits, and as they cannot be put asunder, so neither will our disclaiming merit stand in place of a Christian life. The mould of circumstance so fashions us, that whoever dwells on it will be in danger of merging personality in nature, but if we rescue from nature's tyranny some moral initiative, however faint, with so much freedom as responsibility requires, we may conceive that in the realm of grace a real, though limited, agency survives. The Judge of all may be justified, though the Saviour of those that believe be thanked. St. Paul and St. James may agree, either because the first requires living faith, as the second rejects a dead one; or because the second requires Gospel works, as the first rejected works of the law. Again, the first may be contrasting Christ's hearty faith with ceremonial; the second may be changing a Judaic righteousness of forms into the Baptist's life of a new heart and mind. The unseen world, the coming kingdom, of the Epistle to the Hebrews, suggests different objects and modes of action for a kindred or identical affection. It is certain, that in interpreting St. Paul, we are, from the analogy of our controversy with Rome, too exclusive in our apprehension of him as negativing human merit. Yet it may be remembered, none have shewn more merit with man than those who most disclaimed it before God; the most fruitful in good works and virtue would tolerate the name of neither; we ourselves in drawing out harmonious systems, though they have place and use, are in danger of losing the life of self-negation and dependence which true Faith generates; and after trying to make Man a fellow-worker, have need to fall down and accept all as the grace of God. He who punishes by desert, still gives by grace.

Most Christians conceive that Christ's death was in a sense a punishment, or penal satisfaction to Divine justice for the sins of Mankind. This may be so, as undoubtedly it was a true propitiatory sacrifice; but then in the first case, the Divine satisfaction was not in the physical torture, as in the second, the essence of the sacrifice was not the bloodshed. A fair apprehension might be attained by supposing a reprobate family, whom no benefactor has reclaimed, but in whose midst appears a child of nobler race or of singular merit, who, sharing or undergoing eminently the penal consequences of the family's sin, not of his own, is able at length to bring about their restoration. Again the figure of a ransom is appropriate, if we remember that ransom is paid to an enemy; so we are ransomed from the hostile law, from Sin, Death, Darkness, Ruin, but not from God. The necessity of the suffering, *quâ* suffering, is external to the Divine mind, though without that Mind neither necessity nor potentiality could be. That something of parable, or of adaptation to human apprehension, is in all these phrases, appears hence. Christ is our Mediator with God; yet God appoints him, therefore was reconciled in Will from all Eternity. Christ is our ransom, God pays it. The Spirit alone can make all things efficacious, yet God must ever send the Spirit. So as we began, we end; we come back in all things to the Father, of whose will, through whose wisdom, by whose life, comes the economy of salvation.

So then the righteous lives, and always has lived, by faith. This principle, for which idolatry and ecclesiasticism are poor substitutes, has not lost its identity in systems opposed to each other, of which, even when ignored, it has been the salt. Patriarch, Prophet, Gentile Worthy, unlike the Apostles in belief, were alike in this. Our clearer mediation, our more spiritual sacrifice in Christianity, do but strengthen or enliven this; less divine than its sister charity, it is the nearer to earth, the fitter for man. We hold the Protestant sense of justification as a forensic term for acquittal; yet remembering that our acquittal begins with forgiveness, and continues so long as our sincerity, we must see in such terms but images for the Divine reality, which is compassion to our weakness, help to our cry, light to our darkness, life to our death, joy in our repentance, concurrence in our growth, approval in our holiness. God is not mocked; whatsoever man sows he reaps.

If some forms of conception, Hebrew or scholastic, as Adam's Fall, or Merit by congruity, seem to need re-casting for us, the first having traces of a less measurable antiquity in the world, and more sense of parable in Scripture to embarrass us, as we hold it, the other, or things cognate to it amongst Protestants, seeming but a web of speculation, the truths intended do not so much change. The ideal of Plato, the "congenital evils" of Aristotle, the infinite liabilities to degeneracy from its standard which we see in everything earthly, express an abiding reality, may have prompted the ancient expression. We stretch with human performance after a Divine design, fulfilled in Heaven, but aiming at itself on earth; or we restore a likeness which we have seen in One, and paint to ourselves at the beginning, yet which may not be until the end. The artist sees first what he executes last. The idea of our rising by the overflow of a virtue beyond our own, and deriving through sacrificial self-oblation a higher being, is so far from strange, that by experience of its wholesomeness, which is its truth, we verify to some extent histories which the remote past would place beyond cognisance. Dogma, if false, is a stumbling-block, but if true, is more certain than history. So ideas often are more important than facts; sometimes may be their warranty. Our family affections lose none of their sacredness, if their objects are not all which we deem. The feeling may consecrate the belief, or embalm the fact against irreverence. Only if we insist that any history is the foundation of things permanent, and the only instrument of virtue, especially if we embattle a stringent construction of it against conscientious instincts, such a challenge promises exposition of evidence. History has more belief, poetry more faith; as they blend, we should not prejudge questions respecting their limits; and if not bound always to disentangle, we may still observe when they are raised. We should trust that, if essential they will turn out favourably, or if their result is other, their importance will be less than we deemed.

I have written from prepossession, and from my function, upon the assumption that the New Testament account of the origin of Christianity, including its miracles, is a true account. But if the share of imagination in giving poetical shape to that history should ever seem enlarged, (as undeniably a tendency to that effect appears on many grounds,) the parables of Christ would still speak, His character still attract, His atonement, with its present witness of peace, would guarantee the past and the future, the kingdom which He built upon eternal truth and destiny would still remain. The province of belief might be narrowed, but that of faith be no less wide.

Since we find, more and more, that neither knowledge, nor art, nor physical science, nor dialectical subtlety, but Faith, holds the peace of the present, and the promise of the future, it is a great argument of the truth of Christianity that she makes so vital a principle her own. Woe to those who prevent it, by setting it against knowledge and truth.

In the text, ii. 3, (A. V. 4), out of which this Essay has grown, critics who are not theological usually translate "*faith*" as uprightness, or rectitude. They do so, because the word is not any form of *Batach* to be confident, or *Chasah* to trust, but the noun of *Aman* to be firm. In declining to follow them, I abide by my principle of deciding philology on philological grounds. For the word evidently refers to its cognate verb, affirm or *count true*, in i. 4, and so puts on the sense of that verb's causative mood. This is illustrated by Isaiah xxiv. 16 (A. V. xxviii. 16), and vii. 8, (A. V. 9), and by Psalm lxxviii. 22—32, 37 ; Job iv. 18 ; Job xv. 22. Also, conversely, by Psalm xix. 9, xciii. 5 ; whence I always hold, St. Paul Hebraising, Rom. iii. 2, meant the promises of God had been found faithful. So in our text, the Prophet means faith, strictly called, even if he use the word faithfulness, which might be either on man's part, or applied as by LXX. and Vulgate, to God, or to the vision. The idea would be the same.

Can then our salvation depend on verbal criticisms so doubtful, that they divide the best critics? Not so; but if, as St. John teaches, 1 Ep. ii. iii. iv. *passim*, God gives us *the witness in ourselves*, it is a comfort to find it verified by so ancient and sacred a text. Only, it would be a great illusion to imagine that in Habakkuk ii. or in Hebrews xi. the whole Evangelical scheme, as brought out in our pulpits, or even suggested in the Gospels, was intended. The thing meant is what is said, *By faith we live,* for God is faithful.

HABAKKUK.

The burden[1] *which Habakkuk the Prophet saw in vision.*

II. I. 1. How long, ETERNAL, do I cry, and thou not A. V. 1. 2. hearken; cry unto thee of violence, and thou not save?

2. Wherefore shewest thou me iniquity, and makest me behold grievance? and spoiling and violence *are* before me, and strife, and raising up contention?

3. Therefore law slackens, and judgment goes not forth to prevail[2]; for the wicked encompasses the righteous: therefore judgment goes forth perverted.

---

[1] *Burden;* or, utterance, Heb. *Massah.* "nunquam præfertur in titulo, nisi "cum gravo et ponderis laborisque plenum est quod videtur."—*Hieron.*

[2] *To prevail.* Vulg. ad finem. LXX. εἰς τέλος. Isaiah xxii. 8, (A. V. xxv. 8), in sempiternum; as in Psalm xiii. 1, and so perhaps here; where the etymological sense of *completeness* is suggested by the antithesis *perverted.* Comp. 1 Cor. xv. 54.

The Titles which contain the phrase *Burden,* or *Utterance,* Heb. *Massah,* are for the most part of later date than those which use the phrase *Word,* or *Vision.* So here this title may be later than that of the third chapter.

1—3. The Prophet complains of lawlessness, whether it were of home growth in the beginning of Jehoiakim's reign, and so destined to be punished by the Chaldæan invasion; or whether it were that caused by the invaders, and so lamented first in the way of ejaculation, but described at verse 5, in reference to its historical cause.

Ch. I.   4. Behold among the nations, and regard, and wonder A. V. marvellously; for *I* am working a work in your days, *which you will not count true, though it be told.*

5. For behold me raising up the Chaldæans,³ that bitter and hasty nation, that marches to the far places of the earth, to inherit dwelling-places not his own.

6. Terrible is he, and dreadful; from himself proceeds his judgment and his dignity:

7. And his horses are swifter than leopards, and fiercer than wolves of darkness;⁴ and his horsemen spread abroad, yea, his horsemen came from afar; they fly as the eagle *that* hastens to devour.

8. All his *host* comes for plunder: the swoop⁵ of their faces *is as* an east wind, and he gathers captives like sand.

9. Yea, he makes kings a mockery, and rulers his laughing-stock; he laughs at every stronghold, and heaps up earth, until he captures it.

---

³ *Chaldæans.* Heb. Chasdim, descendants of Chesed, the son of Nahor; but here first in Scripture re-appearing, if we except Isaiah xx. (A.V. xxiii.), after long silence. Having been known to the Hebrews only as dependent on Nineveh they began from Esarhaddon's time, B.C. 710, to vindicate independence, and shared under Nabopolassar, with the Medes under Cyaxares, B.C. 626—606, the spoils of the Assyrian empire. See above Note on Isaiah xii. and introduction to Desprez's Daniel.

⁴ *Darkness.* LXX. 'Αραβίας, an error aiding to us detect the similar mistake of the Masora on Isaiah xviii. 13, (A.V. xxi. 13), where see Note.

⁵ *Swoop;* or, thronging, in which case the East wind will mean Eastwards, or forwards, as the affix suggests. Vulg. facies eorum facies urens.

---

4. The account which God gives to the Prophet's divining mind, either of his purpose to punish native wrong, or of his method of introducing foreign oppression, commences here. We should notice the word *count true,* or firm, as preparing us for the truthfulness, or faith, of ii. 3. (A. V. ii. 4.)

5—9. The Babylonians, recruited, as some think, by Kurdish soldiers, certainly rising on the fall of Assyria,

10. Then *his* spirit⁶ freshens, and he transgresses,⁷ A. V. I. 11. and is guilty; this his strength⁸ becomes his god.

11. Art thou not from of old, O ETERNAL, my God, my Holy One? we shall not die. O ETERNAL, for judgment hast thou set him up, and as a rock⁹ for rebuke¹⁰ hast thou established him.

12. Oh thou purer of eyes than to behold evil, and that canst not look on iniquity, wherefore lookest thou on plunderers; *and* art silent while the wicked devours the more righteous than himself?

13. Wherefore makest thou mankind as the fishes of the sea, as reptiles with no ruler over them.

14. He raises all of it with a hook, he assembles it into his net, and gathers it with his drag; therefore he rejoices and is glad.

---

⁶ *Spirit;* or, breeze.

⁷ *Transgresses, and is guilty;* or, passes away, and is desolate.

⁸ *His strength becomes;* or, whose strength is. So instead of a prosperous stride, the verse may describe downful. *Vulg.* Mutabitur spiritus, et pertransibit, et corruet; hæc est fortitudo ejus Dei sui. LXX. αὕτη ἡ ἰσχὺς τῷ Θεῷ μου, as below in ii. 3, ἐκ πιστεώς μου.

⁹ *As a Rock;* or, Thou, O Rock, as all the versions; but comp. Isaiah viii. 14.

¹⁰ *Rebuke* (or offence), is either of rebuking sinful nations; or, as giving the mockers cause to doubt of Providence.

---

and governed by Nabopolassar, but during part of his reign led by his son Nebuchadnezzar (comp. 1 Prideaux, 1, Joseph. Ant. x. 6), were now victorious or dominant, from the Euphrates to the river of Egypt.

10. According to the Hebrew, prosperity elates, and vain-glorious self-dependence makes the Chaldæan guilty, but, as the versions not improbably suggest, a change of breeze, and reverse are anticipated, which shall shew the little might of his gods, the greater might of Jehovah. So Jerome thinks Nebuchadnezzar's madness meant.

11—17. The Prophet, seeing what perplexity the sway

Ch. I.   15. Therefore he sacrifices to his net, and burns incense to his drag; because by them his portion is fat, and his food plentiful.

16. Shall he therefore empty his net, and not spare continually to slay the nations?

17. Let me stand upon my watch-tower, and take A.V post upon the stronghold, and observe, to see what shall be spoken[11] by me, and what I shall answer to my rebuke.

II.

1. Then the ETERNAL answered me, and said, Write the vision, and make it plain upon tablets, that he may run who reads it.

2. For the vision is yet for an appointed time, but at the end it shall burst forth and not lie; though it tarry, wait for it; for assuredly it will come, it will not be retarded.

3. Behold, swollen *the soul of* him whose soul is not up-

---

[11] *Shall be spoken*; or, What Jehovah will speak.

---

of a lawless conqueror will cause to believers in Providence, turns in expostulation to God, trusting in a wise purpose, yet pleading for the time to be shortened, and that the day of rebuke may not justify blasphemy. So Statius, "sæpe mihi dubiam traxit sententia mentem;" for the Psalmist, the riddle of life was too hard, until he went into the sanctuary of God, and considered it, Psalm lxxiii. 17. The importunity of prayer among the Covenanters, as in the life of Peden (though to colder minds seeming irreverent) is conceived in like spirit. Hence Jerome explains the name Habakkuk (*Embrace*) as of striving with God. Comp. Jer. xii. and xiv. with Gen. xxxii. 28, St. Luke xviii. 7.

1—4. God's answer to our cry is, Walk by faith, He will show us faithfulness. The word *Emounah*, translated faith, A.V. does not include evangelical doctrine,

II. right in him; but the righteous shall live by his[12] faith- A.V.II.4.
fulness.

4. Moreover, though his wine[13] is insolent, [*and he*] a

---

[12] *His faithfulness;* or, its faithfulness, *i.e.* of the vision, which should come. Or, my faithfulness, *i.e.* of God, who would be faithful to those who count him faithful and true; as in Isaiah vii. 9. So here LXX. ἐὰν ὑποστείληται, οὐκ εὐδοκεῖ ἡ ψυχή μου ἐν αὐτῷ· ὁ δὲ δίκαιος ἐκ πίστεώς μου ζήσεται, giving for the latter half the idea, if not the words, see Ep. Heb. x. 37, 38.

[13] *Though his wine is insolent*, ὁ δὲ κατοιόμενος (so Jerome reads, though moderns alter into κατοινώμενος) καὶ καταφρονητὴν ἀνὴρ ἀλαζών, οὐθὲν μὴ περάνῃ. Vulg. Quomodo vinum potantem decipit, sic est vir superbus, et non decorabitur; changing the last verb, but catching the sense, better given by the Chaldee, shall not abide; comp. Horat. ' fortunâque dulci Ebria;' and Psalm lxxviii. 65.

---

still less the solifidian side of it; nor is its meaning trust, so much as fidelity or firmness. Hence many translate it honestly. But to find the Prophet's meaning, we should compare his noun, *i.e.* *truthfulness* with his verb, *count true* in i. 4, (A.V. i, 5), and we shall find the sense as in Isaiah vii. 9. Unless we believe in God, we cannot come to Him; unless we count him firm, we cannot be confirmed; by trust in His strength we are strengthened. So, while the soul not upright is swollen, either of the Chaldæan with pride, or of the faithless Jew with alarm, the righteous is refreshed and will be kept alive, either by the truthfulness of the vision which Habakkuk feels, or by that of God the eternal vindicator; or even by his own steadfastness, in that he counts God steadfast. Hence the germ of St. Paul's doctrine, if not exaggerated, is certainly here; though, if it were less so, he might quote the text as against Jews who placed justification in external rites (even when not formal and hollow), instead of in the hidden man of the heart, which God accepts, forgives, purifies. Romans i. 17; ii. 28; iii. 2; and iv. 10, 11. The same argument holds against those who place baptismal grace in the water, divorced from " the answer of a good conscience." 1 Pet. iii. 21.

Ch. II. man elated, yet he shall not abide: who has made his desire large as the grave, and himself as death, and is never satisfied, but gathers to himself all the nations, and heaps up to himself all the populations:

5. Shall not these all of them take up a parable against him, and a taunting proverb against him, and say,

6. Aha! thou that multipliest *what is* not [14]thine: for how long? and thou that ladest thyself with plunder?[15] Shall they not rise up suddenly that sting[16] thee, and awaken that torment thee, and thou become to them for plunderings? Because thou hast spoiled many nations, all the residue of the populations shall spoil thee: because of men's blood, and the violence of the land, of the city, and all the dwellers therein.

7. Ah! thou that art greedy of evil greediness to thine house; setting his nest on high, that he may be delivered from the grasp of evil: Thou hast consulted shame to thy house, cutting off many populations, and sinnest against thy soul. For the stone cries out of the wall, and the beam out of the timber answers it.

8. Ah! thou that buildest towns[17] with blood, and es-

---

[14] *Thine.* Heb. his own.
[15] *Plunder;* or, thick clay, Vulg. densum lutum; which might allude to the ramparts of cities, new, or besieged.
[16] *Sting.* Literally the word means goods pledged; whence Cocceius and others prosaically take the word *stingers* in the next verse as creditors.
[17] *Towns and cities.* Heb. sing.

---

4. The wine of the red cup of conquest is here intended, as Obad. i. 16; Isaiah li. 17—22; Jer. xxv. 15; and Psalm lxxv. 8.

5—7. The desolator is foreseen desolate, Psalm vii. 12, 13.

8. As in Psalms ix. 6—12; x. 6—17; xi. 2; and perhaps in Gen. xlix. 18; so here, the strong prayer of faith goes up for a more just order of society, or for a greater

II. tablishest cities[17] by iniquity: Are not these[18] from the A.V.11.12. ETERNAL of hosts? that the populations labour in the very fire, and the tribes weary themselves for very nought! For the earth shall be filled with the knowledge of the glory of the ETERNAL, as the waters cover the sea.

9. Ah! thou that madest thy neighbour[19] drink, pouring out thy fury,[20] and even making him drunken, to the end that thou art glutted[21] in looking on their nakedness. Drink thou also shame instead of glory, and be stript naked;[22] the cup of the ETERNAL's right hand come round to thee, and vomit of shame be in thy glory. For the

---

[18] *Are not these?* LXX. οὐ ταῦτά ἐστι παρὰ Κυρίου παντοκράτορος; Vulg. Numquid non hæc sunt a Domino exercituum. The Masora introduced the sense BEHOLD (הֲפֹּה for הֵנָּה), which if I followed, I should translate, Is there no vision (no *behold*) from the Eternal. For the weariness of the subject populations in the conqueror's tasks was not the will of Jehovah. The thought of his designing merely frustration of the work arose in later time, and does not express the humanity of the Prophet. Isaiah lxvi. 2.

[19] *Thy neighbour.* Heb. his.

[20] *Thy fury*; or, thy wine-skin, or thy poison, as Vulg. fel; Ewald, *gift*; or thy heated wine, as perhaps LXX, and many moderns. Alibi translatum legi, Væ qui proximo suo dat, ἔκστασιν ὀχλουμένην; *i.e.* amentiam turbidam.—*Hieron.*

[21] *Glutted.* This word belongs in the Hebrew to the next verse.

[22] *Be stript naked*; or, be amazed, according to Kimchi's beautiful conjecture הֵרָעֵל, which would improve the text; comp. Heb. Zech. xii. 2, Isaiah li. 17, and here LXX. σαλεύθητι καὶ σείσθητι.

---

freedom from marauding anarchy, spoil-built palaces, and forced labour than was yet before the seer's eyes. St. James v. 4—6. Such policy as Solomon's, though not blamed in the history written at court, is condemned by the Prophet, as by the people's hatred which it caused.

9. The sentiment as in 5—7: it is disputed, whether the land and city are spoken of Babylon which inflicted, or of Jerusalem which suffered the violence. Most prefer the latter. Possumus vel regem intelligere Judææ, vel

Ch. II.   violence of Lebanon shall cover[23] thee, and the destruc- A.V
tion of *its* beasts terrify thee ;[24] because of men's blood,
and for the violence of the land, of the city, and all the
dwellers therein.

10. What advantages the graven image that its
maker has graven it? *or* the molten image, and the
teacher of falsehood? that the fashioner thereof trusts
therein, *even* in what he has fashioned, making gods of
nought, that are dumb.

11. Ah! thou that sayest to the wood, Awake, to the
dumb stone, Arise, let it teach! Behold, it is laid over
with gold and silver, but any breath is not in the midst
of it at all.

12. But the ETERNAL is in the temple of his holiness;
be silent before him, all the Earth.

---

[23] *Cover.* Heb. יכסה, explained from כסה, but I suspect, from כנס,
with a reference to the cup, כיס.

[24] *Terrify thee.* Heb. terrify them; but LXX. has ταλαιπωρία θηρίων
πτοήσει σε, and *Vulg.* vastitas jumentorum deterrebit eos. This and the
parallelism suggest a change of affix.

---

omnes homines, quod inebriaverit eos malis, ut videret
Sedechiæ et captivorum nuditatem.—*Hieron.*

10—12. What do these conquerors represent, but
blind idolatry? while the oracular silence of the unte-
nanted shrine implies a spiritual and eternal Helper.

III.

A Prayer of Habakkuk the Prophet, upon wandering[25] measures.

1. ETERNAL, I heard thy speech; I trembled: O ETER- A.V.III.2.
NAL, revive thy work in the midst[26] of the years, in the midst of the years make known; in wrath remember pity.

2. God comes from Teman, and the Holy One from mount Paran. *Selah.*[27] His glory covers the heavens, and the earth is filled with his majesty.

3. Yea, his brightness is as the light; horns[28] go forth

---

[25] *Wandering measures;* or, a fantasia, according as the term *Shigionoth* is explained of mental passion, or of musical variations. See Psalm vii. Title.

[26] *In the midst;* or, in the drawing nigh of the years, *i.e.* speedily. LXX. ἐν τῷ ἐγγίζειν τὰ ἔτη, but also ἐν μέσῳ δύο ζώων γνωσθήσῃ, on which Jerome says, Multi putant de Filio intelligi et Spiritu Sancto; but adds, Simplex (!) interpretatio, et opinio vulgi, de Salvatore intelligit. He also suggests, as better, the Old and New Testaments, or their Churches.

[27] *Selah,* a musical direction, as it were, "Lift up the note." Gr. διά-ψαλμα.

[28] *Horns;* or, rays.

As the Psalms are properly Prayers, so this Psalm, which is distinct enough for its connexion with the rest to be doubtful, is entitled, as if in the Psalter.

1. The Psalmist, in time of trouble, perhaps on the advent of the Chaldæans, implores God that years may not pass without some manifestation of Providence.

2. Going back to old time, as men fancy the old was better, and strengthening his faith by instances on which he suffers imagination to play, he paints, as in Psalm lxviii. 7, the glories of the Exodus and of Sinai.

3—5. Infinitely as the Divine Majesty transcends our

CH. III. from his hand, and there the hiding-place[29] of his A.V strength.

4. Before him marches Pestilence; and lightning[29] goes forth at his feet.

5. He stood, and measured the Earth; he beheld, and made nations start; and the everlasting mountains broke asunder, the perpetual hills sank; his are the paths of eternity.

6. I saw the tents of Cushan[30] in affliction; the pavilions of the land of Midian tremble.

7. Wast thou wroth, JEHOVAH, with the streams, or was thine anger on the rivers, or on the sea thine indignation, that thou mountedst on thy horses, thy chariots of victory![31]

---

[29] *Hiding-place.* LXX. ἀγάπησιν.
[29] *Lightning;* or, burning coal. *Vulg.* Diabolus.
[30] *Cushan,* Gr. Αἰθιοπίαν (cp. title of Ps. vii.); but the Chaldee, with certain Jewish interpreters, whom Rosenmüller follows, understands Cushan-rishathaim, the Mesopotamian satrap of *Judges* iii. and the Midianites overthrown by Gideon, *Judges* vi. vii. This interpretation is chiefly worth mention, as turning our minds towards the early date, from which it may be suspected this prayer came down.
[31] *Thy chariots of victory;* or, on thy chariots for deliverance. *Vulg.* Quadrigæ tuæ salvatio. LXX. ἡ ἱππασία σου σωτηρία.

---

conceptions, imagination embodies it as a Person, and poetry makes it visible to the sensuous eye. All things awful in nature would attend, and all things capable of impression tremble at the LORD going forth to battle. Horns are emblems of the strength of God's right hand, or of brightness, as in Michael Angelo's Moses; if the latter, by hiding-place is meant cloud, as in Psalm xcvii. 2.

6. Israel's enemies would feel, or had felt.

7—9. The divine archer predicts his own victory, and wins it.

8. Thou strippest bare thy bow,[32] proclaiming thine A.V. III. 9. arrows satiated. Selah.

9. Thou cleavest the earth with rivers; the mountains beheld thee, and trembled; the storm-flood overflowed; *then* the Deep uttered its voice, the Height lifted up its hands.

10. Sun *and* Moon stood[33] still in their habitation; at the light of thine arrows they depart; at the brightness of the lightning of thy spear.

11. In disdain thou marchest through the land, in anger thou threshest the nations.

12. Thou wentest forth for the salvation of thy people,

---

[32] *Thou strippest bare thy bow;* or, thy bow is left utterly naked. Vulg. Suscitans suscitabis arcum. LXX. ἐντείνων ἐνέτειναξ τόξον. *Proclaiming thy arrows satiated.* This version is suggested by the Syriac, which Schroeder first adopted in part. My share in it is treating אמר as a participle; but if a noun, I would still understand it of oracular command, as in Psalm lxviii. 12, rather than of triumphant pæan, as most critics take it in both places. Such seems to me the best amendment of the very disputable Hebrew, *sevenths of rods,* formerly understood as *oaths to the tribes.*

[33] " Celebris locus, Jos. 10, 12-15, poeticus est; quare poeticè quoque explicandus, nempe Hebræos tantam cladem intulisse Canaanitis, ac si sol cursum stitisset, ac diem æquali rursus temporis spatio æquasset. Orta nempe est, ut Habakuk, iii. 10-12, exponit, post prælium tempestas, quæ hostes plurimos grandine confecit, deinde Hebræis lumine fulgurum Canaanitas conspicuos reddidit, ut eos totâ nocte, non secus ac si dies esset persequerentur. Poeta in sublimi carmine audaci figurâ induxit Josuam soli et lunæ præcipientem, ut cursum sisterent." JAHNIUS vir fidei Catholicæ, et non mediocris eruditionis, hæc scripsit. *Introd. in lib. Vet. Fœd. libr. Jos.*

9—11. In these figures is something to suggest, how faith allies herself to imagination, and how poetry may pass into history. The great deliverances and conquests of the Hebrews could not fail to make the national mind heave, and generate songs, which the chronicler might interweave, not always understanding them.

12. This is the earliest passage in the Prophets in which

Ch. III. for the salvation of thine Anointed;[31] thou smotest the head out of the house of the wicked; thou laidest[35] bare, foundation *even* to neck. Selah.

13. Thou clavest with his [36] shafts the head of his princes, *when* they whirled to scatter me; whose delight *was* as it were to consume the helpless in refuge.

14. Thou strodest through the sea with thine horses, through the heap[37] of mighty waters.

15. When I heard, my belly trembled; my lips tingled at the voice; rottenness enters into my bones, and I tremble beneath me, in that I must rest for the day of distress, for the coming up against my people *of one who* assails with troops.

16. Though the fig tree bloom not, and no fruit be in the vines; *though* the produce of the olive fail, and the

---

[31] *Thine Anointed.* The Greek versions vary from διὰ Ἰησοῦν χριστόν Th. to τοὺς ἐκλεκτούς σου. Ἀλλ. the latter being justified by Psalm cv. 15. 2 Cor. i. 21, 22.

[35] *Thou laidest bare.* Heb. Text Inf. *laying bare.* Vulg. nudasti fundamentum ejus usque ad collum.

[36] *His shafts.* Either the shafts of the bow, above; or the enemy's own; the latter sense being that of the text, as the affix stands.

[37] *Heap;* or, mud. Vulg. lutum; but comp. Exod. viii. 10, and xiv 22.

---

the term, or idea, *Messiah* occurs. Here it certainly means the People, as in Isaiah xli. 8, xliv. 1. Jerome well remarks: " Christi in veteri testamento dicebantur et " patriarchæ . . . . et omnes qui de Ægypto egressi sunt " Christi vocantur . . . postea sacerdotes . . reges. Sed " et Cyrus Persarum rex, *licet multi errent, et de Domino* " *Salvatore dictum putent,* audit per Esaiam, ' Hæc dicit " Dominus Christo suo Cyro' : . . . et ad extremum, " ' Tu non cognovisti me,' quod de Salvatore nefas est in- " telligere." By so much was this ancient Father more reasonable than some of our contemporaries.

15—18. The Prophet trembles, as imagination paints

II. fields yield no food; the flock be cut off from the fold, and no herd be in the stalls;   A. V. III. 17.

17. Yet let me exult in the ETERNAL; let me rejoice in the God of my salvation:

18. The ETERNAL, my Lord, is my strength; and he will make my feet like hinds' feet,[38] and on my high places make me a way.

To the precentor on my stringed instruments.

---

[38] *Hinds' feet*, as in Psalm xviii. 33, where, as here, the phrase is figurative for moral guidance, and not to be strained. "Sicut cervi spinosa transiliunt, ita ego pericula delictorum Domini virtute transcendo."—*Hier.*

---

the Symbols of Eternal Majesty; but amidst earthly loss, calamity, and death, his soul rests upon a faithful stay, who will guide his feet aright. Comp. Psalms xxiii. iv. 7, xvi. 8; Job xxiii. 6, xlii. 7. "Omnem mundanam solemnitatem contemplatione coelestium transcendere me fecit."
—*Hier.*

INTRODUCTION TO ZEPHANIAH.

READERS of Herodotus (iv. 11, and i. 103—106) remember the mention of certain Scythians, who being pressed by the Massagetæ, displaced the Cimmerians, and following them into Asia, became masters of Media for twenty-eight years, after which they were entrapped by Cyaxares in a drunken banquet, and most of them massacred. During their supremacy, which interrupted the siege of Nineveh, they extended their ravages through Syria, leaving their mark specially on Ascalon, but were diverted from Egypt by presents and prayers from Psammitichus. However much critics may question the route of the Scythians or the incentives to their movement assigned by Herodotus, the narrative represents accurately phenomena which have frequently recurred in the existence of the races[1] concerned. We may doubt, whether the name Scythopolis (for Bethshan, the place of exposure of Saul's remains), be a relic of the movement, or, as Reland[2] ingeniously conjectured, arose from confusion, which is etymologically credible, with the neighbouring name Succoth. We can hardly doubt, that a vast tumultuous movement, caused by disturbance among the northern nations, took place in the reign of Cyaxares, or that its extension to Ascalon must have imminently threatened, if it did not fall upon, Judæa.

If we observe how immediately the overthrow of the

---

[1] Gibbon, ch. ix. x. xxvi. Merivale, R. E. ch. v. Thirlwall, H. G. ch. xiv. That the Cimmerians ended their deliberations by an internecine combat among themselves, may afford ground for conjecturing the stem which they must have represented.

[2] Robinson, iii. *Bibl. Res.* § xiv. p. 175-6.

Scythians was succeeded by the last siege of Nineveh, in which the Chaldæans took part with the Medes, we must infer that the Scythian domination had the growth of the Chaldæan power among its contemporaneous events. We have seen in Habakkuk, with what awe this latter phenomenon impressed the prophetic mind. So within the limits of Josiah's reign, B.C. 640—609, we have two vast disturbances of nations, one of brief, the other of longer duration, both of them affecting Palestine, and each of which must have awakened from men who considered contemporaneous events in the light of Providence, an appeal to Heaven for help, or a judicial interpretation to man of whatever disasters became inevitable. A consideration of this state of things prepares us to understand the book of Zephaniah.

We know, as usually happens with the Prophets, too little of the author's personal history. He wrote not for fame, but from that strong impression of events upon his mind, which made the utterance of awe and warning not so much a duty as a necessity. The title may imply, by mentioning no less than four of his progenitors, that he was a person of some social rank; it is a possibility open to indecisive conjecture, that his father's great-grandfather Hezekiah may have been the famous king. Only in that case we should have expected the royal title to be added, and the limits of time barely allow space. *Nomen Sophoniæ*, says Jerome, *alii speculam, alii arcanum Domini transtulerunt; Sive igitur specula, sive arcanum Domini interpretatur, utrumque prophetæ convenit.* That is, the Hebrew name may bear to have forced upon it the sense of Jehovah's watch, or Jehovah's secret, either of which suits a prophet. But if we consider that the name is likely to have been imposed before the prophetic capacity was developed, we may think it better to follow Hebrew analogy, according to which *Tzephán-iah* would mean one whom Jehovah protects, and express the wish of a pious parent.

The zeal of Josiah may have needed no impulse from without, or may have been stimulated to undertake the reformation in the eighteenth year of his reign, 2 Kings xxii. xxiii., by the imminence of calamities, such as quicken men's perception. Zephaniah rather seems to connect the cutting off of Baal and his diviners (as was done by Josiah at Bethel) with the day of the Lord, not as in Joel, a day of darkness and locusts, but a day of alarm and desolation, which in his first chapter he describes at hand. The language may be thought foreboding; for the speaker places himself at a point of view at which the blow seems coming, but not yet come. Still if we bear in mind that the Scythian devastations extended throughout nearly the entire reign of Josiah, and may have had earlier preludes, while there is a distinction between the tone of narrative in which the preacher alludes to ruin consummated elsewhere, and the tone of presentiment with which he warns Jerusalem of what seems approaching her, we shall feel as little justified here, as elsewhere, in pressing predictive theories. See what has befallen other nations; consider what is likely to befall you, seems the key-note to the strain. If the work of reformation proceeded, so that the monitions of the prophet took effect, there would be no reason why, as in the case of Micah (Jerem. xxvi. 19; comp. Joel ii. iii.), the threatenings should not be happily frustrated. Where a modern preacher would threaten ruin upon persistence, the Hebrew emphasised his warning by omitting the condition, which yet by the manner of his country was understood. We may gather this from the commencement of the second chapter.

In brief, the first chapter of our prophet is warning; the second is chiefly commemorative of what has ruined

elsewhere, with some threatenings against Moab, which can only in the most poetical sense have been fulfilled, since the New Testament alone exhibits Peræa as flourishing; the third chapter, down to the thirteenth verse, is a vindication of Jehovah's dealings with his people, and an anticipation that such a quiet God-fearing race as the prophets loved, would spring up, after Josiah's reforms, in place of worldly and violent men. This latter part harmonises with the tenor of Josiah's reign, when we read of the discovery in the Temple of the long-forgotten, perhaps then revised, book of the Law, which it has been attempted not without vague probability, to identify with Deuteronomy.

It is usual to consider the seven closing verses as a promise of blessings upon the obedience just described, and it is still open to any one to do so. But why then does the style so suddenly become jubilant? Why the return from exile, before an exile has been mentioned? Why the rapid transition from the most gloomy of the prophets as into the dancing tone of one of the post-Babylonian Psalms? "When the Lord turned again the captivity of Zion, then were we like unto them that dream; then was our mouth filled with laughter, and our tongue with joy." So Psalm cxxvi. So here, "*Sing, daughter of Zion,* for I bring back your captivity, saith the Lord." Even if Hitzig had not preceded me in doing so, I think I should have relegated these seven verses to a later date, admitting that the evidence for doing so is only internal.

No less a critic than Ewald has pronounced the picture of Nineveh's desolation, ii. 13 (A. V. 13, 14), to have a fresher stamp of originality than the correspondent woe on Babylon in Isaiah xiii. (A. V. xiii.) It may be so. The strokes are briefer, the ideas less expanded. The general impression of Zephaniah is that he was far less original than the earlier Prophets. He neither searches the deep things of God, awe-stricken by calamity, as Habakkuk, nor stoops with lightning-intention upon some pregnant truth, as Isaiah, but adopts the tone of thought and diction current in his time, and upon disaster builds exhortation. Still his book is a poem; not, as seems ordinarily conceived, a series of messages delivered in form, but a poetical recast of reflexions and warnings, suggested by the events of the day, viewed in reference to the Divine Will. The difficulty of reading the world's riddle tends often to make men fall from a recognition of the unseen Ruler. Especially this happens when the expectation of habitual interpositions has created a revulsion of despondency, or when old associations, to which the sacredness of faith had been transferred, are found erroneous. If in such times a priesthood says All, or None, many will answer None. Mr. Palgrave in his *Arabia* has described strongly a certain absorption of thought in Deity. A kindred habit of mind, such as may be implied in the friends of Job, created amongst the Jews a re-action, in which men said, Jehovah does neither good nor evil. They had been led to expect manifestations apart from the phenomena of Nature and History, so could not see that these phenomena come of His Will. To such people, says Zephaniah, the great Day of the Lord will bring an awakening sense of His Providence. As already distant coasts, Gaza and Ashkelon to the West, Moab to the East, even Ethiopia, and the great city Nineveh, have felt the invader's hand, so Jerusalem, polluted and oppressive, will find the indwelling Judge as well as protector of Israel neither dead nor slumbering.

As we can only trace aright Providence in Nature, when we consider it as the underlying principle of the whole, and not as an exceptional interposition in parts, so Inspiration in Scripture becomes intelligible when we view thought and feeling as arising out of it, instead of requiring displacement to make room for it. When disputes about prediction have passed away, we shall begin to learn what the Prophet means, and see if any lesson is hinted to us through his meaning. Two results from Zephaniah stand out with that imperfect degree of clearness which makes an interrogative form appropriate for them, yet not without a preponderance of suggestion. Are political calamities or invasions not mere movements of nations, but instruments of Providential training? In the same limited sense they are so, as the elementary processes of the world in which we live. We cannot say that the good of a particular man, or nation, is the alone end and object of either, but we may extract from both concurrent instruments of admonition and awakenings of wisdom. Napoleon, after aggresive conquests, dying in an island prison, the Southern Confederacy of America freeing their slaves by a war into which they rushed to fetter them, Austria fastening on Italy a yoke of absolutism, in conjunction with which her own sceptre was broken at Sadowa, would have seemed to the Prophets, I know not why they should not seem to us, signs of God's own judgment. Again, is such an inoffensive but unenterprising community of devout people, as Zephaniah and other Prophets aimed at, the plan of Providence for mankind? Or, with a slight variation, are religious people the best people? Again, is there in the Prophet's mind not merely the love of a certain order of things social or hierarchic, but a diviner vision of what is inherently holy and good? Before we answer let us remember that the religious world rejected the Son of Man because He came eating and drinking; and crucified Him in the name of the Temple, the Scripture, the ancient Law. It seems on the whole that God governs the world on a principle of freedom; but while men are free to sow, they are bound to reap. So they have their reward, the violent man violence, the quiet man quietness. Paley shows well, that the virtues to which our nature is least apt, which most emphatically need cultivation, conduce most to human happiness, and must be most acceptable to our God. Yet as His scheme and thought are larger than ours, He has a place in His kingdom for what we dare not recommend. There is a truth in the Prophet holier than would be in any antagonistic position. Yet the narrowness which we may pardonably trace in the " sayings of old time," exaggerated by partisanship in our Saviour's time, paved the way for the death of Christ, the destruction of Jerusalem, the recasting of all that old society into forms ascetic and worldly, but on the whole of greater freedom and variety.

In Zephaniah I have first been able to consult Dr. Ludwig Philippsohn's *Israelitische Bibel* (Leipzig, 1858), a work of great value, which Dr. Ginsburg made known to me, and which must be added to my previously mentioned aids.

Those who wish a fuller account of the opinions of previous critics than seemed here useful to give, will find such in Dr. Davidson's *Introductions* to the Old Testament, which I wish to mention respectfully, though their plan is not that of this work. Some things in them, as *e.g.* the explanation of Nahum ii. 10—12, that the city had "become a hiding-place for lions," are irreconcilable with the supposition of a study of the original text, or much consideration even of the English version.

ZEPHANIAH.

The word of the ETERNAL *which was to Zephaniah son of Cushi, son of Gedaliah, son of Amariah, son of Hezekiah, in the days of Josiah son of Amon, king of Israel.*

I. 1. I will utterly destroy[1] all from off the face of the A. V. i. 2. land, is the saying of the ETERNAL:

2. I will destroy man and beast: destroy the birds of heaven, and the fishes of the sea, and the stumbling-blocks [*with?*][2] the wicked; and I will cut off mankind from off the face of the land, is the saying of the ETERNAL.

3. And I will stretch forth my hand upon Judah, and upon all the inhabitants of Jerusalem; and cut off from this place the remnant of Baal, and the name of the Diviners with the priests:

---

[1] *Destroy.* Heb. gather, as in Micah ii. 12, where see Note, and below Zeph. iii. 18. Vulg. h. l. Congregans congregabo. LXX. ἐκλείψει ἐκλιπέτω.
[2] *The stumbling-blocks with the wicked.* Vulg. Ruinæ impiorum erunt. LXX. ἀσθενήσουσιν οἱ ἀσεβεῖς Either the noun *stumbling-blocks* exerts a pregnant force as a transitive gerund with a case, or else the text has contracted a change.

The title gives, probably from tradition, the Prophet's name and family, without specifying whether his ancestor Hezekiah was the king of that name, and mentions the reign in which he lived.

1—3. Josiah's reign was a time of widely-extended trouble, from the movements of nomad tribes, viz. Cimmerians in the north (Herodot. iv. 11, and i. 103—106), and Scythians whose incursions included Palestine; but also a time of reform, when the king cut off the worship of Baal from Jerusalem, and slew the priests in Samaria (2 Kings xxii. 4—20), though the disaster of Megiddo was not thereby averted. At such a time, Zephaniah traces to the Divine will, both the alarming anarchy and the purifying disaster.

Ch. I. 4. And those that worship upon the house-tops the host of heaven, and those that worship and swear by JEHOVAH, while they swear by their Moloch.[3]

5. And those that are gone back from after JEHOVAH, and who have not sought JEHOVAH, nor enquired for him.

6. Hush, before the face of the Lord, JEHOVAH; for JEHOVAH's day is near, for JEHOVAH has prepared a sacrifice, has consecrated his guests;[4]

7. And it shall be in the day of JEHOVAH's sacrifice, that I will visit upon the princes, and upon the king's sons, and upon all that clothe themselves in the apparel of the stranger.

8. And I will visit in that day upon every one that leaps over the threshold,[5] those that fill their lord's house with plunder and fraud.

9. And it shall be in that day, is JEHOVAH's saying,

---

[3] *Their Moloch;* or, their king, as LXX. Heb. Malcham, as A. V. i. 5, and Vulgate. Comp. 1 Kings xi. 7, 33; Amos iv. 17 (A. V. v. 26.)

[4] *Consecrated his guests.* Isaiah xii. 2 (A. V. xiii. 3.)

[5] *Leaps over the threshold.* Either a superstition of the Philistines, 1 Sam. v. 5, in which case the strange apparel may be the vestments of Baal's worship, as in 2 Kings x. 22; or, as Jerome less probably, arrogant entrance into the temple; or rather as the context implies, housebreaking. Comp. Amos ii. 1, (A. V 4.

4—6. God is jealous, not merely of the mixing of faith and worship, which breeds confusion, but of the hypocrisy which unites sin to a show of piety. We cannot serve two masters. Judicial slaughter, though wrought by blind instruments, is as a sacrifice to offended Heaven.

7, 8. The blow is merited by luxury effeminate in the palace, and by robbery in private houses (or, as some, by superstitious adoption of Philistine worship). Jehoahaz and Jehoiakim need not be aimed at in the denunciation, though their fate exemplifies it.

9. Either two gates, or else the fish-gate, and the city's

1. *shall be* voice of crying from the fish gate, and howling A.V.I.10. from the second *gate*,[6] and a great crash from the hills.

10. Howl, inhabitants of the pounding pot,[7] because all the Canaanitish[8] people is destroyed; all the laden with silver[9] are cut off:

11. And it shall be in that time, I will search Jerusalem with torches, and visit upon the men that curdle on their lees, that say in their hearts, Neither good does the ETERNAL, nor evil:

12. So shall their substance become a booty, and their houses a desolation: though they build houses, they shall not dwell in them, though they plant vineyards, they shall not drink the wine of them.

---

[6] *Second gate;* or, part of the city, 2 Kings xxii. 14, with some, the height of Ophel. Nehem. iii. 3—26.

[7] *Pounding pot.* Heb. Maktesh; Vulg. Pilæ. lit. a mortar, whether a name given in irony, or gravely.

[8] *Canaanitish,* probably in the sense of trading, as A.V. merchant people.

[9] *Laden with silver,* like suspensi loculos. Comp. *Natol* and *Toul,* Latin tollo.

---

second quarter (in which Huldah lived, 2 Kings xxii. 14), and the farther region of the hills re-echo all around with cries of alarm.

10. The pounding-pot (*Maktesh*), is either the valley, compared to a mortar, or (as Ewald) a contemptuous name for the place of traders and retailers. Canaanitish, used metaphorically, as we say Lombard, or Jewish.

11. The Epicurean disbelief or despair of Providence, such as comes to men immersed in traffic, or hardened, instead of softened, by calamity unblest, (Rev. xvi. 9), will have to learn the lesson of disaster.

12. The language of Amos iv. 8 (A.V. v. 11), is adopted by the Prophet, as later writers habitually employ familiar phrases.

13. The great day[10] of JEHOVAH is near; near, and rapid a. exceedingly; the voice of JEHOVAH's day is bitter; there wails the warrior;

14. A day of wrath is that day, a day of trouble and distress, a day of wasteness and desolation, a day of darkness and gloom, a day of clouds and lowering, a day of trumpet and alarm against the fenced cities, and against the lofty towers.

15. And I will make it grievous for mankind, and they shall walk like blindlings, because they have sinned against JEHOVAH, and their blood shall be shed as dust, and their flesh as dung.

16. Neither their silver nor their gold shall be able to deliver them in the day of JEHOVAH's wrath; but in the fire of his jealousy shall the whole land be devoured; for a complete *work* and a speedy one will he work on all the dwellers of the land.

---

[10] *The great day, &c.* Juxta est dies Domini magnus, juxta est et velox nimis; vox diei Domini amara, tribulabitur ibi fortis. The reader who weighs these words either in Hebrew, or the Vulgate or Anglican, without any punctuation, will observe that the Grammar suggests a construction different from that of the Masora; and perhaps less decidedly a different one from that which strong advocates of parallelism would prefer. For the end, the LXX. have φωνὴ ἡμέρας Κυρίου πικρὰ καὶ σκληρὰ τέτακται.

13, 14. The constant cry of the Prophets, hailing calamity as a *Day of the Lord*, (from whence we symbolise the eternal activity of God's inexorable judgments under form of a Day), is here raised.

15, 16. The misery of mankind's darkest helplessness is connected with forgetfulness of God, and his estrangement from the godless is painted as an avenging decree. Comp. Isaiah x.

II.

1. Make yourselves pale, and wither,[11] nation un-   A. V. II. 1.
ashamed.

2. Before the decree bring forth the day passing[12] as the chaff; while yet is not come upon you the fierceness of JEHOVAH's wrath, while yet is not come upon you the day of JEHOVAH's anger,

3. Seek the ETERNAL, all the quiet of the land, which have wrought his judgment; seek righteousness, seek quietness; if it may be ye shall be hidden, in the day of JEHOVAH's anger;

4. For Gaza[13] shall be forsaken, and Ashkelon become desolation: they shall drive out Ashdod at noon-tide, and Ekron shall be rooted up.

---

[11] *Pale* and *wither;* or, Gather yourselves, as in sheaves; as the Versions, and the older critics. *Vulg.* Convenite, Congregamini. LXX. συνάχθητε; but the word, having the sense of harvest-dryness, by Ewald and others now explained of withering with shame. So the word, translated *un-ashamed,* but Vulg. non amabilis, has the sense of silver-whiteness, or silver-clearness. My preference is not free from doubt. .

[12] *Passing;* or, pass, retaining the vocalisation as of a verb. *Vulg.* Priusquam jussio pariat quasi pulverem transeuntem diem. Cf. Hosea xi. 15. (A. V. xiii. 3.)

[13] *Gaza,* &c. The Hebrew has a word-play, which might be Anglicised thus: *Gaza* shall be left *ghastly,* and *Ashkelon* become *ash*-heaps; they shall *dash* Ashdod at noon-tide, and *Ekron* shall be *excavate.*

1, 2. Writing amidst disasters imminent, but not yet crushing, the Prophet bids either the scattered assemble for prayer, or the hardened bleach with awe, before the day is born sweeping chaff with storm.

3. A touch of Christ's teaching (Matth. v.) appears in the invocation to a quiet and inoffensive type of men, such as the Prophets would have seen their people become, and such as might bend to the storm, or hush while it passed.

4—6. The Scythian invasion fell heavily on the Philis-

Ch. II.   5. Ah! dwellers of the coast of the sea, nation of Cretans, the word of JEHOVAH is upon you: Canaan, land of Philistines, thee too I destroy that there be no inhabitant.

6. And the sea-coast shall be folds, the cutting of shepherds,[14] and enclosures of flocks, and it shall be a coast for the remnant of the house of Judah; thereupon shall they pasture; in the houses of Ashkelon at even shall they lie down; for JEHOVAH their God will visit them, and turn their captivity.

7. I have heard (*saith He*) the reproach of Moab, and the tauntings of the sons of Ammon, wherewith they reproached my people, and wrought mightily against their border.

8. Therefore, as I live, is the saying of JEHOVAH of hosts, the God of Israel, surely Moab shall be as Sodom, and the sons of Ammon as Gomorrah, a tract of nettles,[15] and a digging of salt, and a destruction for ever: the remnant of my people shall spoil them, and the remainder of my nation inherit them.

9. This shall be to them instead of their pride, because they reproached and spake mightily against the people of JEHOVAH of hosts.

---

[14] *Folds, the cutting of shepherds:* so Heb. but LXX. ἔσται κρήτη νομὴ ποιμνίων, as if כרת as a local name had preceded נות.

[15] *A tract of nettles.* Vulg. siccitas spinarum. The word rendered *tract* is either a dreary length, as of desert, or more simply a possession. Isaiah xxvii. 20. (A. V. xxxii. 14.)

---

tine towns, as they also suffered from Assyrian and subsequently from Chaldæan.

7—9. Many an old feud with the half-dispossessed, half-encroaching, nations east of the Jordan, makes the Hebrew writer regard disaster on them as divinely merited, and as opening a way for his own nation's dominion over them. The key-note is not prediction, but denunciation.

II. 10. JEHOVAH is terrible upon them, for he has humbled A.V.11.11. all the gods of the earth, and they bow down to him, every one from his place; all the coasts of the nations, even you Ethiopians,[16] are wounded of my sword.

11. Yea,[17] he stretches forth his hand upon the north, and destroys Assyria, and makes Nineveh a desolation, a desert as the wilderness, and in her midst lie down flocks, every beast[18] of the herd: both pelican and bittern[19] lodge in the coronals; a howl[20] sounds in the windows, the

---

[16] *Even you Ethiopians.* As in the first half of this clause, the bowing of heathen deities, *humbled*, (lit. Heb. *made lean*,) by Jehovah is the subject; so in the second half the reaching of Jehovah's sword to far coasts, even to Ethiopia, is mentioned. Our A. V. v. 12, had no right to insert the future *shall be*.

[17] Jerome and Ewald seem to concur in suggesting that the destruction of Assyria is described as already come, not as future. "Post eversionem insultans ruinæ sermo propheticus loquitur." "Nineveh damals schon seine erste belagerung ausgehalten hatte, und mit der zweiten bedroht wurde."

[18] *Beast of the herd.* Heb. of the nation. Vulg. omnes bestiæ gentium. LXX. τῆς γῆς; I conceive it to mean gregarious. Cf. Ps. lxviii. 30.

[19] *Bittern;* or, hedgehog, as most critics, but with little certainty. Vulg. ericius. LXX. ἐχῖνοι. I find it difficult, on comparing the passages, Isaiah xii. 20, xxix. 11-14, (A. V. xiii. 21. xxxiv. 11-14,) not to suppose some bird meant, though the sense may have been derivative, as the Latin Milvus is a kite, and a pike.

[20] *A howl sounds.* Heb. A voice sings. *Vulg.* Vox cantantis. LXX. θήρια φωνήσει; Ewald and Hitzig, the owl; I believe the name of some bird meant, but know not what.

---

10. The path of wild conquerors may be conceived as traversed by Jehovah's sword, and the fall of their idols as his triumph, reaching even to far Ethiopia; as already (11) he has overthrown Nineveh, and (12) made her exulting palaces dens for wild beasts.

Philippsohn's translation of v. 11, is "Und seine hand streckt er gen Mitter-nacht, und richtet Aschur zu grunde, und wandelt Nineveh zur Oede, zur dürre wie wüste."

Ch. II. raven[21] on the threshold, for her cedar-work[22] is laid A.V. bare.

12. *Is* this the exulting city, that abode confidently, that said in her heart, *here am* I, and beyond me none? how is she become a desolation, a couching-place for beasts! every one passing by her hisses, tosses his hand.

III.

1. Ah! rebellious[23] and polluted, thou oppressive[24] city!

2. She hearkened not to the voice, she received not instruction; she trusted not in JEHOVAH, she drew not near to her God.

3. Her princes within her *were* roaring lions, her judges wolves of darkness: they spared not a bone till the morrow.

---

[21] *The raven.* So *Vulg.* LXX. Ewald, κόρακες, corvus, Krähe; yet the Heb. *Choreb* for *Oreb*, requires straining into that sense.

[22] *Her cedar work is laid bare;* so the Masora, with verb impers. but *Vulg.* attenuabo robur ejus, points to the fut. of *Razah*, to *make lean*, used above in ver. 10, for humbling, and here perhaps a truer reading than the Masora, *her cedar*, which however gives sense, and has the LXX. κέδρος, to aid it.

[23] *Rebellious;* or, filthy, or made a spectacle.

[24] *Oppressive;* or, a Dove. LXX. περιστέρα, *Vulg.* Columba, cf. Hosea vi. 12. (A. V. vii. 11.) We must not think of Ionians here, which would have been Javan.

---

12. The last verse at least implies the ruin of Nineveh consummated; as in the last verse of Nahum. The colouring is as in Isaiah xii. and xxix. (A. V. xiii. and xxxiv.) but whether by imitation or only community of phrase, not certain.

1—6. Here seems a transition of warning from Nineveh to Jerusalem; though, except for the mention of priest and prophet, it might, still possibly may, be

III. 4. Her prophets *were* wanton, men of wiles; her A.V. III. 4.
priests polluted the sanctuary, violated the law.

5. JEHOVAH is righteous in her midst, he worketh no iniquity; morning by morning he brings his judgment to light; the wicked is not hindered,[25] and knoweth not shame.

6. I have cut off nations, their towers are desolate; I laid waste their streets, that none passes by; their cities are destroyed that there is no man, so that there is no inhabitant.

7. I said, Surely thou wilt fear me, thou wilt receive instruction; so shall not be cut off her abode, [*nor happen*] all that I visit upon her;[26] alas! they hastened early to corrupt all their doings.

8. Therefore, wait for me, is JEHOVAH'S saying, till the day of my rising to the prey, when my judgment[27] is to

---

[25] *The wicked is not hindered;* or, Jehovah is not missed, *i.e.* fails not in his judgment. So the punctuators and the critics hitherto; but the primary sense of the verb is setting in order, and the twin negatives suggest the rhythm here preferred.

[26] *All that I visit upon her.* These words are most simply explained by having the negative carried on from the preceding clause, nearly as in Psalm i. 5; or it may be, notwithstanding all my visitation.

[27] *When my judgment is;* or, because my judgment is. These words may govern the following clause, which I have connected with the preceding one.

---

considered a continuous reflexion on Nineveh's ruin. If, as most, we prefer the transition, the disdainful tone towards the prophetic order is remarkable. It would be still more so if we translated פותים wanton, with the LXX. πνευματοφόροι. Whatever the wickedness of religious people, the All-seeing, all-righteous, Object of their unworthy homage is not mocked, however little their wayward course is checked by his awe.

6—8. God's design in punishing sinners is to warn

Ch. III. gather nations: [*wait*] until I assemble kingdoms, to A.V. pour upon them mine anger, all the fury of my wrath: for in the fire of my jealousy shall all the land be devoured.

9. For then will I change the speech of populations *so that it shall be* pure,[28] that they may all call upon Jehovah's name, to serve him with one consent;[29]

10. From beyond the rivers of Ethiopia my[30] incensers, the daughter of my dispersion,[31] they shall bring my offering.

11. In that day thou shalt not be ashamed for all thy doings, whereby thou hast transgressed against me; for then will I remove from thy midst the rampant ones[32] of thy haughtiness, and thou shalt not continue to be lofty any more on my holy mountain;

12. But I will leave a remnant in thy midst, a people poor and humble, that shall trust in the name of Jehovah;

13. The remnant of Israel shall neither work iniquity

---

[28] *Pure lip.* Vulg. labium electum.
[29] *One consent.* Heb. one shoulder.
[30] *My incensers;* or, my incense, Ezek. viii. 11.
[31] *Daughter of my dispersion;* or, the daughter of Nubia; for *Putz*, following so closely Ethiopia, suggests an older reading *Put*, which Ewald adopts. Vulg. Inde supplices mei, filii dispersorum meorum, deferent munus mihi. The idea *dispersion* savours of later copyists.
[32] *Rampant ones of thy haughtiness.* See Isaiah xii. 2. (A. V. xiii. 3.)

---

the less hardened; so it might be hoped, ruin of many nations would have roused Jerusalem to a sense of duty.

9, 10. Even barbarians may unlearn their rude accent, and worship God with pure lip, bringing incense from afar.

11—13. What a happy ending of our trouble, if it reforms us; of invasion and anarchy, if they leave a

nor speak falsehood, nor shall a tongue of deceit be found in their mouth; but they shall pasture and lie down, and there shall be none to make them afraid.

A. V. III.
13.

14. Sing, daughter of Zion; shout you, Israel; be glad and exult with all the heart, daughter of Jerusalem. 15. The ETERNAL has removed thy judgments; the king of Israel[33] has cast out thine enemy; the ETERNAL is in thy midst; thou shalt not see[34] evil any more. 16. In that day shall it be said to Jerusalem, Fear not: Zion, let not thy hands be faint. 17. The ETERNAL thy God is in thy midst, mighty to save: he will rejoice over thee with joy; he will rest[35] in his love; he will cause to rejoice over thee with singing the mourners away from the congregation.[36]

---

[33] *King of Israel.* The Masora points this noun into the next clause, and thereby leaves a verb with no nominative in the first, a noun with no verb in the second member, as the English reader may see from the A. V.

[34] *See;* or, *fear.* The MSS. and Versions differ.

[35] *He will rest.* So Heb. but LXX. from a change of letter, καινιεῖ, shall renew thee.

[36] *Mourners away from the congregation.* LXX. ὡς ἐν ἡμέρᾳ ἑορτῆς. Vulg. Nugas, qui a lege recesserant, congregabo, quia ex te erant: ut non ultra habeas super eis opprobrium. Jerome fancied the Latin *nugas* derived from נוגי, which means mourners or exiles removed, and that it proved Hebrew the source of all tongues. Though the above versions are but curiosities, the Greek suggests that *the mourners for the solemn assembly* were to be rejoiced in the first verse, instead of gathered in the second. When Zephaniah elsewhere uses אסף to *gather,* he does it in the sense of destruction, see i. 1, 2.

---

realm conscious of its true strength; of Scythian and other invasions, if under Josiah's pious rule Judah returns to primitive simplicity of manners, and quiet piety. Here probably ended Zephaniah, his poem being thus rounded off.

14—19. A Psalm is appended, full of triumph on the return from Babylon, or in some like time of restoration.

Ch. III. 18. I have destroyed out of thee *those who in their* utterance[37] were a reproach upon her; behold me working all thy oppressors their shame,[38] in that time when I save the halting, and gather the exiled, and make them a praise and a renown in all the earth. 19. At that time *when* I bring you *again*, and in the time of my gathering you; surely I will make you a renown and a praise among all populations of the earth, when I turn your captivity before your eyes, saith the ETERNAL.

---

[37] The word *Utterance* might mean burthen.
[38] *Their shame.* The Hebrew collocation of these words would be as in A. V. in every land of their shame; but the word *Land* ought not then to have the article, while the verb *do*, or *work* (עֹשֶׂה; A. V. undo, *Vulg.* interficiam,) seems to require a noun. So the transposition followed above, though harsh, seems possible.

The pious will no longer mourn, like our own colonists, or others, afar from the means of grace, longing for the Temple's high chant once more, or for the sober voice of preaching, but Jehovah will be exalted, while he restores his people, and they who hoped in Him against hope will be justified.

HIERONYMUS IN HIEREMIAM PROPHETAM.

LIBELLUM Baruch, qui vulgo editioni LXX copulatur, nec habetur apud Hebræos, et ψευδόγραφον epistolam Hieremiæ, nequaquam censui disserendam, sed magis Hieremiæ ordinem, librariorum errore confusum, multaque, quæ desunt, ex Hebræis fontibus digerere, ordinare, deducere, ac complere, ut novum ex veteri, verumque pro corrupto atque falsato prophetam teneas: parvi pendens obtrectatorum rabiem, qui non solum verba, sed syllabas quoque nostrorum verborum calumniantur : in eo se scire aliquid arbitrantes, si de alienis operibus detrahant : ut nuper indoctus calumniator erupit . . . . . . nec intelligit leges commentariorum . . . . . in quibus multæ diversorum ponuntur opiniones . . . . . . Quod non videns præcursor ejus GRUNNIUS olim nisus est carpere. Cui duobus respondi libris; quæ iste quasi sua profert . . . . . . Sed jam propositum opus aggrediendum est.—*Proëmium.*

INTRODUCTION TO JEREMIAH.

The relation of Jeremiah in point of time to Habakkuk and Zephaniah is not unlike that of Isaiah to Micah. Commencing his career as early, and witnessing with them the inroads of Scythian marauders, (Herod. i. 15 and 105, iv. 11. vii. 20,) whose devastations preluded the Chaldæo-Babylonian conquests, he descends to a far lower date, and describes the fall of Jerusalem, which he had foretold, the migration into Egypt, which he shared. Born perhaps but a few years before Josiah became king, and beginning to teach in the thirteenth year of that reign, he enjoys eighteen years of prosperous activity before the sad battle of Megiddo; teaches with less acceptance, and with ever-deepening presentiments, during the eleven years of Jehoiakim, the creature of Egypt, though reluctant tributary of Babylon; he bestows a few bitter oracles on the three months' reign of Jehoiachin, with whom he sees the direct dynasty of David end, and the true exile begin: he then alternately comforts the well-meaning Zedekiah and warns him against vain resistance; when the eleven years of a wavering reign terminate, after a year and a half's siege, with the storming of the city and the blinding of the king, Jeremiah accompanies the relics of his countrymen in their fluttering for two or three months about the ruins of their country, and then, against his will, in their recourse for shelter to Egypt. We thus trace him for a period of about sixty years, B. C. 647?—587—6.

Anathoth, the prophet's birthplace, not 'poor Anathoth,' but the walled town, whose echoes made answer to startled Laish, in the tribe of Benjamin, at the third milestone north of Jerusalem, says Jerome, is (as Anâta) one of the places rescued from monkish topographers by the traveller Robinson, ii. B. R. p. 109. Whether Hilkiah, the father, is with the aid of another family name Shallum, most naturally identified with the high-priest of the day, or whether the connexion of Abiathar,[1] the dispossessed priest of Solomon's time, with Anathoth would exclude Jeremiah from inheritance there, if his father, as high-priest, had been of the rival line of Zadok and Eleazar, seems not quite certain. The proneness of tentative critics to connect Jeremiah as author with the book of Deuteronomy, (which may have been the book produced by Hilkiah from the Temple,) would, if made out, be in favour of the identification. In either case the descent of our prophet would accord with his devout, and in the innocent sense of the word, priestly type of mind. Connected by sympathy, though not by office, with the Temple, he was, in a way not unlike analogous instances among our Academic clergy, favourably placed for the task of criticism, while the events of the period above defined would profoundly agitate one who surveyed them with religious anxiety. We ought not to think of the Jews as living normally apart from the world, until a judgment of exile fell upon them suddenly. They shared all the perturbations caused by the Scythian invasion. Egypt, under the enterprising Necho, was in a position to grant or threaten interference. Babylon, which had once sought their alliance, was in the closing years of the Assyrian empire a power daily encroaching, and destined, as had been foreseen, to become a hard mistress. At home was the phenomenon, explained in earlier times by the survival of creeds more

[1] 1 Kings ii. 26—35 ; 1 Chron. xxiv. 2—6 ; 1 Chron. vi. 13 ; Jer. xxxii. 7.

native to the soil, but still, and now more than ever, anomalous, of a people summoned to a pure religion by spiritual teachers, yet suffering their women to honour with incense the Queen of heaven, nature-worship in some of its forms revelling on every green hill, the name and attributes of Baal ascribed as freely to GOD, as those of Jehovah. The very language and metaphors of Jeremiah, though free from taint of allurement, imply as general a state of morals in which coarse terms seemed natural. Amidst the strife of teachers we imagine it must have been easy to distinguish the false prophets from the true. Far otherwise it seemed to their contemporaries. When the sanctity of the priesthood was confronted by Seer's denunciation, which was the more divine? When two prophets, with like figure of inspiration, 'Thus saith the LORD, God of Israel,' enjoined opposite policy in respect of Egypt or Babylon, the keener patriotism would sound the more sacred; years might elapse, before the verdict of events could be decisive. Once, in the five centuries over which our specimens extend, the disaster of Sennacherib in the desert gave a splendid sanction to the counsels of Isaiah. We shall find Jeremiah's presentiments on the side of Babylon confirmed by the result: but also open to the remark, that less divided counsels might have offered a more successful resistance. Neither the piety of Josiah, nor the tears (we may suppose the counsels) of his prophets saved him from disaster on the side of Egypt. The death of a rival, within a few months of a collision between two seers, would be explained by his friends as accidental. No such epithet as 'False' was applied to Hananiah by his hearers. In short, the impression, deepening with study of the prophetic records, is that a common zeal in the cause of Jehovah, a like employment of oracular terms, accompanied considerable diversity of views, for each of which might be pleaded a partial, barely for any a complete, justification. Thus the acceptance of a prophet by his people, as that of a council by the church, nay, even as that of a canonical epistle by the Fathers, would have in it at first a problematical element, and being weighed by a composite process of instinct and experience, might grow with distance. Jeremiah, intrigued against by his neighbours, or ignominiously put in "the stocks" by an apparitor, as a Puritan might have been under Whitgift, and worst of all, rescued with clouts under his arms out of a dirty dungeon by an Abyssinian, appears less venerable than in his later years, when the exiles treat him as a national conscience, whose sanction they desire, even while they disobey his monitions; he will still have to suffer rejection, and threat of stoning in Egypt, before he becomes emphatically above all the Prophet, recognised as such by his people, when not named; his works holding the first place in their canon; his gray form seen in vision[2] in their darkest hours, interceding in heaven for those who had rejected him on earth. It is beyond reasonable doubt, that the main causes of this elevation are to be found in the strength of his religious and patriotic affections, his infinite pathos, his spiritual vision in harmony with the deepest ethical instincts—these are the main causes—whether such prediction of events, as we ordinarily imagine, had a causative place among them, or was an appendage, chiefly an aftergrowth, from misplacement, gratuitous imagination, or misunderstanding, is a question less momentous than is thought, but sufficiently interesting to require a systematic exposition.

Not even a mere English reader can throw an intelligent glance through Jeremiah's book, without being

[2] 2 Macc. xv. 13, 14.

struck by the disorder, in which the prophecies stand. He would have expected those of Josiah's reign to come first, and those of the intermediate Jehoiakim to precede those of Zedekiah's reign. Instead of this, he finds nearly twenty chapters with little precise note of time: in the 21st chapter he is launched upon the reign of the last king Zedekiah; in the 24th, and if he looks closely, in the 27th chapter, more obviously in the 28th and 29th, he discerns traces of the same late period; nearly the same is to be said of the 34th. But in the 25th chapter, and again in the 36th, he is transported into the fourth year of Jehoiakim; in the 22nd he finds a review of the same reign, with the addition of Jehoiachin or Jeconiah's: once more, in the 45th he finds Jehoiakim's fourth year named, and in the subsequent group of four chapters against the nations, he finds more to suggest to him the same, than any later year. Hence even in the rhetorical thunders of Bishop Watson[3] against a rude assailant, we find some dislocation in our prophet's works reluctantly admitted. St. Jerome had long before incurred the reproach of neology by observing it. A well-meant attempt is made in Dr. Blayney's version to present a more satisfactory order. Critics have exhausted their ingenuity in conjecturing reasons, intermittent recollection, error of amanuensis, subsequent confusion, to explain a disarrangement on the surface.

The difficulty assumes a graver character on our turning to the Greek. We there find the four chapters *Against the Nations* grouped together in the midst of the xxvth chapter. If we look narrowly, we find differences not merely of order, but of text. Nebuchadnezzar and Babylon are mentioned in our Hebrew of chap. xxv., but omitted in the Greek. In other places, as in xxiii. 7, 8,

[3] *Apology*—Letter vi.

the precise verses, which we read as they stand in our Hebrew with a sense of their inappropriateness to their position, are absent in the Greek. Again, in the four chapters *Against the Nations*, the order is different. Elam, last in the Hebrew, as it would naturally be, is placed by the Greek translators first in order, probably under the impression, which Alexander's conquest of Persia had made in their time. We must discern traces of a like impression in their translating the sword of the oppressor (c. l. v. 16) as the Hellenic sword. Where there is no bias from this impression, the variations of the Greek translators have commonly the appearance of genuineness in their favour, as in their omission of the erroneous title, suspicious also in form, at the head of the 27th chapter. The same is to be said eminently of making the embassy to Babylon (c. li. v. 59), sent by Zedekiah, instead of, as in the Hebrew, making it include the king. The same holds good of the omission of the Cabalistic term *Sheshach*, in cc. xxv. and li., since the prophet needed not to use, if he had even known, the term; and it holds good in a vast number of minute instances. This remark must not be understood as exonerating the Greek translators from habitual proneness to error, but as pointing to their possession of an older text than our Hebrew. In some cases, as in chap. x., we may admit the claims to preference to be nearly balanced.

Again, the Hebrew scholar, who scrutinises closely his text, will find in Jeremiah signs, more than commonly frequent, of change upon change. The problem is not quite, as in Isaiah, of various authors erroneously combined under one name; for about nine-tenths of our book are substantially due to one author, though not to one of an original cast. Nor is the confusion, which we have to explain, such as would arise from transcription, as in the case of Psalm xviii. taken in comparison with 2 Sam. xxii. Hence it is childish to talk of the book having been much read, and therefore altered. Nor does the supposition of attempts to arrange the prophecies according to their subject matter grapple with the philology of the question, though such attempts may be traced. For why have just those titles (cc. 27, 29) which are otherwise suspicious, a later form of the name Jeremiah (*ah*, instead of *ahu*), or the added title of *the prophet*, as if the context would not distinguish him? Why have we a verse of a Chaldee Targum (unless we prefer the LXX. omissions) in the 10th chapter? Why are the four chapters *On the Nations* so much a reproduction of older poems, of Obadiah on Edom, of the unknown poet adopted by Isaiah on Moab, and of others? What suggested the Cabalistic cypher (*Athbasch*) in the words *Sheshach* and *Leb-kamai* (cap. li. v. 1), to a prophet before the Exile? How came just the chapter, containing this last, to be a cento compiled from an author who passes as Isaiah, and in an order less natural or original, than in the book from which it is taken? Still more, why are verses of an encouraging strain, but in a style otherwise resembling that of the latter Isaiah, introduced in the midst of calamities, where they disturb the context, unless because the feelings of an early editor required for himself or for his readers the solace of an expression of confidence? It is remarkable, if even a single instance of this kind is marked by the LXX for suspicion. We may go farther, and see in the xxxth and xxxist chapters an elevation of thought and expansion of horizon, for which in Jeremiah we have little precedent, and which not only bears to him a relation resembling that of the latter Isaiah to the earlier, but recalls in type of expression those glorious chapters, whose place in time is towards the end of the Exile. And, although some things may have been too confidently said about Baruch, it is not without significance, that the avowed transcriber of Jeremiah should have left amid his master's works expressions and sentiments not quite like his master, and very like a book which some critics assign, but conjecturally, to himself. The dissonance of the two notes sounded in the xxxth chapter, the evangelical promise in the xxxist, the return described as following on the great day, when every man was seen with his hand upon his loins, present us with phenomena resembling the commencement of Hosea, less cogent perhaps than some in Isaiah, but suggestive of editor's work amounting to a share in authorship. This much at least is not doubtful, that the question with which we have to deal, is one of editing. Some approach to a consistent theory, if not without supplement of conjecture, may be derived from the following considerations.

Twenty-two full years had passed over Jeremiah as speaker, when in Jehoiakim's fourth year he began to be a writer. Suppose a statesman, without aid from distinct debates, reporting his own speeches after such a time. He would recast many things. More appropriately, a preacher, if accustomed to rhythmical or chanted rhetoric, would first concentrate his teaching in summary, with perhaps a prelude on the nature of his vocation, and proceed to dwell on particular facts of his career. Such is the stamp of book presented to us by about the two first decades of our prophet's chapters, if we take seventeen (with the exception of a passage in the tenth) as the message, and from the eighteenth onward, omitting parts evidently later, find illustrative incidents.[4] But we must observe,

[4] There are frequent repetitions, as in xxii. 4, of xvii. 18, or 25, if we retain so far the order; but the piece in xvii. has some appearance of being subsequently moulded upon xxii.

that the great battle of Carchemish, in which Nebuchadnezzar overthrew the power of Egypt, had just been fought, when Jeremiah began to write. It would be impossible for him, with the stormy career of the Chaldæan conqueror before his eyes, to omit mention of whatever warnings he had uttered respecting foreign nations. For it had been his mission to hold out the symbolical cup of wrath to the nations, as to Judah. It cannot be accident, that the Greek Version places the warnings to the nations, in the centre of the xxvth chapter, about the place in which the warnings to Judah ended. This arrangement is too likely to have been original, not to furnish a dazzling testimony to the Septuagint. But it has not been sufficiently noticed, that all this chapter consists of titular preface, or of summary, by way of index, such as might close the warnings to the nations. Here then, I apprehend, we have in outline, the book, which Baruch read, in Jehoiakim's fifth year (chap. xxxvi.) first in the Temple to the people, secondly in the Court to the king. When the king had burnt it, Jeremiah enlarged, but restored it, we have no reason to doubt, with preservation of the outline. The Seer's vocation, his message, incidents in his life, his warnings to the nations, and a summary of the whole, may be gathered with tolerable distinctness from the Greek, (cc. 25—32), as they must originally have stood. Only we must except for many reasons the chapters on Babylon, here placed for symmetry by the Greek, but reserved more faithfully by the Hebrew for the end. We may waive endeavour to decide, what incidents, or what oracles on the nations, were first added to the second book; and only remark, that nothing in Jeremiah's cast of mind, or in the custom of the prophets, forbade him to use as an ornamental vehicle of sentiments which had been his own, poems fragmentary or entire, which he found handed down. Hence the diction of the group of chapters *On the Nations* is frequently more poetical than Jeremiah's own. Our theory has made its first step.

Eighteen more years were to elapse, before the presentiments which so often tinged with awe the prophet's language, were fulfilled in the city's ruin. During this time, having received the impulse of writing, and enjoying now the aid of an amanuensis, he would cause leading events, his collision with priests, his interviews with successive kings, his imprisonments, and the final crash, to be set down, as we find from ch. xxxvi. to xliv. in tolerable order. Nothing would prevent him from recurring to an earlier period, and expanding the outline, as with the account of the Rechabites, chap. xxxv. or of the dangers he had undergone, xxxvi. and xxxviii. It deserves especial remark, that these narrative chapters may be read as illustrations in parallel with the poetical summary which has preceded, *e.g.* in xxii. xxiii. They are as it were the justificatory notes on the poem. Nor is it an unlikely suggestion, that the two months, which followed the city's fall, would be a time of writing. We are on more solid ground, when we add that the transactions in Egypt, chap. xliv. must have required Baruch's aid to record them; and feel a strong assurance, that with the xlvth chapter from his pen, (notwithstanding the date which has crept in,) our book, originally in its Egyptian form, ended. Thus far was Jeremiah. Thus we should still find him, if those most ancient copies, which the Greek translator first used, could by possibility be recovered.

The tradition among the Fathers of the Church, that Jeremiah was stoned in Egypt, was too certain to arise out of the groundwork in chap. xliv. and is otherwise too little confirmed, to have any historical value. We must judge not more favourably the Jewish supposition of his going from Egypt to Babylon. We leave as probable the suggestion that the second half of chap. xlvi. vv. 13 —26, did not belong to the book of Jehoiakim's fourth year; but was added by Baruch, or his master, while they dwelled in Egypt. More certainly we may affirm this of the last two verses, 27, 28, on "my servant, Jacob."

But if Jeremiah died, as his faithful disciple disappears from view, in Egypt, there must have been an Egyptian Recension. This would be preserved in the many synagogues, as at *Tel Foudich*, and in the temple afterwards built by Onias. To the copies of this recension, though subjected to vigilant comparison by jealous eyes in Babylon, Jerusalem, Tiberias, we owe our Septuagint. Must there not also have been during the Exile a recension at Babylon? The chapters on that city, and the cabalistic cyphers *Sheshach* and *Leb-kamai*, incline us to the belief that there was. We may reckon more confidently on assent, in claiming a recension for Jerusalem after the return. Although tradition, Jewish and Christian, ascribes such things to Ezra, I prefer, with Movers, letting 2 Macc. ii. guide me in naming Nehemiah (yet not improbably with Ezra's literary aid), as the most determinable author. His tendencies, and the assertion to that effect, indicate him as the man under whom our book might take its present form. For then pieces written during the Exile, as the pæan over Babylon, or the chapters resembling the second Isaiah, xxx. xxxi. might easily be added. The arrangement might be dislocated from imaginary connexion of subject; and so slight a feature as a name borne by two persons might bring pieces of different date together. The titles would be supplemented with such criticism as the age could master; and then the name Jeremiah would have assumed its shorter form, (*i.e. ah* for *ahu.*) If any one chooses, on the strength of 2 Macc. ii. or from minuter criticism, to bring down a farther process of editing as late as Judas Maccabeus, I think the supposition antecedently likely; but see no strong evidence of it, except as regards the Macedonian allusions in the LXX. The conditions of our Hebrew Text are on fair, if not the minutest possible, examination, satisfied by acceptance of the tradition, that its form dates from Nehemiah. Such words as *Sheshach* may be due to the later school of Babylon.

From what has been said it must be clear that Jeremiah opens a more than ordinary field for minute criticism. The great acuteness in this domain of Hitzig and Movers deserves eminent recognition; though the attempt of the former[5] to appropriate Psalm xl. with its strongly spiritual imagery, to Jeremiah in his dungeon, is surely very prosaic. Nor will I quite maintain, that the happier endeavour of Movers[6] to find our 30th and 31st chapters quoted as the works of the former prophet in Zech. viii. 7, 8, 9, can be regarded as having taken its place among certainties. I agree, however, as to the date and authorship, which this eminent critic assigns to those chapters. If our insular taste ran that way, the Prophet might yet furnish materials for a monograph. My notes will furnish the reader with what seems sufficient to complete a sketch. The bibliography of recent commentators may be found in Dr. Davidson.

Such being our literary premisses, the question of demonstrable prediction in Jeremiah admits a distinct answer. Instead of evidence, that the battle of Carchemish, for instance, had been foretold, the Prophet pledges

[5] Der Prophet Jeremia, von F. Hitzig. Leipzig, 1841.
[6] Commentatio Critica, § 17, p. 37. scripsit F. C. Movers. Hamburg, 1837.

us his assurance, that he put his poem on record in the year after the battle. Must he not have intended it for (what its style bespeaks it,) a judicial song, a strain of triumphant acknowledgment to the arbiter of destiny? Is it not doing him an injustice, as well as bringing ridicule on ourselves, if we accustom men trained in severer thought to expect a foresight neither apparent, nor claimed? The spirit of this question may be extended to the utterances upon Moab, Ammon, Edom. For, however vivid may have been the presentiment, with which a mind accustomed to interpret history by Providence saw the feuds of lawless clans, and a city whose sins were ripening, come daily within the minitant network, which the Lady of Nations spread, the blow had fallen, before his feelings took written shape; the expression which he then gives them has a borrowed form; our only evidence of minute fulfilment is the presumption that war and its description would generally correspond. As regards the second half of chap. xlvi. vv. 13—26, we have not even so much. For, unless we build upon the fragmentary allegations from Berossus in Josephus against Apion, i. 19, a heavier fabric than they bear, secular history offers little guarantee for the occupation of Egypt by Nebuchadnezzar; not even a sign of its subsequence to any prediction. The assumption of fulfilment in such a case may be a largess, but is not a debt.

A weightier possibility suggests itself in connexion with the Babylonian exile. From our infancy it has been ingrained into us that Jeremiah predicted the duration seventy years. We find to that effect two passages in chaps. xxv. 11, xxix. 10. Unfortunately, the first is a passage in which the Greek translators introduced, or found, a signal displacement of text, a displacement

INTRODUCTION TO JEREMIAH. 67

traceable to didactic considerations. The second has not so direct a witness against it; though here also five verses, 16—20, are wanting in the LXX., as Jerome observed; and when our attention is directed to the point, we observe that the five verses 10—14, if not 8—14, interrupt the warning against prophetic disturbers in Babylon, and lessen, if not destroy, its symmetry. Suppose both places genuine; the Captivity, commencing under Jehoiachin (as xxix. 2 tells us), lasted but fifty-nine, say sixty years; then why the period seventy? It is ingeniously replied, that the absence of precision would not have been introduced after the event; so that it is a sign of genuineness. But this is not a confirmation. The book of Daniel, i. 1, may give us nine years more, if we accept from it a deportation of selected youths early under Jehoiakim. It is unfortunate, that a book, with so many other signs of a later date, should stand alone against contemporary sacred history in furnishing an event to correspond with predictions, the meaning of which was disputed in Daniel's day, and their text in our own. We must grant to those who insist on the antiquity of Daniel, and on the genuineness of Jeremiah's text, a possibility of prediction; but the opposite probabilities remain, that the period seventy years here, as in Isaiah xx. 16 [A.V. xxiii. 15] was observed by Hellenistic chronologers in connexion with the dynasty of Nebuchadnezzar in Babylon; that it was derived into our text from Egypt, perhaps through the Septuagint; and that the writer of Daniel treated it as a problem which he connected with Jerusalem. The historical Exile, from the end of Zedekiah's reign, lasted forty-nine years, from Jehoiachin's captivity about eleven more.

Whether the chapters upon Babylon, which close the collection of Jeremianic prophecies, ought to be connected with the second capture of Babylon, after its revolt against Darius Hystaspes (B.C. 520) appears to my own mind an open question; although in my Notes I have acquiesced in the reference to the more famous capture by Cyrus. Popular writers (*e.g.* Mr. Clabon, in his book of Family Devotions), who press to the uttermost poetical terms of desolation from the prophets, would do well to remember, that both Arab pitches tent, and shepherd pastures flock, within the circuit of Babylon; and a recent traveller[7] (calling 10,000 an exaggerated estimate) implies that the population of Hilleh, a fragment of the area, is counted by thousands. Again, the ruins of many Asiatic cities, such as Seleucia, unmentioned by any prophet, are no less striking in their completeness. The general lesson of 'the desolator desolate' is what we should more wisely urge.

The two passages commonly regarded as predictive of our Lord under the character of Messiah, are xxiii. 5, 6, xxxiii. 15. It is my duty to remark, that if both are connected with their context, their meaning appears to be this. The first is an anticipation which may be regarded as a promise, that in place of the dethroned Jehoiachin, whose race should be disinherited, a successor of the Davidical dynasty should still arise. Whoever wrote the 7th and 8th verses, seems to have conceived of this promise as taking effect on the return from Babylon. Nothing but the name *Josedec* (or *Yahveh-tzidkeynoo*), which to Hebrew ears was a titular association, applied in ch. xxxiii. to Jerusalem, should lead us to dissociate the text in meaning, or range, from the preceding chapter, in which by critical sequence it should be included. The second passage comes obviously under a like interpreta-

---

[7] Ussher's *London to Persepolis*, p. 475; London, 1865. Mr. Ussher mentions owls, also a large tamarisk tree of immense age; he makes the usual reflexions.

tion; the City, the Temple, the Levites, the time, furnishing signs too manifest to dwell upon. Only, if it be asked, whether a comparison of Zech. vi. 11, 12, imports a Messianic rendering of our first passage, I answer that if it did, the interpretation might be an after-thought; but in truth, time and place, person, priest and temple, are so clearly designated in the later prophet, as to demonstrate the natural sense of the earlier. The strong necessity which I feel, as explained in my first volume, of primarily restricting all prophecies ordinarily deemed Messianic to the contemporaneous horizon, and subsequently elevating them, not by verbal legerdemain, but by perception of the eternally ideal in the temporarily accidental, so as to find in the New Testament the Providential transfiguration of the Old, is confirmed by my study of Jeremiah. Apt as we all are to exaggerate a favourite hypothesis, I hope that this conception (obscure as Stygian darkness though it may remain to those who imagine it to inculcate "Natural Religion" in the after-sense of the negation of miracle,) may be useful in enabling men to understand Christ, and to believe in God.

The great evangelical promise of the Old Testament is treated in the Notes on c. xxxi. Critically, we may regard it as rising above the level of our prophet, as well as inconsistent with the Levitical tinge of his existing text; but any uncertainty of its authorship illustrates the affluence of that 'Spirit which breathes where it lists'; it may be taken as a sign of the spiritual stamp of weapons, (neither might, nor power, nor fleshly sign or name), which God has consecrated in Prophecy to overthrow in us the strongholds of evil.

The collapse, first of popular predictions, and at last of those which seem well-grounded, until they are brought into contact with tests of priority or meaning, teaches us the depth of Gibbon's sarcasm, that with all the resources of Miracle at their disposal the Fathers of the Church betray an unaccountable preference for the argument from Prophecy. The sting of the remark depends upon the supposition that religious faith must have a ground external to its own sphere; it disappears, when we recollect that Deity is revealed to us by moral attributes more evidently than by power or wonder. Hence prediction of events would not be so properly inspiration, as the strong religious sentiment which enables a writer to awaken a kindred sense in his readers. Above all things this is a gift. In such a gift consists Jeremiah's power. His book commences with a claim to sacred vocation, such as religious bodies, notwithstanding allowance for temperament, desire in their teachers, and such as our Church should never be persuaded quite to expunge from her Ordinal. It proceeds to point the rightful relation of Judah to Jehovah, including references to the fate of the northern kingdom, and traces in calamities the signs and scourges of falling away. The arrangement resembles so strikingly that of Isaiah and Ezekiel, as to imply that the greater prophets, or the editors who arranged their works, had a common type of outline before their mind. As the drama has its conventional number of acts, and the epic its plunge into the centre of events, with episodes leading up to a climax, so Prophecy has its prelude, its poem, its circumstantial narrative, and its co-ordination of domestic with foreign events.

It has been usual with critics from St. Jerome downwards, to compare Jeremiah unfavourably with Isaiah. He is less an artist, perhaps more a prophet. His strongly practical life implies less care of expression. Yet Scripture never stirs us with a deeper touch than in some of his more plaintive notes, "Oh thou sword of the

"ETERNAL, for how *long wilt* thou take no rest? gather "*thyself into* thy scabbard, rest, and be still." And if we retain for him the Lamentations, though more studied than his style elsewhere, "Is it nothing to you all you "passers by the way? behold, and see, if there be any "sorrow like my sorrow, wherewith the ETERNAL has "afflicted me in the day of the fierceness of his anger :" where Jerusalem, Poland, Ireland, each seems to cry to us in turn. Or again, "I am the man that has seen "affliction by the rod of his anger : me he led, and "brought into darkness, and not light ; yea, against me "he turns again and again his hand all the day :" where the intensity comes of simplicity, in a way converse to 'Me, me, adsum qui feci.' But the true depth of Jeremiah lies in the ethically religious, which he shares with Isaiah, only in a form, in which ornament gives way to plaintiveness, and this, under the corroding influence of persecution, to fierceness. The iron had entered into his soul, when he cried, "Accursed the man, who acquainted "my father, saying, A man-child is born to thee, making "him very glad ; Yea, let that man be as the cities which "the ETERNAL overthrew without relenting ; Yea, let him "hear crying in the morning, and battle-shout at noon-"tide ; because he slew me not from the womb ; that my "mother might have been my grave, and her womb "burdened for ever! wherefore came I thus forth from "the womb, to behold weariness and sorrow, that my "days should waste with shame?" But the purposeless Lamentation, ordinarily associated with our prophet's name, has not so much place in the book certainly his own. Like most of the prophets, he is a man of action. The stern denunciation, and the more than acquiescence in a rival's death, are not (if we remember Amos) confined to him. They may be explained in part from the connexion, which seemed to him indissoluble, between the Divine cause and his own plea for it; in part, by the effect of repeated strokes on the feelings of a man. Hardly any great sufferer from others, certainly not the early Christian martyrs, nor even the Divinest figure in the New Testament, will not need the first of these explanations, if we are to avoid the application of the second. "God smite thee, thou whited wall;" cries St. Paul, though he recalls the words.

The familiar instance of Zechariah being quoted in the New Testament as Jeremy the prophet, Matth. xxvii. 9; is but an index to the circumstance that popular estimate assigned him the foremost place. Not only was he more than others the representative of the nation in its sacredness and humiliation; but the manuscripts of Palestine and Babylon agreed in placing his writings first, those of Ezekiel second, Isaiah but third, in the Canon.[8] This arrangement is justified by what we now know of the aggregation of later writers under the name of Isaiah, to which the earliest framers of the Canon may have been guided by historical instinct, if not by more express tradition than has come down to us.

The order of chapters in my Version does not profess to represent anything that ever stood in any MS. but endeavours to reproduce the natural sequence of pieces so as to furnish the best history of the prophet, as well as a collection of his works. The absence, not so much of readers, as of critics who would estimate any change in version on its proper, that is its philological, ground, has induced me to pass over with light step the prosaic or historical parts, for which the Anglican Version is less

---

[8] In Tract. *Baba Bathra*, fol. 14, b, ordo prophetarum ita se habet: Josua, Judices, Samuelis et Regum libri; *Jeremias*, Ezekiel, Jesaias, et duodecim prophetarum volumen.—*Rosenm.* ad J. et alii passim.

inadequate than for the poetry. A like rule will govern me henceforward. The strophical arrangement, as in a periodic flow and reflow of verse, on which an eminent scholar has laid stress, will not by me have its reality denied in face of the authority which affirms it; but I have not with close attention been able to discern such connexion as ought, if the writers designed the arrangement, to make it illustrate their meaning; nor even if the copyists did not devise it, do the interspaced paragraphs with which they represent it, coincide with the natural division; nor can their paragraphs always be adopted by those who believe in the strophical arrangement. Hence I am inclined to think such paragraphs due to mistaken transfer from poems intended for music, or else to methods of transcription; at least I cannot adopt them for hermeneutical guidance. There is no break of sense in at least half the cases where the Anglican follows the Hebrew in making pauses in the first chapter of Isaiah. The same remark might be made elsewhere. Amongst minor improvements, my removal of an unnatural division between chapters iii. and iv. will correct an error older than St. Jerome's time, though we may half miss the lively encouragement to repentance, which Mason and others extracted out of it. Could it avail for some, were it needed for others, I would repeat my disclaimer of insensibility to touching thoughts, though my duty to the reality of my author touches me more. The striking explanation of Shallum in chap. xxii. I owe to Movers.

It is time to let the priestly reformer of Anathoth speak for himself. He will be found 'a type of Christ,' not in the formally paradigmatical manner of an algebraic equation; but in spirit, power, suffering, as teacher, reformer, man; both warning their nation against a ruin, which came before that generation passed away; both having characteristics, which make a most touching chapter (whether written, or not, of either) applicable as history to one, as forecast to the other; both at last glorified in a circle wider than that in which they had been rejected; both held to have merit in the sight of God, overflowing for those who needed it; both subordinating their own wills to a higher will; both ascribing (though it seems to us the more perfect might have claimed, yet he ascribed) the glory in nature and grace to our Father in Heaven. But what Jeremiah was for Israel, Christ is for Mankind. And if on critical grounds we are right in detaching from any known prophet, the larger aspiration of evangelical freedom which in the 32nd chapter outsteps the Levitical strain of the known Jeremiah, we have but reached a conclusion in harmony with the best estimate of Him whose legacy to His followers was another advocate, the Comforter who should ever abide, the Spirit of Truth.[9]

ILLUSTRATIVE DATES.

	B.C.
Jeremiah's birth	about 657 to 647?
Josiah's accession	640 — 639
Josiah's thirteenth year	626
Scythians in Palestine	623?
Religious Reform in Judah—Book of the law produced	621
Battle of Megiddo and Jehoiakim's accession	608
Fall of Nineveh	606
Battle of Carchemish	605
Jehoiakim's fourth year	604

[9] St. John xiv. 1—17.

INTRODUCTION TO JEREMIAH.

Jeremiah's works written, and restored	603
Jehoiachin's accession—Same year, his dethronement and the first exile	597
Zedekiah's accession	597
Fall of Jerusalem and Temple	586
Babylon's capture by Cyrus	539
Zerubbabel prince, Joshua high-priest	539
Restoration of Temple	536
Babylon's capture by Darius	520

ORDER OF CHAPTERS.

This Version.	A. V.
Usual Order.	I—XX.
XXI	XXII.
XXII	XXIII.
XXIII	XXV.
XXIV—XXVII	XLVI—XLIX.
XXVIII	XXVI.
XXIX—XXX	XXXV—XXXVI.

In deference to date in Text.

XXXI	XLV
	otherwise
XXXII	XXXVII.
XXXIII—XXXVII	XXI, XXIV, XXVII—XXIX.
XXXVIII	XXXIV.
XXXIX—XL	XXXII—XXXIII.
XLI—XLVII	XXXVIII—XLIV.

Here, with Appendix of XLV. its date altered, Jeremiah ends.

XLVIII—XLIX	XXX—XXXI
L—LII.	L—LII.

ORDER OF LXX.*

Heb. A. V.	LXX.	Heb. A. V.	LXX.
xxv, 15—xlv	xxxii—li.	xlix, 34—39	xxv, 14—19.
xlvi . . .	xxvi.	l—li . .	xxvii, xxviii
xlvii . . .	xxix, 1—7.	lii . .	lii.
xlviii, 1—44	xxxi.	xxvii, 19—22	
xlix, 1—5 .	xxx, 1—5.	xxxiii, 14—26	Missing.
7—22 .	xxix, 7—22.	xxxix, 4—13	
23—27 .	xxx, 12—16.	xlviii, 45—47	
28—33 .	xxx, 6—11.		

* Added by Rev. W. W. Harvey.

JEREMIAH.

The words of Jeremiah the son of Hilkiah, of the priests that were in Anathoth in the land of Benjamin; to whom the word of the ETERNAL *came in the days of Josiah, son of Amon, king of Judah, in the thirteenth year of his reign, and came in the days of Jehoiakim, son of Josiah, king of Judah, up to the ending of the eleventh year of Zedekiah, son of Josiah, king of Judah, up to the exile of Jerusalem in the fifth month. Then the word of the* ETERNAL *came to me,[1] saying:*

CH. I. 1. Before I formed thee in the belly, I knew thee, and A. V. before thou camest forth from the womb, I consecrated thee; I ordained thee a prophet to the nations;

---

[1] To me; or, to him. LXX. πρὸς αὐτὸν, which I cannot doubt is the true reading or rendering, though Vulg. ad me.

The title from its own wording "*In the days of Josiah,*" and again "*the days of Jehoiakim,*" as well as from the circumstances of the composition of the book (see ch. xxx. (A. V. xxxvi.) and Introduction above), seems to be of later date than the book; later probably than Jeremiah; yet we cannot say how early it may have been prefixed to a collection of the words ascribed to the Prophet; possibly by Baruch, more probably in a recension after the return from Babylon. At the earliest, the least interval between the Prophet's call and the collection of his sayings would be twenty-three years. Ch. xxiii. (A. V. xxv. 3.)

1. The eternal law that fitness is the gift of God, though human officers or assemblies may consign to it sphere, appears in Jeremiah's sense of consecration from his birth. Hence the rightful indelibility of holy Orders, when deliberately accepted.

2. Then said I, Ah! Lord, ETERNAL, behold, I know A. V. i. 6. not *how* to speak; for I am a child.

3. But the ETERNAL said to me, Say not, I am a child, for to whomsoever I send thee, thou shalt go, and whatsoever I command thee, thou shalt speak;

4. Fear not before them;[2] for I am with thee to deliver thee, is the saying of the ETERNAL;

5. Then the ETERNAL put forth his hand, and touched my mouth; and the ETERNAL said to me, Behold, I have put my words in thy mouth;

6. See, I have appointed thee this day over the nations and over the kingdoms, to uproot and break, to destroy and shatter, to build and plant.

7. Then the word of the ETERNAL came to me, saying, What seest thou, Jeremiah; and I said, I see a rod of an early almond tree;[3]

8. And the ETERNAL said to me, Thou hast well seen, for I am watching early over my word, to perform it.

---

[2] *Before them.* Heb. from their faces. Vulg. a facie corum.

[3] *An early almond tree*; the tree taking its name from a verb of waking. Vulg. virgam vigilantem. LXX. βακτηρίαν καρυίνην. Floret prima omnium Amygdala, mense Januario. Plin. H. N. xvi. 25.

2—4. A sense of the inadequacy of Man, without Divine blessing, makes the Prophet hold back, as Moses and Isaiah; but woe is unto him, as to St. Paul, if he does not obey the Life-giver, who, when he sends, also accompanies.

5, 6. The gift of fitness accompanies, as it attests, the mission. The visible sign is but figurative, as in the living fire which touches Isaiah's lips. So in more playful, less earnest, yet not unmeaning form, the Latin, Cynthius aurem Vellit, et admonuit. He who sees the destiny of nations, is the interpreter of a Divine counsel.

7, 8. The early bloom of the almond tree is a type of the Divine wakefulness in performing.

Ch. I.   9. And the word of the ETERNAL came to me a second time, saying, What seest thou? And I said, I see a pot seething, with its face from the face of the North.

10. And the ETERNAL said to me, From the North shall burst forth the calamity upon all the dwellers of the land;

11. For behold me calling⁴ to all the families of the kingdoms of the North, is the ETERNAL's saying, till they come, and set everyone his throne at the entering of the gates of Jerusalem, and against all her walls round about, and against all the cities of Judah,

12. And I will utter my judgments against them, for all their wickedness, in that they have forsaken me, and burnt incense to other gods, and bowed down to the works of their own hands.

13. And thou, gird up thy loins, and arise, and speak to them all that I command thee; be not dismayed at their faces, lest I confound thee⁵ before them;

---

⁴ *Behold me calling.* In no way can the Hebrew more vividly express the present instant, than by the participle here used. So LXX. ἰδοὺ, ἐγὼ συγκαλῶ, but Vulg. convocabo.

⁵ *Lest I confound thee.* Vulg. Nec enim timere te faciam. Either the prophet is not to fear being terrified; or, if he does fear, God will terrify him. Better the latter.

9, 10. The pot seething northwards typifies the agitation of northern realms.

11. The Chaldæans, notwithstanding their southern site, would enter Judæa from the north. The Scythians, over-running Palestine, may also have been present to the mind's eye of the prophet, as to Zephaniah.

12. The speech turns abruptly to the people of Judæa.

13—15. The Prophet is nerved by trust in God to a life of conflict, in which he will testify of sin, and speak of judgment, and be rejected, as is often the Cassandra-like fate of the Seer, yet enduring in faithfulness he will

Ch. I.   14. And I, behold, have made thee this day a fenced A.V.I.18. city, and an iron pillar, and brazen walls, against all the land, against the kings of Judah, against her princes, against her priests, and against the people of the land;

15. And though they fight against thee, they shall not prevail against thee; for I am with thee, is the ETERNAL's saying, to deliver thee.

II.

1. And the word of the ETERNAL came to me, saying, Go, and cry in the ears of Jerusalem, saying, Thus saith the ETERNAL, I remember of thee the tenderness of thy youth, the love of thy betrothal, thy following me in the wilderness, in a land not sown;

2. *When* Israel *was* consecrate to the ETERNAL; all the devourers of the first-fruits of his increase[6] should be guilty; evil should come upon them, was the saying of the ETERNAL.

---

[6] Heb. The first fruits of his increase, all his devourers shall be, [or *were*] guilty, or desolate, see Note on Joel i. 17. Authority and etymology are for the sense of guilt; idiom, I think, for that of desolation. The whole verse may describe the past; or the future, may be as it were edicts, dependent on Jehovah's saying.

---

know the spirit of his warnings true, and trust to Providence their event. If he had shrunk from his task, his shame would have been greater.

1, 2. As the sense of fall makes sin more shameful, and sorrow more bitter, the Prophet reminds his nation of the time when her youth was betrothed to a heavenly lord. So St. John rebukes the Ephesine Church for leaving her first love, Rev. ii. 4. Natural, and even inevitable, as is the ripening of the emotional into a reflective stage, which should also be a practical and disciplined

Ch. II. 3. Hear the word of the Eternal, house of Jacob, and A. V. 1 all kindreds of the house of Israel;

4. Thus saith the Eternal, What have your fathers found in me evil, that they went afar from me, and walked after the vain[7] thing, and became vain?

5. And they said not, Where is the Eternal, that brought us up out of the land of Egypt, that guided us in the wilderness, in a land waste and sunken,[8] in a land of drought and death's-gloom, in a land which neither man traversed, nor man abode there?

6. And I brought you into a land which is a garden,[9] to eat its fruit and its goodness; and you came, and you defiled my land, and made my inheritance an abomination.

7. The priests said not, Where is the Eternal; and the handlers of the law knew me not; and the shepherds transgressed against me; and the preachers preached by Baal, and walked after *things* which could not vantage them.

---

[7] *Vain;* or, false; i.e. Idol. So *became vain,* or false, as their gods.
[8] *Waste and sunken;* or, of desert and of pits.
[9] *Which is a garden;* or ploughed land. Heb. Ha-Carmel; see Note above. Isaiah xiv. 19.

---

one, the subsidence of all higher aspiration, as it were a fall from our first vows, is the great peril of souls and churches. So in advanced life we should try to revive the dew of our youth.

3, 4. If we are wearied, God has not deserved of us that we should so forsake Him, (5) who brought the Israelites out of bondage, and brings all men out of perplexity, (6) crowning them with blessings, which they too often make means of sin. 7. Priest and Scribe, Ruler and Prophet, having mementoes of office against infirmity, seem to sin more, if they yield to it largely. This is the earliest mention of the Law in so definite a form as the Mosaic Code is

Ch. II.   8.   Therefore will I yet plead with you, is the ETERNAL'S A.V. II. 9. saying, and with your sons' sons will I plead.

9.   For cross over to the isles of Chittim, and see ; and send to Kedar,[10] and observe diligently, and behold, has there been such a thing ?

10.   Has a nation changed its gods, though they are no gods ?   Yet my people has changed its glory into that which cannot vantage *it* !

11.   Be amazed, Heavens, at this, and shudder ; be utterly desolate, is the ETERNAL'S saying.

12.   For two evils have my people wrought ; they have forsaken me, the fountain of living waters, to hew for themselves cisterns, broken cisterns, which hold no water.

13.   Is Israel a slave ? is he a houseborn serf ? wherefore has he become a spoil ?

---

[10] *Chittim* and *Kedar*, i. e. West and East ; the first being Citium in Cyprus, or generally the Mediterranean coasts ; the second Arabia.

---

usually supposed to have held in Israel. There were earlier laws, traditions, maxims, and in Isaiah a reference to unwritten right as the mind of God ; but from Josiah's reign downward we have the full Levitical code, as a theory to which it was desired the people should conform.

8.   The servant who knows his Master's will, and does it not, is beaten with many stripes.

9, 10.   West and East, from the Ionian isles to Arabia, the nations had kept each its ancestral system.   11, 12. More astonishing was the Hebrew fall from a higher to a lower.   The Prophet conceives ideally his people to have been higher, (though the histories of the Judges and Kings imply that the comparison is like our fond retrospect of childhood,) because he wishes them to become so.

13, 14.   If patriotic poetry could personify Israel as the first-born child of God, (Ex. iv. 22), and again with strong change of figure, as his bride, spouse, wife, why does the

Ch. II.   14. The young lions roar over him, they utter their A. V. 1
yell, and make his land a desolation; his cities are burnt,   15.
till they are without inhabitant.

15. Even the sons of Memphis[11] and Tahapanes feed
bare thy skull.

16. *Is* not this *what* thy forsaking the ETERNAL thy God
brings upon thee, in the time when he guided thee in the
way?

17. And now what hast thou to do with the way of
Egypt, drinking the waters of the dark stream,[12] and
what hast thou to do with the way of Assyria, drinking
the waters of the river?

18. Thy own wickedness shall correct thee; and thy
backslidings rebuke thee; and thou shalt know and see *it*
evil and bitter, thy forsaking the ETERNAL thy God, with
no fear of me in thee, is the saying of the Lord, the
ETERNAL of hosts.

19. For of old time thou brakest[13] thy yoke, and burstest

---

[11] *Memphis.* Heb. Noph. *Feed bare,* or break. Vulg. constupraverunt.
LXX. ἔγνωσαν καὶ κατέπαιξαν, misreading the first word, and if not the
second, misunderstanding it.

[12] *Dark Stream.* Heb. Shichor. LXX. Γηῶν, as if they understood the
Gihon of Gen. ii. 13, to be the Nile.

[13] LXX. Ὅτι ἀπ' αἰῶνος συνέτριψας τὸν ζυγόν σου, καὶ διέσπασας τοὺς
δεσμούς σου, καὶ εἶπας, Οὐ δουλεύσω σοι, ἀλλὰ πορεύσομαι ἐπὶ πάντα
βουνὸν ὑψηλόν, κ.τ.λ.—*Vulg.* A sæculo confregisti jugum meum, rupisti
vincula mea, et dixisti, Non serviam. In omni enim colle sublimi, &c.
The Hebrew Text, from its Aramaising addition of *Yod,* as in Micah, Heb. iv.
13, got the verbs *brakest* and *burstest,* treated as first persons; therefore the
Masora suggested the substitution of אֲבוֹר for אֶעֱבוֹד, which however
held its ground in the Text. The versions here give manifest aid and light.

---

fate of slaves befall him from the raveners of Assyria,
Scythia, Babylon; nay, from Egyptian allies, or invaders?

16, 17. Foreign alliance or refuge is not Jeremiah's
idea of his country's policy; seems mistrustful, tending
to strange fashions and religious innovations.

18—21. The bitterness which sinners feel in wandering

thy bonds; and thou saidst, I will not obey; but upon A.V.11.20. every high hill and under every green tree thou wast crouching, seeking hire.

20. Though I planted thee a choice vine;[14] altogether a genuine seed; how then art thou turned for me into the degenerate shoots of the vine *that is* a wilding?

21. For though thou wash thyself with nitre,[15] and take to thee borax[15] abundantly, thy iniquity is ingrained before me, is the Lord's, the ETERNAL's saying.

22. [16]How canst thou say, I am not polluted, I have not gone after the Baals? behold thy path in the valley;

---

[14] *A choice vine.* Heb. vine of Sorek, as Isa. v. 2. The name is thought to mean purple colour, and to have been transferred to Samson's valley, Judg. xvi. 4. Ges. in v. V. d. Velde, *Mem.* Lowth, on Isa. v.

[15] *Nitre and borax.* Heb. *Neter* and *Borith;* the latter also taken as soap, alkali, anything purifying; but the connexion with *Barar* must be only seeming. Comp. Isa. i. 20 (A. V. 25). *Ingrained.* LXX. κεκηλίδω-σαι. *Vulg.* maculata es.

[16] The LXX. and Vulg. differ much in this verse, but nothing would be gained by dwelling on them. ἴδε τὰς ὁδούς σου ἐν τῷ πολυανδρίῳ, καὶ γνῶθι τί ἐποίησας· ὀψὲ φωνὴ αὐτῆς ὠλόλυξε, τὰς ὁδοὺς αὐτῆς ἐπλάτυνεν ἐφ' ὕδατα ἐρήμου, ἐπιθυμίαις ψυχῆς αὐτῆς ἐπνευματοφορεῖτο, παρεδόθη, τίς ἐπιστρέψει αὐτήν; πάντες οἱ ζητοῦντες . . . . ἐν τῇ ταπεινώσει αὐτῆς εὑρήσουσιν αὐτήν. Vide vias tuas in convalle; scito quia feceris; cursor levis (where for קַלָּה the LXX. read קֹלְלָה) explicans vias suas.

---

from God, when either they suffer the consequences of sin, or learn its nature, is by the Prophet ascribed to Israel for leaving Jehovah. For he speaks not as the partisan of a national deity, but as the servant of Him who is righteous and true. He blames the bridal nation for her unfaithfulness, the choice vine for her wild grapes, (Isa. v.) and rejects the self-justifying pleas which wayward men urged for themselves or their nation.

22—25. Imagery coarsely vivid, but congenial to the people's temper, or the time's manners, paints the wan-

Ch. II. consider what thou hast done; a wanton she-camel, turning her course to and fro, 23. a wild ass used to the wilderness, in the eagerness of her desire snuffing up the wind; in her impulse who can turn her back? all her suitors have no trouble; in her season they find her.

24. Withhold thy foot from nakedness, and thy throat from thirst; but thou saidst, There is no hope:[17] No: for I have loved strangers, and after them I will go.

25. Like the shame of a thief when he is caught, so the house of Israel are ashamed, they, their kings, their princes, and their priests, and their prophets, that say to the stock, Thou art my father, and to the stone, Thou hast brought me forth;

26. For they have turned to me the neck,[18] and not the face; but in the time of their calamity they will say, Arise, and deliver us.

27. Then where are thy gods, which thou hast made thyself; let them arise, if they can deliver[19] thee in the

---

Onager assuetus in solitudine, in desiderio animæ suæ attraxit ventum amoris sui . . . . omnes qui quærunt eam, in menstruis ejus invenient eam. The Vulg., though not faultless, is, as usual, far the better of the two. Virgil's description, Georg. iii. 273, of the mares snuffing the breeze,

"Ore omnes versæ in Zephyrum stant rupibus altis,
Exceptantque leves auras," is sufficient illustration. I will not dispute, whether for *wild ass*, we should read *heifer*.

[17] *There is no hope.* Vulg. Desperavi. Hebr. as Isa. lvii. 10. A.V.
[18] *The neck*, i.e. the back, as 2 Chron. xxix. 6.
[19] *If they can deliver;* or interrogatively, Can they deliver thee?

---

derings, the false disclaimers, the depraved and despairing self-abandonment, of the people not fulfilling its vows of dedication to Jehovah.

26—28. As, after all their philosophies or imaginings, men utterly depend upon a Power mysterious, irrespon-

11. time of thy calamity, for *as* the number of thy cities, A.V. II.28. Judah, have been thy gods.

28. [20]Wherefore do you plead with me? all of you have transgressed against me, is the ETERNAL's saying.

29. In vain smote I your sons; they received not correction; your own sword devoured your prophets; like a lion destroying are you, your generation.[21]

30. Behold the ETERNAL's plea; have I been a wilderness to Israel? have I been a land of darkness? wherefore say my people, we are lords, we will come to thee no more?

31. Can a maiden forget her ornaments, a bride her girdle? yet my people have forgotten me, days without number.

---

[20] The LXX. in this verse had a fuller text; πάντες ὑμεῖς ἠσεβήσατε, καὶ πάντες ὑμεῖς ἠνομήσατε εἰς ἐμὲ, κ. λ.

[21] *Like a lion destroying are you, your generation.* *Vulg.* quasi leo vastator generatio vestra; rightly, I believe, though the construction is harsh, and the Masora points *You, your generation* into the next verse, as A.V. The illustration quoted from Numbers xv. 15, seems to me itself doubtful. Internally the words mean, *The generation, You.* Substantially, my version seems anticipated by Maurer. The LXX. καὶ οὐκ ἐφοβήθητε, may suggest that the original text is still open to conjecture.

---

sible, and all-controlling, so (however much we may rightly widen the range of effort), yet in calamity transcending all effort they can only turn to One. If they have forgotten him in the bright time, they have no claim on his faithfulness in the dark hour.

29. If men were deaf when God called by earlier monitions (as in Manasseh's time the sword had silenced the Prophet, and again did so under Jehoiakim), then when they pray, God's answer is this; (30) in his light they might have seen light; if they have been their own masters; (31) forsaken their rightful lord;

Cн. II.   32. Why makest thou thy way delicate, to seek love? A. V. 11
therefore also thou hast made thy ways learn wicked-   33.
nesses;

33. Even in thy robes are found the blood stains of the souls of the poor innocents: not in place of robbery I found them,²² but upon all these *thy robes*.

34. Yet thou sayest, Surely I am innocent; yea, his anger is turned from me: Behold me in judgment with thee, for thy saying, I have not sinned.

35. Why flittest thou so much to change thy way? thou shalt be shamed also out of Egypt, as thou wast shamed out of Assyria; even from hence shalt thou go forth, with thy hands over thy head.

36. ²³ For JEHOVAH hath rejected thy confidences (so

---

²² *Not in place of robbery I found them.* *Vulg.* Non in fossis inveni cos, sed in omnibus quæ supra memoravi. Or, Thou foundest them not in act of house-breaking, (which would have justified their slaughter, Ex. xxii. 2,) and after all these things yet thou sayest I am innocent. So Maurer, and in part Rosenmüller. But the transition of the verb *found* to a different sense and person would be violent. The LXX. reading of ὁρῶ אֶלָּה for אֵלֶּה deserves consideration, and is sanctioned by Jerome, whose mode of speaking implies here, as elsewhere, that the Masoretic punctuation did not exist for him.

²³ Ver. 36 is in the Prophet's thought a coherent sentence, but is broken in our Bibles by a division of chapters, which goes I know not how far back. If it can be as old as St. Jerome, it would prompt his version, *Vulgo dicitur*; if it is as late as the 14th or 15th century, it may have been suggested by

---

(32) invented delicate refinements of sin; (33) caused the death physical, or spiritual, of those who should not have died, and to whom the houses of pleasure became as shambles, or decoy-places; (34) yet the nation assumed a hypocritical air of religious innocence, God will tell them by events, whether He counts them innocent; (35) He has provided for them shame and wailing with up-raised hands in each new refuge; (36) and rejects their

that thou shalt not prosper in them) saying, Lo, if a man A.V. III. 1. send away his wife, and she go from him and belong to another man, shall he return unto her again?

37. Shall not that land be greatly polluted? and hast thou played the harlot with many lovers, and yet return[24] to me again? is the ETERNAL's saying.

38. Lift up thine eyes upon the high places, and see, where hast thou not been a concubine. In the ways hast thou waited for them, as the Arab[25] in the wilderness and thou hast polluted the land with thy harlotries and with thy wickedness.

39. So the showers have been withholden, and the latter rain has not been; yet the brow of a whorish woman has been thine; thou hast refused to be ashamed.

---

his misconception of the passage. The latter seems the more probable. Certainly the Heb. לֵאמֹר introduces the speech with which Jehovah rejects the wanton's illusive confidence. In ver. 37, *And yet return*,[24] is the infinitive becoming consecutive by conjunction with the preceding verb. So in the first verse of the Welsh Prayer-book, the idiom by which an infinitive is appended to a subjunctive, is not unlike. If any one takes the infinitive here more as a substantiated idea, the sense comes to the same, Jehovah rejects (instead of as A. V. encouraging) the often defiled adulteress.

[25] *As the Arab.* Hieron. quasi latro: adding in Comm. Gens latrociniis dedita usque hodiè incursat terminos Palæstinæ, et descendentibus de Jerusalem in Jericho obsidet vias.

---

self-deluding hypocrisy with this strong plea; as the wife, vainly forgiven, again abandoned, cannot return, (37) so Zion has exhausted her chances, and in vain talks of returning to Jehovah.

38. Eastern manners, such as Lady H. Stanhope has painted, furnish an intense illustration of the wanderings of Jehovah's wicked wife.

39. Shortcomings of mercy, tokens of divine displeasure, had failed to awaken shame in the abandoned wife;

Ch. II.   40. Hast thou not from this time called to me,[26] My A.V.III. father, thou art the guide of my youth?
   41. Will he, *thou sayest*, resent for ever? will he remember continually? behold, thou hast spoken, yet doest thy wickedness, and art hardened.

III.

   1. And the ETERNAL said to me in the days of Josiah A.V.III the king,[27] Hast thou seen what did refractory Israel? she went upon every high mountain, and beneath every green tree, and sold herself there.

---

[26] *Hast thou not from this time called to me.* So Heb. though *Vulg.* and others, "Ergo saltem a modo voca me, Pater meus, dux virginitatis meæ tu es," as if it were exhortation. In this verse, as above, vers. 20—33, we have the Paragogic, or Aramaising *Yod* added to the fem. sec. per. I fully concede this may have been archaic, and the oldest form, but in Biblical Hebrew it is suspicious, as a sign of later age, when the purer Hebrew was Aramaising. Hence the Masora in the margin says, *Yethir Yod*, the Yod is superfluous. The Prophet is not exhorting, but condemning inconsistency.

[27] *Josiah the king.* So here, but in earlier books, *the king Josiah*, as 2 Sam. xvii. 17, 21; the exception in 2 Sam. xiii. 39 (where perhaps for דוד we should read דוה) being betrayed by the feminine verb conjoined. So henceforward we have refractory Israel, for which the earlier Hebrew would be Israel refractory. No doubt we can refine a slight distinction in the meaning; the king, namely David, is a different idea from the days of David the king; and the refractory one, Israel, is different from Israel that is refractory. To my own ear, however, it seems that the idiomatic collocation from Jeremiah downwards differs from that of the earlier books.

---

and yet, (40, 41) she thought and spoke of herself as one retaining claims on the relenting goodness (Psalm ciii. 9) of God, (Nahum i. 1, A. V. 2) while she remained unrepentant, and hard of brow.
   1—5. In Josiah's reign, the Prophet, comparing what he saw of Judah's sin with the memory handed down of that of Israel a century earlier, begins to think his own

III. 2. And I said, after her doing all these things, Re- A.V. III.7.
turn to me; but she returned not, and her treacherous
sister Judah beheld.

3. And I saw, when for all the instances wherein refractory Israel was adulterous, I dismissed her, and gave
her the record of divorce, yet her treacherous sister
Judah feared not, but went, and sold herself also.

4. So it was, for the lightness²⁸ of her harlotry, that
she polluted the land, and was adulterous with stones and
with stocks; yet for all this her treacherous sister Judah
returned not to me with all her heart, but feignedly, is
the saying of the ETERNAL.

5. Then the ETERNAL said to me, Refractory Israel has
justified herself more than treacherous Judah;

6. Go, proclaim these words toward the North,²⁹ and
say, RETURN, refractory Israel, is JEHOVAH's saying;
I will not make my face lowering upon you: for I am
gracious, is JEHOVAH's saying, I will not resent for ever.

7. Surely, acknowledge thy transgression, that thou
hast sinned against the ETERNAL thy God, and hast scattered thy ways to strangers beneath every green tree,
and you have not listened to my voice, is JEHOVAH's
saying.

8. Return, refractory sons, is JEHOVAH's saying, for I
am your lord; and I will take you one out of a city, and

---

²⁸ *Lightness.* So the Masora, LXX., Vulgate, and Rabbinical expositors:
but most modern scholars understand *voice*=sound.

²⁹ *North,* Heb. *Tzaphon,* perhaps so called, as the quarter of midnight,
where the sun is most hidden.

---

country worse from hypocrisy, than Israel from rebellion.
Idolatry is intended by imagery drawn from the opposite
of the rightful union between Jehovah and his betrothed
people.

6—8. Out of this comparison arises a hope that the

Ch. III. two out of a family, and will bring you to Zion, and will give you shepherds after my heart, which shall feed you knowingly and skilfully:

A. V. 15.

9. And it shall be, when you multiply and are fruitful in the land, in those days, is JEHOVAH's saying, you shall speak no more of the Ark of JEHOVAH's covenant; neither shall it come to mind; neither shall they remember it; nor shall it be visited,[30] nor wrought any more;

10. In that time they shall call Jerusalem JEHOVAH's throne, and to it shall be gathered all the nations, to the renown of JEHOVAH in Jerusalem; neither shall they walk any more after the obstinacy of their evil heart.

11. [31]In those days shall the house of Judah come to the house of Israel, and they shall come together out of the northern land to the land which I made your fathers inherit, 12. When I had said, How shall I place thee

---

[30] *Nor shall it be visited.* Masora, nor shall they visit. *Vulg.* nec visitabitur, nec fiet ultra.

[31] Compare, for the sentiment of the joint return, Hosea i. 10, and the Note there. At the end of this verse 11, here, the Greek translator, out of the fulness of his heart, interjected γένοιτο, Κύριε, So be it, Lord, which has passed into the LXX. text, as in 1 John iii. a transcriber who read of the Father's love in making us sons, could not refrain from appending, καὶ ἐσμεν, *And we are so*, which appears in some MSS.

The twelfth verse goes back to Jehovah's thought in planting the Hebrews in Canaan. *Beauty of beauties ;* or, of the *hosts*, more regularly.

---

fallen sister may be restored to the one which seemed still standing; nay, that she have precedence, and (11) Judah come to her.

9, 10. A wider field of vision may be hoped in the extension of the Divine presence from the Ark to the entire city, which Christ, outstepping Jeremiah, will extend from the city to the whole earth.

11. Judah may join Israel, (12) as in the days when

among sons, and give thee a desirable land, an inheritance of the beauty of beauties of the nations, and I said, You will call me Father, and you will not turn away from me : A. V. III. 19.

13. Truly, [as] woman[32] goes treacherously from her lover, so dealt you treacherously by me, House of Israel, is JEHOVAH's saying.

14. A voice is heard on the high places, weeping of supplications of the sons of Israel; because they perverted their way; forgot JEHOVAH their God.

15. Return, refractory sons; I will heal your refractoriness.

16. Behold we come to thee; for thou art the ETERNAL our God. Truly in vain from the hills; *in vain* a crying[33] *from* the mountains; truly in the ETERNAL our God is the salvation of Israel. 17. But shamefulness[34] has devoured the labour of our fathers from our youth; their flocks and their herds; their sons and their daughters. 18. We lie down in our shame, and our confusion covers us;

---

[32] *Truly, as woman,* &c. The comparative, quomodo, ὡς, is given in Vulg. and LXX. not in Hebrew, unless we render אך Even as.

[33] *A crying;* or, a multitude; hardly, as some, prosperity. We have to carry on the prep. from hills to mountains.

[34] *Shamefulness;* or, that shame, (baseness). Heb. *Ha-bosheth*, with the article: hence interpreted of Astarte, the infamous Deity, against Jehovah the Saviour. But seeing shame used naturally in the next verse, I think this explanation strained.

Jehovah gave Palestine to the race, (13) which afterwards fell from him so grievously.

14. The prayers of the reunited tribes, (15) encouraged by God's promise, or goodness, (16) will disclaim hopes of prosperity from turning to idols on high places, (17) having found Astarte, *That baseness,* or whatever false deity they had crowded to honour on the mountains, (18) impotent to help, and apt to leave them prostrate.

Ch. III. because we sinned against the ETERNAL our God, we and our fathers, from our youth even to this day, and hearkened[35] not to the voice of the ETERNAL our God.

19. If thou wilt return,[36] Israel, is JEHOVAH's saying, return to Me; and if thou wilt remove thy abominations [out of thy mouth], and not wander from before my face, 20. but swear, As JEHOVAH LIVES, in truth, and in judgment, and in righteousness, then shall nations bless themselves in him [*Israel*], and make their boast by him.

---

[35] *Hearkened*, with dative, in the sense of obeying.
[36] The punctuation and balance of clauses in vv. 19, 20, are disputable. Which is the first respondent or answering clause? "If thou returnest to me, Israel, thou shalt return *to thy home*," said the Masora, playing wrongly on the words. The LXX. and Vulg. agree in finding the first response, at the second *Return*, whether fut. or imperat. So far, I think, both rightly. Most modern critics make five projecting clauses in succession, before they find in nations *blessing* themselves the first response. It seems to me, in that case, the second verb *return* must have had some connecting particle of hypothesis, instead of resuming nakedly. Again, the LXX. insert ἐκ στόματος αὐτοῦ, which the subsequent oath, against the abominations, shews must have been in the original. This being admitted, we naturally join *wander* with *from my face*, as had occurred to me before I found that Movers and Hitzig do so. Still the preposition almost requires moving. Lastly, the harsh transition of pronoun from *thee*, Israel, to *him*, viz. *Israel*, convinces me the LXX. have here preserved throughout the true clue: 'Ἐὰν ἐπιστραφῇ 'Ισραὴλ, λέγει Κ. πρὸς μὲ, ἐπιστραφήσεται· καὶ ἐὰν περιέλῃ τὰ βδελύγματα αὐτοῦ ἐκ στόματος αὐτοῦ, καὶ ἀπὸ τοῦ προσώπου μου εὐλαβήθῃ, καὶ ὀμόσῃ Ζῇ Κύριος, κ.τ.λ. καὶ εὐλογήσουσιν ἐν αὐτῷ ἔθνη, καὶ ἐν αὐτῷ αἰνέσουσι τῷ Θεῷ ἐν 'Ιερ.—Compare the blessing to Abraham and his seed, Gen. xii. 3; xxii. 18; xlviii. 20. An innocent unconsciousness of the connexion between the chapters appears in Dr. Davidson's *Introduction*, iii. p. 90, which the Editor of Avrillon must have read with benevolent pleasure.

---

19. If the turning of heart were really to Jehovah, with oaths by other deities cast aside, (for to invoke God in a solemn oath is a form of worship), then might be fulfilled the ancestral promise to Abraham, that in his better seed, Isaac, Israel, and an upright or spiritual people,

IV.

1. For thus saith the ETERNAL to the men of Judah A.V.IV.3. and Jerusalem, Break up[37] for yourselves a clean fallow, and sow not on to thorns.

2. Be circumcised to the ETERNAL, and put away the outer skin of your heart, men of Judah and inhabitants of Jerusalem; lest my fury come forth like fire, and burn so that there be none to quench *it*, because of the evil of your doings.

3. Announce in Judah, and proclaim in Jerusalem, and say, Blow trumpet[38] in the land; cry loudly,[39] and say, Assemble yourselves, that we may go into the cities of defence.

4. Rear a standard toward Zion; seek refuge,[40] stay not; for *it is* evil *that* I am bringing from the north, and a great destruction.

---

[37] *Break up*, &c. LXX. νεώσατε ἑαυτοῖς νεώματα.

[38] *Blow trumpet.* The Heb. has a superfluous conjunction, omitted by LXX. by Jer. in Comm. and by Hitzig.

[39] *Cry loudly.* Heb. cry, fill, i.e. cry with a full voice. *Vulg.* clamate fortiter, Gr. κεκράξατε μέγα.

[40] *Seek refuge,* as Isa. xi. 8. [A. V. x. 31], or, hurry. LXX. σπεύσατε. *Vulg.* Confortamini.

---

though not in Ishmael, Esau, or any unfaithful people, all the families of the earth should bless themselves, saying, The Lord make us as Israel, or we are glorious as Jacob.

1, 2. As in Hosea, ix. 11, (A. V. x. 11), the Prophet bids the heart be cleansed for the good seed of the word, and for the rain of increase; so here Jeremy bids prepare an honest and good heart; with that preparation of turning to God which He looks for, while men perform an outward rite.

3—5. Else a cry of alarm and siege must go forth as the wrath of God, when he calls the shepherd races of the

Ch. IV.   5. A lion is gone up from his thicket, and a destroyer A.V. 1 of nations is on his way;[41] he goes forth from his place, to make thy land desolate; *so that* thy cities be stript, that there be no inhabitant.

6. For this gird on sackcloth, lament, and howl; because the fierceness of JEHOVAH's anger is not turned back from us.

7. And it shall be in that day, is JEHOVAH's saying, the heart of the king shall perish, and the heart of the princes; and the priests shall be astounded, and the prophets amazed.

8. And I said,[42] Ah, Lord, ETERNAL, Surely, thou hast utterly deceived this people, and Jerusalem, saying, Peace shall be to you, whereas the sword has pierced to the life.

9. [*In that time it shall be said to this people and to*

---

[41] *Is on his way.* These words may be punctuated into closer connexion with the following.

[42] *And I said.* LXX. καὶ εἶπα. *Vulg.* et dixi, but Ewald, *So that men say*; making the verb impersonal, against the Masora, and less appropriately. The Prophets intended are certainly not "false prophets," but in connexion with the Priests, the rightful instructors, whose hopeful presentiments, to Jeremiah's embarrassment failed.

North, probably Scythia, to prowl for prey, (6) unheeding penitential sackcloth, and, (7) astounding the official expounders of destiny.

8. Either they will then complain, or perhaps it seems to Jeremiah now, as if Providence had not made good its presages, but left those who trusted it to suffer embarrassment of mind, as well as trouble of estate. O unhappy Virtue, said Brutus, thou then wert a phrase, though I cherished thee as a thing in deed; but thou wast bondswoman of Chance.

9—11. Like the stormy wind, and lowering clouds,

IV. *Jerusalem,*]¹³ A scorching wind from the dry places of the wilderness toward the daughter of my people, not *a wind* to fan, nor *a wind* to cleanse—a fuller *wind* than those comes for me; now will even I utter judgments against them.

A. V. IV. 11.

10. Behold he comes up as clouds, with his chariots as a whirlwind; swifter than eagles are his horses: Woe to us, for we are destroyed.

11. Wash thy heart, Jerusalem, from wickedness, that thou mayest be saved: How long wilt thou lodge⁴⁴ in thy midst thy imaginations of folly?

12. For *there is* a voice proclaiming from Dan, and *one* announcing affliction from Mount Ephraim; 13. proclaim among the nations; behold, announce to Jerusalem, besiegers are coming from a land far away, and utter over the cities of Judah their voice.

14. As watchers of a field, are they against her round about, because she rebelled against me, is JEHOVAH's saying.

15. Thy way and thy doings have procured these things unto thee; this is thy wickedness, that [*the stroke*] is bitter, that it pierces to thy heart.

---

⁴³ The words in parenthesis belong to the Heb. text, but are removed by Ewald, as a gloss. They have an air of suspicious redundancy, as if they had crept in from the margin.

⁴⁴ *Wilt thou lodge*, i.e. thou people of Jerusalem; or intransitively, shall dwell. *Folly.* Heb. *Aven.* Vulg. noxiæ, LXX. πόνων, as in the next verse, where the word recurs, with perhaps its sense varied.

---

the invader impends in the far horizon, suggesting unsoundness in the prey awaiting him.

12—15. What can bring besiegers, but the will of Heaven? and what cause that will, but Israel's wickedness?

Ch. IV. 16. I have pangs in my very bowels,[45] the walls of my heart; my heart is in a tumult; I have no peace, for the trumpet's sound; O my soul, thou hast heard the alarm of war.

A. V. 19.

17. Crash upon crash is cried; for the whole land is devastated; suddenly are spoiled my tents, in a moment my pavilions; 18. how long shall I behold the banner, hear the trumpet's sound?

19. Because my people is foolish, me they have not known; ignorant sons are they, and not intelligent they: wise to do evil they are, but to do good they know not.

20. I beheld the earth, and lo, it was shapeless and empty:[46] and toward the heavens, and their light was no more: 21. I beheld the mountains, and lo, they trembled, and all the hills were in commotion: 22. I beheld, and lo, mankind was no more, and all the birds of the heavens fled away: 23. I beheld, and lo, the fruitful spot was the wilderness, and all its cities were destroyed before JEHOVAH, before the fierceness of his anger.

24. For thus hath JEHOVAH spoken, The whole land shall be desolate, and a full end will I not[47] make: 25.

---

[45] *My very bowels*, lit. my bowels, my bowels, but dependent on the verb *I am in pangs*, though by the Masora wrongly made exclamatory. I follow nearly the LXX. and Vulg. *My heart is in a tumult.* LXX. τὰ αἰσθητήρια τῆς καρδίας μαιμάσσει ἡ ψυχή μου. Comp. Hom. μαιμάω.

[46] *Shapeless and empty;* without form and void. Heb. *Tohu vabohu*, as in Gen. i. 2.

[47] *Not.* So the text, interpreted as a mitigation of doom; but the context, compared with Isa. x. 19 (A. V. x. 23) renders the reading suspicious.

16—23. The human feelings of the Seer are profoundly stirred, and he cries out at the vision in words of passion, which are clearly the words of a man, and would be inappropriate, if treated as God's word.

24—26. He proceeds to paint the destruction as in

IV. For this the earth mourns, and the heavens are darkened from above, because I have spoken, I have purposed, and have not relented, and will not turn back therefrom. A. V. iv. 28.

26. At the sound of the horsemen[48] and the archers[48] all the cities[48] take to flight: they enter into thickets, and climb upon the crags: all the cities are forsaken, and there is no man a dweller therein.

27. And thou, bespoiled one,[49] what wilt thou do? though thou robe thyself in scarlet, though thou adorn thyself with ornaments of gold, though thou widen thine eyes with paint, thou makest thyself fair in vain; thy lovers have rejected thee, seek thy life.

28. For I hear a voice as of one in pangs, anguish as of one bringing forth her first-born; the voice of the daughter of Zion, sighing, spreading forth her hands, Woe to me, woe, for my soul is faint for the slayers.

V.

1. Run to and fro in the streets of Jerusalem, and see now, and know, and search in her broad places, if you can find a man, if there be one that does justice, that seeks uprightness; that I may pardon her.

---

[48] *Horsemen, archers, cities.* Heb. sing.
[49] *Despoiled one.* Heb. gen. masc. though Sion, or her people, is addressed: there is something of the pendent noun, denoting accompaniment. *Widen thine eyes;* or, tear them, with pinching in the paint.

---

the words of a Divine decree: (27) Turning to Zion's daughter, he asks what in the time of spoiling (*masc. gen.*) she will do, and foretells for her contempt from her foreign masters, with (28) anguish of mental spasm, as she gives her children, or prepares herself, for the slayer. Hosea viii. 13. (A. V. ix. 13.) Jer. vii. 32, xix. 6. (A. V. xxxi. 15.)

1. A re-action from Romish corruptions makes us

Ch. V. 2. And if they say, As JEHOVAH LIVES, surely they swear *by Him* in vain.[50]

3. ETERNAL, are not thy eyes towards uprightness? thou hast stricken them, but they have not grieved: thou hast consumed them, they have refused to receive instruction; they have made their faces harder than the rock, they have refused to return.

4. Then I said, Ah! these are simple;[51] they are foolish: for they know not the way of the ETERNAL, the judgment of their God: let me get me to the great men, and bespeak them; for they know the way of the ETERNAL, the judgment of their God.

[50] *In vain*, i.e. falsely, as in 3rd Commandment.   [51] *Simple*, or poor.

confine the technical term Propitiation to Christ's work, as in English we do not ascribe merit to human devotion, though in Latin we may so apply *mereri*. If practice did not bias theory, we should see some confusion of thought in thus treating Christ's divine excellence as if it were not exhibited in human form, or as if goodness, prayer, striving, even in a human degree, were not also appeasements of God. Scripture teaches plainly, that Jehovah spared Jerusalem for David his servant's sake, and Phinehas made atonement for the people by his zeal: as Abraham's prayer might have saved Sodom, if it had contained but ten righteous men. Indeed, it is a matter of experience that merit and demerit of men affect well or ill the estate of their neighbours. It was an extreme rottenness in which Noah, Daniel, and Job, could have availed nothing to save. So in our text, the Prophet implies, speaking rhetorically, for he overlooks himself and all his disciples or friends, yet still he implies, that one righteous man, or a few, might have won grace for the guilty city; (2, 3) but no such intercessor by good life appears.

4. The Prophet was willing to hope, only the poor

V. 5. Alas! these together with those have shivered the A. V. v. 6.
yoke, broken the bonds: therefore lion out of the forest
slays them, wolf of the desert places⁵² lays them waste,
panther watches against their cities, *so that* every one
going out from them is torn; because their transgressions
are many, and their fallings away increased.

6. How shall I pardon thee for this? thy sons have
forsaken me, and swear by gods of naught: though
I adjured them,⁵³ yet they became adulterous, and in
the house⁵⁴ of her that is for hire they assemble themselves.

7. They became as stall-fed horses, going astray;⁵⁵
every one neighed after his neighbour's wife.

⁵² *Wolf of the desert places*; or, less probably, of the evening, as in Hab. i. 7.

⁵³ *I adjured them.* So the Hebrew is pointed, from the causative of *Shaba*' to swear, as in Beer-sheba', (comp. *seven*,) but the Versions, Gr. Lat. Angl. take it as from *Saba*', to feed to the full. *Vulg.* Saturavi, perhaps rightly. LXX. *ἐχόρτασα*.

⁵⁴ *House*; or, Temple.

⁵⁵ *Going astray*, as if from שָׁנָה=שָׁגָה, or early in the morning, as if from an adverbialised form of שְׁכֶם, to be early. Tu noli fœda Rabbinorum deliramenta sequi.

sinned by ignorance; (5) but finds the great and wealthy no better than the lower class; hence judgments come upon them, literally of beasts, as the Samaritan colonists suffered, 2 Kings xvii. 25, 26, (comp. Ezek. xiv. 15,) or else from the Assyrian, Scythian Nomad, and Chaldæan, symbolised as lion, wolf, and panther. We must not with Jerome introduce Persians and Greeks; but may treat the words as literal or symbolical of calamities.

6. In vain by solemn marriage vow, as by an oath, Jehovah betrothed Zion to himself: her sons go astray, as in temple of Ashtaroth, or by idolatry, which with rapid progress, (7) becomes demoralisation desecrating homes.

Ch. V.   8. Shall I not visit for these things, is the Eternal's A. V. saying; and shall not my soul avenge itself on such a nation as this?

9. Mount upon her walls,[56] and destroy, [*yet make not a full end*]; take away her battlements,[56] for they are not Jehovah's.

10. For the house of Israel and the house of Judah have dealt very treacherously by me, is Jehovah's saying.

11. They have belied Jehovah, and said, It is not He; and evil shall not come upon us; neither shall we see sword nor famine; but the prophets shall become wind, and the word[57] is not in them; thus shall it be done to themselves.

---

[56] *Walls* and *battlements.* LXX. προμαχῶνας and ὑποστηρίγματα. *Vulg.* muros and propagines. Since the latter word is highly metaphorical, its true sense being branches or suckers, it has been proposed to take the first as vine-rows, palm-branches, blossoms, which would give symmetry to the figure. Certainly the feminine plural savours more of *Sorah* a row, than *Shour* a wall (as the latter is misread for *Shor*, a bull = a mighty one, in Gen. xlix. 6), but Jeremiah's diction is often peculiar, and it suits the passage best to understand branches, or off-shoots, metaphorically, and to follow the clue of the versions.

[57] *The word,* i. e. prophetic utterance, ῥῆμα, Ephes. vi. 17—19. Or here, quasi-verbally, He who should speak.

8—10. That Eternal Being, who is not only Almighty, but All-righteous, will not overlook a betrayal of social duty, which is rebellion against his will, but summons by his Providence avenging invaders, whom, (as perhaps Jeremiah wrote,) he bids make a full end of the polluted city; or, as our text now stands, probably from some reviser, who, like the Pharisees on hearing Christ's threatening, exclaimed *God forbid,* the denunciation is of punishment stopping short of destruction.

11. The threatened people, though not doubting the existence of God, will not believe that his spirit becomes vocal in such denunciations, but ascribes them to a zeal

Ch. V.   12.   Therefore thus saith the ETERNAL, the God of hosts, A. V. v. 14. Because of your speaking this word, behold I make my words in thy mouth fire, and this people wood, so that it devour them.

13.   Behold me bringing upon you a nation from afar, House of Israel, is the ETERNAL'S saying; it *is* a mighty nation, it *is* an ancient nation; a nation whose tongue thou knowest not, neither understandest what they say; his quiver[58] as an open sepulchre, all of them valiant.

14.   And *they* shall devour thy harvest and thy bread; they shall devour thy sons[59] and thy daughters; devour thy flocks and thy herds; devour thy vines and thy fig-trees; and thy fenced cities wherein thou trustest, shall *they* demolish with the sword.

[15.   Yet even in these days, is JEHOVAH'S saying, I will not make a full end of you.]

---

[58] *Quiver.* Hebr. *Ashpah*, an exotic term, as other words of military art, though the root *Ashaph* is invented for it. More probably it represents the Greek σπάθη in the sense of sheath; it being the manner of Hebrew to prefix a vowel to borrowed words. Similarly suspicious, though disputed, is the appearance of μάχαιρα in Gen. xlix. 6.

[59] *Devour thy sons*, &c. LXX. κατέδονται τοὺς υἱοὺς. Vulg. devorabit filios tuos et filias tuas.

---

more likely to hurt itself: (12) whereas Jeremiah feels his fervid impulse as a fiery force of truth and perception. 13, 14.   Already he sees hovering in the horizon the wild hordes of Scythia, uncouth of tongue, and quivered as Death; or perhaps, without nice distinction, he may in after years have adapted his description to the Chaldæans of old renown, who carried out what the earlier invaders threatened.

15.   Jeremiah, or his editor, shrinks from painting an utter excision: the sentiment marches more characteristically without this verse.

Ch. V. 16. And it shall be, when you say, Wherefore has A.V.v. Jehovah our God done all these things to us? Then shalt thou answer them, Inasmuch as you have forsaken me, and served strange gods in your own land, so shall you serve strangers in a land not your own.

17. Announce this in the house of Jacob, and proclaim it in Judah, saying, Hear now this, Population foolish, and without heart; who have eyes, and see not; who have ears, and do not hear;

18. Will you not fear me, is the ETERNAL's saying, or before me will you not tremble? who placed the sand a boundary for the sea, a perpetual limit, that it should not cross over;[60] though its waves dash themselves, they cannot prevail; though they rage, they cannot cross over it.

19. But this people has a revolting and rebellious heart; they are revolted and gone, and do not say in their heart, Let us fear now the ETERNAL our God, who gives rain, both early shower and latter rain in its season; who reserves for us plentiful the periods of harvest.[61]

20. Your iniquities have turned away these things, and your sins have withholden good from you; for among

---

[60] *They* cannot cross over.—So the Heb. punctuators; but better the LXX. οὐχ ὑπερβήσεται, carrying the construction back to the Sea.

[61] *Who reserves for us plentiful the periods of harvest.* Not the weeks of harvest, from Nisan to Pentecost; for this is not only artificial, but an inversion of substantive and adjective. Either *Shebu'oth* means *sworn*, as pledged by the Creator's Covenant to his earth; or *Sebe'oth* means abundant, and in that sense might well be joined to the early and latter rain, in the antecedent clause. LXX. κατὰ καιρὸν πληρώσεως προστάγματος θερισμοῦ. *Vulg.* plenitudinem annuæ messis custodientem nobis.

---

16. Guilt ever exclaims, What have I done? but, (17) the Divine judgment, or its human interpreter, eloquently confounds the false plea of men, who, (18) neither feared their Creator's power, (19) nor had heart to thank him for all his goodness, (20) and so provoked his withdrawal of it,

Ch. V. my people are found malefactors; *each* lies in wait, like A.V.v.26. the lurking of fowlers, they set snares, they entrap men; as a cage is full of birds, so their houses are full of plunder.

21. Therefore they become great, and get wealth; they fatten *and* glisten; yea, they overpass deeds of evil; they judge not the cause, the cause of the fatherless, to make it prosper; and the right of the needy they do not set aright.

22. Shall I not visit for these things, is the ETERNAL'S saying; shall not my soul avenge itself on such a nation as this?

23. A wonder and a horror is come to pass in the land; the prophets prophesy falsely, and the priests rule by their means;[62] and my people love *it* so; but what will you do[63] at its latter end?

VI.

1. Hurry, sons of Benjamin, from the midst of Jerusalem, and sound trumpet in Tekoa,[64] and over Bethcerem

---

[62] *Rule by their means;* or, according to their guidance, following their lead. LXX. ἐπεκρότησαν ταῖς χερσὶν αὐτῶν. Vulg. applaudebant manibus suis. Neither rightly.

[63] *But what will ye do,* i. e. a threat.—Or, how far will you go, what not do, unless smitten?

[64] *Tekoa, i.e.* Sounding-town; *Bethcerem, i.e.* Vinetown, in Jerome's time Bethcharma, both towards the southern wilderness beyond Bethlehem.

---

(21) which they heeded little in a short-lived prosperity, swollen by haste to be rich, and by deeds of injustice, or superciliousness.

22. Judgment will come, (23) however little flattering preachers (or orators) bid men expect it, and however much a hierarchical system may be compacted by a low standard of truth, mercy, integrity.

1. Jeremiah wants his tribesmen to retreat from the

Ch. VI. make the beacon[63] blaze; for disaster appears out of the north, and great destruction; the comely one, the delicate one, have I destroyed :[66]

A. V. 1, 2.

2. The daughter of Zion, to her come shepherds and their flocks; they have pitched their tents against her, round about; they pasture each one in his place :[67]

3. *Saying,* Commence[68] against her war; arise, and let us go up at noontide : Alas for us ! that the day is turned, that the shadows of evening are declining; Arise, and let us go up by night, and destroy her palaces.

4. For thus hath the ETERNAL of hosts said, Hew down timber, and pile up a mound against Jerusalem; this is the city,[69] all the oppression in whose midst is visited.

5. Like a fountain's casting forth her waters,[70] so she casts forth her wickedness : violence and spoil is heard in her; before me continually *are* sickness and wounds.

6. Be chastened, Jerusalem, lest my soul be loosened

---

[65] *Beacon,* Judges xx. 38-40.
[66] *Have I destroyed.* As Isa. xv. 1.
[67] *His place,* Heb. his hand.
[68] *Commence.* Lit. Consecrate, or inaugurate.
[69] *The city, all the oppression in whose midst is visited;* or, as the text stands, *the city to be visited;* she is wholly oppression in the midst of her; but such a construction of הַפְּקֹד is strange in respect of gender and verbal form. Hence Israel כָּל הָעֹשָׁה for כֻּלָּהּ, &c.
[70] *Casting forth her waters;* or, keeping them fresh, as a cistern.

---

city about to be beleaguered towards the ruder villages southward, since the delicate place seems sentenced; (2) the Nomads of the desert literally, or figuratively the Captains and their troops (if of Chaldees) strip the suburban spots : (3) by day, if possible, or else by night, they pant for the city's ruin.

4. A Divine thought must have forecast the siege, since (5) the city is a well of wickedness, and (6) heeds

VI. from thee; lest I make thee desolate, a land unin- A.V. VI. 8.
habited.

7. Thus saith the ETERNAL of hosts, They shall thoroughly glean the remnant of Israel, as a vine; turn again thy hand, as a grape-gatherer into the baskets.

8. To whom shall I speak, and warn, that they may hear? behold their ear is closed with skin, and they cannot hearken; behold the word of the ETERNAL becomes to them a reproach; they have no delight in it.

9. So I am filled with the ETERNAL's wrath; I am weary of refraining, from pouring[71] out upon child in the street, and upon the gathering of youths together; for even husband with wife shall be taken, the elder with the full of days;

10. And their households shall be brought round to others, lands and wives together; for I am stretching forth my hand upon the inhabitants of the land, is JEHOVAH'S saying;

11. For from the least even to the greatest[72] every one is greedy of gain, and from prophet even to priest every one deals falsely.

12. And [*they*] heal the wound of the daughter of my people lightly, saying, Peace, Peace, when there is no peace.

---

[71] *From pouring*; or, with pause at refraining, *Pour out thou*, my soul.
[72] *Least to the greatest.* Vulg. a minore usque ad majorem. LXX. ἀπὸ μικροῦ αὐτῶν. The Heb. punctuators give both words the pronominal affix, but the simple plural would be as natural.

---

not warning, therefore, (7) must be plucked by unsparing hand.

8, 9. Mocked by those whom he warns, the Prophet overflows with zeal, and prophesies, (10) utter ruin, (11) of utter guilt.

12. Feeble warnings attest, (13) feeble shame of

Ch. VI. 13. They were put to shame,[73] because they wrought abomination : even with shame they were not ashamed ; they could not even blush ; therefore shall they fall among the falling ; in the time when I visit them they shall be cast down, saith the ETERNAL.

14. Thus saith the ETERNAL, Stand in the ways, and look, and ask for the old paths, where is the way of good, and walk therein, and find rest for your souls ; but they said, We will not walk *therein*.

15. And I set over you watchmen ; Hearken to the sound of the trumpet : But they said, We will not hearken.

16. Therefore hearken, O nations, and learn, congregation, that which [*I will do*][74] by them.

17. Hearken, Earth ; behold me bringing evil upon this people, the fruit of their imaginations, because they have not attended to my words ; and even my law, they rejected it.

18. To what purpose comes to me incense from Sheba,

---

[73] *They were put to shame,* &c. ; or, Were they ashamed, because they had wrought abomination ? *Nay,* they were not at all ashamed, &c. Instead of making the first clause interrogative, I understand it, that they had reason for shame—ought to have felt it. The reiterated term shame is an idiom for utter negation.

[74] *That which I will do.* Vulg. quanta ego faciam eis. The Hebrew, as it stands, is elliptic. The LXX. extracted οἱ ποιμαίνοντες from a misreading.

---

blunted consciences. 14. God ever invites men to the old paths of piety and rectitude, which, unchangeable as their Divine Author, do not depend on fashion or convenience, but transmit everlasting lives through the flux of generations and their shortcomings.

15. Men may reject their rightful teachers, (16, 17) but God punishes at length those whom he has warned in vain. 18. He does not value incense so much as

and cinnamon[75] from a land afar? Your burnt-offerings A.V.vi.20. are not acceptable, nor your sacrifices sweet to me?

19. Therefore thus saith the ETERNAL, Behold me laying upon this people stumbling-blocks, that they may fall upon them, fathers and sons together; that neighbour and his friend may perish.

20. Thus saith the ETERNAL, Behold a population comes from the land of the North, and a mighty nation is raised from the extremities of the earth; 21, they lay hold on bow and spear; fierce are they and have no compassion; their voice roars like the sea, and they ride upon horses, arrayed as men for war against thee, daughter of Zion.

22. We heard his rumour; our hands grew faint, distress took hold of us; pain, as one travailing.

23. Go not forth into the field, and walk not along the way, because of the enemy's sword; panic is on every side; daughter of my people, gird on sackcloth, and besprinkle thyself[76] with ashes; make thee a wailing, as for an only child, a very bitter lamenting; for the spoiler comes suddenly upon us.

24. I have set thee an assayer[77] among my people,

---

[75] *Cinnamon*. Hebr. pleasant cane. LXX. κινάμωμον. *Vulg.* Calamum suave-olentem.

[76] *Besprinkle thyself;* or, roll thyself, Micah i. 9. (A. V. 10.) Comp. Christ's warnings, Matt. xx. 17—34.

[77] *An assayer,* and *severing metal.* So essentially Ewald, Maurer, Hitzig,

---

prayer, nor sacrifice so much as good deeds of thankfulness. 19. Those whom God destroys he infatuates, or entangles in circumstance.

20. As the Tartar host is described, (22) the rumour makes men's hearts sink, (23) and panic crowds the city with fugitives, whose signs of mourning are sackcloth and ashes.

24—26. The warning comes from one who as monitor

108   THE HEBREW PROPHETS.

Ch. VI. severing metal; that thou mayest know and assay their A.V.vi
way;

25. They are all grievous revolters, walking for slander; brass and iron, running to dross all of them, are they;

26. The bellows are burned with their fire; the smelter in vain smelts lead; and the wicked are not severed *therefrom*; refuse[78] silver men pronounce them, for the ETERNAL has rejected them.

---

and as regards the first, *Bachon*, many others, as Vulg. *Probatorem te dedi*; but the second has been pointed and taken usually as *Mibtzar*, a tower, whence Grotius and the older critics made *Bachon* also mean a fortress (comp. Isa. xxii. 14, Heb.); but the passage becomes more coherent, if we compare *Betzer*, Job xxii. 24, xxxvi. 19, and from its cognate, pointed as noun or participle here, get the sense of metal, or severer of metal.

[78] *Refuse*, Heb. *Maas*.

---

of his people had overlooked them as one watches the smelting of metal, and instead of fine gold, when the test of lead is applied, finds only coarser metals running to dross. God rejects that which by experiment is found refuse. Such is from internal coherence a more probable version of these verses, than one, also possible, which represents the Prophet as a tower and fortress, as in Isaiah xviii. 6—8. (A.V. xxi. 6—8.)

Here ends the first consecutive section of the Prophet's reminiscent Poem, or biographical aggregation of past warnings. Treating at least chapter i. as Proem, I consider ii., iii., iv., v., vi., as mainly consecutive, though a break in iv. 1 (A.V. iv. 3) implies a sub-division, in which the Prophet passes from reasoning to threatening. The Prophet having, after a description of his ideal consecration to a divine work, expostulated with his people generally, and iv. 1,—vi. 26, threatened them with avenging invasion, proceeds in chap. vii. to reprobate as hollow the confidence which the nation placed in her solemn temple,

VII.

The [79] word that came to Jeremiah from JEHOVAH, *saying, Stand in the gate of the house of* JEHOVAH, *and proclaim there this word, and say,* Hear the word of the ETERNAL, all Judah, *you enterers at these gates to worship* JEHOVAH.

1. Thus saith the ETERNAL of Hosts, the God of Israel, Amend your ways and your doings, that I may cause you to dwell in this place.

A. V. VII. 3.

2. Put not your trust in words of falsehood, saying, The temple of JEHOVAH, the temple of JEHOVAH, the temple of JEHOVAH these.

3. For if you thoroughly amend your ways and your doings; if you thoroughly execute judgment between man and between his neighbour; (4) the stranger, fatherless, and widow oppress not, and innocent blood shed not[80] in this place, and walk not after other gods to your hurt,

---

[79] The LXX. have as Title only the words, 'Ακούσατε λόγον Κυρίου πᾶσα 'Ιουδαία. The fuller Hebrew title seems appropriate to the mention of the Temple, if not suggested by it.

[80] *Innocent blood shed not.* Hebr. *Al.* Do not shed; the prohibitive amongst the negatives giving energy to the sentence, with a slight loss of consecutiveness.

---

and in her separation from the world at large as peculiarly dedicate to God.

1—9. Anticipating Christ in spirit, as his contemporaries were a forecast of Christ's contemporaries in their doings, the Prophet teaches that God is not mocked, nor religious pomp avails, without deeds answering to prayers. He redeems men from sin, not into a license of sinning. The place where He sets His name, He jealously reserves for other prayers than those offered in the spirit

Ch. VII. 5. Then will I cause you to dwell in this place, in the A. V. 7.
land that I gave to your fathers, from time of old and for
time to come.

6. Behold, you put your trust in words of falsehood,
to be of no advantage:

7. Will you steal, murder, and be adulterous, and
swear yourselves falsely, and burn incense to Baal, and
walk after other gods, whom you have not known; 8. and
then come and stand before me in this house, over which
my name is called, and say, We are delivered[81] that we
may do all these abominations?

9. Is this house over which my name is called, become
a den of robbers in your eyes? Behold, even I have seen
it, is the saying of the ETERNAL.

10. But go now to my place which was in Shiloh,[82]
which I made the dwelling-place of my name at the first,
and see what I did to it, because of the wickedness of
my people Israel:

11. And now, because of your doing all these works,
is JEHOVAH's saying, and I spoke to you, rising early and
speaking, but you hearkened not; and I called you, but
you answered not;

12. Therefore I do[83] to this house, over which my name
is called, in which you trust, and to the place which I
gave to you and your fathers, even as I have done to
Shiloh;

---

[81] *We are delivered;* or, redeemed; as when Christians make negation of
their own merit a licentious substitute for striving and obeying.

[82] *On Shiloh,* vv. 10, 12, see Psalm lxxviii. 60; Judges xviii. 31. xxi.
19; 1 Kings ii. 27; 1 Sam. iii. 21.

[83] *I do;* or, will do.

---

of guile, and will not count peculation or nepotism as devotion. St. Matt. xxi. 13, xviii. 20.

10—13. The northern realm of the ten tribes had
deemed itself guarded by the sanctity of Shiloh (Gen.

VII. 13. And I cast you out from before my face, as I have cast out all your brethren, namely all the seed of Ephraim.

A. V. VII.
15.

14. And thou, neither pray for this people, nor lift up cry nor supplication for them, neither intercede with me; for I am not hearkening to thee.

15. Canst thou not see what they do in the cities of Judah, and in the streets of Jerusalem? 16. The sons gathering wood, and the fathers kindling the fire, and the women kneading dough, to make cakes for the Queen of Heaven,[84] and to pour out libations to other gods, to vex me to anger?

17. Is it me that they vex? is JEHOVAH's saying. Is it not themselves, to the confusion of their own face?

18. Therefore thus saith the Lord, the ETERNAL, Behold my anger and my fury is poured out upon this place, upon man, and upon beast, and upon the trees of the field, and upon the fruit of the ground; so that it burn, and shall not be quenched.

---

[84] *The Queen of Heaven.* The Moon; or more ideally the principle of feminine life in Nature, worshipped under many names, as Ceres, (in some aspects Diana,) Cybele, Idæa Mater, Urania, (the Alma Venus of Lucretius,) here probably as Ashtoreth, whether identified with the Assyrian Ishtar, or Egyptian Athor, is disputed. The new-moon feasts of the Jews were among the points of contact between their system and the rites less pure of surrounding nations.

---

xlix. 10), which Samuel after Eli's fall had reconsecrated, yet the Assyrian ruin came on Samaria and all her people.

14—18. Jeremiah, characteristically about to intercede for his people, is checked by the signs of their falling back from Jehovah to Ashtoreth; that is, from a worship, associated with human history, and moralised by human feeling, into one in which the largeness of Nature should give license to impulses. We conceive unworthily of God, if we think our most ennobling order or discipline not designed by Him; yet (17) we hurt ourselves, not Him by

Ch. VII.   19. Thus saith the Eternal of hosts, the God of Israel; A. V. 21.
Add your burnt-offerings to your sacrifices, and eat flesh :

20. For I spake not to your fathers, nor commanded them, in the day they were brought out of the land of Egypt, on account of burnt-offering or sacrifice;

21. But assuredly this thing I commanded them, saying, Obey my voice, and I will be your God, and you shall be my people; and walk in all the way that I shall command you, that it may be well with you :

22. But they hearkened not, nor inclined their ear, but walked in the counsels—in the obstinacy of their evil heart, and went backward and not forward, even from the day when your fathers went forth out of the land of Egypt up to this day :

---

degrading ourselves to what He potentialises in nature, but does not sanction in man.

19—22. Animal bloodshed, as ritual pomp, is with God subordinate to the offered heart. Psalms l. 8—16, li. 16, 17. Some of the Mosaic sacrifices expressed a sense of sin, and were burnt, whether as unclean, or as suffering penalty; others were thank-offerings, and were eaten in sacrificial feast by priest and donor and family. Lev. vi. and xxiii., Heb. xiii. 11. Again, in Deuteronomy, a book conjecturally ascribed to Jeremiah's time, if not to himself, 2 Kings xxii. 8—13, the sin-offerings consumed by fire have disappeared, and only burnt-offerings of thankfulness, eaten in eucharist, are prescribed; even these rather permitted; while the distinction between clean and unclean meats vanishes. Deut. xii. 15—22, x. 12. Farther, it is doubted, by how many gradual accessions the system called Mosaic, or subsequently Levitical, may have grown. Hence some critics taking this passage literally, understand Jeremiah to deny that in God's great deliverance of Israel by Moses He encumbered his people with Levitical rites, however much they may have been added

VII. 23. And I send to you all my servants the prophets, A. V. VII.
daily rising up early and sending, but they hearkened not 25.
to me, nor inclined their ear, but hardened their neck;
they have done worse than their fathers.[83]

24. So speak thou to them all these words; but they
will not hearken to thee: and call to them, but they will
not answer thee.

25. So say unto them, This is the nation which has
not hearkened to the voice of JEHOVAH its God, nor received instruction: faithfulness is perished, and is cut off
from its mouth.

---

[83] 22, 23. If the reader compares this division of these verses with that of the Hebrew and Anglican, he will find the change required by the conjunction beginning v. 23, as well as by the rhythm and sense. Our translators turned *and* into *even*, because the punctuation misled them. *Obstinacy* is the afterthought, explanatory of *counsels*; or, as Hitzig seems to think, one of the two is redundant.

---

later. Others have recourse to a figure, and suppose, as in Hosea, v. 5, (A. V. vi. 6,) that only the subordination of ritual to moral is taught; which, however, is a great softening of the words. Thirdly, I would suggest, that the idea of sacrifice was undergoing in Jeremy's time a change analogous to that expanded and enforced in the Epistle to the Hebrews, and such a change appears in Deuteronomy, and in this passage. Instead of fancying that the blood of bulls and goats can put away sins, the Prophet conceives God saying, Eat freely whatever you please to sacrifice; such feasts of thanksgiving with charity, (Deut. xii. 18, 19,) neither offend nor appease; but bring me the sincere contrition and obedience which your fathers have forgotten. The reader may compare Amos, iv. 17, (A. V. v. 25), where some think the negative of the act of sacrifice in the wilderness stronger than my comment makes it.

23—26. Since continued warnings profit not this ge-

114   THE HEBREW PROPHETS.

CH. VII.   26. Shear, *Nation*, and cast away thy dedicated locks,[86] and lift up a wailing on the bare heights; because JEHOVAH has rejected and forsaken the generation of his wrath.

A. V. 29.

27. For the sons of Judah have done evil in my sight, is JEHOVAH's saying; they have set their abominations in the house over which my name is called to pollute it;

28. And have built the high places, Tophet,[87] which are in the valley of the son of Hinnom, to burn their sons and their daughters in the fire; which I commanded not, neither came it into my heart:

29. Therefore, behold days coming, is JEHOVAH's saying, when it shall no more be called Tophet, nor the valley of the son of Hinnom, but the valley of slaughter:

30. For they shall bury in Tophet, until there be no room; and the corpses of this people shall be food for the

---

[86] *Dedicated locks;* or, diadem, a sense less appropriate with the verb *shear*.
[87] *Tophet,* if a Hebrew word, the *pleasant place*, "qui Siloe fontibus irrigatus, et est amœnus et nemorosus;" but, if of Persian or foreign origin, it may mean the *burning-place,* as suits Isa. xxvi. 32. (A. V. xxx. 33.) Neither the sense of Tympanum, nor that of abomination, suits well. The son of Hinnom was probably some owner, whose history is lost; for the derivation *groaning* (Hitzig) seems little applicable.

---

neration, the nation may lay aside her coronal, or unshorn locks of dedication to Jehovah, and suffer with the Heathen; (27) whose ill deeds they have brought into Jehovah's temple. 28. Tophet, pleasant valley, watered by Siloe, but also a place of burning bones, has been the scene of such unnatural sacrifice as Abraham the father of the faithful changed into symbol and obedience, (Psalm cvi. 37—39, with Gen. xxii. 2, 6, 14; Ex. xxix. 31; Lev. xx. 2); (29) therefore shall be a place of slaughter, as Jerusalem (30) of mourning; and the sepulchres shall

VII. birds of heaven, and for the beasts of earth, with none to scare them away. ^{A. V. VII. 33.}

31. And I will cause to cease out of the cities of Judah and out of the streets of Jerusalem voice of mirth, and voice of gladness, voice of bridegroom, and voice of bride; for the land shall become a desolation.

32. In that time, is JEHOVAH's saying, then shall they bring out the bones of the kings of Judah, and the bones of its princes, and the bones of the priests, and the bones of the prophets, and the bones of the inhabitants of Jerusalem, out of their graves, 32. and spread them before the sun and the moon and all the host of heaven, whom they loved, and whom they served, and after whom they walked, and whom they sought, and whom they worshipped; they shall neither be gathered, nor be buried; they shall be for dung upon the face of the earth; ^{A. V. VIII. 1.}

33. And death shall be chosen rather than life by all the remnant of those who survive of this evil family, [who survive] in all the places whither I have driven them, is the saying of JEHOVAH of hosts.

VIII.

1. Moreover thou shalt say to them, Thus saith JEHOVAH, Do *men* fall, and not rise again? does *a man* turn, and not turn again?

---

be violated, (31) and the remnant (32) surviving suffer exile. Such outrage on the dead, (for whom the Eastern reverence might well not be trifled with by tourists,) will be the last grief of the living.

VIII. The next two chapters are thought separable from the preceding four, iv. v. vi. vii. yet hardly introduce new topics, but mingle continuous expostulation with mourning.

1. Since men ordinarily try to recover from a fall,

I 2

Ch. VIII. 2. Wherefore is this people of Jerusalem fallen off with a perpetual falling away? *why* persist they in deceit, refuse to return?

3. I attended and hearkened; nothing upright they spake; not a man, *who* repented of his wickedness, saying, What have I done? every one turned to his courses,[88] as the horse bounding to the battle.

4. Yea, the stork[69] in the heavens knoweth her seasons, and the turtle and the swallow and the crane observe the time of their coming; but my people know not the judgment of the ETERNAL.

5. How can you say, We are wise, and the law of JEHOVAH is with us? Behold, surely in vain has wrought the lying pen of the scribes.[90]

6. Ashamed are the wise; dismayed are they and captured; they have rejected the word of the ETERNAL, and what kind of wisdom have they?

---

[88] *Courses*, as from רִיץ, or desires, as from רָצָה.

[89] *The stork*, Heb. the pious bird; better stork, than bittern, or kite. LXX. ἡ ἀσίδα, Grecising the Heb. Vulg. Milvus in cœlo cognovit tempus suum; turtur, et hirundo, et ciconia custodierunt tempus adventûs sui.

[90] *The lying pen of the scribes*; or, changing the punctuation, and I think, better, " Surely in vain has wrought a vain (or lying) pen ; the scribes are " ashamed, the wise are dismayed, and captured." We can hardly suppose falsehood imputed to the earlier Scriptures ; but neither can we conceive written traditions, in opposition to Scripture, at so early a date. Again oral

---

(2) why is Jerusalem obstinate, (3) unrepentant, (4) unlike the wild birds, whose instincts lead them aright across the heavens.

5. They boast, like St. Paul's contemporaries, of written laws, (John v. 38—40, Romans ii. 17—27,) which the Prophet, in reply, disparages, if not in themselves, yet in comparison of God's fresh imprint on conscience and utterance by voice; (Comp. Rom. as above, 2 Cor. iii. 3—6—17.); (6) learning, without fear and love of God, is unblest wisdom.

JEREMIAH. 117

7. Therefore will I give their wives to others, their A. V. VIII. 10.
fields to inheritors; I will utterly consume them, is JE-
HOVAH's saying, *until* no grapes are on the vine, and no
figs on the fig-tree, and the leaf fades; and *the things* I
give them,[91] *invaders* shall overtread them.

8. Wherefore are we sitting still? Assemble yourselves, and let us enter into the fortified cities, and there
be silent;[92] since JEHOVAH our God has brought us to
silence, and made us drink the waters of gall, because we
sinned against JEHOVAH.

9. [93]Waiting for peace—but welfare is not—*waiting for*
a time of healing, and behold trouble.

---

glosses are not the thing intended here ; for the fresh living word is conceived
to be on the Prophet's side, and the written text on his opponents. We may,
as the least difficulty, suppose the contrast as between the living spirit and
formal literalism ; though the expression is intensely emphatic, since the very
sacred document itself seems disparaged, and not merely its exposition. It
is natural to attempt to find here the Protestant antithesis of Scripture and
Tradition ; but something quite different is implied by the whole passage.

[91] *And the things I give them, invaders shall cross over them;* or, And I
will appoint to them *invaders* to overflow (cross over) them. The far greater
coherence of this verse, as given in the LXX, has induced me to follow here
the Greek, without for a moment raising its authority to that of the Hebrew :
the reader will please to notice, that the Hebrew Text, as the A. V. has in
the middle of this verse, a passage taken from above, vi. 11—13 (A. V. vi.
13—15.) but less appropriate here, and disturbing the coherence. *"For
" from little even to great every one is greedy of greed ; from prophet even
" to priest every one worketh falsehood. And they healed the bruise of the
" daughter of my people lightly, saying, Peace, Peace, where was no peace.
" They were put to shame, because they wrought abomination ; they are not
" even at all ashamed, and they know not how to blush. Therefore they shall
" fall among the falling, in the time of their visitation they shall be cast
" down, saith Jehovah."*

[92] *Be silent;* or, be cut off, as Isa. xiv. 1. (A. V. xv. 1.)

[93] *Waiting*, an ellipse=we waited.

---

7. The prophet multiplies threats, repeating, as the
Heb. text now stands, his reasons for threatening, from
vi. 11—13 (A. V. 13—15), but see margin above.

Cн. VIII. 10. The snorting of his horses is heard from Dan; at A. V. vii 16.
the sound of the neighing of his mighty ones the whole
land trembles; and they come to devour land and its
fullness; city, and dwellers therein.

11. For behold me sending among you serpents,
basilisks,[94] against which there is no charm, and they shall
sting you, is JEHOVAH's saying.

12. When I would refresh me[95] over sorrow, my heart
sickens within me.

13. Lo! the sound of the crying of the daughter of
my people from a land of far regions; Is JEHOVAH not in
Zion? is her king therein no more?

14. Wherefore have they vexed me with their graven
images; with the idols of the stranger?

15. The harvest is passed, the summer is ended, and
we are not saved.

16. For the hurt of the daughter of my people am I
hurt: I go mourning:[96] astonishment has taken hold on
me.

---

[94] *Basilisks;* or, vipers. Vulg. regulos. LXX. h. l. θανατοῦντας, alias κεραστάς.

[95] *When I would refresh me;* or, better, I am confounded; the idea of the Hebrew is *blazing forth*, as in Amos iv. 6. (A. V. v. 9.) Most critics extract the sense of reviving; wrongly, I think. Vulg. Dolor meus. LXX. ἀνίατα.

[96] *I go mourning*, lit. put on black. LXX. ἐσκοτώθην. Vulg. contristatus. At the end of this verse, the LXX. have a simile, "as one in childbirth," which has dropt out of the Hebrew.

8—10. A cry of panic summons to refuge, (11) at the stings of Divine wrath, (12) and the Prophet's heart sickens, remediless, or confounded. 13. The cast off bride cries out of exile to her Lord, and, (14) hearing his inexorable plea of cause and effect, (15) compares herself to the shocks of corn, un-gathered, un-saved, when life's harvest is over. (Matt. xiii. 38—43). 16—18. What can the Prophet do but

VIII. 17. Is balm not in Gilead; is healer not there? why then is not the health⁹⁷ of the daughter of my people restored?

18. Oh! that my head were waters, and my eyes a A.V. ix. 1. fountain of tears; that I might weep day and night for the slain of the daughter of my people.⁹⁸

IX.

1. Oh! that I had in the wilderness a way-farer's lodge; that I might leave my people, and go from them away.

2. For they are all adulterous, an assembly of traitors, and bend their tongue, their bow, for falsehood, and not for truthfulness.⁹⁹

3. They are mighty in the land, because they have gone from evil to evil; but me they have not known, is the saying of the ETERNAL.

4. Beware you every one of his neighbour, and trust not in any brother; for every brother is an utter supplanter, and every neighbour walks in slander;

---

⁹⁷ *Health restored.* Vulg. obducta cicatrix; the healing process as of a wound.

⁹⁸ According to our common Hebrew Bibles, as according to the marginal letter in the Bomberg Rabbinical, (Ven. 1525), this verse ends a chapter; though the Vulgate and Anglican, with far less propriety, make it commence a new one.

⁹⁹ *For falsehood and not for truthfulness.* Vulg. quasi arcum mendacii, et non veritatis. So the Hebrew texture of words had persuaded me, before I saw the Vulgate, or knew that Eichhorn (neque id "temerè," ut ait Maurerus,) had preceded me.

---

weep, wondering that no remedy of human art, or Divine goodness, has healed the self-cast-away.

1. The Prophet sighs for rest, away from (2) a people sensual and false, (3) who make money the test of right, and (4—6) deceive each other, as they are themselves

Ch. IX.   5. And they deceive every one his neighbour, and   A. V.
speak not the truth; they have accustomed their tongue   5.
to speak falsehood, with doing evil they are wearied.

6. Thy abode is in the midst of deceit; through deceit they refuse to know me, is JEHOVAH's saying.

7. Therefore thus saith the ETERNAL of hosts, Behold I will smelt them, and assay them;[100] for how shall I do on account of [*the wickedness of*][101] the daughter of my people?

8. Their tongue is a murderous[102] arrow; it speaks deceit; a man speaks peace to his neighbour with his mouth, but in his heart he lays his ambush.

9. Shall I not visit them for these *things?* is JEHOVAH's saying; shall not my soul be avenged on such a nation as this?

10. For the mountains I will raise a weeping and a wailing, and over the pastures of the wilderness a dirge; because they are burnt up, so that no man passes through, neither do men hear the sound of cattle; both birds[103] of heaven and beasts are fled; they are gone:

11. And I will make Jerusalem heaps, a den of jackals :[104] and I will make the cities of Judah a desolation, without an inhabitant.

---

[100] *And assay.* LXX. ἐγὼ πυρώσω αὐτοὺς καὶ δοκιμῶ αὐτούς.

[101] *The wickedness of.* LXX. πονηρίας, which must have been genuine, though unknown to the Vulg. and our present Hebrew. Ewald and Hitzig have preceded me in approving it.

[102] *Murderous;* or, as the Jewish doctors, shot out, 'hujusmodi conjecturis facilè caremus.' R.

[103] *Both birds;* or, lit. from bird to beast.

[104] *Jackals,* Heb. *Tanim.* A.V. dragons, from Vulg. draconum, and LXX. δρακόντων. So even Bochart, iii. xiv. II.A. who explains synonymous or correspondent names accurately. From Pocock downwards the sense jackal has become the accepted one.

---

deceived into alienation from God, (Psalms, iv. v. xiv. lii. lvii.). The word *supplanter,* reiterated in the Hebrew, alludes to Jacob taking his brother by the heel. 7—11.

IX.   12. Who is the wise *man*, to understand this, and to whom the mouth of the ETERNAL has spoken, that he may declare it; wherefore is the land ruined, scorched like a wilderness, so that none passes through?

13. So the ETERNAL saith, Because of their forsaking my law which I set before them, and they listened not to my voice, neither walked therein;

14. But they walked after the perverseness of their heart, and after the lords [*i.e. Baalim,*] which their fathers taught them.

15. Therefore, thus saith the ETERNAL of hosts, the God of Israel, Behold me feeding them, this people, with wormwood, and making them drink waters of gall;

16. And I will scatter them among the nations, whom neither they nor their fathers have known; and will send the sword after them, until I destroy them.

17. Thus saith the ETERNAL of hosts, Take you counsel, and call for the mourning-women, that they come; and send for the wise women, that they come,

18. That they may hasten, and lift up over us a

Therefore judgment must come of him who severs true metal from alloy, and wheat from tares when he purges his floor, and who makes the fruitful land desolate, the city a heap, for the wickedness of its inhabitants.

12, 13. Who has the spirit of vision, to discern in human calamity Divine visitation? Here the will of God is conceived not so ideally, as in the earlier Prophets, but in its written embodiment of moral or religious code, whereby man gives shape to Divinely-breathed instincts. 14—16. Forgetfulness of God, as of one afar, or of his law as a thing out of sight, engenders shame, sinking of heart, and exile. The Prophet speaks even of extinction, though this extreme will be often revoked by the relenting of his human feeling. 17—20. Let signs of funeral

Ch. IX. wailing; that our eyes may run down with tears, and our A. V. 19.
cyelids gush out waters;

19. For a voice of wailing is heard out of Zion, How are we destroyed; *how* confounded utterly, because we have left *our* land, because *men* have cast down our dwelling-places!

20. Yea, hearken, women, to the ETERNAL's word, and let your ear receive his mouth's utterance; so teach your daughters wailing, and each her neighbour a funeral song.

21. For Death is come up into our windows; it has entered into our palaces; to cut off children out of the street, the young men out of the broad places;[105]

22. So that the carcases of men fall as dung upon the face of the field, and as the sheaf behind the harvester, when there is none to gather it.

23. Thus saith the ETERNAL, Let not the wise glory in his wisdom, and let not the valiant glory in his valiancy, and let not the wealthy glory in his wealth:

24. But let him that glories glory in this, that he is wise to know me, that I, the ETERNAL, do mercy, judgment, and righteousness in the earth; for in these I delight, is the saying of the ETERNAL.

25. Behold days coming, is the ETERNAL's saying,

---

[105] 21, 22. Between these verses the Heb. text has, *Speak, thus is Jehovah's saying,* but the unidiomatic junction of *thus* and *saying,* כֹה נְאֻם, the interruption of the sentence, and the absence of the words in the Greek, betray the interpolation.

---

mourning attend the nation's fall. 21, 22. Instead of children playing in the streets, a harvest of neglected corpses seems imminent under the invader's scythe.

23, 24. The true remedy would be in turning to God, (25, 26) not in formal religious rites, which God values

IX. when I will visit upon all consecrate for unconsecra- A. V. ix. 25.
tion;[106]

26. Upon Egypt and upon Judah, and upon Edom, and upon the sons of Ammon, and upon Moab, and upon all the shorn round the crown,[107] the dwellers in the wilderness; because all the nations are unconsecrate, and all the house of Israel are unconsecrate of heart.

X.

1. Hear you the word, which the ETERNAL speaks to you, House of Israel:

---

[106] *Will visit upon all consecrate for unconsecration.* LXX. ἐπισκέψομαι ἐπὶ πάντας τοὺς περιτετμημένους τὰς ἀκροβυστίας αὐτῶν. Vulg. visitabo super omnem qui circumcisum habet præputium. However the construction here may be disputed, the meaning is as if we said, God will treat the baptized as unbaptized: or, he will punish both together; see the converse, Rom. iii. 30, where faith is first appended as the instrument, secondly as the condition.

[107] In v. 26, the *shorn round the crown*, or corners of the head, (as all the old Greek and Latin Versions take it,) are the Arabs described by Herodotus, iii. 8, as receiving a certain tonsure in honour, he supposed, of Dionysus. For the Egyptian circumcision (probably adopted thence by the Hebrews,) see Herod. ii. 36—104. Religious " unbelief" does not consist in acknowledging the providential continuity of usages and ideas amongst nations, but in fearing that the religious sentiment will not rise always to the level of scientific observation.

---

only as expressions of a feeling underlying them, and which, without such feeling, will be no distinction in His pure eyes, no safeguard against His doom. Matt. iii. 9, Rom. iii. 20—30, Gal. v. 6, vi. 15, Philipp. iii. 9: " not having as my righteousness that which is legal, but that which is spiritual." Col. ii. 8—17, where the philosophy condemned is not metaphysical, but Judaically legal; " the rudiments of the world," meaning the Levitical system.

The Xth chapter brings questions of the dislocation of Jeremiah into prominence. The Greek Version places

Ch. X. 2. Thus saith the ETERNAL, Towards the way of the A. V nations learn not, and at the signs of the heavens be not dismayed, though the nations are dismayed at them:

the 9th verse in the midst of the 5th, which it seems as if it might precede; it omits vv. 6, 8, 10, and omits *Israel the rod* in v. 16. Again the 11th verse has a character of its own, being Chaldee instead of Hebrew, and disturbing the context by being thrown into the midst of a sentence, whereas if restored to the margin it becomes a fair paraphrase of the whole piece. Hence it seems our earliest specimen of a *Targum*, not so alien to the text as the curious gloss, *The Burden of the beasts of the South* in Isaiah xxvi. 6 [A. V. xxx. 6.] because it does not violate the sense, but still a Targum, or a tradition, not 'scripture.' So far the most moderate critics go. Yet since this marginal gloss, for such it originally was, is rendered by the LXX. it must be old, if not quite as old as the Exile. Belonging to such an age, it represents the earlier Biblical Chaldee, as Ezra and Nehemiah do, from which the later Daniel is with a preponderance of reasons, as I believe, conceived to decline. (See the *Introduction* to Desprez's *Treatise on Daniel*, and the authorities there quoted.)

Again, others, not without reason, divide (as Movers and Hitzig,) our chapter into two portions. They observe in the portion down to v. 16, some characteristics of the later Isaiah, while from v. 16 they find Jeremiah again. Certainly the injunction 'not to fear the signs of Heaven' savours of the time of the Chaldees, or of the Exile; while v. 16, continues, or resumes, the warnings of ix. 16, 17, 22, 26. Hence a presumption of divided authorship, almost amounting to a proof; but if any one conceives that Baruch, the editor of our Prophet, (see xxxvi. 32. xlv. 1,) added during the Exile this monition to his people, that they should not adopt Chaldee usages,

JEREMIAH.   125

3. For the customs[108] of the populations are folly; for A. V. x. 3. they hew timber[108] out of the forest, the work of the craftsman's hands, with the axe;

4. With silver and gold they bedeck, with nails and hammers they fasten them, that they may not totter;

5. They are as a polished column, and speak not; they are borne of bearers, because they step not; be not adread of them, for they do no hurt, neither again is it in them to do good.

6. There is none[109] like thee, JEHOVAH; great art thou, and great thy name in might.

7. Who must not dread thee, King of the nations? for thee it becomes; for among all the wise of the nations, and in all their kingdoms, there is none[109] like thee.

8. But they are altogether brutish and foolish; the stock is a doctrine of folly.

---

[108] *For they hew timber;* or, as Heb. punctuation, *For they are but timber, which one hews out of the forest.* It seems, as if the punctuators took חקות *customs,* by perhaps a later usage, in the sense of idols, as if we interpreted *statutes* as *statues:* they then pointed the verb *hew,* as a singular, with a pronominal affix. I have preferred a simpler, more running, construction. By customs are meant religious customs, as Gr. τὰ νόμιμα.

[109] *There is none.* Docent interpretes מאין duplicis negativi vim habere. Sed cum vox rarissima post ם *Mem* tam versu priore quam altero (quod jure mireris) occurrat, longè verisimilius fit *Mem* finalem ex antecedente voce oscitantiâ scribarum bis irrepsisse.

---

he will have the analogy of 2nd Isaiah, xl. and xliv. in his favour, and I should be inclined to assent. This chapter and the xxvth, together with the different arrangement of xxv—xxxii, or xlvi—li, in the Greek and Hebrew, show eminently on comparison, how complex a problem of dislocated text meets us in Jeremiah. There is some probability that the LXX. order may be the more ancient.

1—15. Jeremiah, or a later editor, warns the Israelites against adopting Chaldæan dread or worship. Idolatry

Ch. X. 9. [110]Silver beaten out[111] is brought from Tarshish, and gold from Uphaz,[112] the work of the craftsman, and of the founder's hands; blue and purple their vestments; the work of cunning *men* all of them.

10. But JEHOVAH is God in truth; he *is* the living God, and king eternal; at whose wrath the earth trembles, and the nations cannot endure his anger; 12. [114]who [11. *On this wise shall ye say unto them,*[113] *The Gods who the heavens and the earth made not, these shall perish from the earth, and from beneath the heavens.*] made the earth by his power, established the world by his wisdom, and in his understanding expanded the heavens.

13. At the voice of his utterance, is a sound of waters in the heavens, and he makes the mists mount from the end of the earth; he prepares the lightnings for the rain; and brings forth the wind out of his treasures.

---

[110] This ninth verse would seem, as the LXX. suggest, fitter after v. 4; but the whole chapter is too loosely coherent for corrections to be self-evident.

[111] The word *beaten out*, as into plates of silver, is the root רקע, from whence the idea of 'firmament' comes in Gen. i. 6, 7.

[112] *Uphaz*, probably a variation of Ophir.

[113] Not merely the supposed address to the Chaldæans, but the clause, *On this wise shall ye say*, is in the Chaldaic dialect, whence, as well as from the interruption of the sentence which the Prophet ran through, vv. 10—12, we see that verse 11 is an ancient paraphrase, crept in from the margin.

[114] The four or five verses, 12—15, "who made the earth—his name," will be found repeated in Jer. li. 15—19.

---

is described in *Wisdom* xiii. as coming of "a desire to find" God. Embodying man's thought in shape, or imitating some object of awe, it gives a visible symbol to the yearnings of worship, and may either rise into conscious art, or fall through the stage of symbolism (in which most teachers would arrest it) into blind superstition. The

14. Every man is imbruted out of knowledge; every A.V. x.14. founder is ashamed because of graven image; for his molten image is a lie, and they have no breath in them; folly are they, the work of errors; in the time of their visitation they shall perish.

15. Not like them is the portion of Jacob, for the framer of all things is [and[115] *Israel the rod of*] his inheritance; JEHOVAH of hosts his name.

16. Gather thy wares out of the land, thou that dwellest in siege; 17. for thus saith JEHOVAH, Behold me slinging out the inhabitants of the land this time, and I bring distress upon them, that they may find[116] *it*.

---

[115] Heb. וְיִשְׂרָאֵל שֵׁבֶט Vulg. et Israel virga hæreditatis ejus. LXX. ὁ πλάσας τὰ πάντα αὐτὸς κληρονομία αὐτοῦ, κύριος ὄνομα αὐτῷ. I believe the Greek is genuine, as most coherent.

[116] That they may *find*, i.e. taste it; or, that their foes may reach home to them. Vulg. tribulabo eos ita, ut inveniantur.

Hebrews view it on its degrading side, both from their stage of cultivation, and from the evils which they saw result from it. Pure rationalism (which while it continues negative fails to fire the religious instincts,) never sounded a loftier strain than in the later Isaiah, ch. xl—xliv. An uncertain prelude to that voice of power runs through these verses, as if the writer's thoughts were broken, or his expressions borrowed. The sentiment often recurs, being paraphrased in verse 11, and sinking into prosaic depths in the Apocrypha. The insertion in v. 15 belongs to the Asmonean age, when the idea of God being devout men's portion was narrowed into that of Israel being the elect. The grand lesson of the chapter is, that superstition is not protected by reverence against righteous scorn. For the details comp. *Baruch*, vi. 3—69.

16—21. Though we cannot confidently follow those who fix this piece in the fourth year of Jehoiakim, or the

Ch. X. 18. Woe is me for my wound! my stroke is grievous; A.V.x and I said, Truly this is my sickness, and I must bear it.

19. My tent is spoiled, and all my cords are broken; my sons are gone forth of me, and are no more; there is no one that stretches my tent any more, or fixes my pavilions.

20. For the Shepherds,[117] are imbruted, and sought not the ETERNAL; therefore were they unskilled, and all their flocks are scattered.

21. A voice of rumour lo! comes, and a great tumult out of the northern land; to make the cities of Judah a desolation, a haunt of jackals.

22. I know,[118] ETERNAL, that his way belongs not to man; it is not man's, to walk and set firm his steps.

23. Correct me, ETERNAL, but with judgment; not in thine anger, lest thou bring me to nothing.

24. Pour out thy wrath on the nations, which know thee not, and upon the races which call not on thy name: because they have devoured Jacob; even devoured and consumed him, and his habitation they have wasted.

---

[117] *Shepherds*, i.e. Princes.
[118] 22—24. 'Quod a Babyloniis sustinemus, non est eorum fortitudinis, sed nostri meriti, et indignationis tuæ.' *Hieron.* LXX. τὴν νομὴν αὐτοῦ ἠρήμωσαν.

---

eighth of Nebuchadnezzar, 2 Kings xxiv. 12, we see in it such a foreboding of imminent ruin as invasion or siege would awaken. It seems not to predict, but to interpret.

22. It is doubtful whether the Prophet speaks here of the nation's upholding its course in strength, or of man's walking spiritually aright; the latter sentiment, stopping short of the morbid tone, which weakens character, would suit him; the former, as an ascription of Israel's hope to Jehovah, may satisfy the context. The 24th verse is identical with Psalm lxxix. 6, 7.

XI.

XI.   1. A word that came to Jeremiah from the ETERNAL, A.V. xi. 1. saying,

2. Hear you the words of this covenant, and speak to the men of Judah, and to the inhabitants of Jerusalem;

3. And say thou unto them, Thus saith the ETERNAL, the God of Israel, Cursed the man that hearkens not to the words of this covenant,

---

1—5. Comparing 2 Kings xxii. 8, xxiii. 3, we see that a revival of the law, perhaps a recast of it in the form of Deuteronomy, took place in the 18th year of Josiah. In such an event Jeremiah must have borne his part, and seems here to point his warnings from the ancient history.

3. The form of the nation's devotion is that of a league with its Creator. Although our dependence on God's gifts suggests the view of a dispensation, Divine Grace is pleased in Scripture to exhibit itself as entering into contract with man, Gen. xviii. 19. So our power of free action is quickened, and our answerableness preserved. So in the case of Abraham, and in our own Baptism, the troth of God and Man is mutually pledged. The curse may be taken as liturgical, or monitory. The consequences of sin, from the side of God, are judgments, although in the way of nature. Our habit of wishing, directed towards Heaven, is normally prayer for good: but as an assent to retribution, or a cry for it, has the nature of a curse. Strong warning and monition, tinged with horror of evil and sympathy with judgment, express the judicial side of calamity. Yet Christ, as he forbids wishing evil to any one, Matt. v. 44, takes away from all external laws and codes soever the least power of hurting with a curse, Gal. iii. 13, which on Ash-Wednesday we ought to remember.

Ch. XI. 4. Which I commanded your fathers in the day of my bringing them forth out of the land of Egypt, out of the furnace of iron, saying, Obey my voice, and do them, according to all which I command you; so shall you be my people, and I will be your God;

5. That I may establish the oath which I sware to your fathers, to give them a land flowing with milk and honey, as this day; And I answered and said, Amen, ETERNAL.

6. So the ETERNAL said to me, Proclaim all these words in the cities of Judah, and in the streets of Jerusalem, saying, Hear you the words of this covenant, and do them;

7. For I earnestly protested to your fathers in the day of my bringing them up out of the land of Egypt to this day, rising early and protesting, saying, Hearken to my voice;[119]

---

[119] Verse 7, and all but the last clausula of verse 8, are omitted by the LXX. who, restricting the passage to Jeremiah and his age, made it more symmetrical.—"Proclaim to the people, Hear the words of this covenant, "and do them—But they did *them* not." LXX. ἀκούσατε τοὺς λόγους τῆς διαθήκης ταύτης, καὶ ποιήσατε αὐτοὺς Καὶ οὐκ ἐποίησαν. The Hebrew, probably more genuine, makes Jehovah describe his dealings with an earlier generation. Hence, *I brought*: not, I will bring. *Vulg.* et induxi.

---

5. *Amen* is either the assent of obedience; or, rather, the prayer of desire that the good mentioned may come about.

7. God's *rising early*, as if that unsleeping vision needed wakening, is manifestly anthropomorphic, Psalm lxxviii. 65, 1 Kings xviii. 27. What does not strike us often as it should, is that God's speaking is as figurative as his wakening. Divine words are events. It is less figurative to consider a Person as expressing Deity; far more so, to call a body of literature the Word; for this overlooks the intermediated conceptions and instrumentalities.

8. But they hearkened not, neither inclined their ear, A.V. XI. 8. but walked each in the obstinacy of their evil heart; so I brought upon them all the words of this covenant, which I bade them do, and they did not.

9. And the ETERNAL said to me, Treachery[120] is found among the men of Judah, and the dwellers of Jerusalem; they have turned to the iniquities of their forefathers, who refused to hear my words:

10. So are these[121] gone after other gods to serve them; the house of Israel and the house of Judah have broken my league which I struck with their fathers.

11. Therefore thus spake the ETERNAL, Behold me bringing upon them evil, from which they shall not be able to escape; and when they cry to me, I will not hearken to them;

12. But the cities of Judah and the men of Jerusalem shall go and cry to those gods whom they burn incense to; but with no salvation will they save them in the time of their trouble.

13. For *as* the number of thy cities, Judah, were thy gods; and *as* the number of Jerusalem's streets, have you set up[122] altars to Shamefulness,[123] altars to burn incense to Baal.[124]

14. And thou, intercede not for this people, neither lift

---

[120] *Treachery;* or, conspiracy.

[121] *These,* so Heb. LXX. Vulg. et hi ergo abierunt.

[122] *Have you set up;* or, hast thou set up. *Vulg.* posuisti aras confusionis, but Gr. ἐτάξατε.

[123] *Shamefulness;* i.e. probably Astarte, the feminine analogy of Baal; or more generally Idolatry. See above iii. 17, and Note.

[124] 13 and 17 for *Baal, Vulg.* has Baalim.

---

8. As the ancient Hebrews disobeyed, so (9—11) this generation provokes judgments, from which (11—13) neither Ashtoreth nor Baal will preserve them, nor, (14)

Ch. XI. up for them cry, nor prayer; for I am not hearkening in the time of their crying to me because of their trouble.

15. Wherefore is my beloved in my house? Is it for her to accomplish her wickedness? The vows[125] and the consecrated flesh pass away from thee; because of thy wickedness, then thou exultest.

16. A green olive tree, fair, of goodly fruit, the ETERNAL called thy name; with the sound of a mighty roaring, fire is kindled upon it, and its branches are broken; 17. And the ETERNAL of hosts, that planted thee, has pronounced upon thee evil; because of the evil of the house of Israel and the house of Judah, which they wrought against themselves in provoking me, in burning incense to Baal.

18. Yea, JEHOVAH gave me knowledge, that I might

---

[125] *Vows;* or, crowds. Heb. הָרַבִּים for which תרנים *cries,* has been conjectured, but the LXX. give τί ἡ ἠγαπημένη ἐν τῷ οἴκῳ μου ἐποίησε βδέλυγμα: μὴ εὐχαὶ καὶ κρέα ἅγια ἀφελοῦσιν ἀπὸ σοῦ τὰς κακίας σου, ἢ τούτοις διαφεύξῃ: they read נדרים vows. Ewald, Hitzig, Blayney, and others wholly or partly adopt this. De Wette, with unswerving fidelity, keeps to the Hebrew, and makes *Many* qualify the Mass of Israel, in continuous construction. I cannot follow these who violently join the sing. fem. *wickedness* with the masc. plur. *many,* as the Masora, Vulg. (scelera multa,) and A. V. Nor yet dare I turn the inf. verb *accomplish* into a past tense, nor the simple verb *pass away* into a causative, (cause to pass), as many follow the Greek in doing, and the latter is very natural. Least of all could I adopt the frightful Rabbinism quoted from Jarchi, that neglect of circumcision is intended. Either the sense is, what the Greek suggests, Shall prayers and sacrifices avail against wicked worship? or else the removal of the temple and its sacrifices is threatened; or the transient effect of worship on the mind is blamed, as De Wette seems to have understood it.

---

will the Prophet's intercession avail. 15. In vain the Temple is crowded with worshippers whose vows and sacrifices are interspersed with sins; but, (16—17) the goodly olive tree grows for the flame and the axe.

18, 19. Either with sudden transit to a new topic, in a piece which perhaps should be arranged apart, or else as an instance of the national wickedness, the Prophet

XI. know; then thou shewedst me their doings, when I was as a tame lamb,[126] that is led to the slaughter. A. V. XI. 18.

19. When I knew not that they devised devices against me, *saying*, Let us destroy the tree with its fruit,[127] and let us cut him off from the land of the living, that his name be remembered no more.

20. But thou, JEHOVAH of hosts, that judgest righteously, that triest the reins and the heart, let me see thy vengeance upon them; for to thee have I revealed my cause.

21. Therefore thus saith JEHOVAH of the men of Anathoth who seek thy life, saying, Thou shalt not prophesy in JEHOVAH's name, lest thou die by our hand,

22. Therefore thus saith JEHOVAH of hosts, Behold me visiting upon them: their choice youths shall die by the sword, their sons and their daughters die by famine,

23. and remnant of them shall be none; such evil I bring upon Anathoth in the year of their visitation.

---

[126] *A tame lamb.* *Vulg.* agnus mansuetus. Gr. ἀρνίον ἄκακον. Ew. ein zahmes Schaf. but others, as A. V. like a lamb, an ox, &c., as in Psalm l. mountains of oxen—compare for the sentiment, Isaiah liii.

[127] Destroy the tree with its *fruit.* Heb. *bread.* Hence some understand it of putting poison in his food. Unlikely; but likelier than Jerome's comment: Mittamus lignum in panem ejus: *Crucem* videlicet in corpus Salvatoris; ipse enim est qui ait, Ego sum *panis* qui de cœlo descendi!! . . . . Judæi, et nostri Judaizantes hæc ex personâ Hieremiæ dici intelligunt: . . . . sed nescio quomodo approbare possint crucifixum Hieremiam.

---

relates his own townsmen's plot against himself. When he was a sacrificial lamb, or passive as some unsuspecting house pet, Divine Providence shewed him the plot: comp. Isa. liii. Psalms xxvii. xxxi. xxxv. xxxvii. xli. lv.

20—23. The Prophet anticipates utter retribution, such evil will Jehovah bring on Anathoth in the year of his visiting it.

XII.

Ch. XII. 1. Righteous art thou, Eternal, when I plead with A.V thee; yet let me talk with thee of thy judgments:[128] Wherefore is the way of the wicked prosperous, all the treacherous revolters at peace?

2. Thou hast planted them, yea, they are rooted; they grow, yea, they bear fruit:[128] near art thou in their mouths, but far off from their reins.

3. But thou, Eternal, knowest me; thou beholdest, and triest my heart towards thee:[128] drag them out like sheep for the slaughter, and devote them for a day of massacre.

4. How long shall the land mourn, and the grass of all the field wither, for the wickedness of the dwellers therein?[128] (the beasts are consumed, and the birds,) in that they say, He will not look upon our utter end.[129]

5. If thou hast run with footmen, and they have wearied thee, then how wilt thou strive with horses? and if in a land of peace thou trustest, then how wilt thou do in the swelling[130] of Jordan?

---

[128] It is a question of arrangement, whether the first three, or first four, verses would not be better broken in the middle, at the words *judgments, fruit, towards thee, therein.* As we have the verses, the transition of sentiment seems to be in the middle of each. But does verse 4 belong here, Hitzig asks.

[129] *Utter end.* So Heb. LXX. οὐκ ὄψεται ὁ Θεὸς ὁδοὺς ἡμῶν. Vulg. novissima.

[130] *Swelling.* So most naturally: but many critics understand by the *pride* of Jordan the forest banks, haunted by lions, therefore opposed to a land of peace. The phrase seems a proverb.

Verses 1—6 form a piece, connected closely with the preceding passage on the men of Anathoth, more loosely with the subsequent description of the land. The Pro-

XII. 6. Since even thy brethren, and the house of thy A.V.XII.6. father, even they have dealt treacherously by thee; even they call after thee loudly; trust them not, though they speak to thee fair words.

7. I have forsaken my house, I have deserted my heritage; I have given the dearly loved of my soul into the hand of her enemies;

8. My heritage has become to me as a lion in the forest; she roars with her voice against me; therefore I hate her.

9. Beast of prey, hyæna,[131] is to me my heritage; beasts of prey *be* round about against her: come, gather together, all beasts of the field, assemble to devour her.

10. Shepherds[132] in numbers have destroyed my vine-

---

[131] *Hyæna*. LXX. [σπήλαιον] ὑαίνης. So, for the 2nd word, Gesen. de Wette, Maur. but Vulg. avis discolor ; so A.V. Ew. Hitz.

[132] *Shepherds*, *i.e.* chieftains, as in Homer.

---

phet, alarmed and angry, questions the ways of God, asking why judgment tarries. The answer is, that the bitterness of his spirit makes him complain, more than the greatness of his trouble. Apt to trust appearances, or querulous for small troubles, he now knows what it is to have his kinsmen and brother priests raise a full cry against him. The fourth verse is observed by Hitzig to be strangely out of place; but the speaker's thought seems to pass from the local instance to the national guilt.

7. Not only Anathoth, but Judah's land is ripe for vengeance, and the neighbouring tribes (2 Kings xxiv. 2), in the interest of Nebuchadnezzar, to whom Jehoiakim had renounced his homage, commence the destruction, B.C. 605-600, which in Jehoiachin's reign the great King will complete. 8. Disobedience makes the rebellious people wild against their lord: so he lets loose on them destroyers, (9) as ravenous as themselves; (10) many

Ch. XII. yard; they have trampled my portion; they have made the portion in which I delighted a wilderness of desolation.

A. V. 10.

11. They have made it a desolation; it makes mourning upon me, desolated; the whole land is desolated, yet is there no man that layeth it to heart; 12. spoilers are come upon all the bare heights in the wilderness; for the sword of JEHOVAH devours, from land's end to land's end: there is no peace for any flesh.

13. They have sown wheat, and reap thorns: they have laboured,[133] and get no advantage; but be disappointed out of your produce, for the fierceness of JEHOVAH's anger.

14. Thus saith JEHOVAH against all my borderers,[134] the shepherds that encroach on my heritage which I made my people Israel inherit, Behold me plucking them from off their land, and the house of Judah will I pluck from out of their midst;

15. And it shall be, after my plucking them out, I will have compassion on them again, and will bring them again, each to his heritage, and each to his land;

16. And it shall be, if they thoroughly learn the ways of my people, to swear by my name, AS THE ETERNAL LIVES, as they taught my people to swear by Baal, then shall they be built in the midst of my people; 17. but if

---

[133] *They have laboured;* or, inherited. *Vulg.* hæreditatem acceperunt; not amiss. The first clause may be imperative. LXX. σπείρατε πυρούς, καὶ ἀκάνθας θερίζετε· οἱ κλῆροι αὐτῶν οὐκ ὠφελήσουσιν αὐτούς.

[134] *My borderers;* or, my enviers. *Shepherds,* so I first point. Other versions and critics '*my evil neighbours.*'

---

chieftains, (12) bearing the sword of divine wrath, (13) reap the unhappy land bare, until the Prophet mourns, and (14) Jehovah loathes his own instruments.

14—17. The too great envy and cruelty of the border

they will not hearken, then will I pluck up that nation utterly and destroy, is JEHOVAH's saying.

XIII.

XIII. 1. Thus spake JEHOVAH to me, Go and buy thee a linen girdle, and put it upon thy loins, but let it not come into water. A. V. xiii. 1.
2. So I bought a girdle according to the word of JEHOVAH, and put it upon my loins;
3. And the word of JEHOVAH came to me the second time, saying, 4. Take the girdle which thou hast bought, which is upon thy loins, and arise, go to Ephrathah,[135] and hide it there in a cleft of the rock.
5. So I went, and hid it at Ephrathah, as JEHOVAH commanded me.
6. And it came about after many days, that JEHOVAH said to me, Arise, go to Ephrathah, and take from thence the girdle, which I commanded thee to hide there.
7. Then I went to Ephrathah, and dug, and took the girdle from the place where I had hidden it; and behold, the girdle was marred, it was no good for anything.

---

[135] *Ephrathah*, at Bethlehem, six miles from Jerusalem; therefore reasonably near. Heb. *Phrat.* whence LXX. Vulg. and most versions and critics, *Euphrates*; but since the Heb. has neither article nor fluvial title, and the distance is extreme, Bochart, followed by Dathe, Hitzig, and in part by Ewald, understands Bethlehem Ephrathah; or, as Ewald, some place in the vicinity.

---

nations will provoke Heaven to include them within the remoter conqueror's net, until, instead of perverting Judah, they are converted themselves to Judah's God.

1—11. As a man cherishes the girdle, which clings round his loins, but if it is spoiled, gives it up as lost, so by a striking image Jeremiah places before men's eyes his

Ch. XIII. 8. And the word of JEHOVAH came to me, saying, Thus A. V. 8.
saith JEHOVAH, Even thus mar I the pride of Judah, and
the pride of Jerusalem, which is great.

9. This evil people, men who refuse to hear my words,
who walk in the obstinacy of their heart, and who go after
other gods, to serve them and bow down to them, shall be
as this girdle which is no good for anything;

10. For as the girdle clings to the loins of a man, so
made I the whole house of Israel and the whole house of
Judah cling to me, is JEHOVAH'S saying: that they might
be to me a people, and a name, and a praise, and a glory;
but they would not hearken:

11. So speak to them this word; Thus saith JEHOVAH
God of Israel, Every bottle shall be filled with wine;
and when they say to thee, Do not we know assuredly that
every bottle shall be filled with wine,

12. Then say to them, Thus saith JEHOVAH, Behold
me filling all the inhabitants of this land, both the kings
that sit upon David's throne, and the priests, and the
prophets, and all the inhabitants of Jerusalem, with
drunkenness;

13. And I will dash them, each man against his
brother, and fathers and sons together, is JEHOVAH'S
saying; I will not pity, and not spare, nor refrain in
compassion from destroying them.

---

own thought of Israel cherished, but depraved, and then
abandoned. Buying a girdle, he buries it in a spot near
Jerusalem, perhaps Ephrathah, (here called *Phrat*, with
symbolical play on the name of the river Euphrates,) and
on finding it spoiled, sees in it an emblem of Judah's
pride marred, her closeness to Jehovah broken.

11—13. From the acted image of the girdle, Jeremiah
passes to the verbal emblem of a bottle filled with wine.

XIII. 14. Hearken, and give your ears: be not haughty, for A.V. xiii. 15. Jehovah has spoken.

15. Give glory to JEHOVAH your God, before he make darkness, and before your feet stumble upon the dark mountains; and while you long for the light he turns it into death's shadow, yea, makes it thick darkness.

16. But if you will not hearken to it, my soul shall weep in secret places because of *your* pride; and mine eye shall weep sore, and run down with tears, because JEHOVAH's flock is carried captive.

17. Say to the king, and to the Royal Lady, Set your seats low, since fallen is your principality, the crown of your glory; 18. the cities of the south are enclosed, with none to open; captive is Judah all of her; carried captive completely.

19. Lift up[136] *thou city, thy people's* eyes, and behold

---

[136] *Lift up.* Heb. text, in sing. addressing Zion; but in margin altered into plural. The rapid transition from the city to the people creates a confusion of affixes, which the LXX. render, ἀναλάβε ὀφθαλμούς σου, Ἱερουσαλήμ, but *Vulg.* Levate oculos vestros, et videte qui venitis ab aquilone, ubi est grex qui est datus tibi?

As Christ's disciples, and their aged contemporaries, or the forms and usages to which they had been accustomed, were as old bottles, which could hardly bear infusion of the new wine of spiritual freedom, so the men of Israel are here bottles, to be filled with the wine of wrath, as *Obad.* i. 16, and drink the wine of conquest, as *Habak.* ii. 15, 16.

14—16. Jeremiah's plaintive spirit invokes despondently an attention which he hardly hopes to receive.

17. Already in Jehoiakim's reign, invasion has laid waste the South sufficiently to invite humiliation. The Queen may be his mother Zebudah. The LXX. render *rulers*. 19. Let Zion look for the more terrible invader

Ch. XIII. these coming from the north; where is the flock that was given thee, the flock of thy glory?

A. V. 20.

20. What wilt thou say when thou art visited?[137] whereas thou hast trained them thyself as captains for rule over thee; will not pangs seize hold of thee, as a woman in travail?

21. And when thou sayest in thine heart, wherefore are these[138] come upon me? for the greatness of thine iniquity are thy fringes laid bare, thy heels violated.

22. Will the Negro[139] change his skin, or the leopard his spots? you also will skill to do good, accustomed to evil.

23. So scatter I them as driving chaff to the wind of the wilderness.

24. This is thy lot, the portion of thy measures from me, is JEHOVAH'S saying; in that thou hast forgotten me, and trusted in falsehood.

25. Therefore also I have stript thy fringes over thy face, that thy reproach be seen; thy adulteries, and thy neighings, the sin of thy whoredom; 26. upon the hills in the field have I seen thine abominations; wilt thou not be pure after me?[140] How much longer?[141]

---

[137] *When thou art visited.* Heb. when one visits thee.
[138] *These.* Vulg. hæc.
[139] *Negro.* Heb. Cushite.
[140] *Wilt thou not be pure after me?* or, thou wilt not be pure.
[141] After how much longer? LXX. ὀπίσω μού. Vulg. non mundaberis post me.

---

from the north, who tramples the people she boasted of, (20) in requital for ignominious submissions from Ahaz and Hezekiah downwards.

21. These strange reverses do not befall without cause a nation fallen from her God; (22) whose evil habits have become ingrained instincts, (24) and to whom God apportions meet destiny. 25. So she is stript in naked-

XIV.

That which was JEHOVAH's *word to Jeremiah on account of the drought.*[142]

1. Judah mourns, and her gates languish; her people are blackened to the ground,[143] and the cry of Jerusalem is gone up;

2. For their nobles have sent their lesser ones to the waters; they come to the pits, they found no water; they returned, their vessels empty; they were abashed, and confounded, and covered their heads.

A.V. XIV. 2.

---

[142] *Drought;* or, sieges. Heb. *withholdings;* the sense probably as below in xvii. 4 [A. V. 8] not as in Psalms ix. 9, x. 1, where the word and thought are different. Except for xvii. 4, the sense here might well follow the etymology, which suggests circumvallation.

[143] *Blackened to the ground,* i.e. sit in mourning robes on the earth ; the persons to be supplied out of the preceding Judah, or the subsequent nobles.

---

ness, which in event leaves her desolate, and in image discovers her idolatries, which are adulterous apostasies from her lord. " Unde revelantur femora ejus, ut videat " ignominiam suam .... cernatque ipsa quæ fecit, et ap- " pareat ignominia ejus .... Rogemus Iesum, ut nec in " præsenti nec in futuro sæculo revelet femora et posteriora " nostra ; sed ut deleat omnes iniquitates nostras, et " omnia scelera apparere non faciat."—*Hieron*. With equal emphasis Jerome has taken occasion from the image of the vessels to affirm the positive and not (ut veteres et novi hæretici volunt) the comparative depravity of man ; but also to wrest the image of the Negro not changing his skin from those who made the depravity irremediable ; and this he does, as Pelagius would, by showing that habit implies pursuit and will : quicquid discitur, non naturæ est, sed studii, et propriæ voluntatis.

1—5. As previously in xii. 4, and ii. 39, [A. V. iii. 3,]

Ch. XIV. 3. Because the land is shattered, since there has been no rain on the earth, the plowmen are ashamed, they cover their heads.

4. Yea, even the hind calves in the field, and forsakes *it*, because there is no grass.

5. And the wild asses stand on the bare heights, they snuff the wind, like jackals;[144] their eyes are wasted, because there is no grass.

6. Though our iniquities testify against us, Eternal, work for thine own name's sake; because our backslidings are many, we have sinned against thee.

7. O hope of Israel, his saviour in time of distress, wherefore shouldst thou be as a stranger in the land, and as a traveller bending[145] to lodge?

8. Wherefore shouldst thou be as a man confounded, as a warrior that has no strength to save? when thou, Eternal, art in our midst, and thy name is called over us; forsake us not.

9. Thus saith the Eternal to this people, Thus have this people loved to wander, they have not restrained their feet, and Jehovah has no pleasure in them; now will he remember their iniquity, and visit their sin.

---

[144] *Jackals;* or, crocodiles, or dolphins, Hitzig. *Vulg.* dracones.
[145] *Bending,* i.e. either as pitching tent; or, as turning aside from his way.

---

drought and dearth awaken prayer. The time is fixed under Josiah or Jehoiakim, according as the earlier pieces or the latter verses of this chapter sway interpreters. Not merely in the city with its single spring ill supported by cisterns, but in field and fell, beast suffers with man.

6—8. Prayer turns to God, as to one who of right should be a familiar dweller, not a stranger, which Jerome applies to Christ's sojourn on earth. 9—11. The con-

XIV. 10. So the ETERNAL said to me, Intercede not for this people for good; 11. when they fast, I am not hearkening to their cry; and when they offer burnt-offering and oblation, I have no pleasure in them: but by sword, and by famine, and by pestilence will I consume them.

12. Then said I, Ah, Lord, ETERNAL, Behold, the prophets tell them, ye shall not see sword, neither shall famine come upon you; but assured peace will I give you in this place:

13. And the ETERNAL said to me, The prophets prophesy falsehood[146] in my name: whereas I neither sent them, nor commanded them, nor spake unto them; a false vision, and a divination, and a thing of nought, and the deceit of their own heart, are they prophesying to you.

14. Therefore, thus saith the ETERNAL concerning the prophets that prophesy in my name, when I sent them not, yet they say, Sword and famine shall not be in this land; By sword and famine shall these prophets be consumed; 15. and the people to whom they prophesy shall be cast forth in the streets of Jerusalem before the famine and the sword, with none to bury them; *even* they, their wives, and their sons, and their daughters; and I

---

[146] *The prophets prophesy falsehood.* The verb *prophesy* is Masoretically punctuated as a passive, (Niphal poet.) in the sense of *inspired;* and this is the received usage or interpretation; but it is a fair question, whether the prophet did not intend an active participle, in the sense of bubbling and babbling; for this is as natural an interpretation of the word; a certain furor of utterance having been the prophetical manner; though perhaps chiefly so with the inferior and pretentious sort.

---

tinuance of drought, and the sight of his people's unworthiness, make the Prophet's heart eloquent with a sense of God's refusal to be entreated.

12. Pleading with Providence, the good Prophet lays the blame on ill teaching, but (13) the stern answer, admitting the plea as true, (15) rejects it as inadequate,

Ch. XIV. will pour upon them their wickedness. So speak thou unto them this word.   A. V. 16.

16. Let mine eyes run down with tears night and day, and let them not cease; for with a great ruin is ruined the virgin daughter of my people, with a stroke exceedingly grievous.

17. If I go forth into the field, then behold the slain with the sword; and if I enter into the city, then behold the sickenings with famine; yea even prophet and priest are vagrants to a land that they know not.[147]

18. Hast thou utterly rejected Judah? has thy soul loathed Zion? why hast thou smitten us, that there is no healing for us? that we look for peace, and *there is* no good; and for a time of healing, and behold confusion?

19. We acknowledge, ETERNAL, our guilt, the iniquity of our fathers; yea, we have sinned against thee.

20. Do not abhor, for thy name's sake; do not degrade the throne of thy glory; remember, break not thy covenant with us.

21. Are there givers of showers among the idols of the nations? or can the heavens give dropping rain? Art not thou, ETERNAL, our God,[148] and he in whom we will trust? for thou hast made all these things.

---

[147] *Are vagrants to a land that they know not.* Heb. "*wander*, (*i.e.* as traders or mendicants,) *to a land, and know not.*" On these words it is disputed, whether the copula can have the sense of a relative, as with the Greek, Latin, Anglican, and Philippsohn's version I take it, (comp. Gen. iii. 19, iv. 25); or whether, after the verb *know*, we should *supply* the direction *whither*, as Rosenm. de Wette; or, as Ewald, understand, *know no help*; or, as Hitzig, *know not yet* the lot coming upon them. If the first of these modes is not permissible, I should adopt the second.

[148] *Art not thou, Eternal, our God.* LXX. εἰ ὁ οὐρανὸς δώσει πλησμονὴν αὐτοῦ, οὐχὶ σὺ εἶ αὐτός; *Vulg.* nonne tu es Dominus Deus noster, quem expectavimus. Ambigitur, spectetne Heb. pron. הוא ad præcedentem pluviæ

---

and denounces sorrows, which (16—21) the prophet passionately deprecates.

XV.

1. And the ETERNAL said to me, If Moses stood, and Samuel before me, my soul is not towards this people: cast them out[149] from before me, and let them go forth.

2. And let it be, when they say unto thee, Whither shall we go forth, say thou unto them, Thus saith the ETERNAL, That which is for death, to death; and that which is for the sword, to the sword; and that which is for famine, to famine; and that which is for captivity, to captivity.

3. And I will appoint over them four kinds, is the saying of the ETERNAL; the sword to slay, and the dogs to tear, and the birds of the heavens and the beasts of the earth, to devour and to destroy; 4. and I will give them to be scattered[150] to all the kingdoms of the earth, because of Manasseh, son of Hezekiah king of Judah, for what he did in Jerusalem.

5. For who will have pity on thee, Jerusalem; or who bemoan thee? or who will turn aside to bid thee hail?

6. Thou hast forsaken me, is the ETERNAL's saying, thou fallest backward; so stretch I out[151] my hand against thee, and destroy thee; I am weary of relenting.

A. V. xv. 1.

datorem, an meræ copulæ parte fungatur et ad sequentia debeat produci. Malo posterius.
[149] *Cast them out.* Vulg. ejice illos. LXX. ἐξαπόστειλον τὸν λαὸν τοῦτον, κ. ε.
[150] *To be scattered.* Heb. for a scattering.
[151] *So stretch I out, and destroy.* The tense past, future, or illative, is disputed.

1. Although ordinarily fervent prayer of the faithful avails in intercession, it is here no longer so, but still the frowning face of destiny implies an unrelenting God. 2. In nearer prospect of exile, therefore, it would seem in Jehoiakim's reign, prayers are only answered by (3—8) an

Ch. XV. 7. Yea I winnow them with a winnowing fan in the A.V. gates of the land;[152] I bereaved and destroyed my people; they returned not from their ways.

8. Their widows are multiplied to me beyond the sand of the seas; I brought them, upon mother *and* youth,[153] a spoiler at noonday; I let fall upon her suddenly fury and terrors; 9. She that had borne seven sons languishes; she breathes out her life; her sun is gone down, while yet day-time; she is ashamed and confounded: and their remnant will I give to the sword before their enemies, is the ETERNAL's saying.[154]

10. Woe to me, my mother, that thou gavest me birth, a man of pleas and a man of struggles with all the land; I neither lend, nor have they given me loan; all of them reproach me.[155]

11. The ETERNAL said to me, Surely I have made thee strong for good;[156] surely I have made the enemy thy suppliant in the time of evil, and in the time of distress.

---

[152] *Gates of the land,* i.e. of Palestine, as elsewhere; or the cities of the earth in general; or the portals of Earth and Hades.

[153] *Upon mother and youth;* or, on the mother of the warrior; or, on the mothers (collectively) I brought a warrior spoiling at noon-day. We are not to understand the city.

[154] After verse 9, should perhaps be continued, as by Ewald, the passage 12, 13, 14, the 10th and 11th verses, if understood of Jeremiah, being more appropriate before verse 15.

[155] *All of them reproach me.* Very beautifully, and most certainly, J. D. Michälis, followed by Hitzig, transferred the מ, from the verb קִלְלוּנִי where it was senselessly prefixed, to the preceding adjective כֹל, where it belonged as prenominal affix.

[156] *I have made thee strong for good;* or, thy remnant shall turn out well;

---

enumeration of judgments, or of sins which provoked them.

10. The Prophet feels his isolation, as one with whom men avoid intercourse of charity or business; as in Isaiah liii., the Lord's servant is one who hides his face from men in shame. 11. He is encouraged by an answer to his

12. Can we break iron, the northern iron, and brass? A.V. xv. 12.

13. Thy substance and thy treasures I give for spoil without ransom,[157] and for all thy sins, even in all thy borders, even so will I make thee serve[158] thine enemies in a land thou knowest not.

14. For a fire is kindled in mine anger, *which* shall burn upon you [*for ever*. See A. V. xvii. 4.]

15. Thou ETERNAL knowest, remember me, and visit me, and avenge me of my persecutors; take me not away in the endurance of thy anger;[159] know that for thy sake I have suffered rebuke.

16. Thy words were found, and I ate them; and thy words were to me the joy and gladness of my heart; yea, thy name was called over me, *thou* ETERNAL, *thou* God of Hosts.

17. I sat not in the assembly of the merry-makers,

---

as Vulg. reliquiæ tuæ in bonum: but the correspondent clause has a verb. Ewald and Maurer happily suggest שָׁרֵר; but it must remain a question, whether the verb is not better taken infinitively, as by Hitzig, *thy striving*, or participially, *thy assailants*; in which case, we may bring back the verb out of the second clause.

[157] *Without ransom;* or, taking no price, because setting no value upon them, as in Psalm xliv. 12.

[158] *Make thee serve.* So the sense, and some MSS. but more MSS. *deliver thee to.* With this verse and the next, compare xvi. 21 (A. V. xvii. 4).

[159] *Endurance of thine anger;* or, in thy too great patience with our enemies, I take it, as Nahum i. 2 (A.V. 3.) Ezek. xvii. 3.

---

heart from Jehovah, and as vv. 12, 13, 14, now stand, by an assurance that the iron of the North, the avenging host, will make good the Divine threats through him; but Ewald, with a moral certainty, which I am too weak to follow, relegates these three verses as here misplaced; (15) more naturally then the Prophet's plea with God continues. (16—18) He pleads, as men of prayer are wont,

L 2

148   THE HEBREW PROPHETS.

Ch. XV. neither exulted, because of thy hand; I sat alone, because   A. V.
thou hast filled me with indignation.[160]   17.

18. Why is my pain[160] perpetual, and my wound grievous, that refuseth to be healed? wilt thou be to me altogether a failing spring, waters that are not steadfast?

19. Therefore thus saith the ETERNAL, If thou turn again, I will bring thee again, that thou shalt stand before me; and if thou bringest forth the precious out of the vile, thou shalt be as my mouth; let them return to thee, but return not thou unto them.

20. And I will make thee to this people a fenced brazen wall; and when they fight with thee, they shall not prevail against thee; for I am with thee to save thee and to deliver thee, is the saying of the ETERNAL,

21. And I will deliver thee out of the hand of the wicked, and redeem thee out of the hand of the violent.

---

[160] In verse 17, and less strikingly in the next, the arrangement of the clauses suggests change of punctuation. The LXX. have also in v. 18, ἱνατί οἱ λυποῦντές με κατισχύουσί μου; and the Vulg. quare qui contristant me confortantur? hence they must have read. *My pain* as a plural participle, and we may almost suspect that the verbs היה and חי have changed places in the text, with some other confusion. Throughout Jeremiah questions of misplacement suggest themselves too frequently for mention.

his experience of mental struggle; and (19) in the reaction of hope and conscience becomes assured, that God will stand by him, if he will himself subordinate passion to duty, distinguishing the strong truth from his own weakness, and, instead of yielding to threats or jeers, abiding (20) under the shadow of the Almighty. 'Nempe statu suo excidisse indignusque prophetico munere videbatur Jer. tam intemperanter conquerens et vindictam exigens.' *Ros.* This is better than others, distinguishing the good men from the bad, the choice from the mass, &c.

XVI.

XVI. 1. The word of the ETERNAL came also to me, saying, A. V. xvi. Thou shalt not take to thee a wife; neither shalt thou have sons or daughters in this place.

2. For thus saith the ETERNAL of the sons and of the daughters that are born in this place, and of their mothers that bear them, and of their fathers that beget them in this land, of grievous deaths shall they die;

3. They shall neither be lamented nor buried; they shall be for dung upon the face of the earth; and they shall be consumed by the sword and by famine, until their carcases became food for the birds of the heavens, and for the beasts of the earth.

4. Yea, thus saith the ETERNAL, Enter not the house of wailing,[161] neither go to lament, nor condole with them; for I have taken away my peace from this people, my kindness and my compassions, is the saying of the ETERNAL.

---

[161] *Wailing;* or, funeral banquet; the liche-wake, or death-wake. The radical idea is shrieking. Comp. Amos, v. 5. [A. V. vi. 7.] Prov. xxxi. 6. LXX. h. l. θίασον. *Vulg.* convivium.

1—3. As St. Paul, 1 Cor. vii. 26, in a present distress, with the time short before the end, would not advise marriage, the Prophet in prospect of war and exile dissuades from ties which would embitter trouble. So Hosea had seen Ephraim bearing children for slaughter, and our Lord counts blest the breasts that give no suck. We need not with Jerome introduce arguments against marrying more than once, but rather read the counter-promise in Zech. viii. 5, of the streets filled again with boys and girls playing.

4—8. All lesser mourning will be absorbed in so vast a calamity.

Ch. XVI. 5. Both great and small in this land shall die; they A. V. x
shall not be buried, nor shall *men* mourn for them; neither 6.
shall any one gash himself, nor become bald for them.

6. Neither shall men break bread[162] for them in mourning, to comfort each for the dead; nor shall they give them to drink the cup of consolation, for their father or their mother.

7. And banquet-house thou shalt not enter, to sit with them, to eat or to drink.

8. For thus saith the ETERNAL of hosts, the God of Israel, Behold me causing to cease out of this place in your eyes, and in your days, the voice of mirth and the voice of gladness, the voice of the bridegroom and the voice of the bride.

9. And it shall be, when thou shalt declare to this people all these words, and when they say unto thee, Wherefore has the ETERNAL pronounced upon us all this great evil; and what is our iniquity, or what is our sin, which we have sinned against the ETERNAL our God:

10. Then shalt thou say unto them, Because your fathers forsook me, is the ETERNAL's saying, and went after other gods, and served them, and worshipped them, while they forsook me, and observed not my law:

11. You too have wrought evil more than your fathers; and behold you walking each man after the obstinacy of his evil heart, so as not to hearken to me;

12. Therefore I hurl you forth from this land on to a

---

[162] *Break bread.* The word bread is in some MSS. expressed; in others, implied.

9—12. The Prophet reads the secret meaning of a ruin which is a sentence from One who not only controuls natural processes, but designs the moral results of His world.

XVI. land which neither you nor your fathers have known, and you shall serve there those other gods day and night, since I will grant you no grace¹⁶³ .... + ... ¹⁶⁴

A. V. XVI.
13.

13. Behold me sending for many fishers, who shall fish them, is the ETERNAL's saying; and afterwards will I send for many hunters, who shall hunt them from off every mountain, and from off every hill, and out of the caverns of the rocks.

14. For my eyes are upon all their ways; they are not hidden from my face; nor is their iniquity secret from before my eyes;

15. And I will requite the foretime¹⁶⁵ *and* the repeating of their iniquity and their sin; for their defiling my

---

¹⁶³ *Since I will grant you no grace.* Vulg. qui non dabunt vobis requiem. LXX. οἱ οὐ δώσουσιν ὑμῖν ἔλεος, both pointing, doubtless, to a more genuine text.

¹⁶⁴ ... + ... *Text.* 'Therefore behold the days come, saith Jehovah, that it shall no more be said, As the Lord liveth that brought up the sons of Israel out of the land of Egypt; but as the Lord liveth, that brought up the sons of Israel from the land of the north, and from all the lands whither he had driven them; and I will bring them again into the land that I gave to their fathers:' as below in xxiii. 7, 8, where the verses suit better than here; but are also there omitted by the LXX. as in fact they have the air of the later Isaiah, and are almost certainly of post-Babylonian date.

¹⁶⁵ *The foretime and the repeating.* Vulg. reddam primum duplices iniquitates, &c. The LXX. omit *foretime;* most interpreters take it adverbially.

12, 13. Either, as the Heb. text stands, a far off restoration is mentioned as bringing out clearly the calamity first to come; or as the Versions of v. 12, imply by their suggestion, the deities whom Judah runs after will not help her exile, but Jehovah will bring fishers of men, not such as the apostles, but such as Nebuchadnezzar.

14—17. God's unsleeping eye has watched a nation, which being predestinate to serve him, and refusing the form of obedience with blessing, will have the harder form

Ch. XVI. land with the carcases of their abominations, and *because* ʌ they have filled my inheritance with their detestations.[166]

16. O Eternal, my strength, and my fortress, and my refuge in the day of distress, to thee shall come nations from the ends of the earth, and say, Surely our fathers inherited falsehood, things of nought, wherein was no helper.

17. Should man make gods to himself, that are no gods? Therefore behold me making them learn, this time; I will make them learn my hand and my might, that they may know my name is the Eternal.

18. The sin of Judah is written with pen of iron, graven with point of diamond, upon the tablet of their hearts, and to the horns of their altars.[167]

19. [As their children remember their altars and their Moon-statues,] upon green trees, upon lofty hills, upon the mountains of the field.

20. I give thy substance, all thy treasures, to the spoil; thy high-places *that were* for sin throughout all thy borders.

21. And thou shalt cease even through thyself[168] from off thy inheritance which I gave thee, and I will make

---

[166] *Detestations*, i.e. detestable idolatry.

[167] 18—21. These four verses, though quoted from some Greek versions, were omitted by the LXX., through tenderness, as Jerome suggests; more probably from the unsettled state of the text. The first clause in v. 19, can, as I suspect, be only an ancient gloss.

[168] *And thou shalt cease, even through thyself.* Comp. Levit. xxvi. 34, 35, but the *Vulg. relinqueris sola* ab hæreditate tuâ, and a Gr. V. ἀφαιρεθήσῃ μόνη καὶ ταπεινωθήσῃ, suggest an originally simpler text, possibly לבדך, or לבדך. A like inference might be drawn from the *Vulg.* rendering of mountains by the word *sacrificantes*.

---

of warning nations afar by its suffering, and glorify God as an unwilling missionary.

18—21. While strange populations hear and obey, as St. Paul writes to his countrymen at Rome, the Jews

thee serve thine enemies in a land which thou knowest not; since you have kindled a fire in my nostril, which shall burn for ever.

XVII.

XVII. 1. Thus saith the ETERNAL,[169] Accursed the man, who trusts in mortal, and makes flesh his arm, and whose heart departs from the ETERNAL.

A.V. xvii. 5.

2. For he shall be like a juniper[170] in the desert, that sees not when good comes; that abides in parched places in the wilderness, in a salt and uninhabited land.

3. Blessed the man that trusts in the ETERNAL, and to whom the ETERNAL is his confidence.

4. For he shall be as a tree planted upon the waters, and that shoots forth its branches upon the stream; that fears[171] not when heat comes, but its leaf is green; and in the year of drought it fails not, nor ceases from bearing fruit.

---

[169] *Thus saith the Eternal*, om. LXX.

[170] *A juniper;* or, tamarisk. LXX. ἀγριομυρίκη, *Vulg.* myricæ. Tu noli de ruinis, ut Ges. ex Isa. xvii. vel de homine destituto, ut alii ex Ps. 102. 18, cogitare. Docet contextus.

[171] *Fears;* or, sees. *Vulg.* non timebit. LXX. οὐ φοβηθήσεται. The whole passage seems moulded on Psalm i, which belongs to the same age, or not much earlier.

---

betray an ingrained obstinacy; as if diamond pen, (this *schamir*, is the word which Mr. Baring Gould, *Myths of M.A.* fancifully distorts to mean lightning,) had traced on heart and altar, on green tree and hill, their waywardness and their idolatry. So Judah dispossessed, or resting for her own pain, instead of for worship, from off a desecrated soil, will learn how hard to quench are the flames of God's anger.

1. The Prophet, seeing perhaps Jehoiakim trusting in Egyptian allies, or (7) cut off after a short and evil reign, contrasts the (2) fading bloom of the godless, with the abiding lot (4) of the faithful.

Ch. XVII. 5. He that is crooked of heart[172] above all, and frail, who shall know him?

6. I, the ETERNAL, search the heart, I try the reins; even to give each after his ways, after the fruit of his doings.

7. A bird of cry,[173] that broods, and hatches not, is he that gathers wealth, but not by right; in the midst of his days he leaves it, and in his latter end becomes despised.

8. A throne of glory on high from of old is the place of our sanctuary, the hope of Israel.

9. ETERNAL, all that forsake thee shall be ashamed; and they that depart from thee[174] be written in earth, because they forsook the ETERNAL, the fountain of living waters.

---

[172] *He that is crooked*, i.e. deep. Symm. ἀνεξεύρητος. LXX. βαθεῖα ἡ καρδία παρὰ πάντα, καὶ ἄνθρωπός ἐστι. The sentiment is not a declamation on human depravity, but an invocation of Divine discrimination. "Solent quidam nostri, bono quidem voto, sed non secundum scientiam uti h. l. contra Judæos; quum homo sit dominus atque salvator," . . . . . "nullusque posset nativitatis ejus scire mysterium, ut Esai. liii. 8. *Generationem ejus quis enarrabit?* Melius autem est ut simpliciter accipiamus, quod nullus cogitationum secreta cognoscat, nisi solus Deus." *Hieron.* omnino rectè; nisi quod ipso loc. cit. Esai. abutitur.

[173] *A bird of cry.* LXX. πέρδιξ; the partridge, having the credit, which I believe is undeserved, of sitting on other birds' eggs. For its slinking gait, comp. Ar. Av. 768, ἐκπερδικίσαι.

[174] *They that depart from thee.* So LXX. and Vulg. but Heb. they that depart from *me*. This is one of numerous cases, in which we must decide as we can, whether the transcribers made a slip, while the versions preserve the older text; or whether the Prophet wrote, with abrupt transition, introducing Jehovah as speaker. My mind inclines to the former; Judaic authorities maintain persistently the latter.

---

5. Hard as men's hearts to discern, (whence our Saviour with divine wisdom makes religion secret, but its tests moral,) (6) God can read hearts, and make deep schemes, (7) like eggs addled, or broods thankless. 8. Wisely Israel bases her hope on that throne, (9) to leave

XVII. 10. Heal me, O Eternal, and I shall be healed; save A.V. xvii. 14.
me, and I shall be saved; for thou art my praise.

11. Behold, they say unto me, where is the word of the Eternal? let it come now.

12. But I have not hasted from being pastor after thee, nor longed for hire of man:[175] thou knowest; the issue of my lips was before thee.

13. Be not a terror to me; be thou my refuge in the day of evil: let my pursuers be confounded, and let me not be confounded: let them be dismayed, and let me not be dismayed: bring upon them the day of evil, and with repeated destruction destroy them.

14. Thus said the Eternal to me, Go and stand in the gate of the sons of the people, by which the kings of Judah enter in, and by which they go forth, and in all the gates of Jerusalem,

15. And say to them, Hear the Eternal's word, kings of Judah, and all Judah, and all inhabitants of Jerusalem, that enter in by these gates,

16. Thus saith the Eternal, Take heed to your lives, and bear not burthen on the day of rest, nor bring

---

[175] *Hire of man.* Heb. *day* of man, as LXX. οὐκ ἐκοπίασα κατακολουθῶν ὀπίσω σου, καὶ ἡμέραν ἀνθρώπου οὐκ ἐπιθύμησα. *Vulg.* diem hominis non desideravi; but here the punctuators introduce *evil* day, thereby evidently contradicting the next verse.

---

which is to be written in dust, and to thirst without the heart's true water.

10—13. Turning to God from thankless toils, the Prophet still pleads that he had not desired to be man's day-labourer, or hireling, instead of God's shepherd; but embittered by mockery desires the warnings he has vainly given to be fulfilled. We must point, אֱנוֹשׁ not אָנוּשׁ.

14—21. A separate piece, out of place at least here, and

Ch. XVII. burthen through the gates of Jerusalem; neither carry forth from your houses on the day of rest, nor do any labour, but hallow the day of rest, as I commanded your fathers, A.V. x 22.

17. Though they hearkened not, and inclined not their ear, but hardened their neck against hearing, and against receiving instruction:

18. Now it shall be, if you truly hearken to me, is JEHOVAH'S saying, so as to bring no burthen through the gates of this city on the day of rest, but hallow the day of rest, so as to do therein no labour,

19. Then shall enter by the gates of this city kings and princes sitting upon the throne of David, riding upon chariot and upon horses, they and their princes, men of Judah and inhabitants of Jerusalem, and this city shall abide for ever;

20. So shall come from the cities of Judah, and from the circuits of Jerusalem, and from the land of Benjamin, and from the Plain,[176] and from the mountains, and from the south, bringers of burnt offering and victim and oblation and incense, and bringers of praise, to the house of JEHOVAH.

21. But if you will not hearken to me, to hallow the

---

[176] *Plain.* Heb. *ha-Shephelah*, here, as in Isa. xxvii. 24, (A. V. xxxii. 19), the usage seems general; but in the close of Obadiah, a special locality, as the seaward lowland and Western Palestine, may be meant, as explained by Mr. Grove, D. B. It may be observed here also that the horizon is narrow; so that a definite region may lurk in the general expression.

---

belonging apparently to the time of the Return, describes the Sabbatical observances required by the restorers. With it should be compared the close of Obadiah, the books of Ezra, Nehemiah, Zech. vii. viii., Mal. iii., Ezek. xlvii. In the last verse there is a faint echo of Amos. Yet compare also chap. xxii. below.

day of rest, or not to bear burthen and enter through the gates of Jerusalem on the day of rest, so kindle I a fire in her gates, that shall devour the palaces of Jerusalem, and not be quenched.

A.V.xvii. 27.

XVIII.

1. The word which came to Jeremiah from JEHOVAH, saying,

2. Arise, and go down to the potter's house, and there I will cause thee to hear my words:

3. So I went down to the potter's house, and behold, he wrought a work on the double stone.[177]

4. And the vessel that he was making[178] became marred in the hand of the potter; so he made it over again a different vessel, as seemed good in the eyes of the potter to make.

5. And the word of JEHOVAH came to me, saying, Can I not deal with you as this potter, House of Israel? is JEHOVAH'S saying: behold, as clay in the potter's hand, so are you in my hand, house of Israel.

6. The moment I pronounce upon a nation, or upon a

---

[177] *Double stone;* or, two wheels; here of the potter's implements; in Ex. i. 16, of the place of childbirth, or bathing-troughs: quanquam sunt qui de sexûs signis intelligunt.

[178] *He was making*; here the Heb. inserts *as clay*, rightly omitted by the LXX. as might perhaps be the two next words.

---

1. An impression on Jeremiah's mind leads him to a potter's house, (3) where a vessel broken, and recast, (5) seems an image of God's building or breaking Israel.

6—9. Not by race, nor by chance, but by his own

kingdom, to root up, and to pull down, and to destroy, 7. if that nation turn from its evil, whereof I spake against it, so repent I of the evil which I designed to do to it.

8. And the moment I pronounce upon a nation or upon a kingdom, to build and to plant, 9. if it do evil in my eyes, so as not to hearken to my voice, so repent I of the good wherewith I promised to treat it well.

10. So now, speak thou to the men of Judah, and to the inhabitants of Jerusalem, saying, Thus saith JEHOVAH, Behold me devising against you evil, and counselling upon you destiny; return now each from his evil way, and make your ways and your doings good.

11. But they say, All in vain; for we will walk after our own counsels, and do each the obstinacy of his evil heart.

12. Therefore thus saith JEHOVAH, Inquire now among the nations, who has heard things like these; the virgin of Israel has wrought shuddering exceedingly.

---

will, (Rom. ix. 21) which takes account of conduct and fitness, God creates, destroys, restores. The train of thought here helps those who find in St. Paul's election a favourable state, instead of an absolute destiny. Again, the modern notion of marred lives perishing, and of their materials being re-cast, answers the image more nearly than the theological conception of souls created to endure probation and doom.

10. Though no predestination can be excluded from the Infinite Mind, God is pleased to let us conceive of our own will as entering into the links of causation, (11) though nothing is more hopeless than the impotence of men depraved by habit instinctive or acquired.

12. Yet the Prophet thinks all depravity unnatural: for nature (13), with her summits faithful to snow in mid-

13. Does the snow[179] of Lebanon fail from the rock of the fell? or can the bubbling watersprings, welling, flowing, be uprooted? that my people have forgotten me;   A. V. xviii. 14.

14. That they burn incense to a thing of nought, and make them stumble in [their ways, *even*] the ancient fathers, to walk in tracks of a road not embanked;

15. To make their land a desolation, a perpetual hissing; *that* every passer over it be astonished, and mock with his head:

16. Like an east wind, will I scatter them before the enemy; turning away, and not with face, will I gaze on them in the day of their calamity.[160]

17. Then said they, Come, let us devise against Jeremiah devices; for law shall not perish from priest, nor counsel from wise, nor word from prophet. Come, and let us smite him with the tongue, and not give heed to any of his words.

---

[179] *Does the snow; &c.* LXX. μὴ ἐκλείψουσιν ἀπὸ πέτρας μαστοί, ἢ χιὼν ἀπὸ τοῦ Λιβάνου; μὴ ἐκκλίνῃ ὕδωρ βιαίως ἀνέμῳ φερόμενον; Vulg. Numquid deficeret de petrâ agri nix Libani? aut evelli possunt aquæ erumpentes frigidè et fluentes? Comp. Tac. Hist. v. 6. Libanum, tantos inter ardores opacum fidumque nivibus.

[180] Cf. Jer. ii. 26 (A. V. 27).

---

summer, and with perennial depth of fountains, suggests to man like loyalty by his Maker's design. 14. Whereas Israel, in self-chosen paths, leaves the old solid road of piety, (15) preparing for herself evil, and (16) that blindness which thinks that God sees not, with hopelessness on the side of heaven, amidst disasters on earth.

17. Irritated by blame, the other side attack the Prophet, as if they had the advantage of him in dignity and orthodoxy; though he too was of priestly stem, and his intercession for his people, (implied perhaps, Isa. liii. 12, and transferred to the spirit-world in . . . . . *)

* Blank in MS. 2 Macc. xv. 13, 14.

†

18. Give thou heed to me, ETERNAL, and listen to the voice of them that strive with me.

19. Should evil be recompensed for good? that they have dug a pit for my life; remember my standing before thee to speak good for them, to turn away thy wrath from them.

20. Therefore, give over their sons to famine, and deliver them to the edge of the sword; and let their wives be bereaved and widowed; and let their men be slain of death; their youths slaughtered of the sword in battle.

21. Let a crying be heard from their houses, because thou bringest a troop upon them suddenly; because they dug a pit to take me, and hid snares for my feet.

22. But thou, ETERNAL, knowest all their counsel against me for death; cover not over their iniquity, nor blot out their sin from thy sight; but let them be overthrown before thee; in the time of thy anger deal with them.

XIX.

1. Thus saith JEHOVAH, Go, and get a potter's earthen bottle,[181] and *with thee*[182] of the elders of the people, and of the elders of the priests;

---

[181] *Bottle;* Vulg. lagunculam. Heb. bok-bok, considered onomatopœic, more probably one of the household words widely spread by trade. Gr. βικὸν, Eng. beaker, as sack, pepper, wine, &c.
[182] *With thee.* LXX. καὶ ἄξεις.

---

became mediatorial in tradition. 20—22. Indignant in turn, the Prophet joins his own wrongs with the sins against God, so that they embitter and darken each other, until to foresight of calamity he adds prayer that it may come.

1. Fresh from the potter's wheel, the Prophet feels

XIX. 2. And go forth to the valley of the son of Hinnom, A. V. xix. which is at the entrance of the gate of the sunrise,[183] and proclaim there the words which I speak unto thee;

3. And say, Hear JEHOVAH's word, kings of Judah, and inhabitants of Jerusalem, Thus saith JEHOVAH of hosts, the God of Israel, Behold me bringing evil upon this place, which whoso hears, his ears shall tingle:

4. Because they have forsaken me, and have estranged this place, and burned incense in it to other gods, whom they knew not; they, and their fathers, and the kings of Judah, and have filled this place with innocent blood:[184]

5. And have built the high places of Baal,[185] to burn their sons in the fire, burnt-offerings to Baal, which I neither commanded nor spake, neither entered it into my mind;

6. Therefore behold days coming, is JEHOVAH's saying, when this place shall no more be called the pleasant place,[186] (*Tophet*) nor the valley of the son of Hinnom, but the valley of slaughter,

7. And I will make void the counsel of Judah and of

---

[183] *Gate of the sunrise*; i.e. east, or south-east; as in Nehemiah iii. 29; or, with a different etymology, the gate of the pottery. Vulg. portæ fictilis. The LXX. do not translate the term, which is perhaps unique.

[184] *Innocent blood*; or, as Masora, blood of innocents.

[185] *Baal*, with the article; as a Phœnician name, the supreme Lord, or owner of heaven and earth; but anciently applicable to Jehovah, until contrasted by polemical usage; also appropriated with variation in more than one local worship.

[186] *The pleasant place*; i.e. Tophet, as originally desirable from *Yaphah*, to be fair; but, as a burning-place, adapted to *Aphah* to burn. Here, leaving etymology, the Prophet makes slaughter give it a descriptive title.

---

impelled to enact the symbol, and taking Jewish elders (2) through the S.E. gate, (3—5) teaches them to connect the signs of the times with their own and their fathers' misdeeds.

6, 7. Tophet (which ought to have been eastward, but

Ch. XIX. Jerusalem in this place, and cause them to fall by the sword before their enemies, and by the hand of them that seek their life, and I will give their carcases for food to the bird of the heavens, and to the beast of the earth,   A. V. 7.

8. And I will make this city a desolation[187] and a hissing; that every passer thereby shall be amazed and hiss over all her wounds;[188]

9. And I will cause them to eat the flesh of their sons and the flesh of their daughters; and they shall eat every one the flesh of his friend; in the siege and straitness, wherewith their enemies and they that seek their life shall straiten them.

10. Then break thou the bottle before the eyes of the men that go with thee, and say to them, Thus saith Jehovah of hosts,

11. So break I this people and this city, as one breaks the potter's vessel, that it can not be restored again; and they shall be buried[189] in Tophet, till *there be* no place to bury.

12. So do I to this place, is Jehovah's saying, and to its inhabitants, even to make this city as Tophet, that the

---

[187] *A desolation;* or, an amazement, as in the following verb.

[188] *Her wounds,* as in Solomon's prayer, the *stroke* of every man's heart, but from the Gr. πληγῆς several modern versions have got the word plague, which in 1 Kings viii. 38, has led to misinterpretation.

[189] *They shall be buried;* or, men shall bury, as Mas. punct. *Vulg.* sepelientur. The clause is omitted by LXX. in which Tophet is curiously rendered as τὴν διαπίπτουσαν, and ὁ τόπος ὁ διαπίπτων.

---

as in Hinnom's vale is now placed by our maps south-westward), had been pleasant, till defiled by Josiah, 2 Kings xxiii. 5—10, and as the place of battle or burial during the siege, will be more defiled with slaughter.

8—13. The city, no less than its neighbourhood, defiled by bloody rites and slaughter, will become a thing to stare and mock at, as the shivered bottle in the Pro-

ii. xix. houses of Jerusalem and the houses of the kings of Judah be as the places[190] of Tophet that are defiled;

A. V. xix. 13.

13. Even [*so do I*] to all the houses upon whose roofs they have burnt incense to all the host of the heavens, and poured libations to other gods.

14. Then Jeremiah came from Tophet, whither JEHOVAH had sent him to prophesy, and he stood in the court of JEHOVAH's house, and said to all the people,

15. Thus saith JEHOVAH of hosts, the God of Israel, Behold me bringing upon this city, and upon all her towns, all the evil which I have spoken against her; because they hardened their neck, not to hearken to my words.

XX.

1. Now Pashur, son of Immer, the priest, who was officer ruling in JEHOVAH's house, heard Jeremiah prophesying these things. 2. So Pashur smote Jeremiah the prophet, and put him upon the turn-stock[191] that was

---

[190] *Places.* I get the plural out of the defining article with the word *defiled*; as above in verse 4, I found reason to make the string of nominatives follow the leading verb. I am not convinced that the lengthened form Tophet, for a burning pile in general, in Isaiah xxvi. (A.V. xxx.) will apply here. Of Hinnom we know nothing but that he gave name to the Vale, which, in its degraded stages, as sepulchral and penal, supplies the New Testament with its local image for spiritual ruin.

[191] *Turn-stock.* Vulg. nervum. Symm. βασανιστήριον, al. Græc. στρεβλωτήριον.

---

phet's hand foreshows, and houses of incense will become charnel-houses of stench. 14, 15. After the dramatic symbolism outside, the result is narrated in the court of the Temple.

1—2. Pashur, being responsible for the peace of the temple, and dreading (like Amaziah on hearing Amos at Bethel,) the effect of the Prophet's cry, put him for a day in the stocks, an instrument which confined the legs and arms, and contorted the body. 3—5. Smarting with

Ch. XX. in the upper gate of Benjamin, that is in JEHOVAH's A.V. house. 3. And it was so on the morrow, that Pashur brought forth Jeremiah from the turn-stock; and Jeremiah said to him, JEHOVAH calls thy name not Pashur, but *Panic all around*.[192] 4. For thus saith JEHOVAH, Behold I turn thee to panic [for] thyself and [for] all thy friends; so that they fall by the sword of their enemies, with thine eyes beholding; and I give all Judah into the hand of the king of Babel, and he transports them to Babel, and smites them with the sword. 5. And I give all the strength of this city, and all its labour, and all its costliness, and all the treasures of the king of Judah give I into the hand of their enemies, to plunder them, and take them, and carry them to Babel. 6. And thou, Pashur, and all the dwellers of thy house, shalt go into captivity; and to Babel shalt thou come, and there die, and be buried there, thou, and all thy friends, to whom thou hast prophesied in falsehood.

7. Thou hast misled me, JEHOVAH, and I was misled; thou wast stronger than I, and hast prevailed; I am become a derision all the day, every one mocks me.

8. For since I spake,[193] I cry out violence, and com-

---

[192] *Panic-all-around*; or, removal from all around; as LXX. μέτοικον and μετοικία, rather perhaps the more probable rendering, though little favoured, unless by Hitzig.

[193] *Since I spake, &c.* Vulg. jam olim loquor, vociferans iniquitatem, et vastitatem clamito. The Masora punctuates, as A. V.

---

pain, Jeremiah, released on the morrow, imprecates on Pashur and all his friends migration into exile, or, as the Hebrew editors understood, panic and terror on all sides.

7. Seeing no immediate effect of his warning or imprecation, except the suffering it has brought on himself, the Prophet turns to plead with the God who impelled, as if to desert, and (8) lets him suffer, as well as foresee,

plain of oppression; for the word of JEHOVAH became to A. V. xx. 8.
me a reproach and a derision all the day.

9. Then I said, I will not mention him, nor speak any more in his name; but it was in my heart as a burning fire; *it was* shut up in my bones, that I was weary with containing, and could not endure.

10.[194] While I heard the reproach of many, the gathering all around; Denounce, and we will denounce him, *said* every man of my acquaintance, the companions of my side: Perchance he will be misled, and we shall prevail over him, and take our revenge of him.

11. But JEHOVAH is with me, as a man of might, terrible; therefore my pursuers shall stumble, and not prevail; they are ashamed exceedingly, because they had not understood,[195] with a perpetual confusion, *that* shall not be forgotten.

12. Yea, JEHOVAH of hosts proves the righteous, beholding the reins and heart: let me behold thy vengeance on them, for to thee have I laid bare my cause.

13. [*Let me say*] Sing to JEHOVAH, praise JEHOVAH; because he has delivered the soul of the poor from the hand of the wicked.

---

[194] LXX. ἤκουσα ψόγον πολλῶν συναθροιζομένων κυκλόθεν, Ἐπισύστητε, καὶ ἐπισυστῶμεν ἐπ' αὐτῷ πάντες ἄνδρες φίλοι αὐτοῦ. *Vulg.* Audivi contumelias . . . ab omnibus viris, qui erant pacifici mei, et custodientes latus meum; si quo modo decipiatur.

[195] *Not understood*; or, not prospered.

---

disaster; until, (9) if the burning impulse within would permit, he would fain be silent.

10. Those who should have befriended, watch for a place of striking the proscribed Prophet, (11) who can but trust in God and the future; and in that faith (12) meditates thanksgiving.

Cн. XX.   14.[196] Accursed the day, whereon I was born; the day on which my mother bare me, be unblest.   A.V. 14.

15. Accursed the man, who acquainted my father, saying, A man child is born to thee; making him very glad;

16. But let that man be as the cities which JEHOVAH overthrew, and relented not; yes, let him hear crying in the morning, and shouting at noon-tide;

17. Because he slew me not from the womb; that my mother might have been my grave, and her womb burdened for ever!

18. Wherefore thus came I forth from the womb, to behold weariness and sorrow, that my days should waste with shame?

XXI.[197]

Cн. XXI.   1. Thus said JEHOVAH, Go down to the king of Judah's house, and speak there this word, and say,   A.V. 1.

2. Hear JEHOVAH's word, king of Judah, that sittest on David's throne, thou, and thy servants, and thy people that enter by these gates:

---

[196] The symmetry resulting from transposition of the two pieces, 14—18, and 7—13, is more manifest than our right to create it.

[197] XXI. For chapter xxi. (A. V.) and its natural appendages, see after chapter xxxii. though it may be questioned, as by Hitzig, whether verses 11—14, of xxxiii. (A. V. xxi.) should not be connected with xxi. (A. V. xxii.) I think not.

14—18. Reverting from anticipation to reality, (unless with Ewald we make the thought continuous by inverting the order of the hopeful and the dolorous passage,) the Prophet curses the day of his birth, and (like Job sitting in ashes amongst the formalists,) paints the tragedy of his life.

1—5. In connexion of thought, though not in close

XXI. 3. Thus saith JEHOVAH, Do judgment and righteous- A.V.XXII. ness, and deliver the spoiled out of the hand of the 3. oppressor; and neither wrong nor violate the stranger, fatherless, and widow, nor shed innocent blood in this place:

4. For surely as you do this saying, shall enter by the gates of this house kings sitting to David upon his throne, riding in chariot and on horses, king,[198] and his servants, and his people;

5. But if you will not hearken to these words, by myself I swear, saith JEHOVAH, surely this house shall become a desolation.

6. For thus saith JEHOVAH over the king of Judah's house; Gilead *art* thou to me, the summit of Lebanon; I have sworn to make thee a wilderness among cities,[199] uninhabited,

7. And I consecrate against thee destroyers, each with his weapons; to cut down the choice of thy cedars, and fell *them* on the fire;

8. Until many nations pass by this city, and say every one to his neighbour, Wherefore has JEHOVAH wrought thus to this great city?

---

[198] *King*; Heb. he.
[199] *A wilderness among cities.* This is an instance of a flowing text of Scripture broken Rabbinically into antithesis. For the singular verb נושבה must originally have referred to מדבר, wilderness; but the Masoretic punctuators, having paused at wilderness in their conception of clauses, altered the verb into a plural to agree with cities. The *Vulg.* and LXX. however, had equally joined the verb with cities.

---

coherence, with preceding pictures of ruin, Jeremiah sums up, (whether under Zedekiah, or before,) the result of his warnings to Josiah's two sons and grandson.

6—9. Either the likeness of the king's palace to

Ch. XXI.   9. And men answer, Because they forsook the covenant of JEHOVAH their God, and bowed down to other gods, and worshipped them.

10. Weep not for the dead, and lament not for him; weep, weep for him that goes away; for he shall return no more, nor behold the land of his birth.

11. For thus saith JEHOVAH of Shallum,[200] the son of Josiah king of Judah, that reigned instead of Josiah his father, that went forth from this place; he shall not return there again; 12. but in the place where they led him captive, there shall he die, and not behold this land any more.

13. Ahah! he that builds his house by unrighteousness, and his chambers by injustice; who has service of his neighbour gratis, and renders him not his earning; 14. that saith, I will build me a spacious house and airy chambers; and cutteth him out its windows,[201] jointing with cedar, and painting with vermilion.

15. Shalt thou reign, because thou pridest thyself[202]

---

[200] *Shallum*, the name of an Ephraimite king, who reigned but a month, 2 Kings xv. 13, is applied in enigma to Jehoahaz (1 Chron. iii. 15. Johanan), who reigned but three months. Jezebel, 2 Kings ix. 31, salutes Jehu as Zimri, because he slew his master. But the genealogist in 1 Chron. iii. 15, not understanding the passage before us (ex loco perperam intellecto, as Maurer and Hitzig rightly after Junius) inserts Shallum as a fourth son of Josiah, after the genuine three, Jehoahaz or Johanan, Jehoiakim or Eliakim, Zedekiah or Mattaniah. This is curiously suggestive.

[201] *Cutteth him out its windows;* or, cutteth out windows for it, and joints, &c. Conjecturam levissimâ mutatione retrahentium ך ex verbo insequente meam feci.

[202] *Pridest thyself;* or, viest, art emulous, ἀμιλλᾶσαι πρὸς τὴν κέδρον,

---

balmy hill and cedrous mount will not save it; or better, the destroying God will turn its dwelling-place to bare mountain peak.

10. King Josiah's fate in battle seems less deplorable (11) than that of Jehoahaz, captive to Necho, and exiled in Egypt for life; and his memory more precious (15)

XXI. in cedar? Did not thy father eat and drink, and wrought A.V. xxii. 15. judgment and righteousness? then was well with him:

16. Judged he [*not*] the cause of the afflicted and poor? then was well with him; is not this the knowing me? is JEHOVAH's saying.

17. But thine eyes and thine heart *are* nought but upon thy booty; and upon the innocent blood for shedding, and upon oppression and upon violence for doing.

18. Therefore thus saith JEHOVAH of Jehoiakim, the son of Josiah king of Judah, They shall not lament for him, Ah! my brother, or Ah! sister; they shall not lament for him, Ah! lord, or Ah! his majesty.

19. With the burial of an ass[203] shall he be buried, drawn forth and cast beyond the gates of Jerusalem.

20. Go up Lebanon, and cry, and in Basan lift up

Aquila. So many, as Ewald; but others, as Theodoret, understand Josiah as the fallen cedar; others introduce the idea of raging against the cedars; as in Isai. xii. (A. V. xiv.) The simplest way of carrying on the idea from the preceding verse is the best. Professor Noyes, and others, labour to reduce these verses to rhythmical symmetry; for this chapter is supposed to be poetry; while the xxi[st] is to be prose: but if without preconception we compare the two, we may find a certain frequent antithesis in both; but symmetrical rhythm in neither. I suspect the subject-matter of determining the degree of antithesis, more than any Rabbinical rule. The Sermon on the Mount might be turned into parallel clauses.

[203] *Burial of an ass,* i.e. be unburied; thrown to birds and dogs. But in 2 Kings xxiv. 6, Jehoiakim sleeps with his fathers, *i.e.* in their tombs; again in 2 Chron. xxxvi. 6, he is bound as a captive for Babylon. Either then the Prophet here speaks before the event, with vague presentiment and denunciation; or we must imagine with some, that on his way to Babylon, Jehoiakim died, and was left contemptuously unburied. Or, in the Prophet's mind, exile is burial.

---

than that of Jehoiakim, whose pomp of buildings and costly timbers, (17) stained by violence, will win (18) no plaintive cry for him, (19) whether his carcase be ejected from its tomb, or whether he die on his way to exile.

20. Widowed Zion sees her sons fugitive in rocks, or

Ch. XXI. thy voice, and cry from the farther heights,[204] because destroyed are all thy lovers. A.V. 20

21. I spake to thee in thy prosperity; thou saidst, I will not hear: this was thy way from thy youth, that thou hast not hearkened to my voice.

22. All thy shepherds shall be a flock for the storm, and thy lovers shall go into captivity; surely then shalt thou be ashamed and confounded for all thy wickedness.

23. Thou enthroned on Lebanon, nestling in cedars, how pitiable art thou,[205] when pangs come on thee, pain as *of one* child-bearing.

24. As I live, is JEHOVAH's saying, though Coniah, son of Jehoiakim, king of Judah, be the signet on my right hand, yet will I pluck thee thence, 25. and give thee into the hand of those that seek thy life, and into the hand of those whose face thou dreadest, and into the hand of Nebuchadrezzar[206] king of Babel, and into the hand of the Chaldæans.

26. And I will cast thee out, and thy mother that bare thee, into the land strange,[207] where you were not born;

---

[204] *Farther heights*. Heb. Abarim, the Peræan heights, including Pisgah.
[205] *How pitiable art thou, &c.* LXX. καταστενάξεις ἐν τῷ ἐλθεῖν σοι ὀδύνας ὡς τικτούσης. Vulg. Quæ sedes in Libano, et nidificas in cedris, quomodo congemuisti, quum venissent tibi dolores. I doubt, with Hitzig, the derivation from הנן.
[206] *Nebuchadrezzar*. This form is frequent in Jeremiah.
[207] *Into the land strange*. The noun only has the def. article, because the adjective is defined by the subsequent clause.

---

dragged across the hills beyond Jordan, in spite of Egyptian allies, or troth-breaking idols. 21. Her sin was not new; (22) she will understand it, when her princes are driven before the blast, and her objects of trust shivered. 23. Queenly pomp turns to outcry of pangs.

24—27. More popular than his father, Jeconiah is still

XXI. and there shall you die ; 27. but upon the land, whereon they lift their soul to return thither, there shall they not return.

28. Is this man Coniah a despised, shattered, piece of pottery ? or is he a vessel wherein is no delight ? Wherefore are they hurled forth, he and his seed, and cast on to the land which they know not ?

29. [208] O land, land, land, hear the word of JEHOVAH ; Thus saith JEHOVAH, Enrol you this man childless, a man that prospers not in his days ;

---

[208] 29, 30. Compare 2nd Sam. vii. 12—19, 26—29, with Psalm lxxxix. 19—37. Jeconiah, though replaced temporarily by his uncle Zedekiah, was the last lineal inheritor of the throne of David. Though Nature, lawless in her gifts, gave him offspring, and his grandson Zerubbabel was prince of the returned exiles, the Prophet counts him dynastically childless, (ἐκκήρυκτον ἄνθρωπον, LXX.) because his fathers' land and people would enrol no child of his in the list of kings of David's line. So the glory of the throne is departed ; though a reviving hope, or a transfer to the spiritual domain, appears in the next chapter. See the fifth of Davison's brilliant, but unsatisfactory Discourses on Prophecy.

---

destined to a hopeless exile, with his mother Nehushta, who may have helped to shape his policy. (Herod. vii. 3 ; Xen. An.; 1 Kings ii. 19 ; 2 Kings xi. 1, xviii. 2 ; Daniel v. 10, 29.)

28. Can this outcast thing be the gracious representative of David's line ? 29. Let the land cease henceforward to record her kings. Here one view would be, that God's most faithful promises and awful threatenings are spoken to man as accountable, and so are contingent on his conduct. Another may be, that David's faith, making the Divine counsel vocal in his presentiment of a splendid yet God-fearing dynasty, could not secure a like faith in his descendants, and so could not bind a righteous Providence to uphold their unworthiness. Again, on the strongly-Messianic view of Scripture, the Davidical line

30. For no man of his seed shall prosper, sitting upon the throne of David, or ruling any more in Judah.

XXII.

Ch.XXII. 1. Ahah![209] shepherds that destroyed and scattered the flock of my pasture, is JEHOVAH's saying;

A.V.
1.

2. Therefore thus saith JEHOVAH the God of Israel, of the shepherds that fed my people, You scattered my flock, and drove them away, and visited them not; behold me visiting upon you the evil of your doings, is JEHOVAH's saying;

3. But I will gather the remnant of my flock out of all the lands whither I drove them; and I will bring them back again to their folds, that they may be fruitful and increase;

4. And I will establish over them shepherds to feed them; and they shall neither fear any more, nor be dismayed, nor shall they be lost;[210] is JEHOVAH's saying.

---

[209] *Ahah!* or, Ho! LXX. ᾦ not a denunciation of woe, but an invocation of the three kings before described. Comp. Hosea xii. 7 (A. V. xiii. 11.)

[210] *Nor shall they be lost.* Vulg. nullus quærctur ex numero. LXX. omit the word.

---

had now fulfilled its purpose by generating the idea of a national king and deliverer, whom in the end men would discover must be a spiritual king. Once more, if we ask the Scripture what form of government is preferable, we find many recorded, with traces of their development. Royalty was not the first choice of Samuel, or of the earlier prophets; but the later prophets had cordially adopted it, and regretted it when lost.

1—4. Having described the fate of the three princes who followed with brief or ill-starred reigns after Josiah, the Prophet sums up their conduct and destiny, and expresses the Divine requirement of better governors, who shall be truly shepherds of men.

XXII. 5. Behold days coming, is JEHOVAH's saying, when I raise up to David a righteous branch, and a king shall reign and prosper, and execute judgment and righteousness in the land;

A.V.xxiii. 5.

6. In his days shall Judah be saved, and Israel dwell in confidence; and this is the name whereby men shall call him, JEHOVAH *is* our righteousness.

7. [Therefore, behold days coming, is JEHOVAH's saying, when they shall no more say, As JEHOVAH lives, who brought up Israel's sons out of the land of Egypt; 8. but As JEHOVAH lives, who brought up, and who led the seed of the house of Israel from the land of the north, and from all the lands whither I had driven them; that they may dwell in their own land.]²¹¹

---

²¹¹ 7, 8. After translating these verses with an uneasy sense of suspicion in my mind, both because they savour of the later Isaiah, and the formula of *Behold days coming* is rather indicative of touched passages, I find Hitzig pointing out that they do not occur in the LXX. and as he acutely remarks, the contexture of the Greek shows they must have been wanting in the Hebrew which formed the basis of that Version, e.g. τοῦτο τὸ ὄνομα αὐτοῦ, ὁ καλέσει αὐτὸν Κύριος, Ἰωσεδὶκ ἐν τοῖς προφηταῖς. He might have added, that we hence see the Hebrew had been edited, for it had titles inserted, even before the Greek Version was made. See margin of xvi. 14, 15 above.

5, 6. Yearnings for a better prince, and perhaps, (as himself a Babylonian partisan,) seeing such in *Zedek-i-jah* (*Jehovah is my righteousness*) who had been set up by Nebuchadnezzar the agent of Jehovah's will, the Prophet anticipates a brighter day, when Jehovah would maintain his people's cause. In two verses (7, 8,) not impossible in Zedekiah's reign, but not so coherent as to preclude question of insertion in the time of Cyrus, and in fact wanting in the LXX. from the first, the return from Babel is painted, and compared with the outcoming from Egypt.

To the Prophets.

Ch. XXII. 9. My heart is broken within me; all my bones quiver; I am become as a man drunken, and as a man whom wine has overcome, because of JEHOVAH, and because of the words of his holiness.   A.V. xx 9.

10. Since the land has filled with adulterers; since because of blasphemy[212] the land mourns, the pastures of the wilderness wither; and their course is become evil, and their mightiness not aright;

11. Since alike prophet, alike priest, have been defiled,[213] even in my house have I discovered their wickedness, is JEHOVAH'S saying, 12. Therefore their way shall be to them as slippery places in the darkness; they shall be thrust forward, and fall therein; for I will bring upon them evil, the year of their visitation, is JEHOVAH'S saying.

13. Both in the prophets of Samaria I have seen folly; they played the prophet to Baal, and led astray my people Israel;

14. And in the prophets of Jerusalem I have seen a

---

[212] *Blasphemy*, i.e. Worship, in the sense of swearing by other deities than Jehovah, nearly as in Levit. v. 1, Prov. xxix. 24, Psalm lix. 12; and possibly, but ? Isaiah xxiv. 6. So here the sequence of thought, and the absence of the article persuade me; but most versions take it of a divine Curse, as in Zech. v. 3, Deut. xxvii—viii—ix, and perhaps Isaiah xxiv. 6. So *Vulg.* a facie maledictionis luxit terra.

[213] *Defiled;* or, *profane;* the sense of hypocrite given to this word by A. V. in Isaiah xxxiii. 14, and elsewhere, seems not to belong to it.

9—11. Turning from priests to prophets, and treating them as a class without regard to exceptional instances of zeal, Jeremiah is bewildered, till his mind reels, at the shocking inconsistencies of professed teachers, and imprecates on them darkness of counsel and of fate, as of life. 13. Little better than the Ephraimite worshippers of Baal, were (14) those who named Jehovah in Zion,

horrible thing; adultery, and walking in lies; and they strengthened the hands of evil-doers, so that they returned not each from his wickedness; they are all of them to me as Sodom, and her inhabitants as Gomorrhah. A.V.xxiii. 14.

15. Therefore thus saith JEHOVAH of hosts against the prophets; Behold me feeding them with wormwood, and making them drink the waters of gall;[214] since from the prophets of Jerusalem has gone forth defilement to all the land.

16. Thus saith JEHOVAH of hosts, Hearken not to the words of the prophets that prophesy to you; they make you fools; they speak a vision of their own heart, not out of the mouth of JEHOVAH say they,

17. When they say, to them that mock at me, JE-HOVAH has said, Peace be to you; and to every one that walks after the obstinacy of his own heart they say, Evil shall not come upon you.

18. For who has stood in the secret counsel of the ETERNAL, and seen, and heard his word? [*who gave heed to my word, and heard?*[215]]

19. Behold the tempest of JEHOVAH gone forth in

---

[214] *Gall.* Heb. Rôsh, usually translated hemlock, or colocynth; by Gesenius opium, *Vulg.* felle. LXX. ὕδωρ πικρόν.

[215] The words *italicised* are taken by some as an answer to the preceding question; but have more the air of an explanatory gloss upon it.

---

but whom their God looked upon, as upon the guilty cities of the plain, and who should be pre-eminent in ruin, as in defilement. 16, 17. Babbling, as if inspired, these worldly politicians promise success to a policy of arms, (18) because they have no insight into the designs of a righteous Providence.

19. The storm comes, (20) teaching late wisdom to

Ch. XXII. fury; and the whirling storm sweeps down on the head of the wicked.

20. The anger of Jehovah will not turn back, until he accomplish, and until he establish the counsels of his heart; in the aftertime of days you shall understand therein wisdom.

21. I sent not these prophets, yet they ran; I spake not to them, yet they prophesied.

22. But if they had stood in my secret counsel, and had caused my people to hear my words, then they would have turned them from their wicked way, and from the wickedness of their doings.

23. Am I a God at hand, is Jehovah's saying, and not *also* a God afar?[216] 24. Can any hide himself in hiding-places, that I should not see him? is Jehovah's saying. Do not I fill heaven and earth? is Jehovah's saying.

25. I have heard what the prophets say, that prophesy in my name falsely, saying, I have dreamed, I have dreamed.

26. How long shall it be in the heart of the prophets that prophesy falsehood, and that are prophets of the delusion of their own heart,

27. That they devise to make my people forget my name for the dreams which they tell each to his neighbour, as their fathers forgot my name for Baal?

---

[216] Hitzig understands this question of time afar off and near. The context points to place. The LXX. by omitting the interrogation, invert the sense, Θεὸς ἐγγίζων ἐγώ εἰμι, καὶ οὐκὶ Θεὸς πόρρωθεν.

---

politicians, (21) who had overlooked the deep moral disease, and the Eternal, (23, 24) whom conditions of time and place had been idly thought to fetter, (25—27)

XXII. 28. Let the prophet that has a dream, tell a dream: and let him that has my word, speak my word in truth; what is the chaff²¹⁷ to the wheat? is JEHOVAH's saying. A.V.xxiii. 28.
29. Is not such my word, as the fire? is JEHOVAH's saying, and as a hammer that shatters rock?
30. Therefore, behold me against the prophets, is JEHOVAH's saying, who steal my words each from his neighbour; 31. behold me against the prophets, is JEHOVAH's saying, who use their tongues, and say, It is *God's* saying;²¹⁸ 32. behold me against the prophesiers of dreams falsely, is JEHOVAH's saying, who tell them to lead my people astray with their lies and with their frenzy,²¹⁹ when I neither sent them nor commanded them, and they shall not advantage this people at all, is JEHOVAH's saying.
33. And when this people, or the prophet, or priest, ask thee, saying, What is the burden of JEHOVAH, then

---

²¹⁷ *Chaff;* or, more properly straw, as Isa. xi. 18, (A. V. 7), but also Job xxi. 18. LXX. h. l. τί τὸ ἄχυρον πρὸς τὸν σῖτον; *Vulg.* quid paleis ad triticum.

²¹⁸ *And say it is God's saying;* or, who are oracular, and say, it is an oracle; *i.e.* who in impulse of humour call their impulse inspiration, not distinguishing passion from the vision of truth.

²¹⁹ *Frenzy;* or, pride of display. *Vulg.* in miraculis suis, curiously joined with mendacio. LXX. ἐν τοῖς πλάνοις αὐτῶν.

---

turns upside down the policy of the worldly-wise. 28—32. Let men learn to distinguish their dreams, fancies, and schemes, from the awful inspiration of the alone true God, and not put chaff for wheat, excitement for vision of right and truth. His word sways its true speaker, and finds its destined issue. Not so with excited fancies, or with tricky plots.

33—38. And, since the phrase *Massah*, meaning anything lifted in song and strain, or in denunciation, was

Ch. XXII. say thou to them this, What burthen: I will even cast A.V. xx 33.
you forth, is JEHOVAH's saying;

34. And the prophet, and the priest, and the people that shall say, The burden of JEHOVAH, I will visit upon that man, and upon his house.

35 Thus[220] shall you say, each one to his friend, and each one to his brother, What has JEHOVAH answered, or What has JEHOVAH spoken; 36, but the burden of JEHOVAH you shall mention no more, [*because the burthen to each is his word*] neither pervert the words of the living God, of JEHOVAH of hosts, our God.

37. *Thus shalt thou say to the prophet, What has Jehovah answered, or what has Jehovah spoken?*

38. But if you say the burden of JEHOVAH; therefore thus saith JEHOVAH, Because of your saying this word, The burden of JEHOVAH, while I sent to you saying, You shall not say, The burden of JEHOVAH,

---

[220] 35–38. This passage, with some appearance of confusion in the Hebrew, and still more in the Greek, seems to have suffered dislocation, and perhaps (though not so evidently as ch. x. 11) introduction from an early Targum. At least verse 37, wanting in the LXX. and interrupting the personal verbs by a singular thrown in, has the air of a paraphrase of verse 35; and the parenthesis, "*because the burthen is to each his word*," or each calls Jehovah's word a burthen, seems an interpreter's marginal explanation, and interrupts the grammatical sequence "*neither shall you pervert.*" Similarly the LXX. καὶ διατί ἐλάλησε κ. ὁ Θ. ἡμῶν.

---

now applied (see Isaiah xii. 1, A. V. xiii. 1, &c.) to prophetic sayings, (Prov. xxx. 1; xxxi. 1) either in a fashion which through mannerism became cant, or else in the retort of scoffers, with mockery, or again with a sense of weariness, expressed by its double meaning of what is lifted or borne, so the Prophet, resenting affectation, or rebuking profaneness, or reminding men of their dependency on God, forbids the word *Massah*, burden, as utterly as Hosea forbade Baal, Baalim, previously used in Israel.

XXII. 39. Therefore behold, I, even I, will utterly forget you, A.V. xxiii. 38. and cast forth you, and this city, which I gave to you and to your fathers, from before my face;

40. And I will lay upon you an eternal[221] reproach, and an everlasting[221] ignominy, which shall not be forgotten.

XXIII.[222]

XXIII. 1. The word that was to Jeremiah concerning all the A.V. xxv. 1. people of Judah, in the fourth year of Jehoiakim, son of

---

[221] *Eternal* and *everlasting*. Heb. *Olam*, as in Micah iv. 7 (where see note in this version) of ancient princely descent; and in general indefinitely of extreme antiquity or futurity. LXX. δώσω ἐφ' ὑμᾶς ὀνειδισμὸν αἰώνιον καὶ ἀτιμίαν αἰώνιον, ἥτις οὐκ ἐπιλησθήσεται. Here in the LXX. appear vv. 7—8, marked above as doubtful, yet suiting there better than here, perhaps there better than in xvi. 14, 15, yet considering both their incoherency, and the doubtfulness caused by their absence from the Greek, our earliest version, we can but say if they are anywhere genuine, they most seem to be so above, as vv. 7, 8, of this chapter, but they lie under a very strong suspicion of post-Babylonian insertion. No sincere person, I am sure, will ever follow the steps of my reasoning on these verses, and suppose that my desire to obey evidence is the same thing as prejudice against prediction.

[222] For the xxivth chapter (A. V.) see after chap. xxxii. (A. V. xxxvii), the group of narratives belonging to the last king Zedekiah. The brackets above represent but partially the words not occurring in the Greek, whether omitted in it, or rather added in a recension of the Hebrew.

39, 40. As a punishment for profaneness, is denounced exile with reproach, as perpetual as man's language can paint, or his wrath under strong impulse conceive; yet relentings elsewhere shew that this perpetuity may be understood with all the conditions of contingency, and as spoken in a career of impulse. The *ipsissima Dei fata* know no relenting; but while their possibilities float in the form of monitory presentiment, they may be modified by conditions moral or external.

Chapter XXIII (A. V. XXV), forming an index and summary of the preceding chapters, and of the four here

Ch.XXIII. Josiah, king of Judah, [that was the first year of Nebuchadrezzar, king of Babylon,]

2. Which *he* [Jeremiah the prophet] spake to all the people of Judah, and to [all] the inhabitants of Jerusalem, saying,

3. From the thirteenth year of Josiah, son of Amon, king of Judah, and up to this day, that is three and

---

next appended, has in the Greek those four chapters against the Nations inserted in its midst. In such a form it may have come originally from the pen of Baruch the prophet's secretary. Only in that case, we must question whether the mention of Nebuchadrezzar and the Chaldæans in the Hebrew, or their omission in the Greek, represent most the original form; and if we so far prefer the Hebrew, we must still regard with suspicion the whole passage, from the middle of the 11th verse to the end of the 14th, of which the 12th and 13th verses form the central key; and more especially we may affirm the first half of verse 14 (A.V.) which gives the contents of Jeremiah's book, and the last clause of verse 26 (both wanting in the Greek) to represent at highest a secondary recension, if not a much later moulding and departure from the original form. My own conviction that neither the Hebrew nor the Greek gives quite the oldest text, prevents me from doing more towards its restoration than bracketing suggestively some points of difference, and appending at the end of the chapter, instead of in its midst, which might be their proper place, the predictions against the Nations. A comparison of Ewald with Hitzig will best aid those who are sanguine of a more minute arrangement, or of its interesting English readers, if it were obtained. Suffice it, that an editor's handling marked the earliest form, and still more marks the variations.

1—3. We read below, chap. xxx. (A. V. xxxvi), the history of which we have here the result in summary.

twenty years, the word of JEHOVAH has been to me and I have spoken to you, rising up early and speaking,²²³ but you hearkened not: A.V. xxv 3.

4. [As JEHOVAH] sent to you all his servants the prophets, rising up early, and sending: (though you hearkened not, neither inclined your ear to hear,)

5. Saying, Turn now each from his evil way, and from the evil of your doings; so dwell upon the soil which JEHOVAH gave to you and to your fathers from everlasting to everlasting;

6. And go not after other gods to serve, and to bow down to them, and provoke me not with the work of your hands; so will I do you no hurt:

7. But you hearkened not to me, is JEHOVAH's saying, in order to provoke me to anger with the work of your hands, to your own hurt.

8.²²⁴ Therefore, thus saith JEHOVAH of hosts, Because you hearkened not to my words, 9. behold me sending to take all the families of the north [is JEHOVAH's saying, and

---

²²³ Rising up early and speaking; or, I rose up early, and spoke; Jehovah's speech then continuing in verse 4.

²²⁴ 8—11. Hoc in conciliabulo malignantium et hodiè comprobant: ut magistri eorum non doceant verbum Dei, sed instar colubri sibilent;

After preaching for twenty-three years, the Prophet addresses a poetical recast of his discourses to the king, who treats it contemptuously. Not the less, Jeremiah sums up the substance of what he has addressed to Judah, and of what he is about to address to the Nations. Only the arrangement is one of subject-matter, and hardly, if at all, chronological.

4—7. As the keepers of the vineyard in time past had rejected other preachers, so now Jeremiah.

8—10. After recalling the earlier, specially the 2nd and 3rd chapters of the collected book, the editor pro-

182   THE HEBREW PROPHETS.

Ch. XXIII.

Jer. XXV. Heb.	Jer. XXV. Greek LXX.	A. V. xx 9.
to Nebuchadrezzar, king of Babel, my servant,] and I will bring them against this land, and against its inhabitants, and against all these nations round about, and utterly destroy them, and make them a desolation, and a hissing, and perpetual deserts: 10. and I will destroy from among them the voice of joy and	I send, and will take a family from the north, and bring them against this land, and against its inhabitants, and against all the nations round about her, and will exterminate them, and make them a desolation, and a hissing, and an everlasting reproach; 10. and I will destroy from among them the voice of joy and the	

peritque in iis vox gaudii voxque lætitiæ, ut nunquam audiant illud Apostoli, *Gaudete et iterum dico, gaudete:* Voxque sponsæ, ecclesiasticæ fidei, et vox Sponsi, Domini Salvatoris : Qui eam habet sponsam, Sponsus est : Vox molæ, ut non conterant in iis frumenta, et populis vescenda tribuant: et lumen lucernæ, doctrina videlicet et scientia prophetarum. Denique et de Joanne baptistâ dicitur, Ille erat lucerna lucens ..... Universa inquit terra hæreticorum erit in solitudinem et in stuporem ; cum novissimum ei incipiens fuerit demonstratum. *Hieron.* i. b. l. ; but again also, Denique usque hodiè urbis Babylonis reliquiæ tantum manent. *Ib.* The comparison of the two modes of worship is one of the many signs in Jerome, and elsewhere, as in Justin Martyr, and in Augustine, of a more subdued solemnity of ritual having been retained, or adopted, by the sects, such as the Montanists, than in the broader or less severe, perhaps less pure, development of the Church had come about. A meeting-house of "Friends," and the Cathedral of Cologne, may present analogies to each.

ceeds to summarise the associated threatenings, specially from the 4th, 5th, 7th, 8th chapters, including also the 15th and 19th. The name of Nebuchadrezzar is added, either because in Jehoiakim's fourth year the minister of Jehovah's judgment was revealed, or because the book received a later recast; while in the Greek it is omitted, because when the LXX. made their version, hatred had

JEREMIAH.

XXIII.	JER. XXV. Heb.	JER. XXV. Greek LXX.	A. V. xxv. 10.
	the voice of gladness, voice of bridegroom and voice of bride, sound of grinding-stones and light of torch; and all this land shall become a wilderness, a desolation.	voice of gladness, voice of bridegroom and voice of bride, the fragrance of incense and light of torch; and the whole land shall be a desolation.	
	11. And these nations shall serve [the king of Babel] seventy years; and it shall be when seventy years are fulfilled, I will visit [upon the king of Babel, is JEHOVAH's saying, and] upon that nation their iniquity, [and upon the land of the Chaldæans,] and make it perpetual deso-	11. And they shall serve among the nations seventy years, and when the seventy years are fulfilled, I will judge that nation, and make them an everlasting desolation, 12. and I will bring upon that land all the words which I proclaimed against it, which are written in this book.	

ceased with fear of Babylon, and Elam, or Persia, seemed from Alexander's reign downward a more special object of Divine denunciation.

11—13. At all events, the assignment of a seventy years' term to the Nino-Babylonian empire, and by inference to Judah's exile, savours of invention near or after the end of the exile, not merely from its predictive character, but from the mention of Jeremiah's book, with an editor's summary of its character,. and also from the incoherence of the paragraph, its unintelligibility without disintegration of its parts, and the presence in it of words which are absent from the Greek; while here they only round off the insertion (v. 14).

Ch.XXIII.　　Jer. XXV. Heb.

lations, 12. and I will bring upon that land all my words which I have pronounced against it, all that is written in this book which Jeremiah prophesied against all the nations [that these also, *even* many nations and great kings, should serve amongst them;]

13. And I will recompense them according to their deeds, and according to the work of their hands.

14. Since thus spake the Eternal, the God of Israel, to me, Take this wine-cup of wrath from my hand, and offer it to drink to all the nations to whom I send thee; 15. that they may drink, and be bewildered and maddened, because of the sword which I send among them.

Jer. XXV. Greek LXX.　　A. V. x: 13.

The things which Jeremiah prophesied against the nations.

The things of Elam.

13. Thus saith the Lord, A.V. xl 35. The bow of Elam is broken, the rule of their supremacy.

14. And I will bring upon Elam the four winds from the four corners of heaven, and scatter them throughout all these winds, and there shall be no nation whither the outcasts of Elam shall not come. . . .

[The Greek continues with Elam nearly as Heb. xlix. 34—39, then turns to Egypt, nearly as Heb. xlvi. 1. It then inserts the Babylon, as Heb. l. and appends the rest of Jeremiah's denunciations of the nations.]

14—24. Ten or eleven verses combine in summary the 1st chapter of Jeremiah's collected works with the four chapters now about to follow, stretching with free adaptation of words from the older prophets the circle of Nebuchadrezzar's conquests. The form of this paragraph implies that its outline was given by Jeremy to Baruch;

XXIII. 16. So I took the cup from the ETERNAL's hand, and offered it to drink to all the nations to whom the ETERNAL sent me;

A.V. xxv. 17.

17. Jerusalem, and the cities of Judah; her kings [and] her princes;[225] to make them a desolation and an amazement; a hissing and a curse; [as at this day:]

18. Pharaoh, king of Egypt, and his servants, and his princes, and all his people, and all the mixed multitude;[226]

19. And all the kings of the land of Uz, and all the kings of the land of the Philistines, and Ashkelon, and Azzah, and Ekron, and the remnant of Ashdod;

20. Edom, and Moab, and the sons of Ammon, 21. and all the kings of Tyre, and all the kings of Zidon, and the kings of the isles,[227] which are in the border of the sea,

22. Dedan, and Tema,[228] and Buz, and all those shorn of the poll,[229] 23. and all the kings of Arabia,[230] and all

---

[225] *And her princes.* *Vulg.* et principibus ejus. The Heb. has the conjunction before *her kings.*

[226] *Mixed multitude.* Gr. τοὺς συμμίκτους. Theodor. μετοίκους. Comp. Exod. xii. 38, Ezek. xxx. 5—7, where on the part. סְמָכֵי the Targ. Chald. has מַלְכֵי סוֹמְכְוָתָא, allies *(quasi συμμάχους?)*

[227] *Isles;* or, coasts; *border,* or beyond. Gr. πέραν. Cyprum et Rhodum et insulas quæ appellantur Cyclades; hæ enim a Babyloniis occupatæ sunt. *Hier.*

[228] *Dedan and Tema,* as in Isaiah xviii. [A.V. xxi.] Buz, notwithstanding the LXX. Ρῶς, is the land implied in Gen. xxii. 21, and Job i.

[229] *All those shorn of the poll;* i.e. as above in ix. 25, the Arabs mentioned Herod. iii. 8, as receiving the tonsure in honour of Dionysus.

[230] *Arabia.* If we accept the Hebrew text in preference to the Greek,

---

but its position in a spot whence the book against the Nations has been dislocated in the Hebrew, savours of an editor.

Ch.XXIII. the kings of the mixed tribes, that pitch tent in the desert, A.V. xxv. 24.

24. And all the kings of Zimri,[231] and all the kings of Elam, and all the kings of the Medes, and all the kings of the north, those that are nigh and those that are far, one with another, and all the kingdoms of the earth, which are upon the face of the soil,

25. [And the King of Sheshach[232] shall drink after them.]

---

which omits the name altogether, and if we understand the word in Isaiah xviii. 13, to mean evening, and regard a later date of Isaiah xii. 19, [A.V. xiii. 20,] as more probable than an earlier, this passage may claim, with ii. 38 (A. V. iii. 2,) to be one of the earliest uses of this word geographically for the land of Ishmael and Joktan. Was it given to the land of mixed tribes, distinct from the pure Ægyptians, or is the common derivation from dryness and sterility right?

[231] *Zimri*, not in the LXX. no longer Arabs, but probably a Medo-persic race, whose name is found in the Achæmenian inscriptions.

[232] *Sheshach.* This word means Babel, as explained by Jerome, according to the *Ethbasch*, or cabalistic cypher, which inverted the order of the Alphabet for enigmatic purposes. But (1) this technical cypher was not known in Jeremiah's time; (2) nor would it have been useful amidst plain enough denunciations to affect mystery. (3) What is still more significant, is, that the whole verse, interjecting a nominative amidst accusatives, disturbs the syntax and sequence of thought. (4) The Greek version happily does not contain this clause, or the word by which it is defended in c. li. 41. (5) We must conclude that the verse was inserted here in the table of contents, perhaps to correspond with the later chapter on Babylon; inserted at least by a subsequent editor. (6) This conclusion may confirm presumptions against prediction, but in no way whatever depends upon them.

---

25. Either to complete the circle of Divine judgments, or to correspond with the enlarged form of the book, when denunciation against Babel had been added, a Hebrew editor here adds Babel under an enigmatic name to the kingdoms threatened. Explanations from the Persians, as meaning *king's-house*, or from Arabic, as *fortified*, *warlike*, are idle attempts to explain a title, which from

.XXIII. 26. And say to them, Thus saith JEHOVAH of hosts, A.V. xxv.
the God of Israel, Drink you, and be drunken, and vomit, 27.
and fall, that you rise no more, because of the sword,
which I send among you;

27. And it shall be, when they refuse to take the cup
at thine hand to drink, that thou shalt say to them, Thus
saith JEHOVAH of hosts, You shall certainly drink:

28. Since behold, upon the city over which my name
is called, I am beginning to bring evil; and shall you go
utterly unpunished? You shall not go unpunished; since
I summon a sword against all the inhabitants of the earth,
is the saying of JEHOVAH of hosts.

29. So prophesy thou to them all these words, and
say to them, JEHOVAH from on high thunders, and from the
abode of his sanctity utters sound;

30. He thunders terribly against his dwelling-place:
shouting as of tramplers, echoes against all the inhabitants of the earth; the noise reaches to the end of the
earth.

31. For JEHOVAH has a quarrel amidst the nations; he
is entered into judgment with all flesh; he has given[233]
over the wicked to the sword, is JEHOVAH's saying.

---

[233] *He has given*. *Vulg.* impios tradidi gladio, dicit Dominus, LXX.
ἐδόθησαν εἰς μάχαιραν.

---

the non-existence in his time of the alphabetical cabala,
and for various reasons, Jeremiah could not have written.
Compare the Greek here, and in li. 41, and note the objective cases of the syntax.

26—36. In a loftier strain, and not unworthy of Baruch,
but still referring manifestly to the earlier portions of the
book, which as its scribe he handed down (comp. ii. 2, iii.
16, iv. 5, vi. 22, xv. 4, xvi. 2—16, xxiii. 2—20), the editor,

Ch.XXIII.   32. Thus saith JEHOVAH of hosts, Behold, evil goes A. V. 3: forth from nation to nation, and a mighty whirlwind is roused from the sides of the earth, so that the slain of JEHOVAH in that day be from one end of the earth to the other end of the earth.

33. They shall neither be lamented, nor gathered, nor buried; they shall be for dung on the face of the ground.

34. Howl, O shepherds, and cry; and roll yourselves in dust,[234] lords of the flock;[235] for your days are accomplished for slaughtering, and your scatterings, for you to fall, like costly vessels.

35. Yea, refuge perishes from the shepherds, and escape from the herds of the flock.

36. *There is* a voice of crying of the shepherds, and howling of the lords of the flock; since JEHOVAH destroys their feeding-place, and the peaceful pastures are laid waste; 37. because of the fierceness of JEHOVAH's anger, he has left as a lion his thicket:

---

[234] *Roll yourselves in dust.* Micah i. 9, (A. V. 10.)
[235] *Lords of the flock*; or, prime, *Vulg.* optimates. LXX. κρίοι τῶν προβάτων. Hieron. optimatibus, sive arietibus.

---

or the Prophet prompting him, condenses under images Nebuchadrezzar's conquests.

27. Comp. Obad. 16.

32. Jerome thinks this passage spoken of by our Lord in St. Luke, xxi. 10; and that it may be understood as fulfilled in Nebuchadrezzar's siege, or as awaiting a remote fulfilment in the bringing of the world to a close. So little fettered is his chronology.

37. Cap. iv. 5 [A.V. iv. 7] Jehovah's anger is the unseen cause which urges the ravager of nations as a lion ravening from his covert. The invader's sword is ideally in Jehovah's hand; it is called for by the voice of His will.

38. Yea their land is become a desolation, because of the fury of the oppressor,²³⁶ and because of the fury of his anger.

XXIV.

Ch.XXIV. That which was the word of JEHOVAH to Jeremiah the prophet concerning the nations. To Egypt, concerning the host of Pharaoh-necho king of Egypt, which was at the river Euphrates by Carchemish, which Nebuchadrezzar king of Babel smote in the fourth year of Jehoiakim son of Josiah king of Judah. A.V.xlvi. 1.

1. Array shield and buckler, and draw nigh to battle:
2. Harness the horses, and mount, O horsemen, and

---

²³⁶ *Fury of the oppressor*, should be *sword* of the oppressor, as in the LXX. τῆς μαχαίρας, reading in the Heb. חרב for חרון—*Vulg.* a facie iræ columbæ, understanding Nebuchadnezzar as the dove! It is uncertain whether the destroyer, on whose emerging from covert the shepherds and flocks howl, is Jehovah himself, or the oppressor going forth because of Jehovah's anger. The distribution of the clauses is disputable; my own feeling is, that the logical syntax of thought is not precisely represented by the rhythm of the respondent clauses; but that there is a carrying through of the mental subject-matter, as in Isaiah xii. 23. [A.V. xiv. 2.]

Proem.—After a summary of the utterances of Jeremiah over Judah and the nations, none could so properly open the collection, as the song of triumph over the great battle of Carchemish, in which Necho atoned for the death of Josiah, and the dominion of south-western Asia passed from the Nile to the Euphrates, B.C. 606. Two pieces compose the chapter, written at different times, and both so essentially, the first so strikingly poetical, as to recall the artist touch of Nahum, and suggest the question, whether some parts of Jeremiah, which from their antiphonal rhythm we take as poetry, were not meant by him for prose.

1—4. Swordsman and horseman hurled backward from

Ch.XXIV. stand forth with helmets; furnish the spears, put on the coats of mail.

3. Wherefore have I seen them dismayed, retreated backward? and their warriors are smitten, and fugitive in flight, and shew not face; panic *is* all around, is Jehovah's saying.[237]

4. Let not the swift flee, nor the valiant escape; northward, on the side of the river Euphrates, they are stumbled and fallen.

5. Who is this that comes up as the river; as streams, whose waters are stirred?

6. Egypt comes up as the river, and as streams whose waters are stirred; and he says, I will go up, I will cover the land; I will destroy cities,[238] and the dwellers therein.

7. Go up, O horses, and whirl, O chariots, and go forth the warriors; Ethiopia and Nubia[239] grasping the shield; and Lydians[240] [grasping] bending the bow.

8. And that day *shall be* a day of vengeance to the

---

[237] *Vulg.* Quid igitur? vidi ipsos pavidos, et terga vertentes, fortes corum cæsos; fugerunt correcti, nec respexerunt; terror undique, ait Dominus. LXX. φυγῇ ἔφυγον, καὶ οὐκ ἀνέστρεψαν, περιεχόμενοι κυκλόθεν, λέγει Κύριος.

[238] *Cities.* Heb. sing.; omitted by the LXX.

[239] *Ethiopia and Nubia.* Heb. Cush and Phut, comp. Gen. x. 6, and notes on Nahum.

[240] *Lydians*, here, as in Gen. x. 13, a Hamite, or African people, which has been one of the stumbling-blocks in the Mosaic genealogies, though Semitic Lydians also occur Gen. x. 22. We may either suppose au homonymous people in Africa, or with Ewald and Hitzig take the word as a variation of Lybians. Still remains the wider question, a solution here, but difficulty otherwise, What was the real difference between Ham and Shem?

---

the mighty stream are surveyed by the holder of the balance of battle.

5—8. Otherwise had seemed the Lybian inundation, Nubian shieldmen, Libyan bowmen, not thinking that

XXIV. Lord, JEHOVAH of hosts, to avenge himself on his adver- A.V.XLVI. 10.
saries; that the sword may devour, and be glutted, and
be drunken with their blood; for the Lord JEHOVAH of
hosts has a sacrifice in the northern land, at the river
Euphrates.

9. Go up to Gilead, and take balm,[241] Virgin[242]
daughter of Egypt: in vain hast thou multiplied to thyself healings, health[243] is not for thee.

10. The nations have heard of thy ignominy, and thy
crying has filled the earth; for warrior has stumbled upon
warrior, together are both of them fallen.

*The word that JEHOVAH spake to Jeremiah the prophet,
that Nebuchadrezzar king of Babel should come to smite
the land of Egypt.*

11. Tell in Egypt, and proclaim in Migdol,[244] yea,
proclaim in Noph[245] and Tahpanhes;[246] say, Take thy

---

[241] *Balm.* Gr. ῥητινήν, i.e. resin. See above, viii. 17 (A. V. 22.)

[242] *Virgin*, here the true word, Bethulah.

[243] *Health*, the result of the healings, either through the closing of the scar, or as some, through bandage and plaster. I prefer the first, as xxx. 13, comp. viii. 22, and xxxiii. 6. (A. V.)

[244] *Migdol*, an Egyptian town, with a Hebrew name, probably as being towards the north-east frontier, and perhaps the Pelusiac camp of the Greek mercenaries; the name is Grecised into Μογδωλός, but must not be confused with Megiddo, notwithstanding what Herodotus says of Necho's battle there.

[245] *Noph* is Memphis, not to be confused with Thebes, the No-Amon of Nahum.

[246] *Tahpanhes*, also a place of garrison, near Pelusium, and distinct from Hanes, which was Leontopolis.

---

their slaughter would reek sacrificially in the nostrils of
Divine vengeance. Isa. xxix. 6. [A. V. xxxiv.]

9, 10. She who wounded Judah at Megiddo, needs
healing balm in Carchemish.

11, 12. Not content with overthrowing Necho, Nebuchadrezzar invades his successor Apries in his own

Ch.XXIV. stand, and prepare thee, for the sword has devoured those around thee.²⁴⁷

12. Why are thy mighty overthrown?²⁴⁸ they stood not, for JEHOVAH cast them down; they went on tottering; yea, are fallen, man upon man, till they said, Arise, and let us return to our people, and to the land of our birth, because of the sword of the oppressor.²⁴⁹

13. They called the name²⁵⁰ of Pharaoh king of Egypt, Destruction; he has passed the appointed time.²⁵¹

14. Surely, as I live, is the saying of the king, whose name is the ETERNAL of hosts, as Tabor is among moun-

---

²⁴⁷ *The sword has devoured those around thee.* LXX. κατέφαγε μάχαιρα τὴν σμίλακά σου. Vulg. quæ per circuitum tuum sunt.

²⁴⁸ *Why are overthrown thy mighty?* LXX. Διατί ἔφυγεν ἀπὸ σοῦ ὁ Ἆπις; ὁ μόσχος ὁ ἐκλεκτός σου οὐκ ἔμεινεν, ὅτι Κύριος παρέλυσεν αὐτόν, καὶ τὸ πλῆθός σου ἠσθένησε καὶ ἔπεσε. This identification of the Heb. *Abir* mighty (or ox), with Apis is accepted by Ewald (comp. Ps. 50, 13), seemingly by Hitzig, Michaelis, Kennicott; better rejected by Rosenmuller, Maurer.

²⁴⁹ *Sword of the oppressor.* LXX. μαχαίρας Ἑλληνικῆς. I must regard this rendering as a sign of the Alexandrine date, as the above introduction of Apis is a sign of the Alexandrian place, of the version; but see last verse of ch. xxv. next preceding here.

²⁵⁰ They called the *name*. So far LXX. ὄνομα, and *Vulg.* nomen, clearly better than the Masora שָׁאוֹן ibi, *there*. But when the LXX. add, Σαὼν ἐσβεὶ μωήδ, did they simply blunder? or did they know Egyptian words, significant of destruction and contempt, such as the prophet may here be playing upon? For the sentiment, compare Isaiah's way of giving the name Rahab, xxvi. 7, and *Magor-missabib*, above. Jer. xx. 3.

²⁵¹ *Appointed time*, means either the hour of Jehovah's destiny; or the engagement with the mercenaries, now nullified, and voided.

---

country. Natural to invoke the Greek mercenaries, who from the time of Psammetichus, (Her. ii. 152—4,) had occupied a camp on the Nile, and had become settled in Memphis. But these men of might fell away, migrating in panic homeward, and contemptuously punning on the name (13) of king Apries, or deeming their engagement elapsed, or his hour come.

v. tains, and as Carmel in the sea, *he shall* come;²⁵² 15. Prepare thyself furniture of exile, inhabitress, daughter of Egypt, for Noph shall become a desolation and be destroyed,²⁵³ so as to have no dweller.

16. Egypt is a heifer fair of aspect;²⁵⁴ a stinging-fly²⁵⁵ from the north comes upon her;²⁵⁶ 17. Yea, her hirelings in the midst of her are like stalled calves; for they too are turned, are fled together; they stood not, since the day of their calamity was come upon them, tho time of their visitation; 18. its sound marches as a brazen *sound*,²⁵⁷ for they march in a host, and with axes are they come upon her; 19. like hewers of wood they have cut down her forest, is JEHOVAH's saying; for it cannot be reckoned,²⁵⁸ for they are more than the locusts, and are beyond numbering.

---

²⁵² *He shall come;* or, As Carmel advances into the sea, so surely shalt thou need to be furnished for flight.

²⁵³ *Destroyed;* or, burnt.

²⁵⁴ *Fair of aspect;* or, as more usually taken, exceeding fair.

²⁵⁵ *A stinging-fly.* Vulg. Stimulator, LXX. ἀπόσπασμα.

²⁵⁶ *Comes upon her.* So the versions Greek and Latin, but the Heb. text, comes assuredly.

²⁵⁷ *As a sound of brass.* Vulg. Vox ejus quasi æris sonabit; taking נחש as נחשה, which suits the context better than the sound of a serpent's hiss, whether applied to the gliding of the invader through the sandy desert, or to the slinking aside of scared Egypt.. *Her sound*, LXX. their sound.

²⁵⁸ *For it cannot be reckoned;* i.e. the calamity, or invading host; or else, *though* it cannot be reckoned; i.e. the Egyptian population.

---

14. Fixed as the hills is Jehovah's design to bring the invader, (15) and lay Memphis desolate, giving Egypt (16, 17) and her soldiers, like the oxen whom they made sacred symbols, to the gadfly and the goad; (18) while with brazen crash (not so well, with serpent's hiss) numberless invaders hew down the human forest, and (20) give Egypt a slave to Babel.

Ch. XXIV. 20. The daughter of Egypt is confounded, she is delivered into the hand of the northern people.

21. [259] [JEHOVAH of hosts, the God of Israel, has spoken,] Behold me visiting upon Amun *god* of No, and upon Pharaoh and [upon Egypt; as well on her gods as on her kings, as well on Pharaoh as] on them that trust in him; 22. [and I will deliver them into the hand of those that seek their life, even into the hand of Nebuchadrezzar king of Babel and into the hand of his servants, and afterwards shall she dwell, as in the days of old, is JEHOVAH'S saying.]

23. [260] [But fear not thou, my servant Jacob, and be not dismayed, Israel; for behold me saving thee from afar, and thy seed from the land of their captivity; so that Jacob returns and is at ease, and there is none to terrify him. 24. Fear not thou, my servant Jacob, is JEHOVAH'S saying; for I am with thee; for I will work a complete work with all the nations whither I have driven thee; but with thee will I not make a full end, but correct thee in measure, though I leave thee not utterly unpunished.[261]]

---

[259] 21—22. The parenthetic marks convey an impression, not quite precise, of the vast difference here between the Greek and the Hebrew. I cannot doubt the Greek is here nearer the original, and rightly avoids plurality of kings, notwithstanding its mistake in rendering Amun of No, Ἀμμὼν τὸν υἱὸν αὐτῆς. Movers discusses this passage in his Critical Essay, Hamburg, 1837.

[260] Verses 23, 24, though present in the Greek, and there serving, as Hitzig remarked, as a transition to the oracle against Babylon, are still here out of place, and belong by style, almost word for word, to the later, or second Isaiah. Ewald throws them into the margin. I ascribe them to a very early Editor.

[261] *Leave thee not utterly unpunished.* Or, as the Targum, and high

---

21, 22. But in all this was accomplished the counsel of Jehovah (not upon "the multitude of Egypt," but) upon the Theban God Amun, whose goat-horns symbolised strength, but whose attribute was living eternity.

23, 24. It comforts the editor, (perhaps Baruch) to

XXV.

That which was the word of JEHOVAH *to Jeremiah the prophet, to the Philistines, before Pharaoh smote Gaza.*²⁶²

XXV. 1. Thus saith JEHOVAH, Behold, waters rising from the north, until they become an overflowing flood, and overflow land and its fulness, city and dwellers therein ; so

A. V.
XLVII. 1.

Jewish authorities, Jarchi, Kimchi, I will not utterly destroy thee ; but Philippsohn, as above, *dich nicht ungestraftet lasse.* Versus supra, xxx. 10, 11, videntur h. l. repetiti, ne Judæi h. l. carerent fausto promisso. *Rosenm.*

²⁶² *Title.*—LXX. ἐπὶ τοὺς ἀλλοφύλους τάδε λέγει Κύριος. Probably an older, perhaps more genuine, form. By the versions a sort of Providence seems mercifully to deliver us from the Rabbins ; though Hitzig here supposes Gaza to be the Kadytis of Herod. ii. 159, and the spoiler therefore to be Necho on his southward return from Carchemish.

---

reflect, that as Egypt herself may by Divine permission recover from the invasion, so at least Israel, the servant of the spiritual God amongst blinded nations, will never be deserted by her Strength, but the old promises (xlviii. 6, 7) come good, with which, as with words of good men, it is pleasant to cover over a page of bitterness.

Title.—Within a duration suggested by Megiddo and Carchemish, 606—604, (though by Perizonius brought later into the reign of Apries,) Jeremiah saw the Philistine towns threatened from the north, *i. e.* we should naturally say, by the Chaldæans ; but whoever prefixed the Hebrew title either knew of *Necho's* assaulting Gaza, on his homeward route, or from some other tradition connects the passage with an Egyptian inroad, of which we know nothing. We may compare Isaiah (A. V. xx.) ch. xiii. of this Version. The prophet judges of the invasion, as one who had seen in the Philistine cities centres of alliance with Phœnicia, and of hostility to his own nation as it emerged from rudeness.

1, 2. The image so frequent in Isaiah, of the invader's

Ch. XXV. that cry aloud mankind, and howls every inhabitant of the land;

2. At the sound of the tramp of the hoofs of his warriors,²⁶³ at the rushing of his chariots, the roar of his wheels, fathers looked not back to sons, for faintness of hands;

3. Because of the day that is come, to destroy all the Philistines; to cut off from Tyre and from Zidon every surviving ally; because JEHOVAH is destroying the Philistines, the remnant of the coast of Caphtor.²⁶⁴

4. Baldness is come upon Gaza; cut off is Ashkelon, the remnant of their valley; how long wilt thou gash thyself?²⁶⁵

5. Ah! Sword of the ETERNAL, for how long wilt thou take no rest? gather thyself into thy scabbard, pause, and be still.

6. How can it be at rest, when the ETERNAL has given it charge against Ashkelon, and against the coast of the sea? There he has appointed it.

A.V. XLVII.

---

²⁶³ *Warriors.* LXX. τῶν ποδῶν. *Vulg.* bellatorum ejus. *Hebr. lit.* his mighty ones, doubtless here, as in xiv. 3, 4, 12, (A. V. xlvi. 5, 6, 12), where the calf-god Apis is wildly introduced by some.

²⁶⁴ *Caphtor*, the mother-country of the Philistines; whether Cyprus and Crete, where, however, as Semitic, they must be regarded as immigrants; or *Copt*-land, E-Gypt, where they would have been akin to the Shepherd-kings; but of their E-Gyptian origin no conscious trace appears remanent in the passage before us, in which the Prophet does not think of Egypt.

²⁶⁵ *Gash thyself,* i.e. mourn. See note on Hosea vi. 15, but question here, if the LXX. do not rightly carry it on to Jehovah's sword?

---

flooding the land with attendant nations and horsemen, is applied to the Philistian coast.

3. Civilised as the Philistines had been, and boasting origin from Caphtor, their pride is shorn. 4. Shall they always be gashing themselves over the slain? *or*, shall God's sword be ever brandished? 5. When will that sword sleep? 6. Alas! how sleep, with such a charge against the populous coast?

XXVI.
To Moab.

Ch.XXVI. 1. Thus saith JEHOVAH of hosts, the God of Israel, Woe to Nebo,²⁶⁶ because it is destroyed; shame-stricken, captured, is Kiriathaim;²⁶⁷ shame-stricken and ruined is Misgab.²⁶⁷

A. V. XLVIII. 1

2. Moab's glory is no more; in Heshbon they expound²⁶⁸ evil against her; Come and let us cut her off from a nation; also, Madmen,²⁶⁸ be made dumb; after thee marches the sword.

3. A sound of crying from Horonaim; with a mighty destruction and crash is shivered Moab; they uttered aloud a crying as far as Zoar.²⁶⁹

---

²⁶⁶ *Nebo*, here, as in Isaiah xiv. 2, (A. V. xv. 2,) a Moabite city, which at times was Reubenite, near Kiriathaim and Baal-Meon, more commonly the mountain over against Jericho, of which Pisgah was the summit; more primarily the Semitic deity, there, as more typically in Babylon, worshipped. The word has been associated with Heb. *Nabah*, to prophesy, but more probably by Hitzig with Sanscr. *Nabhas*, heaven, Lat. *nebula*. C.B. *Nev*.

²⁶⁷ *Kiriathaim and Misgab*, cities and fortress, seem here local names. The LXX. curiously blunder into Hamath and Gath.

²⁶⁸ *In Heshbon they expound*; lit. they devise; here, as in *Madmen*, (qu. if a variation for Meidaba? Isa. xv. 2; 1 Macc. ix. 36,) there is a verbal play.

²⁶⁹ *As far as Zoar.* LXX. εἰς Ζογόρα, as in Isaiah xv. 5, (A. V. xv.) but if so, it suggests taking it so below in xxvii. 20, where critics do not, who do so here; neither here did the Masoretic Hebrews so take it; and it is a question whether their text might mean, her little cities, such as Zoar, uttered a cry; or, whether we are to charge mistake of the text on the manuscripts, or mistake of Isaiah on the prophet; but the supposition here adopted seems borne out by the Greek Version. I had once rendered here "her little ones uttered aloud a cry;" in now preferring the reversion to Isaiah, I have Ewald with me here; but not below in xxvii.(A. V. xlix.) 20, nor Hitzig here.

XXVI. This whole chapter, which reads more clearly with a freer punctuation, is important, as shewing us how the Hebrew prophets worked. Long before Isaiah, some ancient ruin of Moab had called forth a strain of rugged

Ch.XXVI. 4. Yea, in the ascent[270] of Luhith[271] *men* go up weeping bitterly; yea, in the descent[270] of Horonaim they have heard wailings of the cry of ruin; 5. Flee, save your lives, and be as ruined places[272] in the wilderness.

6. For because of thy trusting in thy works[273] and in thy treasures, thou also shalt be captured; and Chemosh[274] shall go forth in captivity; his priests and his princes together;

7. And the destroyer shall come upon every city, and no city shall escape; but the valley shall perish, and the plain be desolated, as JEHOVAH has spoken.

[270] *Ascent and descent*, thought to be steps from some mountain temple, such as we see at the conventual shrines of Italy; but from the antithesis I judge a natural declivity meant.

[271] Luhith has been placed westwards, or to the south near Zoar.

[272] As *ruined places*; or, as heath or juniper, comp. Jer. xvii. 2. (A. V. 6). LXX. h. l. ὥσπερ ὄνος ἄγριος. *Vulg.* quasi myricæ.

[273] *Works. Vulg.* munitionibus. LXX. ἐν ὀχυρώματι. The Versions point to a different text in the Hebrew.

[274] *Chemosh*, comp. Judges xi. 19—24, and Numbers xxi. 29. The name is thought to mean mighty, or conqueror, comp. Lat. Camillus.

description, which the great prophet adapted, associating it with monition, to his own time. When Jeremiah saw the Chaldæan conquest of Peræa, he could find no fitter quarry for digging out expressions of sympathy or denunciation, than the same strain. But he felt for Moab less than for Judah, and as his poetical faculty, when not tinged by feeling, fell short of Isaiah's, besides which his editors would touch, and have left signs of touching, the composite song with snatches from elsewhere, the whole result resembles the poems in which modern Latinists lay the ancients under contribution. It becomes a robe of many pieces.

1—5. The siege of cities and crying of fugitives are described.

6—9. The Divine sentence is recalled, which had denounced the ruin.

8. Give wings[275] to Moab, that she may flee utterly away, and that her cities may become a desolation, with no inhabitant in them;   A. V. XLVIII. 9.

9. Accursed[276] is he that doeth JEHOVAH's work negligently, and accursed he that refraineth his sword from blood.

10. Moab was secure[277] from his youth, and rested still upon his lees, and was not poured from vessel into vessel, nor went into captivity; so his flavour remained in him, and his reek was not changed.

11. Therefore, behold days coming, is JEHOVAH's saying, when I will send to him drawers to draw him,[278] that they empty his vessels, and break their flagons[279] in pieces,

12. So that Moab be ashamed of Chemosh, as the house of Israel was ashamed of Bethel their confidence.

13. How[280] say you, We are warriors, and men of

---

[275] *Wings;* or, signs by way of finger-posts to guide his flight.

[276] *Accursed.* As in the case of Achan, after the *cherem* or denunciation of sacred war.

[277] *Secure.* Comp. Isa. xxvii. 16—18. (A.V. xxxii. 9—11).

[278] *Drawers, to draw him;* or, tilters to tilt him. *Vulg.* stratores.

[279] *Their flagons;* i.e. the flagons of the people of Moab. So *Vulg.* lagunculas corum, but LXX. τὰ κέρατα αὐτοῦ; the affixes being, let it be once for all remarked, either changed by transcription, or varied by abruptness of transition.

[280] 13, 14. Comp. above, ver. 9; Isa. xxix. 5—8. (A. V xxxiv.) Joel iii.

---

10. Notwithstanding that it was wrested of old from Amorite, and subsequently from Moabite alternately, and from Peræan tribes, the east of Jordan had in long peace become fat and easy of life, like wine undisturbed; (11) but displacement is at hand.

13—18. Taunt and scornful pity attend the wandering of homeless fugitives, (19—24) while each hill

Ch. XXVI. might for the battle? 14. The destroyer of Moab and of her cities[281] is gone up, and the choice of his youth are gone down to slaughter, is the saying of the king, whose name is JEHOVAH of hosts.

A. V.
XLVIII. 1

15. The calamity of Moab is nigh of coming, and her affliction hastens exceedingly.

16. Bemoan[282] him, all his neighbours, and all familiar with his name say, How is broken the rod of strength, the staff of excellency!

17. Come down from thy glory, and sit in dust, inhabitress, daughter of Dibon; for the destroyer of Moab has gone up against thee, has destroyed thy strongholds.[283]

18. Stand by the roadside, and watch, inhabitress of Aroer; inquire of the flier and the fugitive; say, What has come about?

19. Moab is confounded, yea, is ruined, howl thou and cry; proclaim in Arnon that Moab is destroyed, 20. and that judgment is come to the land of the plain, to Holon, and to Jahazah, 21. and upon Mephaath, and upon Dibon,

---

[281] *For the destroyer of Moab, &c.*, the Masora, LXX. and *Vulg.* have "Moab is destroyed;" but so the verb *gone up* hardly agrees with cities in number or sense (e. g. gone up in smoke, &c.), and at least 'destroyer' was implied in the verb 'destroyed,' which probably should be read as a participle, and as below in v. 17.

[282] *Bemoan;* or, bemock, wagging the head at him. LXX. κινήσατε αὐτῷ κεφαλήν.

[283] Most of the places named lie between the Jabbok and the Arnon, (some more southward) and most of them so near the track of a subsequent Roman road, that in any age an invader would find them in his way. Robinson, *Phys. Geog. Pal.* pp. 67—124, bids us distinguish the upland plain, *Meishor*, interspersed with, or attached to hill villages, from the *Arabah*, or waste tract, through which the prolongation of the Jordan valley would run; and both from the *Sephelah*, or sea-ward flat of Western Judah.

---

town and upland pasture has its part in the national down-fall.

XXVI. and upon Nebo, and upon Beth-Diblathaim, 22. and upon Kiriathaim, and upon Beth-Gamul, and upon Beth-Meon, 23. and upon Kerioth, and upon Bozrah, and upon all the cities of the land of Moab, both far and near; 24. the horn of Moab is cut off, and his arm is broken, is JEHOVAH's saying.

A. V. XLVIII. 23.

25. Give him the wine-cup,[284] since against JEHOVAH he waxed great, and let Moab stagger[285] in his vomit, and he too become a mockery.

26. For was not Israel a mock to thee? was he counted *by thee* amongst thieves? in that often as thou spakest of him, thou hast wagged the head.

27. Forsake the cities, and dwell in the rocks inhabitants of Moab; and become like the dove that nestles in the side of the cavern's mouth.[285]

28. [286] We heard the haughtiness of Moab, haughty exceedingly; his pride and his haughtiness and the loftiness and exultation of his heart.

29. I have known, is JEHOVAH's saying, his overflowing, and his unfulfilled feignings; not so, *as they spoke*, they wrought.[287]

---

[284] *Give him the wine cup.* Heb. Cause him to drink; comp. above, i. 1—5 (A. V. 5—9); xxiii. 14—26 (A. V. xxv. 15—27); Obad. ver. 16.

[285] *Stagger.* Vulg. allidet manum. LXX. ἐπικρούσαι ἐν χειρὶ αὐτοῦ. 27. For the image Bochart and Rosenm. quote Hom. Il. φ. 495; Virg. Æn. v. 213, 214.

[286] 28—31. Here compare closely Isaiah xiv. 15—21 (A.V. xvi. 6—11).

[287] 29. *Vulg.* Ego scio, ait Dominus, jactantiam ejus; et quod non sit juxta eam virtus ejus, nec juxta quod poterat conata sit facere. So, I think, of vain-gloriousness, exceeding strength; not of deception.

25—29. Those who rejoiced when the red wine-cup of wrath was handed to Israel, drink it in their own turn to the dregs. See Hab. ii. 4—9 (A. V. 5—15).

Ch. XXVI. 30. Therefore over Moab I wail, and for the whole of Moab cry aloud; for the men of Kir-heres *must man sigh*.

31. More than Jahzer's weeping must I weep for thee, O vine of Sibmah; thy suckers branched across the sea, reached to the sea of Jahzer;[288] 32. on thy harvest and on thy vintage destroyer is fallen,[289] so that removed are gladness and joy, from the fruitful field [and from the land of Moab], and wine from the wine-vats; I have caused to cease the cry of joy, *that man* tramples not; the cry is no cry of joy.

---

[288]. *Reached to the sea of Jahzer.* Vulg. usque ad mare Jazer pervenerunt; but LXX. πόλεις Ἰαζὴρ ἤψαντο. Where is this sea of Jahzer? The Eton Atlas gives *Jahzer torrens et mare*, but travellers find a mere source not deserving the name of sea. Hence the reading here is doubted, or even the writer's knowledge of the spot; his imitation of Isaiah, with variations, having perhaps betrayed him into topographical inaccuracy. Gesenius takes the latter, Hitzig the former alternative.

[289] *On thy harvest destroyer is fallen.* In the passage of Isaiah here imitated, for 'destroyer,' we find alarm-cry, by strong inversion, as most critics think, of the vintage joy-cry, though my own version followed the Anglican, in making the joy-cry fail. Here Jeremiah interprets the alarm-cry as meaning destroyer, and adds a fuller paraphrase in the following clause. He is also supposed to have misunderstood *Carmel* (the fruitful field) as a local name, and therefore to have added *the land of Moab;* but my own suspicion is that the writer preserved the true antithesis of fruitful field and wine-vat; then that an editor, misunderstanding him, threw in the land of Moab; which the LXX. translated, and then finding *Carmel*, needless for the rhythm, and locally, as they thought inapplicable, left it out. So arose the Greek συνεψήσθη χαρμοσύνη καὶ εὐφροσύνη ἐκ τῆς Μωαβίτιδος, καὶ οἶνος ἦν ἐπὶ ληνοῖς. Or, if the Greek be the earlier, then a Hebrew editor introduced the Carmel here from Isaiah; but that seems less likely. The whole passage is eminently suggestive for the art of comparative criticism.

30—32. How should the poet have no tears, when he knows the choice vines trampled down, field emptied of joy, and vineyard of vintage-cry, with the war-alarm taking their place?

XXVI. 33. From the crying of Heshbon, to Elealeh, to Jachaz, they have uttered their voice; from Zoar to Horonaim, Eglath Shelishiyah;[290] yea, the waters of Nimrim become desolations; 34. and I will cause to cease from Moab, is JEHOVAH's saying, offerer in the high-place, and burner of incense to his gods. A. V. XLVIII. 34.

35. Therefore my heart sighs for Moab like music-pipes, and my heart sighs for the men of Kir-heres like music-pipes; therefore the riches he had gotten are perished; 36. yea, every head is become bald, and every beard shorn; on all hands are gashes, and on the loins sackcloth.

37. On all the house-tops of Moab, and in her streets throughout is lamentation; for I have shivered Moab as a vessel wherein is no delight, is JEHOVAH's saying.

38. How art thou broken, is their howl; how has Moab turned his back with shame; and Moab is become a mockery and a terror to all his neighbours.

39. For thus spake JEHOVAH, Behold he flies as an eagle,[291] and expands his wings towards Moab; 40. captured are the cities, and surprised the strongholds, and the heart of the warriors of Moab is in that day as the heart of a woman in pangs.

41. So Moab is destroyed from being a people, be-

---

[290] *Eglath-shelishiyah*, either a synonym for Horonaim, or a place not otherwise known, or, not a name, but a simile, from a three-year-old heifer, or the heifer let loose, and lowing as it goes, comp. Isaiah xiv. 5. (A. V. xv. 5).

[291] *He flies as an eagle*, i.e. the invader, Nebuchadrezzar; Jer. xxvii. (A. V. xlix. 22); Isa. xxvii. 5; (A. V. xxxi. 5,) and Deut. xxviii. 49, a passage perhaps referred to here, or belonging, as some critics have argued, to this same age. Hence again the natural application in the Gospels.

33—37. City, water-stream, altar, all defiled, heads shorn, house-tops crowded with mourners, attest ruin.

39—42. The eagle-swoop of the invader, and crash of

Ch. XXVI. cause against JEHOVAH he waxed great; terror and pit and snare[292] are upon thee, inhabitant of Moab, is JEHOVAH's saying; 42. he that flees from the terror shall fall into the pit, and he that climbs out of the pit shall be taken in the snare, when I bring upon her, upon Moab, the year of their visitation, is JEHOVAH's saying.

A. V. XLVIII.

43. [In the shadow of Heshbon stood fleers for lack of strength; but fire came forth of Heshbon, and flame out of the midst of Sihon, and devoured the extreme side of Moab, and the crown of the tumultuous people.

44. Woe to thee, Moab; the people of Chemosh perishes; for thy sons are taken in slavery, and thy daughters in servitude;

45. Though I turn again the captivity of Moab in the aftergrowth of days, is JEHOVAH's saying.][293]

Thus far is Moab's judgment.

---

[292] *Terror and pit, &c.* All this is a cento from Isaiah xxi. 18, 19. (A. V. xxiv. 17, 18).

[293] The three closing verses are wanting in the LXX. and were probably added to the Hebrew after that version was made. They are in fact little more than a cento from Numbers xxi. and xxiv. By rendering 'the children of *Sheth*' as 'the sons of tumult' the compiler shews that he understood in Numb. xxiv. 17, not any patriarch or tribe, but an appellative of Moab, as Rahab is of Egypt.

---

walls, drive fugitives into pitfalls with panic, which the words of Isaiah are borrowed to describe.

43—45. The editor recalls from the Pentateuch ancient fragments, (see also Amos i. 15—17, A. V. ii. 1—3) too painfully appropriate in a crisis, which yet need not be, is in a few years seen not to be, irreparable. The extreme side means the bearded cheek. A marginal note appears in the MS. as a title, and becomes part of our text.

XXVII.

To the sons of Ammon.

1. Thus saith JEHOVAH, Has Israel no sons? or has he no heir? why does Milcom[294] inherit Gad, and his people dwell in his cities?

A. V.
XLIX. 1.

2. Therefore, behold days coming, is JEHOVAH's saying, when I sound alarm of war upon Rabbah of the Ammonites, that it be a desolate heap, and her daughters be burnt with fire; so shall Israel inherit his disinheritors, saith JEHOVAH.

3. Howl, Heshbon, for it is laid waste in ruins; cry, daughters of Rabbah, gird on sackcloth; lament, and run to and fro within the defences; for Milcom goes into slavery, his priests and his princes together.

4. Wherefore gloriest thou in thy valleys, the flow of thy valley, O refractory daughter; that trusted in her treasures, Who can come to me?

5. Behold me bringing upon thee terror, is the saying of the Lord, JEHOVAH of hosts, from all thy circuits; until you are driven out every one before him, with none to rally the runaway.

---

[294] *Milcom*; or, their king. *Vulg.* Melchom. LXX. Μελχὸλ, probably a dialectic variation of *Molech*, king, the name under which the fire-god (perhaps of the oldest Zoroastrianism?) was worshipt, specially in Ammon and Moab: comp. 1 Kings xi. 5—7; 2 Kings xxiii. 10—13; Jer. xxxix. (A. V. xxxii. 35); Zeph. i. 5; perhaps Amos iv. 17, (A. V. v. 26,) where see Note; Psalm cvi. 38; Gen. xxii. 2; Jos. J. Ant. i. 7; Plin. H. N. xxx. 2.

1—5. Slight as is the record rescued by Josephus (c. Apion) from Berossus, that Nebuchadnezzar conquered Egypt and Syria and Phœnicia and Arabia, we can conceive that his career would give Jeremiah ample reason to propound the symbolical cup of wrath to Judah's neighbours in turn. He who was poet of the exile, as

Ch.
XXVII

A.V
XLIX.

6. [Though hereafter I turn again the captivity of the sons of Ammon, is JEHOVAH's saying.]²⁹⁵

To Edom.

7. Thus saith JEHOVAH of hosts, Is wisdom no more in Teman? is counsel perished from the prudent?²⁹⁶ their wisdom vanished?

8. Turn away²⁹⁷ in flight, go dwell in depth, inhabitants of Dedan, for I have brought on Esau his calamity, the time of his visitation.

---

²⁹⁵ Verse 6, wanting in the LXX., is one of the signs of later editorship in our Hebrew text. Events had shewn, or human sagacity would anticipate a revival from the evil day.

²⁹⁶ *From the prudent.* LXX. ἐκ συνετῶν, though *Vulg.* not so well, a filiis.

²⁹⁷ *Turn away, &c.* *Vulg.* fugite, et terga vertite, descendite in voraginem; I conceive there is a triple series of imperatives, with that dual interlinking of verb, common in Hebrew, of which this chapter presents an instance below. With all this part should be compared Obadiah.

---

well as monitor of his people would feel impelled to read to rival nations the lesson of their calamities. He would do so the more, since he found materials at hand in fragments from older prophets, which in the case of Moab seem to overpaint the measure of her sufferings at this period, comp. ch. xxxv. 3, with xliii. 11, and 2 Kings xxiv. 2. The Ammonites, ruder stem-brothers of Moab, having always grudged to Israel the range between the Arnon and Jabbok, would take advantage of troubled times to press down from the tributaries of the northern stream, and re-inherit what had become Israel's inheritance, comp. Judges xi. 13. The daughters I understand literally: most critics as smaller towns. The valley is the Jabbok, over which Rabbah was built.

7—10. This re-adaptation of Obadiah rather implies

9. If grape-gatherers had come to thee, would not they have spared gleanings? if thieves in the night, they would have destroyed *but* their fill.

10. Nay, but I have stript Esau, uncovered his secret places, so that he hides himself, and is not hidden;[298] destroyed are his seed and his brethren; yea, his neighbours, so that there is no one, *who should say,* 11.[299] Leave thy orphans, I will preserve them, or thy widows, let them trust in me.

12. For thus saith JEHOVAH, Behold they whose destiny[300] was not to drink the cup, drink deeply; and shalt thou go utterly unscathed? thou shalt not go unscathed, thou shalt surely drink.

13. For by myself have I sworn, is JEHOVAH's saying, that Bozrah shall become a desolation *and* a reproach, a waste and a curse; and all her cities shall become perpetual wastes.

---

[298] *And is not hidden.* Heb. is not able.
[299] *So that there is no one, who should say.* The Greek runs, ὤλοντο διὰ χεῖρα ἀδελφοῦ αὐτοῦ, γείτονός μου· καὶ οὐκ ἔστιν Ὑπολείπεσθαι ὀρφανόν σου, ἵνα ζήσηται· καὶ ἐγὼ ζήσομαι, καὶ αἱ χῆραι ἐπ' ἐμὲ πεποίθασιν. Kimchi, followed by Schnurrer, suggested the connexion of verse 11, as a speech, with the preceding. I think, though not without misgiving as to the text, that this is more probable than the introduction of a Divine promise; especially as we have just below a speech thrown in with like abruptness.
[300] 12. *Destiny.* Heb. judgment.

---

the higher antiquity of the book passing under that name. Verse 11, is either a relenting promise of mercy to the young, yet so thrown in as to intensify despair for the old; or else it is such a vainly desired comfort as no neighbour will survive to utter.

12. If Judah drinks the cup of deadly wine, hand it on to Edom. 13—18. The bitter hatred of a people

208   THE HEBREW PROPHETS.

Ch. XXVII.

14. [301]I heard a rumour from JEHOVAH, and an embassy sent among the nations, Assemble yourselves, and come against her, and rise up for the battle; 15. for lo, I have made thee small among the nations, despicable amongst men thy terribleness.[302]

A. V XLIX. 1

16. The pride of thy heart deluded thee, dweller in the clefts of the rock, holder of the height of the hill; though thou make thy nest aloft as the eagle, is JEHOVAH's saying, from thence will I pull thee down, 17. and Edom shall be a desolation; every passer thereby shall be amazed, and hiss, at all her wounds; 18. as in the overthrow of Sodom and Gomorrah, and the neighbours thereof, no man, saith JEHOVAH, shall dwell there, neither son of man sojourn there.

19. Behold he comes up[303] as a lion from the overgrowth[304] of Jordan to the perennial[305] pasture; for in a

---

[301] Comp. Obadiah, 1, 2.

[302] *Thy terribleness.* This word belongs by rhythm, and by sufficiency of subject in the next clause, to verse 15, though not by punctuation. I suspect it was originally a causative verb, either ת having taken the place of ה by error, or the form being exceptional, as in Hosea xi. 3, תרגלתי for חרגלתי.

[303] *He comes up.* The invader.

[304] *Over-growth,* either of thicket and overgrown bank, or swell of water. See note above, xii. 5.

[305] *Perennial,* takes its sense from the context, as in Amos iv. 16, (A. V. v. 24,) else it might mean strength, as of fortress, if that suited the metaphor here. However much the Heb. *who,* מי, might be a relative, as in Ex. xxxii. 33, it seems better interrogative throughout here.

---

akin, but subjected, which had thrown off Judah's yoke and revenged itself scoffingly (Psalm cxxxvii.), sees messengers of heaven in the destroyers of Bozrah, a sacred war in the depopulation of the land.

19. The people of shepherds became as a flock to be scared by the invader as he comes in leonine strength to their pasture (or to their impregnable Bozrah), trampling

moment, *he saith*, I will drive him from thereupon; and who is the champion[306] I shall meet thereon? For who is like me? or who is the shepherd that will stand before me? 20. Hearken therefore to the design of JEHOVAH, which he has designed against Edom, and his purposes which he has purposed against the dwellers of Teman; Surely he shall tear even of the little ones of the flock;[307] surely he shall lay waste for them their pasture.

21. At the sound of their fall the earth trembled; *there was* crying, the sound thereof heard in the sea of weeds.[308]

22. Behold, he comes up as an eagle, and soars, and spreads his wings over Bozrah; and the heart of the warriors of Edom shall be in that day as the heart of a woman in pangs.

To Damascus.

23. Confounded is Hamath, and Arpad, for they have

---

[306] *Champion.* Heb. chosen, or youth. The speaker throughout is the leonine invader. Edom is the flock to be driven off the pasture.

[307] *Surely he shall tear even of the little ones of the flock;* i.e. reading, יִסְחָב וּמְצָעִירֵי and comparing Daniel viii. 9, with Ges. Thes. in v. מִן. But in retaining this, as the least modification the text will bear, I acknowledge my own suspicion that Zoar is here meant; at least that this passage must be governed by xxvi. (A. V. xlviii. 4,) and that by Isaiah, xiv. 5. (A. V. xv.)

[308] *Sea of weeds;* or, sea of limit; *i.e.* the narrow, contracted sea. Heb. Yam-sûph; but as it bordered Edom, the red man's land, it became with the Greeks, thence with ourselves, the Red Sea.

---

as he goes, and terrible, and not counting on resistance, nor thinking native chieftain his equal; but (20) by Jehovah's design, tearing even the little ones (or out of the little city Zoar), and leaving the land waste.

21. The air is already full of the sound of ruin, and (22) the eagle swoop imminent.

Ch.
XXVII.
heard evil tidings; they are dissolved [in a sea of] disquiet,[309] that cannot be at rest.

24. Damascus has grown faint, turned round to flee; and dread has taken hold of her, like one bearing child.

25. [310]How is not left the city of praise, the city of [my] delight!

26. Therefore her choice youth fall in her streets, and all the men of war are cut off in that day, is the saying of JEHOVAH of hosts;

27. And I kindle fire on the wall of Damascus, to devour the palaces of Benhadad.[311]

To Kedar and to the kingdoms of Hazor, which Nebuchadrezzar king of Babel smote.[312]

---

[309] *In a sea of disquiet.* I confess this image seems more modern than Hebrew. But what was the sea doing at Damascus? Ewald most ingeniously substitutes a word meaning senses (בְּ from בִּין) and translates, their senses are bewildered.* But if I touched the text, I should rather look for a word rendering the Greek ἐθυμώθησαν. On the whole, not finding the sea mentioned by the LXX., and observing the Hebrew word for disquiet to be connected with the ripple of the waves, I suspect that some Targumist indicated that connexion by inserting or appending the word for sea. Otherwise render; because they have heard evil tidings, they are fainthearted; *as* on the sea disquiet, that can not be at rest.

[310] *Vulg.* Quomodo dereliquerunt civitatem laudabilem, urbem lætitiæ LXX. πῶς οὐχὶ ἐγκατέλιπε πόλιν ἐμήν, κώμην ἠγάπησαν.

[311] V. 27. is from Amos. Hadad, or Hadar (LXX. ᾿Αδερ), is the frequent Syriac appellation of kings, derived from the national deity. Gen. xxv. 15; xxxvi. 39; 2 Sam. viii. 3; 2 Sam. x. 16; Zech. xii. 11; Plin. H. N. xxvii. 11, Adadunephros (a renibus), ejusdem oculus et digitus dei, et hic colitur a Syris; where the text is hopelessly corrupt, and the critics assume, perhaps erroneously, a mortal deified.

[312] Let the reader notice, that the Hebrew title says expressly, *Nebuchad-*

---

23. The Syrian cities hear with agitation (24) of their capital's distress, and (25) her strangely inexorable fate, (26) amidst slaughter, and (27) flames, such as Amos saw.

---

* 'Ihr sinn ist in bekümmerniss—בְּ vielleicht aus בִּין *verstand* verkürzt,

'Vgl. بِي V. auch بَلَى und بَي verstehen, *merken*.'—Ewald, Proph. A. B. II. p. 226, 227.

28. Thus saith Jehovah, Rise you, go up to Kedar, and plunder the sons of the east; 29. Their tents and their flocks shall they take; their pavilions and all their furniture and their camels shall they take to themselves, and raise a cry over them, Terror all around.

30. Flee you, go exceeding far, dwell in depth, inhabitants of Hazor, is Jehovah's saying, for Nebuchadrezzar, king of Babel, has taken counsel against you, and planned a purpose against you.

31. Arise, is Jehovah's saying, go up against the easy nation, dwelling carelessly, which has neither gates nor bars, but with habitations apart.

32. And let their camels be for spoil, and the multitude of their herds for plunder; and I will scatter to every wind the tonsured polls,[313] and assemble from every quarter their calamity, is Jehovah's saying; 33. so that Hazor[314] become a haunt of jackals, a desolation for ever; that neither man dwell there, nor son of man sojourn therein.

A.V. xlix. 28.

---

rezzar smote, so that the Anglican version greatly errs in making the title predictive, whatever the text below may be. Probably the prophet only assigns Divine forecast as cause to an already known event.

[313] *The tonsured polls;* or, the shorn of cheek; *i.e.* certain Arabs, who practised a religious tonsure. See above, Jer. ix. 26, and Herod. iii. 8.

[314] *Hazor.* Not only the frequency of this name, as in Jabin's realm, and in the 'fox-village' of the tribe of Simeon (and specially frequent towards the desert), but the application of the term here forbids us to seek closer identification than with some district of Arabia Petræa, bordering on Edom, and presenting the happier aspect of pastoral life in village-like cluster of tents.

---

28. The conqueror's mission from Jehovah includes the pastoral tents of the desert, though (31) not provoking war by walls (32) tempting plunder by herds. 33. The ruin is thorough enough to seem lasting, though in the event easily repaired by moving Nomads. The sons of the East remind us of Job i. 3; Numb. xxiii. 7; 1 Kings iv. 30; Isa. xvi. 19 (A. V. xix. 11).

212   THE HEBREW PROPHETS.

Ch. XXVII. *That which was the word of* JEHOVAH *to Jeremiah the* A.V.x 34. *prophet against Elam, in the beginning of the reign of Zedekiah king of Judah, saying:*

35. Thus saith JEHOVAH of hosts, Behold me shivering the bow of Elam,³¹⁵ the chief of their valiancy.

36. And I bring upon Elam the four winds from the four quarters of the heavens, and scatter them towards all those winds; so that there be no nation whither the outcasts of Elam shall not come; 37. and I shatter Elam

---

³¹⁵ *Elam.* This name in the Prophets, here, as in Isaiah xviii. xix. (A.V. xxi. xxii.) stands for quivered Persia, or for Iran, certainly for an Iranian people. Hence it is one of the least explained difficulties in the Mosaic genealogies, that in Gen. x. 22, Elam is with the Assyrians and Chaldees affiliated upon Shem. The simplest explanation seems, that the framer of the genealogies meant by Elam Elymais, at the immediate head of the Persian gulf, or not much more; such part, that is, of Susiana and Syro-media, as lying between Assyria and Persia underwent stages of Semitic occupation. If we choose to add Mr. Rawlinson's favourite Cushites, we may derive some, if hardly adequate, confirmation for doing so, from Strabo's association of Memnon with the people of Susiana under the appellation of Cissians, lib. xv. c. 228. The reader will remember, that the piece against Elam is placed by the LXX. in the xxvth chapter.* Unlike the other prophecies against the nations, it contains in the Greek the promise of restoration. Also in the Greek the date of Zedekiah's reign follows, instead of preceding, the piece; and probably arose out of mistake. If we suppose the piece sprang out of something written by Jeremiah of Persian conquests by Nebuchadnezzar, or components of his force, it would still be adapted by later editors to Alexander's conquest of Persia; and hence, as Movers or Hitzig half suggests, its place in the arrangement may refer to Alexander's movements after the battle of Issus.

This title by its form betrays comparative lateness. That portion of south-western Persia which had been Assyrian, would be claimed by dominant Babel, or by her Median (at first) allies.

37. Either Jeremiah sees the Syro-chaldæan empire appropriating Elymais, or more commensurately with the width of expression, a later collector of fragments places under the name of the most comprehensive of the

---

* See p. 184.

before their enemies and before the seekers of their life, and bring upon them evil, the fierceness of my anger, is JEHOVAH's saying, and I will send after them the sword, until I consume them, 38. and set my throne in Elam, and destroy from thence king and princes, is JEHOVAH's saying,

38. Though it be in the aftertime of days, that I turn again the captivity of Elam, is JEHOVAH's saying.

A.V. xlix. 37.

XXVIII.

1. In the beginning of the reign of Jehoiakim, the son of Josiah king of Judah came this word from JEHOVAH, saying, 2. Thus saith JEHOVAH; Stand in the court of JEHOVAH's house, and speak unto all the cities of Judah, which come to worship in JEHOVAH's house, all the words that I command thee to speak unto them; diminish not a word: 3. If so be they will hearken, and turn every man from his evil way, that I may repent me of the evil, which I purpose to do unto them because of the evil of their doings. 4. And thou shalt say unto them, Thus saith JEHOVAH; If ye will not hearken to me, to walk in my law, which I have set before you, 5. To hearken to the words of my servants the prophets, whom I sent unto you, both rising up early, and sending *them*, but ye have not

A.V. xxvi. 1.

---

prophets, a vivid denunciation of the four battles which broke Persia, and the calamities under him who called himself son of Zeus, though an unseen Judge presided at their distribution. 38. Yet the ruin need not be for ever.

XXVIII. This is the prose summary of the events which attended the teaching already given in poetical form, from chapters i. to ix., especially in chap. vii. Compare vii. title, and vv. 10, 11, 12, with vv. 2, 6, 9, 12, here.

Ch.
XXVIII.
hearkened; 6. Then will I make this house like Shiloh, and will make this city a curse to all the nations of the earth. 7. So the priests, and the prophets, and all the people, heard Jeremiah speaking these words in the house of JEHOVAH.

8. Now it came to pass, when Jeremiah had made an end of speaking all that JEHOVAH had commanded *him* to speak unto all the people, that the priests, and the prophets, and all the people, took him, saying, Thou shalt surely die. 9. Why hast thou prophesied in the name of JEHOVAH, saying, This house shall be like Shiloh, and this city shall be desolate without an inhabitant? And all the people were gathered against Jeremiah in the house of JEHOVAH.

10. When the princes of Judah heard these things, then they came up from the king's house unto the house of JEHOVAH, and sat down in the entry of the new gate of JEHOVAH's *house*. 11. Then spake the priests and the prophets[316] unto the princes, and to all the people, saying, This man *is* worthy to die; for he hath prophesied against this city, as ye have heard with your ears.

12. Then spake Jeremiah unto all the princes, and to all the people, saying, JEHOVAH sent me to prophesy against this house, and against this city all the words that ye have heard. 13. Therefore now amend your ways and your

---

[316] The prophets join the priests in denouncing Jeremiah. This the LXX. characteristically alter into οἱ ψευδοπροφῆται, but no such order existed as distinct from the true; nor, while they and Jeremiah lived, was there criterion between the parties, except the nature of the doctrine of each.

---

9. Shiloh, the old Ephraimite sanctuary, where Eli dwelt, and Samuel grew up (whence the phrase "our living Dread, which dwelleth in Silo,") probably also the city mentioned in Jacob's death-song, had given sad type of Zion's fate.

Ch.
XVIII.
doings, and obey the voice of JEHOVAH your God; and JEHOVAH will repent him of the evil that he hath pronounced against you. 14. As for me, behold, I am in your hand: do with me as seemeth good and meet unto you. 15. But know ye for certain, that if ye put me to death, ye shall surely bring innocent blood upon yourselves, and upon this city, and upon the inhabitants thereof: for of a truth JEHOVAH hath sent me unto you to speak all these words in your ears.

A.V. xxvi. 13.

16. Then said the princes and all the people unto the priests and to the prophets; This man *is* not worthy to die: for he hath spoken to us in the name of JEHOVAH our God. 17. Then rose up certain of the elders of the land, and spake to all the assembly of the people, saying, 18. Micah the Morasthite prophesied in the days of Hezekiah king of Judah, and spake to all the people of Judah, saying, Thus saith JEHOVAH of hosts, Zion shall be plowed *like* a field, and Jerusalem shall become heaps, and the mountain of the house as the high places of a forest. 19. Did Hezekiah king of Judah, and all Judah put him at all to death? did he not fear JEHOVAH, and besought JEHOVAH, and JEHOVAH repented him of the evil which he had pronounced against them? Thus might we procure great evil against our souls. 20. And there was also a man that prophesied in the name of JEHOVAH, Urijah the son of Shemaiah of Kirjath-jearim, who prophesied against

---

18. On the conditional character of Micah's threatenings, so that in his book the presentiment of brighter days appears as immediately following, see notes on Micah iii. iv.

20—23. These verses seem rather an historical illustration, than an argument which could have been addres-

Cн.
XXVIII.
A.V. xx
21.

this city, and against this land, according to all the words of Jeremiah: 21. And when Jehoiakim the king, with all his mighty men, and all the princes, heard his words, the king sought to put him to death; but when Urijah heard it, he was afraid, and fled, and went into Egypt. 22. And Jehoiakim the king sent men into Egypt, *namely*, Elnathan the son of Achbor, and *certain* men with him into Egypt: 23. And they fetched forth Urijah out of Egypt, and brought him unto Jehoiakim the king; who slew him with the sword, and cast his dead body into the graves of the common people. 24. Nevertheless the hand of Ahikam the son of Shaphan was with Jeremiah, that they should not give him into the hand of the people to put him to death.

XXIX.

Cн.
XXIX.
A.V
xxxv.

1. The word which came unto Jeremiah from JEHOVAH, in the days of Jehoiakim the son of Josiah king of Judah, saying, 2. Go unto the house of the Rechabites, and speak unto them, and bring them into the house of JEHOVAH, into one of the chambers, and give them wine to drink. 3. Then I took Jaazaniah the son of Jeremiah,

---

sed to the king. Of this Uriah, says Hitzig, is otherwise nothing known. More sanguine critics (Bunsen, *Gott in d. G.* I. p. 450) see in him the author of the three chapters arranged in our Bibles as the last three of Zechariah. The contents of those chapters do not correspond with the preaching ascribed to Uriah here. He would be more readily surrendered to Jehoiakim, as to an ally of Egypt.

24. Ahikam's son, Gedaliah, appears, xlii. 2, (A. V. xxxix. 14,) as protecting the prophet.

1—19. Jonadab, son of Rechab, a friend of the usur-

the son of Habaziniah, and his brethren, and all his sons, and the whole house of the Rechabites; 4. And I brought them into the house of JEHOVAH, into the chamber of the sons of Hanan, the son of Igdaliah, a servant of God, which *was* by the chamber of the princes, which *was* above the chamber of Maaseiah the son of Shallum, the keeper of the door : 5. And I set before the sons of the house of the Rechabites pots full of wine, and cups, and I said unto them, Drink ye wine. 6. But they said, We will drink no wine : for Jonadab the son of Rechab our father commanded us, saying, Ye shall drink no wine, *neither* ye, nor your sons for ever : 7. Neither shall ye build house, nor sow seed, nor plant vineyard, nor have *any :* but all your days ye shall dwell in tents; that ye may live many days in the land where ye *be* strangers. 8. Thus have we obeyed the voice of Jonadab, the son of Rechab our father in all that he hath charged us, to drink no wine all our days, we, our wives, our sons, nor our daughters; 9. Nor to build houses for us to dwell in :

A. V.
xxxv. 3.

per Jehu, 280 years before this time, had after the fashion of the Kenite stem to which he belonged, 1 Chron. ii. 55; Judges iv. 17; Gen. xv. 19; 1 Sam. xv. 6; strictly charged his posterity to retain pastoral habits, living in tents, and not sowing corn, or planting vine. The fair side of this primitive life struck the prophet, though its weakness comes out in the Rechabite necessity of taking shelter in Jerusalem, (just as our Quakers are protected by armed governments). Comparing their wild faithfulness with the relapses of civilized but refractory Judah, the Prophet takes them into the inhabited precincts of the temple, to which as priest he had access, and presses on them wine. Their refusal points in dramatic symbol the warning against Judah, more favoured, but less obedient.

neither have we vineyard, nor field, nor seed : 10. But we have dwelt in tents, and have obeyed, and done according to all that Jonadab our father commanded us. 11. But it came to pass, when Nebuchadrezzar king of Babylon came up into the land, that we said, Come, and let us go to Jerusalem for fear of the army of the Chaldeans, and for fear of the army of the Syrians: so we dwell at Jerusalem. 12. Then came the word of JEHOVAH unto Jeremiah, saying, 13. Thus saith JEHOVAH of hosts, the God of Israel; Go and tell the men of Judah and the inhabitants of Jerusalem, Will ye not receive instruction to hearken to my words? saith JEHOVAH. 14. The words of Jonadab the son of Rechab, that he commanded his sons not to drink wine, are performed; for unto this day they drink none, but obey their father's commandment: notwithstanding I have spoken unto you, rising early and speaking; but ye hearkened not unto me. 15. I have sent also unto you all my servants the prophets, rising up

---

The theory of a Kenite tradition underlying Scripture as guarding the spiritual in antagonism to the priestly (or Pharisaic) principle, is but a tedious paradox. There is more reason, though little can be derived from this chapter, for the belief that Jonadab had Nazarite affinities (Amos ii. 8, A.V. 11), and that his posterity becoming incorporated in Judah, acquired Levitical privileges. What is most obvious is that the ascetic type of religious Nomad has frequently recurred in Arabia from the Nabathæans of Diodorus Siculus (xix. 94), to the earlier Mahomedans, and the Wahabees with whom Mr. Palgrave has rendered us familiar. The traveller Niebuhr specially identified the Rechabites with the Beni-Kheiber in the hills north-east of Medina. Benjamin of Tudela in the 12th century is quoted as having found them in the same region. Nearer Mecca, or further south, Joseph Wolff

early and sending *them*, saying, Return ye now every man from his evil way, and amend your doings, and go not after other gods to serve them, and ye shall dwell in the land which I have given to you and to your fathers: but ye have not inclined your ear, nor hearkened unto me. 16. Because the sons of Jonadab the son of Rechab have performed the commandment of their father, which he commanded them; but this people hath not hearkened unto me: 17. Therefore thus saith JEHOVAH God of hosts, the God of Israel; Behold, I will bring upon Judah, and upon all the inhabitants of Jerusalem, all the evil that I have pronounced against them: because I have spoken unto them, but they have not heard; and I have called unto them, but they have not answered.

A. V.
xxxv. 15.

18. And Jeremiah said unto the house of the Rechabites, Thus saith JEHOVAH of hosts, the God of Israel; Because ye have obeyed the commandment of Jonadab your father, and kept all his precepts, and done according unto all that he

claims to have recognised them, but under the same name as Niebuhr, and with a circumstantial fulness which needs confirmation. A subsequent traveller *(Bibl. Dict. in v.)* is quoted as finding them in a strangely different spot, by the Dead Sea. The phrase 'stand before Jehovah' might bear a sacerdotal sense, but is satisfied by 'surviving,' as in the presence of Deity. Abstinence from wine is not here enjoined, but recognised as a practice with which the Prophet sympathises, while his stress is on fidelity.

Here, as elsewhere, the LXX. render " my servants the prophets," τοὺς παῖδας μου τοὺς προφήτας. So in Acts iv. 27, "thy holy child, Jesus," has been rendered servant; though the citation of Psalm ii. renders this questionable. The most remarkable variation is that instead of the army of the Syrians, v. 11, the LXX. xlii. 11, give τῆς δυνάμεως τῶν Ἀσσυρίων, which would imply that

Ch.
XXIX. hath commanded you: 19. Therefore thus saith JEHOVAH   A. V
of hosts, the God of Israel; Jonadab the son of Rechab   xxxv. 1
shall not want a man to stand before me for ever.

XXX.

Ch. XXX. 1. And it came to pass in the fourth year of Jehoiakim   A. V
the son of Josiah king of Judah, *that* this word came unto   xxxvi.
Jeremiah from JEHOVAH, saying, 2. Take thee a roll of a
book, and write therein all the words that I have spoken
unto thee against Israel, and against Judah, and against
all the nations, from the day I spake unto thee, from the
days of Josiah, even unto this day.   3. It may be that the
house of Judah will hear all the evil which I purpose to
do unto them; that they may return every man from
his evil way; that I may forgive their iniquity and their
sin.   4. Then Jeremiah called Baruch the son of Neriah;
and Baruch wrote from the mouth of Jeremiah all the
words of JEHOVAH, which he had spoken unto him, upon a
roll of a book.   5. And Jeremiah commanded Baruch,
saying, I *am* shut up; I cannot go into the house of
JEHOVAH: 6. Therefore go thou, and read in the roll,
which thou hast written from my mouth, the words of
JEHOVAH in the ears of the people in JEHOVAH's house
upon the fasting day: and also thou shalt read them in
the ears of all Judah that come out of their cities.   7. It
may be they will present their supplication before JEHO-
VAH, and will return every one from his evil way: for great

Nineveh not having yet fallen, the 'altogether king,'
Nebuchadnezzar, was reckoned among its 'princes,' *i.e.*
vassals, hence the incident falls early in Jehoiakim's
reign.

1—32. B.C. 604, four years from the fatal battle of

JEREMIAH. 221

is the anger and the fury that JEHOVAH hath pronounced against this people. 8. And Baruch the son of Neriah did according to all that Jeremiah the prophet commanded him, reading in the book the words of JEHOVAH in JEHOVAH's house. 9. And it came to pass in the fifth year of Jehoiakim the son of Josiah king of Judah, in the ninth month,[317] *that* they proclaimed a fast before JEHOVAH to all the people in Jerusalem, and to all the people that came from the cities of Judah unto Jerusalem. 10. Then read Baruch in the book the words of Jeremiah in the house of JEHOVAH, in the chamber of Gemariah the son of Shaphan the scribe, in the higher court, at the entry of the new gate of JEHOVAH's house, in the ears of all the people. 11. When Michaiah the son of Gemariah, the son of Shaphan, had heard out of the book all the words of JEHOVAH, 12. Then he went down into the king's house, into the scribe's chamber: and, lo, all the princes sat there, *even* Elishama the scribe, and Delaiah the son of Shemaiah,

A. V.
xxxvi. 7.

---

[317] The most important variation of version in this chapter is, that the LXX. give the fifth year of Jehoiakim, in which the recital took place, as the eighth of his reign, καὶ ἐγενήθη ἐν τῷ ἔτει τῷ ὀγδόῳ. In ver. 24, the princes, instead of not fearing, are said not to have sought out, or rescued, οὐκ ἐζήτησαν.

Megiddo, two from the greater recoil of Carchemish, and downfall of Nineveh, Nebuchadnezzar, hitherto his father's vice-gerent, becomes full king. Jehoiakim, set up by Egypt, had reigned four years. That he must transfer his allegiance to Babylon, or that his little realm would suffer the penalties of contumacy, could escape no sagacious observer, least of all the large party whose sympathies, as those of the pious Josiah, Ahikam, and perhaps Elnathan, had been on the side of alliance with the kindred nations of Assyria and Babylon, instead of with Egypt. In such a crisis, Jeremiah felt impelled to gather

Ch. XXX. and Elnathan the son of Achbor, and Gemariah the son of Shaphan, and Zedekiah the son of Hananiah, and all the princes. 13. Then Michaiah declared unto them all the words that he had heard, when Baruch read the book in the ears of the people. 14. Therefore all the princes sent Jehudi the son of Nethaniah, the son of Shelemiah, the son of Cushi, unto Baruch, saying, Take in thine hand the roll wherein thou hast read in the ears of the people, and come. So Baruch the son of Neriah took the roll in his hand, and came unto them. 15. And they said unto him, Sit down now, and read it in our ears. So Baruch read *it* in their ears. 16. Now it came to pass, when they had heard all the words, they were afraid both one and other, and said unto Baruch, We will surely tell the king of all these words. 17. And they asked Baruch, saying, Tell us now, How didst thou write all these words at his mouth? 18. Then Baruch answered them, He pronounced all these words unto me with his mouth, and I wrote *them* with ink in the book. 19. Then said the princes unto Baruch, Go, hide thee, thou and Jeremiah; and let no man know where ye be.

20. And they went in to the king into the court, but they laid up the roll in the chamber of Elishama the scribe, and told all the words in the ears of the king. 21. So the king sent Jehudi to fetch the roll;

A. V. xxxvi. 1

---

into a volume a summary of his teachings or warnings during the preceding period of three and twenty years. Much of what we now read from the first to about the twentieth or twenty-fourth chapters of our book would enter into this volume. Some may suppose a part of the subsequent utterances over the nations to have been included. We of course exclude all chapters belonging to the reign of Zedekiah. As the composition occupied the

and he took it out of Elishama the scribe's chamber. And Jehudi read it in the ears of the king, and in the ears of all the princes which stood beside the king. 22. Now the king sat in the winterhouse in the ninth month: and *there was a fire* on the hearth burning before him. 23. And it came to pass, *that* when Jehudi had read three or four leaves, he cut it with a penknife, and cast *it* into the fire that *was* on the hearth, until all the roll was consumed in the fire that *was* on the hearth. 24. Yet they were not afraid, nor rent their garments, *neither* the king, nor any of his servants that heard all these words. 25. Nevertheless Elnathan and Delaiah and Gemariah had made intercession to the king that he would not burn the roll: but he would not hear them. 26. But the king commanded Jerahmeel the son of Hammelech, and Seraiah the son of Azriel, and Shelemiah the son of Abdeel, to take Baruch the scribe and Jeremiah the prophet: but JEHOVAH hid them.

27. Then the word of JEHOVAH came to Jeremiah, after that the king had burned the roll, and the words which Baruch wrote at the mouth of Jeremiah, saying, 28. Take thee again another roll, and write in it all the former words that were in the first roll, which Jehoiakim the king of Judah hath burned. 29. And thou shalt say to Jehoiakim king of Judah, Thus saith JEHOVAH; Thou hast burned this

A. V.
xxxvi. 21.

---

prophet a year (ver. 9), we must conceive of him as employed in the toils of authorship. When the perusal of the threatening scroll was transferred from the temple to the palace, the princes treated Baruch with courtesy, inviting him to sit, unless we treat ver. 15, with the LXX. as an injunction to read a second time, πάλιν ἀνάγνωθι εἰς τὰ ὦτα ἡμῶν, which the text might be punctuated to bear. The king, more irritated, threw the volume into

Ch. XXX. roll, saying, Why hast thou written therein, saying, The A. king of Babylon shall certainly come and destroy this xxxv land, and shall cause to cease from thence man and beast? 30. Therefore thus saith JEHOVAH of Jehoiakim king of Judah; He shall have none to sit upon the throne of David: and his dead body shall be cast out in the day to the heat, and in the night to the frost. 31. And I will punish him and his seed and his servants for their iniquity; and I will bring upon them, and upon the inhabitants of Jerusalem, and upon the men of Judah, all the evil that I have pronounced against them; but they hearkened not.

32. Then took Jeremiah another roll, and gave it to Baruch the scribe, the son of Neriah; who wrote therein from the mouth of Jeremiah all the words of the book which Jehoiakim king of Judah had burned in the fire: and there were added besides unto them many like words.

XXXI.[318]

Ch. XXXI. The word that Jeremiah the prophet spake unto Baruch the son of Neriah, when he had written these words in a book at the mouth of Jeremiah, in the fourth year of A. V.

---

[318] The LXX. give this chapter after ch. li.; rightly seeing it to have the nature of an appendix.

---

the fire, and so prepared the way for the many recasts which the book has undergone. The prophet restores and amplifies his work, adding fresh recollections, resembling, as the Hebrew and Greek say, the first, or as the Vulgate says, more than the first, 'multo plures quam antea fuerant;' perhaps further utterance against the nations, perhaps narrative of the circumstances which had attended his original warnings.

1—5. When Baruch had written all his master's

Jehoiakim the son of Josiah king of Judah, saying, 2. Thus saith JEHOVAH, the God of Israel, unto thee, O Baruch; 3. Thou didst say, Woe is me now! for JEHOVAH hath added grief to my sorrow; I fainted in my sighing, and I find no rest. 4. Thus shalt thou say unto him, JEHOVAH saith thus; Behold, *that* which I have built will I break down, and that which I have planted I will pluck up, even this whole land. 5. And seekest thou great things for thyself? seek *them* not: for, behold, I will bring evil upon all flesh, saith JEHOVAH: but thy life will I give unto thee for a prey in all places whither thou goest.

A. V. XLV. 2.

XXXII.

1. And king Zedekiah the son of Josiah reigned instead of Coniah the son of Jehoiakim, whom Nebuchadrezzar king of Babylon made king in the land of Judah. 2. But neither he, nor his servants, nor the people of the land, did hearken unto the words of JEHOVAH, which he spake by the prophet Jeremiah. 3. And Zedekiah the king

A V. XXXVII. 1.

---

warnings, a word of consolation, yet soberness, to his fainting spirit was natural. As our text runs, it came in this place. But he would need it more in his Egyptian exile; and there, as the Hebrew and Greek agree, it came to him, at the end of the last utterance upon Egypt. Only then, we must suppose the words of ver. 1, *in the fourth year of king Jehoiakim*, to be the mistake of an editor, who thought of the scroll burnt and restored. Had I ventured to remove them into the margin, I needed not have altered the place of the chapter.

1—21. Of the latter years of Jehoiakim we hear little from our prophet. But in 597, the eleventh year of his reign, he was dethroned by Nebuchadnezzar, as we must suppose from comparing the simple statement of 2 Kings xxiv. 2—6, that he slept with his fathers, with the ac-

Ch. XXXII. sent Jehucal the son of Shelemiah and Zephaniah the son of Maaseiah the priest to the prophet Jeremiah, saying, Pray now unto JEHOVAH our God for us. 4. Now Jeremiah came in and went out among the people: for they had not put him into prison. 5. Then Pharaoh's army was come forth out of Egypt: and when the Chaldeans that besieged Jerusalem heard tidings of them, they departed from Jerusalem.

6. Then came the word of JEHOVAH unto the prophet Jeremiah, saying, 7. Thus saith JEHOVAH, the God of Israel; Thus shall ye say to the king of Judah, that sent you unto me to enquire of me; Behold, Pharaoh's army, which is come forth to help you, shall return to Egypt into their own land. 8. And the Chaldeans shall come again, and fight against this city, and take it, and burn it with fire. 9. Thus saith JEHOVAH; Deceive not yourselves, saying, The Chaldeans shall surely depart from us: for they shall not depart. 10. For though ye had smitten the whole army of the Chaldeans that fight against you, and there remained *but* wounded men among them, *yet* should they rise up every man in his tent, and burn this city with fire.

---

count in 2 Chron. xxxvi. 6, of his being bound to be carried to Babylon, and with the narrative of Josephus, X. vi. that he was slain, and his carcase cast from the walls; though this last seems to be an assumption moulded upon Jer. xxi. (A. V. xxii.) 19, which implies something of the kind, though hardly reconcilable with 2 Kings xxiv. 6. See above, note on Jer. xxi. 19. At all events, in 597, the great captivity properly begins, Jehoiachin, the stripling-king of eighteen, (for this suits the mention of him in Jer. xxii. better than the later account which makes him a boy of eight,) being carried off with all the notables of Jerusalem. Zedekiah, one of the gentle and helpless beings, in whom dynasties are apt amidst calamities to

11. And it came to pass, that when the army of the Chaldeans was broken up from Jerusalem for fear of Pharaoh's army, 12. then Jeremiah went forth out of Jerusalem to go into the land of Benjamin, to separate himself thence in the midst of the people. 13. And when he was in the gate of Benjamin, a captain of the ward *was* there, whose name *was* Irijah, the son of Shelemiah, the son of Hananiah; and he took Jeremiah the prophet, saying, Thou fallest away to the Chaldeans. 14. Then said Jeremiah, *It is* false; I fall not away to the Chaldeans. But he hearkened not to him: so Irijah took Jeremiah, and brought him to the princes. 15. Wherefore the princes were wroth with Jeremiah, and smote him, and put him in prison in the house of Jonathan the scribe; for they had made that the prison.

16. When Jeremiah was entered into the dungeon, and into the cabins, and Jeremiah had remained there many days; 17. then Zedekiah the king sent, and took him out: and the king asked him secretly in his

---

come to an end, seems to have his accession heralded at first by the prophets, at least by those whose sympathies were with Nebuchadnezzar; but vainly, by subsequent submission to all parties in turn, attempts to avert the catastrophe. Goaded against his judgment into resistance, but in no other way doing evil that we can specify, he undergoes from the ninth to the eleventh year of his reign a siege which terminates fatally for the city of David. To this period, 588—86, the eleven chapters hence following, which place in strong light the internal factions, the vain hopes from Egypt, the prophet's warnings, and the fatal ending, seem mostly to belong. Here also Ezekiel, chap. xvii. and chaps. xxix.—xxxii. should be compared. The allegation of Josephus, X. vii. that Zedekiah was "a despiser of justice and duty," is not only

Ch. XXXII.

house, and said, Is there *any* word from JEHOVAH? And Jeremiah said, There is: for, said he, thou shalt be delivered into the hand of the king of Babylon. 18. Moreover Jeremiah said unto king Zedekiah, What have I offended against thee, or against thy servants, or against this people, that ye have put me in prison? 19. Where *are* now your prophets which prophesied unto you, saying, The king of Babylon shall not come against you, nor against this land? 20. Therefore hear now, I pray thee, O my lord the king: let my supplication, I pray thee, be accepted before thee; that thou cause me not to return to the house of Jonathan the scribe, lest I die there. 21. Then Zedekiah the king commanded that they should commit Jeremiah into the court of the prison, and that they should give him daily a piece of bread out of the bakers' street, until all the bread in the city were spent. Thus Jeremiah remained in the court of the prison.

XXXIII.

Ch. XXXIII.

1. The word which came unto Jeremiah from JEHOVAH,

---

unsupported by facts, but is at variance with the same historian's mention in the same chapter of his justice and kindness to Jeremiah; so that we can only see in it a strong instance of the servile subordination of character to event, to which the Jewish historian is prone. Again, although the prediction in Ezekiel xii. 13, that the king should die in Babylon, but not see it, has a genuine air, and seems remarkably fulfilled, yet, since there is no inconsistency between that prediction as it stands in clear terms, and the warnings of these chapters of Jeremiah, we must conclude that Josephus's account (X. vii.) of the king's disbelieving them both on account of an apparent disagreement between them, is entirely fabulous.

1—14. During the preludes to the siege, the king's

when king Zedekiah sent unto him Pashur the son of Melchiah, and Zephaniah the son of Maaseiah the priest, saying, 2. Enquire, I pray thee, of JEHOVAH for us; for Nebuchadrezzar king of Babylon maketh war against us; if so be that JEHOVAH will deal with us according to all his wondrous works, that he may go up from us.

3. Then said Jeremiah unto them, Thus shall ye say to Zedekiah: 4. Thus saith JEHOVAH the God of Israel; Behold, I will turn back the weapons of war that *are* in your hands, wherewith ye fight against the king of Babylon, and *against* the Chaldeans, which besiege you without the walls, and I will assemble them into the midst of this city. 5. And I myself will fight against you with an outstretched hand and with a strong arm, even in anger, and in fury, and in great wrath. 6. And I will smite the inhabitants of this city, both man and beast: they shall die of a great pestilence. 7. And afterward, saith JEHOVAH, I will deliver Zedekiah king of Judah, and his servants, and the people, and such as are left in this city from the pestilence, from the sword, and from the famine, into the hand of Nebuchadrezzar king of Babylon, and into the hand of their enemies, and into the hand of those that seek their life: and he shall smite them with the edge of the sword; he shall not spare them, neither have pity, nor have mercy.

8. And unto this people thou shalt say, Thus saith JEHOVAH; Behold, I set before you the way of life, and the way of death. 9. He that abideth in this city shall die by the sword, and by the famine, and by the

---

counsellors, desiring a more hopeful word, plead with Jeremiah, as they consult him; but the hour of destiny has sounded to the Prophet; nor will her fortified rock and hill-encircled pleateau or vale protect Jerusalem. The closing verses have a traditional tone, as if echoed, like

Ch. XXXIII. pestilence: but he that goeth out, and falleth to the Chaldeans that besiege you, he shall live, and his life shall be unto him for a prey. 10. For I have set my face against this city for evil, and not for good, saith JEHOVAH: it shall be given into the hand of the king of Babylon, and he shall burn it with fire. 11. And touching the house of the king of Judah, say, Hear ye the word of JEHOVAH: 12. O house of David, thus saith JEHOVAH: Execute judgment in the morning, and deliver *him that is* spoiled out of the hand of the oppressor, lest my fury go out like fire, and burn that none can quench *it*, because of the evil of your doings. 13. Behold, I. am against thee, O inhabitant of the valley, *and* rock of the plain, saith JEHOVAH; which say, Who shall come down against us? or who shall enter into our habitations? 14. But I will punish you according to the fruit of your doings, saith JEHOVAH: and I will kindle a fire in the forest thereof, and it shall devour all things round about it.

XXXIV.

Ch. XXXIV. 1. JEHOVAH showed me, and, behold, two baskets of figs *were* set before the temple of JEHOVAH, after that Nebuchadrezzar king of Babylon had carried away captive Jeconiah the son of Jehoiakim king of Judah, and the princes of Judah, with the carpenters and smiths, from Jerusalem, and had brought them to Babylon.

---

the utterance on Moab, from some ancient strain. They resemble, amidst the prophets remaining, most nearly Amos. Hitzig would connect them in sequence with chap. xxi. (A. V. xxii.) but needlessly. The recurrent name, Pashur, though of a different person and time, is thought to have suggested the arrangement of this chapter after the xxth in the Hebrew.

1—10. During Zedekiah's reign, at a period earlier than most of the chapters in this group, Jeremiah has a

2. One basket *had* very good figs, *even* like the figs *that are* first ripe: and the other basket *had* very bad figs, which could not be eaten, they were so bad. 3. Then said Jehovah unto me, What seest thou, Jeremiah? And I said, Figs; the good figs, very good; and the evil, very evil, that cannot be eaten, they are so evil.

4. Again the word of Jehovah came unto me, saying, 5. Thus saith Jehovah, the God of Israel; Like these good figs, so will I acknowledge them that are carried away captive of Judah, whom I have sent out of this place into the land of the Chaldeans for *their* good. 6. For I will set mine eyes upon them for good, and I will bring them again to this land: and I will build them, and not pull *them* down; and I will plant them, and not pluck *them* up. 7. And I will give them an heart to know me, that I *am* Jehovah; and they shall be my people, and I will be their God; for they shall return unto me with their whole heart. 8. And as the evil figs which cannot be eaten, they are so evil; surely thus saith Jehovah, So will I give Zedekiah the king of Judah, and his princes, and the residue of Jerusalem, that remain in this land, and them that dwell in the land of Egypt: 9. And I will deliver them to be removed into all the kingdoms of the earth for *their* hurt, *to be* a reproach and a proverb, a taunt and a curse, in all places whither I shall drive them. 10. And I will send the sword, the famine, and the pestilence, among them, till they be consumed from off the land that I gave unto them and to their fathers.

A. V. xxiv. 2.

---

vision, evidently suggested by Amos vi. (A. V. viii.) in which good and bad figs represent the happier lot of resignation to destiny, or the evil lot of evasion and resistance. Calamity might regenerate those who traced in it God's finger; resistance would provoke the fate of obstinacy. The symbolical vision is here a mere instrument of monition.

XXXV.[319]

Ch. XXXV.

1. Thus saith JEHOVAH to me; Make thee bonds and yokes, and put them upon thy neck, 2. and send them to the king of Edom, and to the king of Moab, and to the king of the Ammonites, and to the king of Tyrus, and to the king of Zidon, by the hand of the messengers which come to Jerusalem unto Zedekiah king of Judah; 3. and command them to say unto their masters, Thus saith JEHOVAH of hosts, the God of Israel; Thus shall ye say unto your masters; 4. I have made the earth, the man and the beast that are upon the ground, by my great power and by my outstretched arm, and have given it unto whom it seemed meet unto me. 5. And now have I given all these lands into the hand of Nebuchadnezzar the king of Babylon, my servant; and the beasts of the field have I given him also to serve him. 6. And all nations shall serve him, and his son, and his son's son, until the very time of his land come; and then many nations

---

[319] The Hebrew title to this chapter is, as in A. V.: "In the beginning "of the reign of Jehoiakim the son of Josiah king of Judah came this word "unto Jeremiah from Jehovah, saying." Modern editors observing from the verses below that Zedekiah must be the right name, coolly alter Jehoiakim into Zedekiah. But the LXX. more properly omit the title, which is not only erroneous in part, but unnecessary altogether, and which seems due to some early Hebrew editor, who made the same mistake here as probably in xxxi. (A. V. xlv.) 1, in dating the close of Baruch's labour.

1—21. About the fourth year of Zedekiah's reign new hopes were kindled in Jerusalem by a confederacy of the nations east of Jordan and the Phœnicians against Babel. Ambassadors sought Judah's concurrence. (Comp. 2 Sam. xi. 1, "the year from the time of the ambassadors going forth.") Many prophets persuade to join; as four years

and great kings shall serve themselves of him. 7. And it shall come to pass, *that* the nation and kingdom which will not serve the same Nebuchadnezzar the king of Babylon, and that will not put their neck under the yoke of the king of Babylon, that nation will I punish, saith JEHOVAH, with the sword, and with the famine, and with the pestilence, until I have consumed them by his hand. 8. Therefore hearken not ye to your prophets, nor to your diviners, nor to your dreamers, nor to your enchanters, nor to your sorcerers, which speak unto you, saying, Ye shall not serve the king of Babylon: 9. for they prophesy a lie unto you, to remove you far from your land; and that I should drive you out, and ye should perish. 10. But the nations that bring their neck under the yoke of the king of Babylon, and serve him, those will I let remain still in their own land, saith JEHOVAH; and they shall till it, and dwell therein.

11. I spake also to Zedekiah king of Judah according to all these words, saying, Bring your necks under the yoke of the king of Babylon, and serve him and his people, and live. 12. Why will ye die, thou and thy people, by the sword, by the famine, and by the pestilence, as JEHOVAH hath spoken against the nation that will not serve the king of Babylon? 13. Therefore hearken not unto the words of the prophets that speak unto you, saying, Ye shall not serve the king of Babylon: for they prophesy a lie unto you. 14. For I have not sent them, saith JEHOVAH, yet they prophesy a lie in my name; that I

A. V. xxvii. 7.

---

later, when Apries held out delusive hopes from Egypt. Jeremiah, with the burden of hopelessness hanging heavy on his spirit as a Divine decree, takes wooden yokes, and now fitting them on his neck, now presenting them to the ambassadors, exhibits a symbol of what Providence by

Ch.
XXXV.
might drive you out, and that ye might perish, ye, and the prophets that prophesy unto you. 15. Also I spake to the priests and to all this people, saying, Thus saith JEHOVAH; Hearken not to the words of your prophets that prophesy unto you, saying, Behold, the vessels of JEHOVAH's house shall now shortly be brought again from Babylon: for they prophesy a lie unto you. 16. Hearken not unto them; serve the king of Babylon, and live: wherefore should this city be laid waste? 17. But if they *be* prophets, and if the word of JEHOVAH be with them, let them now make intercession to JEHOVAH of hosts, that the vessels which are left in the house of JEHOVAH, and *in* the house of the king of Judah, and at Jerusalem, go not to Babylon. 18. For thus saith JEHOVAH of hosts, concerning the pillars, and concerning the sea, and concerning the bases, and concerning the residue of the vessels that remain in this city, 19. which Nebuchadnezzar king of Babylon took not, when he carried away captive Jeconiah the son of Jehoiakim king of Judah from Jerusalem to Babylon, and all the nobles of Judah and Jerusalem: 20. Yea, thus saith JEHOVAH of hosts, the God of Israel, concerning the vessels that remain *in* the house of JEHOVAH, and *in* the house of the king of Judah and of Jerusalem; 21. They shall be carried to Babylon, and there shall they be until the day that I visit them, saith JEHOVAH; then will I bring them up, and restore them to this place.

Nebuchadrezzar is bringing about. Justified as his warning was by the event, it must have seemed to more fervid spirits timid and unpatriotic. Ewald even places about this period the three closing chapters (saving some verses) of Zechariah; thinking that some sanguine prophet now pointed them against Babel.

XXXVI.

1. And it came to pass the same year, in the beginning of the reign of Zedekiah king of Judah, in the fourth year, *and* in the fifth month, *that* Hananiah the son of Azur the prophet, which *was* of Gibeon, spake unto me in the house of JEHOVAH, in the presence of the priests and of all the people, saying, 2. Thus speaketh JEHOVAH of hosts, the God of Israel, saying, I have broken the yoke of the king of Babylon. 3. Within two full years will I bring again into this place all the vessels of JEHOVAH's house, that Nebuchadnezzar king of Babylon took away from this place, and carried them to Babylon: 4. And I will bring again to this place Jeconiah the son of Jehoiakim king of Judah, with all the captives of Judah, that went into Babylon, saith JEHOVAH: for I will break the yoke of the king of Babylon.

5. Then the prophet Jeremiah said unto the prophet Hananiah in the presence of the priests, and in the presence of all the people that stood in the house of JEHOVAH,

---

1—17. Foremost of those who burned with indignant zeal at Jeremiah's faintheartedness, was Hananiah, the prophet from the priestly city of Gibeon. (Josh. xxi. 17.) Priest, he ill endures subjection to Babel; prophet, he foresees brighter things. Jehovah, he conceives, will shiver the heathen yoke. 11. Jeremiah gives way, as if to a stronger spirit; but reflecting (12—14) on the signs of Providence, and too painfully reassured, he retorts inverting the prediction. He adds, (15, 16) what had not been expressed in the first clear word to himself, that his gainsayer should die. 17. Hananiah died accordingly. We may (1) either suppose, what the frequent editions of our book permit, that verses 15—17, were moulded in recension after the

Ch. XXXVI.

6. Even the prophet Jeremiah said, Amen : JEHOVAH do so : JEHOVAH perform thy words which thou hast prophesied, to bring again the vessels of JEHOVAH's house, and all that is carried away captive, from Babylon into this place. 7. Nevertheless hear thou now this word that I speak in thine ears, and in the ears of all the people : 8. The prophets that have been before me and before thee of old prophesied both against many countries, and against great kingdoms, of war, and of evil, and of pestilence. 9. The prophet which prophesieth of peace, when the word of the prophet shall come to pass, *then* shall the prophet be known, that JEHOVAH hath truly sent him.

10. Then Hananiah the prophet took the yoke from off the prophet Jeremiah's neck, and brake it. 11. And Hananiah spake in the presence of all the people, saying, Thus saith JEHOVAH, Even so will I break the yoke of Nebuchadnezzar king of Babylon from the neck of all nations within the space of two full years. And the prophet Jeremiah went his way.

12. Then the word of JEHOVAH came unto Jeremiah *the prophet*, after that Hananiah the prophet had broken the yoke from off the neck of the prophet Jeremiah, saying, 13. Go and tell Hananiah, saying, Thus saith JEHOVAH ; Thou hast broken the yokes of wood ; but thou shalt make for them yokes of iron. 14. For thus saith JEHOVAH of hosts, the God of Israel ; I have put a yoke of iron upon the

---

event; (2) or may say with Ewald, that Hananiah's death seemed to many (only we must include the writer here), a divine sign of the falsehood of his prediction ; (3) or we may compare those famous instances of the Middle Ages, in which fiery monk, or seer, in the name of humanity, summoned some tyrant to appear within a specified time before God's tribunal ; though this case hardly belongs to the same category ; (4) or we may see a parallel

neck of all these nations, that they may serve Nebuchad- A. V.
nezzar king of Babylon; and they shall serve him: and xxviii. 14.
I have given him the beasts of the field also.

15. Then said the prophet Jeremiah unto Hananiah the prophet, Hear now, Hananiah; JEHOVAH hath not sent thee; but thou makest this people to trust in a lie. 16. Therefore thus saith JEHOVAH; Behold, I will cast thee from off the face of the earth; this year thou shalt die, because thou hast taught rebellion against JEHOVAH. 17. So Hananiah the prophet died the same year, in the seventh month.

XXXVII.[320]

1. Now these *are* the words of the letter that Jeremiah A. V.
the prophet sent from Jerusalem unto the residue of the xxix. 1.

---

[320] In this chapter we may distinguish the original draft, containing (1) the letter to Babylon; (2) Shemaiah's reply, and its reception at Jerusalem; (3) the retort of Jeremiah, on hearing the reply read by the high-priest. Some interval of time is required for these events, before the chapter could be drawn up.

We may then ask, if the title, 1—3, or at least vv. 2—3, (in which the Greek omits the name of Nebuchadnezzar,) be not the work of an editor. More certainly, we see in the verses 16—19, a paragraph about Jerusalem very inappropriate in the letter to the exiles; and we recognise an internal fitness as indicating the absence of this paragraph in the Greek to have arisen probably from following a more genuine, original, text.

Thirdly, we see in the sequence of thought, and in comparison with chap.

---

in that "witty and bold atheist," whom Bp. Hall "bent his prayers against," beseeching God daily to remove that hindrance, until the malicious man was swept away by the pestilence. [Bp. H. *Specialities*]—(5) or we may do well to leave the difficulty unsolved. The name *Hanan-iah, God's grace,* is the same as the N. T. Ananias, also connected with a judicial death.

1—23. As the weight of destiny involved in overwhelming invasions of a guilty land had impressed Jere-

Cн.
XXXVII.

A. V.
xxix. 1

elders which were carried away captives, and to the priests, and to the prophets, and to all the people whom Nebuchadnezzar had carried away captive from Jerusalem to Babylon; 2. (After that Jeconiah the king, and the queen, and the eunuchs, the princes of Judah and Jerusalem, and the carpenters, and the smiths, were departed from Jerusalem;) 3. By the hand of Elasah the son of Shaphan, and Gemariah the son of Hilkiah, (whom Zedekiah king of Judah sent unto Babylon to Nebuchadnezzar king of Babylon) saying, 4. Thus saith JEHOVAH of hosts, the God of Israel, unto all that are carried away captives, whom I have caused to be carried away from Jerusalem unto Babylon; 5. Build ye houses, and dwell *in them;* and plant gardens, and eat the fruit of them; 6. Take ye wives, and beget sons and daughters; and take wives for your sons, and give your daughters to husbands, that they may bear sons and daughters; and that ye may be increased there, and not diminished. 7. And seek the peace of the

---

xxiii. (A. V. xxv.) reasons why the paragraph 10—14, may be suspected, as written subsequently to the Return.

We must not follow the A. V. and Vulgate, v. 10, in translating *at* Babylon, in Babylone, but the Greek, *to* Babylon; i.e. as regards her. Here, as usual, the opponent prophets are with the Greek ψευδοπροφῆται. The whole may be compared with chap. xxxiv. (A. V. xxiv.) We must conceive of the exiles as living Nomad-fashion, in tents, and exhorted to become settled inhabitants. The spirit of the passage might now be adapted to Chiliast upholders of a Palæstinian restoration.

---

miah with a feeling of the uselessness of resistance, so the lot of the leading men carried off with Jeconiah seemed to him happier than that of those who survived to be tempted with vain hopes under Zedekiah. Hence he heard with regret of the spirit of fanatical patriotism awakening amidst the exiles; and unlike Micah, who had looked hopefully on a kindred stirring among the cap-

Ch.
XVII.

A. V.
xxix. 7.

city whither I have caused you to be carried away captives, and pray unto JEHOVAH for it: for in the peace thereof shall ye have peace.

8. For thus saith JEHOVAH of hosts, the God of Israel; Let not your prophets and your diviners, that *be* in the midst of you, deceive you, neither hearken to your dreams which ye caused to be dreamed. 9. For they prophesy falsely unto you in my name: I have not sent them, saith JEHOVAH.

[10. For thus saith JEHOVAH, That after seventy years be accomplished to Babylon I will visit you, and perform my good word toward you, in causing you to return to this place. 11. For I know the thoughts that I think toward you, saith JEHOVAH, thoughts of peace, and not of evil, to give you an expected end. 12. Then shall ye call upon me, and ye shall go and pray unto me, and I will hearken unto you. 13. And ye shall seek me, and find *me*, when ye shall search for me with all your heart. 14. And I will be found of you, saith JEHOVAH: and I will turn away your captivity, and I will gather you from all the nations, and from all the places whither I have driven you, saith JEHOVAH; and I will bring you again into the place whence I caused you to be carried away captive.]

---

tives in Assyria, Jeremiah takes the opportunity of a suppliant embassy from Zedekiah to address a letter to the exiles, exhorting them to patience, and reproving the prophets who fed them with ambitious hopes.

Several paragraphs in this chapter are doubtful. One, vv. 10—14, is open to the same criticism as the kindred, but more evidently altered, passage in chap. xxiii. (A. V. xxv.) It interrupts the sequence of the context. It introduces the period of seventy years, which if applied strictly to the exile (597—538,) will have to be reduced to fifty-

15. Because ye have said, Jehovah hath raised us up prophets in Babylon; [16. *Know* that thus saith Jehovah of the king that sitteth upon the throne of David, and of all the people that dwelleth in this city, *and* of your brethren that are not gone forth with you into captivity; 17. Thus saith Jehovah of hosts; Behold, I will send upon them the sword, the famine, and the pestilence, and will make them like vile figs, that cannot be eaten, they are so evil. 18. And I will persecute them with the sword, with the famine, and with the pestilence, and will deliver them to be removed to all the kingdoms of the earth, to be a curse, and an astonishment, and an hissing, and a reproach, among all the nations whither I have driven them: 19. Because they have not hearkened to my words, saith Jehovah, which I sent unto them by my servants the prophets, rising up early and sending *them;* but ye would not hear, saith Jehovah.]

20. Hear ye therefore the word of Jehovah, all ye of the captivity, whom I have sent from Jerusalem to Baby-

---

nine; while, if we better understand it of the period of the Chaldæan dynasty, (625—555, or 606—538,) it involves a prediction, which as it regarded Judæa had but a partial and secondary fulfilment, and as it regarded the Babylonian empire would require to substantiate it a better settled text than we possess. Looking at the manifold signs of recension in our book, we cannot but feel that an editor after the Return might conceive it an edifying improvement to give the old prophet's presentiment a more definite form. Some confirmation of this doubt, though not so strikingly as in chap. xxiii. (A. V. xxv.) appears also here in the Greek, which runs, "Οταν μέλλῃ πληροῦσθαι Βαβυλῶνι ἑβδομήκοντα ἔτη, ἐπισκέψομαι ὑμᾶς, as if the Alexandrian properly applied the seventy-year term

lon: 21. Thus saith JEHOVAH of hosts, the God of Israel, of Ahab the son of Kolaiah, and of Zedekiah the son of Maaseiah, which prophesy a lie unto you in my name; Behold, I will deliver them into the hand of Nebuchadrezzar king of Babylon; and he shall slay them before your eyes; 22. And of them shall be taken up a curse by all the captivity of Judah which *are* in Babylon, saying, JEHOVAH make thee like Zedekiah and like Ahab, whom the king of Babylon roasted in the fire: 23. Because they have committed villany in Israel, and have committed adultery with their neighbours' wives, and have spoken lying words in my name, which I have not commanded them; even I know, and *am* a witness, saith JEHOVAH.

24. *Thus* shalt thou also speak to Shemaiah the Nehelamite, saying, 25. Thus speaketh JEHOVAH of hosts, the God of Israel, saying, Because thou hast sent letters in thy name unto all the people that *are* at Jerusalem, and to Zephaniah the son of Maaseiah the priest, and to all the priests, saying, 26. JEHOVAH hath made thee priest in the stead of Jehoiada the priest, that ye should be officers in the house of JEHOVAH, for every man *that is* mad, and maketh himself a prophet, that thou shouldest put him in prison, and in the stocks. 27. Now therefore why hast thou not reproved Jeremiah of Anathoth, which maketh himself a prophet to you? 28. For therefore he sent

A. V.
XXIX. 21.

---

to the Babylonian empire, and not to the fifty-nine-year exile of the Jews. Again, in the Greek the paragraph 16—20 is altogether wanting; a sufficient sign of the great fluctuation of our text.

24—29. The letter of Jeremiah having relegated the hopes of the exiles to a remote time, Shemaiah amongst them writes to the high priest at Jerusalem in the tone of an Elizabethan statesman calling the attention of bishops

Cн.
XXXVII.
unto us *in* Babylon, saying, This *captivity is* long: build ye houses, and dwell *in them;* and plant gardens, and eat the fruit of them. 29. And Zephaniah the priest read this letter in the ears of Jeremiah the prophet.

30. Then came the word of JEHOVAH unto Jeremiah, saying, 31. Send to all them of the captivity, saying, Thus saith JEHOVAH concerning Shemaiah the Nehelamite; Because that Shemaiah hath prophesied unto you, and I sent him not, and he caused you to trust in a lie: 32. Therefore thus saith JEHOVAH; Behold, I will punish Shemaiah the Nehelamite, and his seed: he shall not have a man to dwell among this people; neither shall he behold the good that I will do for my people, saith JEHOVAH: because he hath taught rebellion against JEHOVAH.

XXXVIII.

Cн.
XXXVIII.
1. The word which came unto Jeremiah from JEHOVAH, when Nebuchadnezzar king of Babylon, and all his army, and all the kingdoms of the earth of his dominion, and all the people, fought against Jerusalem, and against all the cities thereof, saying, 2. Thus saith JEHOVAH, the God of Israel; Go and speak to Zedekiah king of Judah, and tell him, Thus saith JEHOVAH; Behold, I will give this city into the hand of the king of Babylon, and

---

to Puritan prophesyings, and asks why order is not taken to restrain this frenzy.

30—32. After an interval, Jeremiah retorts threatening in words which resemble those spoken by a man of God to Eli and his house, 1 Sam. ii. 32.

1—7—28. The horizon of this chapter corresponds with that of xxxii. (A.V. xxxvii.) 3—8. The plan of a confederacy in the king's fourth year having failed, and an embassy, or, as would seem from li. (A. V.) 59, a deprecatory

II. VIII.
he shall burn it with fire: 3. And thou shalt not escape out of his hand, but shalt surely be taken, and delivered into his hand; and thine eyes shall behold the eyes of the king of Babylon, and he shall speak with thee mouth to mouth, and thou shalt go to Babylon. 4. Yet hear the word of JEHOVAH, O Zedekiah king of Judah; Thus saith JEHOVAH of thee, Thou shalt not die by the sword: 5. *But* thou shalt die in peace: and with the burnings of thy fathers, the former kings which were before thee, so shall they burn *odours* for thee; and they will lament thee, *saying*, Ah lord! for I have pronounced the word, saith JEHOVAH. 6. Then Jeremiah the prophet, spake all these words unto Zedekiah king of Judah in Jerusalem. 7. When the king of Babylon's army fought against Jerusalem, and against all the cities of Judah that were left, against Lachish, and against Azekah: for these defenced cities remained of the cities of Judah.

8. *This is* the word that came unto Jeremiah from JEHOVAH, after that the king Zedekiah had made a covenant with all the people which *were* at Jerusalem, to proclaim liberty unto them; 9. That every man should let his manservant, and every man his maidservant, *being* an Hebrew or an Hebrewess, go free; that none should serve himself of them, *to wit*, of a Jew his brother. 10. Now when all the princes, and all the people, which had entered into the covenant, heard that every one should let his manservant, and every one his maidservant, go free, that none should serve themselves of them any more, then they obeyed, and let *them* go. 11. But afterward they turned,

A. V. xxxiv. 3.

---

journey of the king to Babylon, having attained its object, a gloomy peace reigned, until alliance with the Egyptian Apries, grandson of Necho, kindled hopes destined to be

Ch. XXXVIII.

and caused the servants and the handmaids, whom they had let go free, to return, and brought them into subjection for servants and for handmaids. 12. Therefore the word of JEHOVAH came to Jeremiah from JEHOVAH, saying, 13. Thus saith JEHOVAH, the God of Israel; I made a covenant with your fathers in the day that I brought them forth out of the land of Egypt, out of the house of bondmen, saying, 14. At the end of seven years let ye go every man his brother an Hebrew, which hath been sold unto thee ; and when he hath served thee six years, thou shalt let him go free from thee : but your fathers hearkened not unto me, neither inclined their ear. 15. And ye were now turned, and had done right in my sight, in proclaiming liberty every man to his neighbour ; and ye had made a covenant before me in the house which is called by my name : 16. But ye turned and polluted my name, and caused every man his servant, and every man his handmaid, whom he had set at liberty at their pleasure, to return, and brought them into subjection, to be unto you for servants and for handmaids. 17. Therefore thus saith JEHOVAH; Ye have not hearkened unto me, in proclaiming liberty, every one to his brother, and every man to his neighbour : behold, I proclaim a liberty for you, saith JEHOVAH, to the sword, to the pestilence, and to the famine; and I will make you to be removed into all the kingdoms of the earth. 18. And I will give the men that have transgressed my covenant, which have not performed the words of the covenant which they had made before me, when they cut the calf in twain,

---

fatal. The king's ninth year in its tenth month saw the city besieged. A release of native bondsmen followed as a measure of policy, and in the Prophet's eye, of deprecation. On the advance of Apries the siege was broken up ; the

JEREMIAH. 245

and passed between the parts thereof, 19. The princes of
Judah, and the princes of Jerusalem, the eunuchs, and the
priests, and all the people of the land, which passed between the parts of the calf; 20. I will even give them
into the hand of their enemies, and into the hand of them
that seek their life : and their dead bodies shall be for
meat unto the fowls of the heaven, and to the beasts of the
earth. 21. And Zedekiah king of Judah and his princes
will I give into the hand of their enemies, and into the
hand of them that seek their life, and into the hand of the
king of Babylon's army, which are gone up from you.
22. Behold, I will command, saith JEHOVAH, and cause
them to return to this city; and they shall fight against
it, and take it, and burn it with fire : and I will make the
cities of Judah a desolation without an inhabitant.

A. V.
xxxiv. 19.

I.

XXXIX.

[321] The word that came to Jeremiah from the ETERNAL
in the tenth year of Zedekiah king of Judah, which *was*

A. V.
xxxii. 1.

---

[321] With this xxxixth (A. V. xxxiind) chapter, Jerome's own version and
commentary on Jeremiah appear to end : whether from some breach or loss
in his works come down to us, I hardly know, or because (as he quaintly says
in his Proem to c. xxx., Prolixitas voluminis Hieremiæ prophetæ vincit nos-
trum propositum, ut, quamvis, breviter, tamen multa dicamus,) his perseverance may have failed him. Can the order in his MSS. have so varied, that he
might have inserted the oracles on the nations, including Babylon, after
chap. xxv, (as he says there, Denique in sequentibus dicit contra Ægyptum,
et Philistim, et Moab, et Ammon, ... et ad extremum contra Babylonem,)

---

city, freed from alarm, resumed her security and her harsh-
ness. Jeremiah's worst presentiments are intensified by
indignation, and he predicts the end.

1—15. When Hannibal drew nighest, being on the
Anio, within three miles of Rome, the ground on which

Ch.
XXXIX.
the eighteenth year of Nebuchadrezzar. 2. For then the king of Babylon's army besieged Jerusalem: and Jeremiah the prophet was shut up in the court of the prison, which *was* in the king of Judah's house. 3. For Zedekiah king of Judah had shut him up, saying, Wherefore dost thou prophesy, and say, Thus saith the ETERNAL, Behold, I will give this city into the hand of the king of Babylon, and he shall take it; 4. And Zedekiah king of Judah shall not escape out of the hand of the Chaldeans, but shall surely be delivered into the hand of the king of Babylon, and shall speak with him mouth to mouth, and his eyes shall behold his eyes; 5. And he shall lead Zedekiah to Babylon, and there shall he be until I visit him, saith the ETERNAL: though ye fight with the Chaldeans, ye shall not prosper.

6. And Jeremiah said, the word of the ETERNAL came unto me, saying, 7. Behold, Hanameel the son of Shallum thine uncle shall come unto thee, saying, Buy thee my field that *is* in Anathoth: for the right of redemption *is* thine to buy *it*. 8. So Hanameel mine uncle's son came to me in the court of the prison, according to the word of

---

and so the group of chapters about xxx—xxxiii, would turn out the latest in his work ? At least, as regards the *Sheshac* clause, if we can so restrict the word *capitulo*, he says, " Longius quam commentariorum brevitas " patitur de hoc Capitulo diximus ; quod Græci Latinique forsitan fastidient " *quia in suis codicibus non habent*. Sed . . . proderit."

---

his camp stood was sold by auction in the city for its full price. This sign of confidence was ill matched by his bravado in selling the silver shops. Liv. xxvi. 11. So Jeremiah, having by the Mosaic law (which aimed at a perpetuity of family freeholds, Levit. xxv. 25) a right of preemption of his cousin Hanameel's field at Anathoth, is encouraged, though a prisoner, to buy it even in the

Ch. XXIX. the ETERNAL, and said unto me, Buy my field, I pray thee, that *is* in Anathoth, which *is* in the country of Benjamin: for the right of inheritance *is* thine, and the redemption *is* thine; buy *it* for thyself. Then I knew that this *was* the word of the ETERNAL. 9. And I bought the field of Hanameel my uncle's son, that *was* in Anathoth, and weighed him the money, *even* seventeen shekels of silver. 10. And I subscribed the evidence, and sealed *it*, and took witnesses, and weighed *him* the money in the balances. 11. So I took the evidence of the purchase, *both* that which was sealed *according* to the law and custom, and that which was open: 12. And I gave the evidence of the purchase unto Baruch the son of Neriah, the son of Maaseiah, in the sight of Hanameel mine uncle's *son*, and in the presence of the witnesses that subscribed the book of the purchase, before all the Jews that sat in the court of the prison. 13. And I charged Baruch before them, saying, 14. Thus saith the ETERNAL of hosts, the God of Israel; Take these evidences, the evidence of the purchase, both which is sealed, and this evidence which is open; and put them in an earthen vessel, that they may continue many days. 15. For thus saith the ETERNAL of hosts, the God of Israel; Houses and fields and vineyards shall be possessed again in this land.

16. Now when I had delivered the evidence of the pur-

A. V. xxxii. 8.

---

straitness of the siege. Not that in his mind was doubt of the imminent ruin, or denial of the national guilt; but trust in the ancient promises, love to his devoted race, taught him confidence that when ill offerings to Baal and Molech have been expiated by the besiegers' fires, God will inspire the repentance which He requires, and restore men's rights from the terror of the sword.

CH.
XXXIX.

chase unto Baruch the son of Neriah, I prayed unto the Eternal, saying, 17. Ah! Lord, Eternal, behold, thou hast made the heaven and the earth by thy great power and stretched out arm, *and* there is nothing too hard for thee: 18. Thou shewest loving kindness unto thousands, and recompensest the iniquity of the fathers into the bosom of their children after them: the Great, the Mighty God, the Eternal of hosts, *is* his name, 19. Great in counsel, and mighty in work: for thine eyes *are* open upon all the ways of the sons of men: to give every one according to his ways, and according to the fruit of his doings: 20. Which hast set signs and wonders in the land of Egypt, *even* unto this day, and in Israel, and among *other* men; and hast made thee a name, as at this day; 21. And hast brought forth thy people Israel out of the land of Egypt with signs, and with wonders, and with a strong hand, and with a stretched out arm, and with great terror; 22. And hast given them this land, which thou didst swear to their fathers to give them, a land flowing with milk and honey; 23. And they came in, and possessed it; but they obeyed not thy voice, neither walked in thy law; they have done nothing of all that thou commandedst them to do: therefore thou hast caused all this evil to come upon them: 24. Behold the mounts, they are come unto the city to take it; and the city is given into the hand of the Chaldeans, that fight against it, because of the sword, and of the famine, and of the pestilence: and what thou hast spoken is come to pass; and, behold, thou seest *it*. 25. And thou hast said

A. V.
xxxii. 1

16—25. Yet what a ground of pleading with the mysteries of the Divine counsel is in this strange injunction; this purchase of redemption out of the jaws of an inexorable ruin.

unto me, O Lord, ETERNAL, Buy thee the field for money, and take witnesses; for the city is given into the hand of the Chaldeans.

A. V. xxxii. 25.

26. Then came the word of the ETERNAL unto Jeremiah, 27. Behold, I *am* the ETERNAL, the God of all flesh : is there anything too hard for me ? 28. Therefore thus saith the ETERNAL; Behold, I will give this city into the hand of the Chaldeans, and into the hand of Nebuchadrezzar king of Babylon, and he shall take it : 29. And the Chaldeans that fight against this city, shall come and set fire on this city, and burn it with the houses, upon whose roofs they have offered incense unto Baal, and poured out drink offerings unto other gods, to provoke me to anger. 30. For the children of Israel and the children of Judah have only done evil before me from their youth : for the children of Israel have only provoked me to anger with the work of their hands, saith the ETERNAL. 31. For this city hath been to me *as* a provocation of mine anger and of my fury from the day that they built it even unto this day; that I should remove it from before my face, 32. Because of all the evil of the children of Israel and of the children of Judah, which they have done to provoke me to anger, they, their kings, their princes, their priests, and their prophets, and the men of Judah, and the inhabitants of Jerusalem. 33. And they have turned unto me the back, and not the face : though I taught them, rising up early and teaching *them,* yet they have not hearkened to receive instruction.

26—44. Not the less, God's counsel stands, and His mysteries come plain. There is no escape from the purifying flame; yet no fear that Divine Pity will not work out its way through healing after ruin to restoration.

How far ' the word of Jehovah,' ver. 6, foretelling the

Ch.
XXXIX.
34. But they set their abominations in the house, which is called by my name, to defile it. 35. And they built the high places of Baal, which are in the valley of the son of Hinnom, to cause their sons and their daughters to pass through *the fire* unto Molech; which I commanded them not, neither came it into my mind, that they should do this abomination, to cause Judah to sin.

36. And now therefore thus saith the ETERNAL, the God of Israel, concerning this city, whereof ye say, It shall be delivered into the hand of the king of Babylon by the sword, and by the famine, and by the pestilence: 37. Behold, I will gather them out of all countries, whither I have driven them in mine anger, and in my fury, and in great wrath; and I will bring them again unto this place, and I will cause them to dwell safely: 38. And they shall be my people, and I will be their God: 39. And I will give them one heart, and one way, that they may fear me for ever, for the good of them, and of their children after them: 40. And I will make an everlasting covenant with them, that I will not turn away from them, to do them good; but I will put my fear in their hearts, that they shall not depart from me. 41. Yea, I will rejoice over them to do them good, and I will plant them in this land assuredly with my whole heart and with my whole soul. 42. For thus saith the ETERNAL; Like as I have brought all this great evil upon this people, so will I bring upon them all the good that I have promised them. 43. And fields shall be bought in this land, whereof ye say, *It is* desolate without

---

cousin's application, and directing the purchase, is to be taken as Divinely objective and oracular from without, is not a simple question. We must observe the emotional play of the Prophet's mind, and need not exclude a natural instrumentality of intelligence; yet the presenti-

man or beast; it is given into the hand of the Chaldeans. 44. Men shall buy fields for money, and subscribe evidences, and seal *them*, and take witnesses in the land of Benjamin, and in the places about Jerusalem, and in the cities of Judah, and in the cities of the mountains, and in the cities of the valley, and in the cities of the south: for I will cause their captivity to return, saith the ETERNAL.

A. V.
xxxii. 44.

XL.

1. Moreover the word of JEHOVAH came unto Jeremiah the second time, while he was yet shut up in the court of the prison, saying, 2. Thus saith JEHOVAH the maker thereof, JEHOVAH that formed it, to establish it; JEHOVAH *is* his name: 3. Call unto me, and I will answer thee, and shew thee great and mighty things, which thou knowest not. 4. For thus saith JEHOVAH, the God of Israel, concerning the houses of this city, and concerning the houses of the kings of Judah, which are thrown down by the mounts, and by the sword; 5. They come to fight with the Chaldeans, but *it is* to fill them with the dead bodies of men, whom I have slain in my anger and in my fury, and for all whose wickedness I have hid my face from this city. 6. Behold, I will bring it health and cure, and I will cure them, and will reveal unto them the abundance of peace and truth. 7. And I will cause the captivity of Judah, and the captivity of Israel to return,

A. V.
xxxiii. 1.

---

ment came out right, and the symbolical act had its counter-type of fulfilment. This will seem to many minds a proof of Providential guidance; hardly any will refuse to trace an inward drama of trust and moral insight.

1—11. As Jeremiah dwells on the promises with which he has been comforted in spirit, and while the nearing

Ch. XL. and will build them, as at the first. 8. And I will cleanse them from all their iniquity, whereby they have sinned against me ; and I will pardon all their iniquities, whereby they have sinned, and whereby they have transgressed against me. 9. And it shall be to me a name of joy, a praise and an honour before all the nations of the earth, which shall hear all the good that I do unto them : and they shall fear and tremble for all the goodness and for all the prosperity that I procure unto it. 10. Thus saith JEHOVAH ; Again there shall be heard in this place, which ye say *shall be* desolate without man and without beast, *even* in the cities of Judah, and in the streets of Jerusalem, that are desolate, without man, and without inhabitant, and without beast, 11. The voice of joy, and the voice of gladness, the voice of the bridegroom, and the voice of the bride, the voice of them that shall say, Praise JEHOVAH of hosts ; for JEHOVAH *is* good; for his mercy *endureth* for ever : *and* of them that shall bring the sacrifice of praise into the house of JEHOVAH. For I will cause to return the captivity of the land, as at the first, saith JEHOVAH. 12. Thus saith JEHOVAH of hosts ; Again in this place, which is desolate without man and without beast, and in all the cities thereof, shall be an habitation of shepherds causing *their* flocks to lie down. 13. In the cities of the mountains, in the cities of the vale, and in the cities of the south, and in the land of Benjamin, and in the places about Jerusalem, and in the cities of Judah,

A. V. xxxiii. 8.

downfall darkens for others the future, he feels that through prayer comes revelation, v. 3, and in trust is strength. So through faith his presentiment of the Return becomes jubilant, and the psalms of Ezra's liturgy already sound in his ears.

12—18. So, what is becoming a desolation before his

XL. shall the flocks pass again under the hands of him that telleth *them*, saith JEHOVAH. A V. xxxiii. 13.

14. Behold, the days come, saith JEHOVAH, that I will perform that good thing which I have promised unto the house of Israel and to the house of Judah. 15. In those days, and at that time, I will cause to bud to David a bud of righteousness,[322] to execute judgment and righteousness in the land. 16. In those days shall Judah be saved, and Jerusalem shall dwell safely : and this *is the name* wherewith she shall be called, JEHOVAH our righteousness. 17. For thus saith JEHOVAH ; David shall never want a man to sit upon the throne of the house of Israel ; 18. Neither shall the priests the Levites want a man before me to offer burnt offerings, and to kindle meat offerings, and to do sacrifice continually.

---

[322] *Cause to bud to David a bud of righteousness ;* the word *Tsemach*, here usually translated Branch, is commonly treated as a Messianic title. It seems to have become such in Zech. vi. 12, at first sight, but less so, if we observe that it is an application (perhaps from this passage) to the high priest of that time. In Jer. xxii. (A. V. xxiii.) 5, it seems used of the revived Davidical dynasty; and in this place of the Levitical priests as well. In Isaiah, iv. 11, (A. V. 2,) its use is still more vague, for offspring of mankind, or of the earth in general, as the parallelism implies. Its natural sense is suggested by Gen. ii. and iii. Psalm cxlvii. 8. Dr. W. H. Mill's argument from the word in his book against " the application of Pantheistic Principles" being often quoted in England, I regret to observe that it is not of the smallest philological value.

---

eyes shall be full of life again, and the new generation of princes sprung from David's stem, and of priests of Levi's lineage (instead of the lowest of the people,) shall present before the eternal Throne the desired spectacle of justice to men, and reverence towards God. Without urging Movers's weighty suggestion as to the interpolated air of the verse and clause 18 and 21, mentioning the Levites, we may say the form of the picture is Judaic, local, Levi-

Ch. XL, 19. And the word of JEHOVAH came unto Jeremiah, saying, 20. Thus saith JEHOVAH; If ye can break my covenant of the day, and my covenant of the night, and that there should not be day and night in their season; 21. *Then* may also my covenant be broken with David my servant, that he should not have a son to reign upon his throne; and with the Levites the priests, my ministers. 22. As the host of heaven cannot be numbered, neither the sand of the sea measured: so will I multiply the seed of David my servant, and the Levites that minister unto me. 23. Moreover the word of JEHOVAH came to Jeremiah, saying, 24. Considerest thou not what this people have spoken, saying, The two families which JEHOVAH hath chosen, he hath even cast them off? thus they have despised my people, that they should be no more a nation before them. 25. Thus saith JEHOVAH; If my covenant *be* not with day and night, *and if* I have not appointed the ordinances of heaven and earth; 26. Then will I cast away the seed of Jacob, and David my servant, *so* that I will not take *any* of his seed *to be* rulers over the seed of Abraham, Isaac, and Jacob: for I will cause their captivity to return, and have mercy on them.

A. V. xxxiii. 1

---

tical; but it may be rendered Christian, *i. e.* spiritual, by the constant key to such passages which St. Paul supplies, detaching the essence from the accident, and so transforming the letter into spirit. The two families are either Ephraim and Judah, or as some think implied, David and Levi, princes and priests.

19—26. To this prisoner, patriot no less than prophet, the endurance of Israel seems guaranteed by the Divine faithfulness, as that of the sun and stars. For where man has covenanted with God, he rises above the mere range of Providential benignity which embraces savage races and

XLI.

XLI. 1. Then Shephatiah the son of Mattan, and Gedaliah the son of Pashur, and Jucal the son of Shelemiah, and Pashur the son of Malchiah, heard the words that Jeremiah had spoken unto all the people, saying, 2. Thus saith JEHOVAH, He that remaineth in this city shall die by the sword, by the famine, and by the pestilence: but he that goeth forth to the Chaldeans shall live; for he shall have his life for a prey, and shall live. 3. Thus saith JEHOVAH, This city shall surely be given into the hand of the king of Babylon's army, which shall take it. 4. Therefore the princes said unto the king, We beseech thee, let this man be put to death: for thus he weakeneth the hands of the men of war that remain in this city, and the hands of all the people, in speaking such words unto them: for this man seeketh not the welfare of this people, but the hurt. 5. Then Zedekiah the king said, Behold, he *is* in your hand: for the king *is* not *he that* can do *any* thing against you. 6. Then took they Jeremiah, and cast him into the dungeon of Malchiah the son of Hammelech, that *was* in the court of the prison: and they let

A.V. xxxviii. 1.

---

wild creatures; so he acquires a claim not merely on the faithful Creator, who is the preserver of all men; but on the God of tenderness and faithfulness, with whom he is in league. But we must note, that if the Christian application of such promises and aspirations to a better land beyond the grave be adopted by us, the Jewish right to a perpetuity of Palestine falls away, and becomes unimportant.

1—6. Since a remote hope, presupposing immediate disaster, could only weaken men's courage, the king's counsellors persuade him to silence the prophet by per-

Ch. XLI. down Jeremiah with cords. And in the dungeon *there was* no water, but mire: so Jeremiah sunk in the mire.

7. Now when Ebed-melech the Ethiopian, one of the eunuchs which was in the king's house, heard that they had put Jeremiah in the dungeon; the king then sitting in the gate of Benjamin; 8. Ebed-melech went forth out of the king's house, and spake to the king, saying, 9. My lord the king, these men have done evil in all that they have done to Jeremiah the prophet, whom they have cast into the dungeon; and he is like to die for hunger in the place where he is: for *there is* no more bread in the city. 10. Then the king commanded Ebed-melech the Ethiopian, saying, Take from hence thirty men with thee, and take up Jeremiah the prophet out of the dungeon, before he die. 11. So Ebed-melech took the men with him, and went into the house of the king under the treasury, and took thence old cast clouts and old rotten rags, and let them down by cords into the dungeon to Jeremiah. 12. And Ebed-melech the Ethiopian said unto Jeremiah, Put now *these* old cast clouts and rotten rags under thine armholes under the cords. And Jeremiah did so. 13. So they drew up Jeremiah with cords, and took him up out of the dungeon: and Jeremiah remained in the court of the prison.

14. Then Zedekiah the king sent, and took Jeremiah the prophet unto him into the third entry that *is* in the

---

mitting his removal from the court of ward; they then throw him into a deep well, where, if not drowned, he may die of hunger.

7—13. An Abyssinian eunuch, forerunner of him whom Philip found reading of God's stricken servant, obtains permission to release the prophet from his lowest dungeon. (Comp. Isa. liii.)

house of JEHOVAH: and the king said unto Jeremiah, I will ask thee a thing; hide nothing from me. 15. Then Jeremiah said unto Zedekiah, If I declare *it* unto thee, wilt thou not surely put me to death? and if I give thee counsel, wilt thou not hearken unto me? 16. So Zedekiah the king sware secretly unto Jeremiah, saying, *As* JEHOVAH liveth, that made us this soul, I will not put thee to death, neither will I give thee into the hand of these men that seek thy life. 17. Then said Jeremiah unto Zedekiah, Thus saith JEHOVAH, the God of hosts, the God of Israel; If thou wilt assuredly go forth unto the king of Babylon's princes, then thy soul shall live, and this city shall not be burned with fire; and thou shalt live, and thine house: 18. But if thou wilt not go forth to the king of Babylon's princes, then shall this city be given into the hand of the Chaldeans, and they shall burn it with fire, and thou shalt not escape out of their hand. 19. And Zedekiah the king said unto Jeremiah, I am afraid of the Jews that are fallen to the Chaldeans, lest they deliver me into their hand, and they mock me. 20. But Jeremiah said, They shall not deliver *thee*. Obey, I beseech thee, the voice of JEHOVAH, which I speak unto thee: so it shall be well unto thee, and thy soul shall live. 21. But if thou refuse to go forth, this *is* the word that JEHOVAH hath shewed me: 22. Then, behold, all the women that are left in the king of Judah's house *shall be* brought forth to the king of Babylon's princes, and those *women* shall say, Thy friends have set thee on, and have prevailed against thee: thy feet are sunk in the mire, *and* they are turned away back. 23. So they shall bring out all thy wives and thy children to the Chaldeans: and thou shalt

A. V. xxxviii. 14.

14—22. The well-meaning king endeavours in the secrecy of a subterranean passage to extract comfort; but

Ch. XLI. not escape out of their hand, but shalt be taken by the hand of the king of Babylon: and thou shalt cause this city to be burned with fire.

24. Then said Zedekiah unto Jeremiah, Let no man know of these words, and thou shalt not die. 25. But if the princes hear that I have talked with thee, and they come unto thee, and say unto thee, Declare unto us now what thou hast said unto the king, hide it not from us, and we will not put thee to death; also what the king said unto thee: 26. Then thou shalt say unto them, I presented my supplication before the king, that he would not cause me to return to Jonathan's house, to die there. 27. Then came all the princes unto Jeremiah, and asked him: and he told them according to all these words that the king had commanded. So they left off speaking with him; for the matter was not perceived. 28. So Jeremiah abode in the court of the prison until the day that Jerusalem was taken.[323]

XLII.

Ch. XLII 1. And it came to pass, when Jerusalem was taken, when all the princes of the king of Babel came in, and sat in the middle gate, Nergal-sharezer, Samgar-

---

[323] The last clause of ver. 28, in the A. V., belongs to the next chapter, by grammatical necessity, though not by the most received accentuation. (Comp. Rosenm.) The Greek text, (chap. xlvi. of the LXX.) has most instructive and suggestive variations from the Hebrew.

---

hears a stern sound predicting the song of reproach in which the women of his own household as captives will make his new counsellors a shame to him. (Comp. Obad. 6, 7.

XLII. This chapter is important as a specimen of the work of early Hebrew editors. Otherwise, its few genuine verses might well have closed the preceding. Jeremiah,

nebo, Sarsechim, chief of the eunuchs,[324] Nergal-sharezer, chief Magian,[325] and all the rest of the princes of the king of Babel;[326] 2. that they sent and took Jeremiah from the court of ward, and committed him to Gedaliah the son of Ahikam, the son of Shaphan, to take him forth to his home; so he dwelt amongst the

A. V.
xxxix. 3.
.... 14.

---

[324] Our Hebrew text, followed by A. V., gives as vv. 1, 2 of this chapter a little chronology of the siege, taken from below lii. 4, as there from 2 Kings xxv. But grammar and idiom require an apodosis or answering clause to the time " when Jerusalem was taken," &c., and it was not taken in the ninth year, so that we cannot get our apodosis till we reach verse 3, A. V., and then the disturbing parenthesis appears to have been introduced, as we have found in so many analogous cases, from the pen of an editor, who perhaps at first placed it in the margin ; or may have wished to be instructive. Comp. "the burden of the beasts of the south," Isa. xxvi. (A. V. xxx.) So essentially, Ewald, Hitzig, Movers. The Greek abridges this chronology, in some MSS., by inserting the ninth month, instead of ninth year ; but below, with greater propriety omits the history between vv. 4—14 (A. V.)

[325] 'Chief of the eunuchs' and 'chief Magian' seem possible translations of Rabsaris and Rabmag. The names are strangely confused in the Greek.

[326] Let it suffice to remind the reader in the margin, that some Hebrew editor, (whom the LXX. if they found his work in their MSS. disdained to follow,) transplanted into this place, so as to disturb the context, the narrative of Zedekiah's fate, found in 2 Kings xxv.; from thence furnishing a supplement to our entire book. (Ver. 4, A. V.) ' And it came to pass, *that* when Zedekiah the king of Judah saw them, and all the men of war, then they fled, and went forth out of the city by night, by the way of the king's garden, by the gate betwixt the two walls: and he went out the way of the plain. (5.) But the Chaldeans' army pursued after them, and overtook Zedekiah in the plains of Jericho: and when they had taken him, they brought him up to Nebuchadnezzar king of Babylon to Riblah in the land of Hamath, where he gave judgment upon him. (6.) Then the king of Babylon slew the sons of Zedekiah in Riblah before his eyes: also the king of Babylon slew all the nobles of Judah. (7.) Moreover he put out Zedekiah's eyes, and bound him with chains, to carry him to Babylon. (8.) And the Chaldeans burned the king's house, and the houses of the people, with fire, and brake down the walls of Jerusalem. (9.) Then Nebuzar-adan the captain of the guard carried away captive into Babylon the remnant of the people that re-

---

released from dungeon, remains in ward until the city is taken, when the Babylonian chieftains or officers hand him over to the friendly care of his old protector Ahikam's

Ch. XLII. people. 3. Now the word of JEHOVAH came to Jeremiah, while he was shut up in the court of ward, saying, 4. Go and speak to Ebed-melech the Ethiopian, saying, Thus saith JEHOVAH of hosts, the God of Israel ; Behold, I will bring my words upon this city for evil, and not for good ; and they shall be *accomplished* in that day before thee. 5. But I will deliver thee in that day, saith JEHOVAH : and thou shalt not be given into the hand of the men of whom thou *art* afraid. 6. For I will surely deliver thee, and thou shalt not fall by the sword, but thy life shall be for a prey unto thee : because thou hast put thy trust in me, saith JEHOVAH.

A. xxxi

XLIII.

Ch.XLIII. 1. The word that came to Jeremiah from JEHOVAH, after that Nebuzar-adan the captain of the guard[327] had let him

A.V

---

mained in the city, and those that fell away, that fell to him, with the rest of the people that remained. (10.) But Nebuzar-adan the captain of the guard left of the poor of the people, which had nothing, in the land of Judah, and gave them vineyards and fields at the same time. (11.) Now Nebuchadnezzar king of Babylon gave charge concerning Jeremiah to Nebuzar-adan the captain of the guard, saying, (12.) Take him, and look well to him, and do him no harm; but do unto him even as he shall say unto thee. (13.) So Nebuzar-adan the captain of the guard sent, and Nebushasban, Rab-saris, and Nergal-sharezer, Rab-mag, and all the king of Babylon's princes.' There is, however, a possibility that the last three verses, 11, 12, 13, may belong to this place, but the grammatical context, and the Greek, (of which the above is virtually a translation,) followed by Ewald, persuade me to edit, as I have done. That something was wrong, had indeed occurred to myself from the mere Hebrew of ver. 28 of the preceding chapter.

[327] *Captain of the guard*, the same title as applied to Potiphar, Gen. xxxix. 1, LXX. ἀρχιμάγειρος. *Vulg.* magister militiæ.

---

son, Gedaliah. His votive presentiment for the eunuch who preserved him, is a proper appendix to the history of his release.

1—16. Jeremiah's release seems not to have prevented

LIII. go from Ramah, when he had taken him being bound in A.V.xl.1. chains among all that were carried away captive of Jerusalem and Judah, which were carried away captive unto Babylon. 2. And the captain of the guard took Jeremiah, and said unto him, JEHOVAH thy God hath pronounced this evil upon this place. 3. Now JEHOVAH hath brought *it*, and done according as he hath said: because ye have sinned against JEHOVAH, and have not obeyed his voice, therefore this thing is come upon you. 4. And now, behold, I loose thee this day from the chains which *were* upon thine hand. If it seem good unto thee to come with me into Babylon, come; and I will look well unto thee: but if it seem ill unto thee to come with me into Babylon, forbear: behold, all the land *is* before thee: whither it seemeth good and convenient for thee to go, thither go. 5. And as yet he was not going back,[328] (*he said*) Then go back to Gedaliah the son of Ahikam the son of Shaphan, whom the king of Babylon hath made governor over the cities of Judah, and dwell with him among the people: or go wheresoever it seemeth convenient unto thee to go. So the captain of the guard gave him victuals, and a reward, and let him go. 6. Then went Jeremiah unto Gedaliah the son of Ahikam to Mizpah; and dwelt with him among the people that were left in the land.

---

[328] *And as yet he was not going back*, &c. Vulg. et mecum noli venire, sed habita apud Godaliam, LXX. εἰ δὲ μή, ἀπότρεχε, ἀνάστρεψον. Hitzig follows Luther in extorting the sense, "but back from Babylon there will be no return." The Vulgate supposes שׁבי.

---

him from being taken in the crowd of captives intended for Babylon. But being dismissed with gifts by the commander at Ramah, he seeks out his patron Gedaliah at Mizpah. Both these names, the *high-place* and the *look-out post*, seem properly placed near N. Jerusalem; but the first (Arimathea?) having a homonym claimed

Ch.XLIII. 7. Now when all the captains of the forces which were A.V in the fields, *even* they and their men, heard that the king of Babylon had made Gedaliah the son of Ahikam governor in the land, and had committed unto him men, and women, and children, and of the poor of the land, of them that were not carried away captive to Babylon ; 8. Then they came to Gedaliah to Mizpah, even Ishmael the son of Nethaniah, and Johanan and Jonathan, the sons of Kareah, and Seraiah the son of Tanhumeth, and the sons of Ephai the Netophathite, and Jezaniah the son of a Maachathite, they and their men. 9. And Gedaliah the son of Ahikam the son of Shaphan sware unto them and to their men, saying, Fear not to serve the Chaldeans; dwell in the land, and serve the king of Babylon, and it shall be well with you. 10. As for me, behold, I will dwell at Mizpah, to serve the Chaldeans,[329] which will come unto us : but ye, gather ye wine, and summer fruits, and oil, and put *them* in your vessels, and dwell in your cities that ye have taken. 11. Likewise when all the Jews that *were* in Moab, and among the Ammonites, and in Edom, and that *were* in all the countries, heard that the king of Babylon had left a remnant of Judah, and that he had set over them Gedaliah the son of Ahikam the son of Shaphan ; 12. Even all the Jews returned out of all places whither they were driven, and came to the land of Judah, to Gedaliah,

---

[329] *To serve the Chaldeans.* Heb. stand before ; *i.e.* to collect the tribute for them. *Vulg.* ut respondeam præcepto.

---

towards Bethlehem, whence the appropriateness of the adaptation of Rachel's weeping, Matt. ii. 18. (Yet the mention of the Ammonites suggests, that the same names might be found east of the Jordan.) The word of Jehovah, ver. 1, must be carried on to the warnings in chap. xlv. (A. V. xlii.) though interrupted here by the compiler's

unto Mizpah, and gathered wine and summer fruits very much. A.V. XL. 12.

13. Moreover Johanan the son of Kareah, and all the captains of the forces that *were* in the fields, came to Gedaliah to Mizpah, 14. and said unto him, Dost thou certainly know that Baalis the king of the Ammonites hath sent Ishmael the son of Nethaniah to slay thee? But Gedaliah the son of Ahikam believed them not. 15. Then Johanan the son of Kareah spake to Gedaliah in Mizpah secretly, saying, Let me go, I pray thee, and I will slay Ishmael the son of Nethaniah, and no man shall know *it* : wherefore should he slay thee, that all the Jews which are gathered unto thee should be scattered, and the remnant of Judah perish? 16. But Gedaliah the son of Ahikam said unto Johanan the son of Kareah, Thou shalt not do this thing: for thou speakest falsely of Ishmael.

XLIV.

1. Now it came to pass in the seventh month, *that* Ishmael the son of Nethaniah the son of Elishama, of the seed royal, and the princes of the king,[330] even ten men with him, came unto Gedaliah the son of Ahikam to Mizpah; and there they did eat bread together in Mizpah. 2. Then arose Ishmael the son of Nethaniah, and the ten men that were with him, and smote Gedaliah the son of Ahikam the son of Shaphan with the sword, and slew him,[331] whom the

A.V. XLI.1.

---

[330] *And the princes of the king.* This clause is wanting in the Greek, and held by Ewald for a gloss.
[331] The day of Gedaliah's death, says Philippsohn, is a synagogue fast.

---

narrative. The old feud of the Ammonites suborns against the Jewish remnant one Ishmael, against whom Johanan the stout son of Kareah warns Gedaliah in vain.

1—18. In the seventh month after the city's fall (or

Ch. XLIV. king of Babylon had made governor over the land. 3. Ishmael also slew all the Jews that were with him, *even* with Gedaliah, at Mizpah, and the Chaldeans that were found there, *and* the men of war. 4. And it came to pass the second day after he had slain Gedaliah, and no man knew *it*, 5. that there came certain from Shechem, from Shiloh, and from Samaria, *even* fourscore men, having their beards shaven, and their clothes rent, and having cut themselves, with offerings and incense in their hand, to bring *them* to the house of JEHOVAH. 6. And Ishmael the son of Nethaniah went forth from Mizpah to meet them, weeping all along as he went : and it came to pass as he met them, he said unto them, Come to Gedaliah the son of Ahikam. 7. And it was *so*, when they came into the midst of the city, that Ishmael the son of Nethaniah slew them, *and cast them* into the midst of the pit, he, and the men that *were* with him. 8. But ten men were found among them that said unto Ishmael, Slay us not : for we have treasures in the field, of wheat, and of barley, and of oil, and of honey. So he forbare, and slew them not among their brethren. 9. Now the pit wherein Ishmael had cast all the dead bodies of the men, whom he had slain because of Gedaliah, *was* it which Asa the king had made for fear of Baasha king of Israel : *and* Ishmael the son of Nethaniah filled it with *them that were* slain. 10. Then Ishmael carried away captive all the residue of the people that *were* in Mizpah, *even* the king's daughters, and all the people that remained in Mizpah, whom Nebuzar-adan the captain of the guard had committed to Geda-

---

of the new year ?) Ishmael's plot succeeds, and Gedaliah is slain. The traitor's weeping is truly Eastern. The survivors, rescued from Ishmael by Johanan, crowd together near Bethlehem, with eyes turned to Egypt for

liah the son of Ahikam : and Ishmael the son of Nethaniah carried them away captive, and departed to go over to the Ammonites.   A. V. XLI. 14.

11. But when Johanan the son of Kareah, and all the captains of the forces that *were* with him, heard of all the evil that Ishmael the son of Nethaniah had done, 12. then they took all the men, and went to fight with Ishmael the son of Nethaniah, and found him by the great waters that *are* in Gibeon. 13. Now it came to pass *that* when all the people which *were* with Ishmael saw Johanan the son of Kareah, and all the captains of the forces that *were* with him, then they were glad. 14. So all the people that Ishmael had carried away captive from Mizpah cast about and returned, and went unto Johanan the son of Kareah. 15. But Ishmael the son of Nethaniah escaped from Johanan with eight men, and went to the Ammonites. 16. Then took Johanan the son of Kareah, and all the captains of the forces that *were* with him, all the remnant of the people whom he had recovered from Ishmael the son of Nethaniah, from Mizpah, after *that* he had slain Gedaliah the son of Ahikam, *even* mighty men of war, and the women, and the children, and the eunuchs, whom he had brought again from Gibeon : 17. And they departed, and dwelt in the habitation of Chimham[332] which is by Bethlehem, to go to enter into Egypt. 18. Be-

---

[332] *In the habitation of Chimham.* Better with Hitzig, reading בְּגִדְרוֹת by the sheep-folds of Chimham. *Vulg.* peregrinantes in Chamaam, taking perhaps בָּרוּת as a hospice from בֵּר, LXX. γαβηρωχαμάα.

---

refuge, in case Babylonian vengeance should pursue them for the murder of the king's officer. During these months we may suppose Jeremiah arranging the records of his life, not without Baruch's help. He seems to have been ignorant of the plot against his patron.

Ch.XLIV. cause of the Chaldeans: for they were afraid of them, because Ishmael the son of Nethaniah had slain Gedaliah the son of Ahikam, whom the king of Babylon made governor in the land.

A. ¹
XLI. 1

XLV.

Ch. XLV. 1. Then all the captains of the forces, and Johanan the son of Kareah, and Jezaniah the son of Hoshaiah, and all the people from the least even unto the greatest, came near, 2. and said unto Jeremiah the prophet, Let, we beseech thee, our supplication be accepted before thee, and pray for us unto JEHOVAH thy God, *even* for all this remnant; (for we are left *but* a few of many, as thine eyes do behold us:) 3. That JEHOVAH thy God may shew us the way wherein we may walk, and the thing that we may do. 4. Then Jeremiah the prophet said unto them, I have heard *you*; behold, I will pray unto JEHOVAH your God according to your words; and it shall come to pass, *that* whatsoever thing JEHOVAH shall answer you, I will declare it unto you; I will keep nothing back from you. 5. Then they said to Jeremiah, JEHOVAH be a true and faithful witness between us, if we do not even according to all things for the which JEHOVAH thy God shall send thee to us. 6. Whether *it be* good, or whether *it be* evil, we will obey the voice of JEHOVAH our God, to whom we send thee; that it may be well with us, when we obey the voice of JEHOVAH our God.

A. ¹
XLII.

7. And it came to pass after ten days, that the word of JEHOVAH came unto Jeremiah. 8. Then called he Johanan the son of Kareah, and all the captains of the forces which

---

XLV. 1—22. The word, promised above, xliii. (A.V. xl. 1,) now commences. For in a weightier design, the countenance of a prophet is important; his counsel, and

XLV. *were* with him, and all the people from the least even to the greatest, 9. and said unto them, Thus saith JEHOVAH, the God of Israel, unto whom ye sent me to present your supplication before him; 10. If ye will still abide in this land, then will I build you, and not pull *you* down, and I will plant you, and not pluck *you* up: for I repent me of the evil that I have done unto you. 11. Be not afraid of the king of Babylon of whom ye are afraid; be not afraid of him, saith JEHOVAH: for I *am* with you, to save you, and to deliver you from his hand. 12. And I will shew mercies unto you, that he may have mercy upon you, and cause you to return to your own land.

13. But if ye say, We will not dwell in this land, neither obey the voice of JEHOVAH your God, 14. saying, No; but we will go into the land of Egypt, where we shall see no war, nor hear the sound of the trumpet, nor have hunger of bread; and there will we dwell: 15. And now therefore hear the word of JEHOVAH, ye remnant of Judah; Thus saith JEHOVAH of hosts, the God of Israel; If ye wholly set your faces to enter into Egypt, and go to sojourn there; 16. Then it shall come to pass, *that* the sword, which ye feared, shall overtake you there in the land of Egypt, and the famine, whereof ye were afraid, shall follow close after you there in Egypt; and there ye shall die. 17. So shall it be with all the men that set their faces to go into Egypt to sojourn there; they shall die by the sword, by the famine, and by the pestilence: and none of them shall remain or escape from the evil that I will bring upon them. 18. For thus saith JEHOVAH of hosts, the God of Israel; As mine anger and my fury hath

A. V.
XLII. 8.

---

through his prayers the sanction of Heaven, are sought. He gives it to reluctant ears; and feeling unable to retract the view he has all along maintained of Judah's

Ch. XLV. been poured forth upon the inhabitants of Jerusalem; so shall my fury be poured forth upon you, when ye shall enter into Egypt: and ye shall be an execration, and an astonishment, and a curse, and a reproach; and ye shall see this place no more. 19. JEHOVAH hath said concerning you, O ye remnant of Judah; Go ye not into Egypt: know certainly that I have admonished you this day. 20. For ye dissembled in your hearts,[333] when ye sent me unto JEHOVAH your God, saying, Pray for us unto JEHOVAH our God; and according unto all that JEHOVAH our God shall say, so declare unto us, and we will do *it*. 21. And *now* I have this day declared *it* to you; but ye have not obeyed the voice of JEHOVAH your God, nor any *thing* for the which he hath sent me unto you. 22. Now therefore know certainly that ye shall die by the sword, by the famine, and by the pestilence, in the place whither ye desire to go *and* to sojourn.

A. V
XLII. 1

XLVI.

Ch.XLVI. 1. And it came to pass, *that* when Jeremiah had made an end of speaking unto all the people all the words of JEHOVAH their God, for which JEHOVAH their God had sent him to them, *even* all these words, 2. Then spake Azariah

A. V
XLIII.

---

[333] *Ye dissembled in your hearts;* better, You sinned against your own lives. LXX. ἐπονηρεύσασθε ἐν ψυχαῖς ὑμῶν. Vulg. decepisti animas vestras.

---

destiny, and the necessity of accepting the Babylonian yoke, he learns in the demeanour of his hearers, how far asking counsel may fall short of obeying it.

1—7. Reverencing the prophet, not enough to obey him, but too much not to wish his countenance, the Jewish fugitives carry him into Egypt, where they settle at

XLVI. the son of Hoshaiah, and Johanan the son of Kareah, and all the proud men,[334] saying unto Jeremiah, Thou speakest falsely: JEHOVAH our God hath not sent thee to say, Go not into Egypt to sojourn there: 3. But Baruch the son of Neriah setteth thee on against us, for to deliver us into the hands of the Chaldeans, that they might put us to death, and carry us away captives into Babylon. 4. So Johanan the son of Kareah, and all the captains of the forces, and all the people, obeyed not the voice of JEHOVAH, to dwell in the land of Judah. 5. But Johanan the son of Kareah, and all the captains of the forces, took all the remnant of Judah, that were returned from all nations, whither they had been driven, to dwell in the land of Judah; 6. *Even* men, and women, and children, and the king's daughters, and every person that Nebuzar-adan the captain of the guard had left with Gedaliah the son of Ahikam the son of Shaphan, and Jeremiah the prophet, and Baruch the son of Neriah. 7. So they came into the land of Egypt: for they obeyed not the voice of JEHOVAH: thus came they *even* to Tahpanhes.

A. V.
XLIII. 2.

---

[334] *And all the proud men.* *Vulg.* et omnes viri superbi. LXX. καὶ πάντες οἱ ἄνδρες, as if men, in contradistinction to women.

Daphnæ (Her. ii. xxx.) south-west of the Pelusiac mouth of the Nile, and thence spread themselves to Heliopolis or On, (here Bethshemesh). Here is an instance, the earliest manifest, of that Jewish influx, which made Egypt one of the literary centres of the race. On Egyptian soil Jeremiah's works reached completion; Isaiah's underwent recension; the book of Nahum perhaps was written; the stories associated with the name of Daniel probably originated. The temple built by the fugitive Onias at Leontopolis, (see note on Isa. xvii. and compare Jos. A. J. xiii. 3,) must have had its own editions and copies. Greek

CH.XLVI. 8. Then came the word of JEHOVAH unto Jeremiah in Tahpanhes, saying, 9. Take great stones in thine hand, and hide them in the clay in the brickkiln, which *is* at the entry of Pharaoh's house in Tahpanhes, in the sight of the men of Judah; 10. And say unto them, Thus saith JEHOVAH of hosts, the God of Israel; Behold, I will send and take Nebuchadrezzar the king of Babylon, my servant, and will set his throne upon these stones that I have hid; and he shall spread his royal pavilion[335] over them. 11. And when he cometh, he shall smite the land of Egypt, *and deliver* such *as are* for death to death; and such *as are* for captivity to captivity; and such *as are* for the sword to the sword. 12. And I will kindle a fire in the houses of the gods of Egypt; and he shall burn them, and carry them away captives: and he shall array himself with the land of Egypt, as a shepherd putteth on his garment; and he shall go forth from thence in peace. 13. He shall break also the images of Beth-shemesh,[336] that *is* in the land of Egypt; and the houses of the gods of the Egyptians shall he burn with fire.

A. V. XLIII.

---

[335] *His royal pavilion.* So not amiss A. V. after Kimchi, some sign of judicial splendour is meant. LXX. ἀρεῖ τὰ ὅπλα ἐπ' αὐτούς. *Vulg.* solium suum.

[336] *The images of Beth-shemesh;* better, perhaps, with Hitzig, the pillars of the temple of the Sun; which, however, might be meant at Heliopolis. LXX. τοὺς στύλους Ἡλιοπόλεως τοὺς ἐν Ὤν. *Vulg.* conteret statuas domus Solis. It is not without interest to find the ancient Version occasionally confirmed by the boldest of modern critics, perhaps the keenest.

---

influences subsequently contributed to give us Philo, Origen, Athanasius, in whom Christ absorbs Plato, and the prophets become Gentile, without being Pagan.

8—13. Haunted by the certainty of the Babylonian conqueror's arm reaching to Egypt, Jeremiah represents in symbol his throne as Jehovah's vicegerent, and foretells ruin and flame.

XLVII.

1. The word that came to Jeremiah concerning all the Jews which dwell in the land of Egypt, which dwell at Migdol, and at Tahpanhes, and at Noph, and in the country of Pathros, saying, 2. Thus saith JEHOVAH of hosts, the God of Israel; Ye have seen all the evil that I have brought upon Jerusalem, and upon all the cities of Judah; and, behold, this day they *are* a desolation, and no man dwelleth therein, 3. Because of their wickedness which they have committed to provoke me to anger, in that they went to burn incense, *and* to serve other gods, whom they knew not, *neither* they, ye, nor your fathers. 4. Howbeit I sent unto you all my servants the prophets, rising early and sending *them*, saying, Oh, do not this abominable thing that I hate. 5. But they hearkened not, nor inclined their ear to turn from their wickedness, to burn no incense unto other gods. 6. Wherefore my fury and mine anger was poured forth, and was kindled in the cities of Judah and in the streets of Jerusalem: and they are wasted *and* desolate, as at this day. 7. Therefore now thus saith JEHOVAH, the God of hosts, the

A. V.
XLIV. 1.

1—15. The tragedy of Jeremiah's life draws to a close. Reaching Egypt in 585, he found his people scattered throughout the towns of the north, perhaps southward, (if Pathros be Upper Egypt,) and adopting Egyptian manners, or retaining nature-worship of the Moon and elements. His spirit felt such a course unblest. He must have foreseen, that Nebuchadnezzar, who on Jerusalem's fall had turned his arms against Tyre, would, whenever that siege ended, be attracted to Egypt; and the battle of Carchemish foreshadowed the result of such invasion. Would it not be better to seek again the Holy Land even

God of Israel; Wherefore commit ye *this* great evil against your souls, to cut off from you man and woman, child and suckling, out of Judah, to leave you none to remain; 8. In that ye provoke me unto wrath with the works of your hands, burning incense unto other gods in the land of Egypt, whither ye be gone to dwell, that ye might cut yourselves off, and that ye might be a curse and a reproach among all the nations of the earth? 9. Have ye forgotten the wickedness of your fathers, and the wickedness of the kings of Judah, and the wickedness of their wives, and your own wickedness, and the wickedness of your wives, which they have committed in the land of Judah, and in the streets of Jerusalem? 10. They are not humbled *even* unto this day, neither have they feared, nor walked in my law, nor in my statutes, that I set before you and before your fathers.

11. Therefore thus saith JEHOVAH of hosts, the God of Israel; Behold, I will set my face against you for evil, and to cut off all Judah. 12. And I will take the remnant of Judah, that have set their faces to go into the land of Egypt to sojourn there, and they shall all be consumed, *and* fall in the land of Egypt; they shall *even* be consumed by the sword *and* by the famine: they shall die, from the least even unto the greatest, by the sword and by the famine: and they shall be an execration, *and* an astonishment, and a curse, and a reproach. 13. For I will punish them that dwell in the land of Egypt, as I

---

in its desolation, and there await the Divine will? So he warns and remonstrates; but (15—19) the exiles, including now the women, to whom the pale Queen of heaven seemed a more accessible object of worship than an invisible Spirit, reject angrily his word. So the prophet (20—28) once more, for the last recorded time, in collision

have punished Jerusalem, by the sword, by the famine, and by the pestilence: 14. So that none of the remnant of Judah, which are gone into the land of Egypt to sojourn there, shall escape or remain, that they should return into the land of Judah, to the which they have a desire to return to dwell there: for none shall return but such as shall escape.

A. V.
XLIV. 13.

15. Then all the men which knew that their wives had burned incense unto other gods, and all the women that stood by, a great multitude, even all the people that dwelt in the land of Egypt, in Pathros, answered Jeremiah, saying, 16. *As for* the word that thou hast spoken unto us in the name of JEHOVAH, we will not hearken unto thee. 17. But we will certainly do whatsoever thing goeth forth out of our own mouth, to burn incense unto the queen of heaven, and to pour out drink offerings unto her, as we have done, we, and our fathers, our kings, and our princes, in the cities of Judah, and in the streets of Jerusalem: for *then* had we plenty of victuals, and were well, and saw no evil. 18. But since we left off to burn incense to the queen of heaven, and to pour out drink offerings unto her, we have wanted all *things*, and have been consumed by the sword and by the famine. 19. And when we burned incense to the queen of heaven, and poured out drink offerings unto her, did we make her cakes to wor-

---

with those whom he had loved in vain, throws the issue into the hands of God, whose word he had spoken. Let the fate of (29, 30) Pharaoh-Hophra (Apries, Her. ii. 161), as it should resemble, or not, that of Zedekiah captured by the besieger, decide the issue of refractoriness or resignation. If the tradition in Epiphanius, vol. ii. p. 239, that the Prophet was stoned by the Jews at Daphnæ, be true, this challenge was a likely prelude to the crime.

Ch.
XLVII.
ship her, and pour out drink offerings unto her, without our men?

20. Then Jeremiah said unto all the people, to the men, and to the women, and to all the people which had given him *that answer*, saying, 21. The incense that ye burned in the cities of Judah, and in the streets of Jerusalem, ye, and your fathers, your kings, and your princes, and the people of the land, did not JEHOVAH remember them, and came it not into his mind? 22. So that JEHOVAH could no longer bear, because of the evil of your doings, *and* because of the abominations which ye have committed; therefore is your land a desolation, and an astonishment, and a curse, without an inhabitant, as at this day. 23. Because ye have burned incense, and because ye have sinned against JEHOVAH, and have not obeyed the voice of JEHOVAH, nor walked in his law, nor in his statutes, nor in his testimonies; therefore this evil is happened unto you, as at this day. 24. Moreover Jeremiah said unto all the people, and to all the women, Hear the word of JEHOVAH, all Judah that *are* in the land of Egypt: 25. Thus saith JEHOVAH of hosts, the God of Israel, saying; Ye and your wives have both spoken with your mouths, and fulfilled with your hand, saying, We will surely perform our vows that we have vowed, to burn incense to the queen of heaven, and to pour out drink offerings unto

---

Here for us, (even if omission of the date in the text permits us to restore here chap. xxxi. (A. V. xlv.) the Prophet disappears. If it be asked, does the last verse, followed by the death of Apries, at the hands of his rival Amasis, in 570, imply clear prediction, we must answer, that (1) we do not know when Jeremiah died, (2) still less, whether Baruch finished the chapter; but more conclusively, that (3) the utterances on Egypt, chap. xxiv. (A. V. xlvi.) shew

Ch. VII.

A. V. XLIV. 25.

her: ye will surely accomplish your vows, and surely perform your vows. 26. Therefore hear ye the word of JEHOVAH, all Judah that dwell in the land of Egypt; Behold, I have sworn by my great name, saith JEHOVAH, that my name shall no more be named in the mouth of any man of Judah in all the land of Egypt, saying, The Lord GOD liveth. 27. Behold, I will watch over them for evil, and not for good: and all the men of Judah that *are* in the land of Egypt shall be consumed by the sword and by the famine, until there be an end of them. 28. Yet a small number that escape the sword shall return out of the land of Egypt into the land of Judah, and all the remnant of Judah, that are gone into the land of Egypt to sojourn there, shall know whose word shall stand, mine, or their's.

29. And this *shall be* a sign unto you, saith JEHOVAH, that I will punish you in this place, that ye may know that my word shall surely stand against you for evil: 30. Thus saith JEHOVAH; Behold, I will give Pharaoh-hophrah king of Egypt into the hand of his enemies, and into the hand of them that seek his life; as I gave Zedekiah king of Judah into the hand of Nebuchadrezzar king of Babylon, his enemy, and that sought his life.[337]

---

[337] At the end of this chapter, unless we append to it chap. xxxi. (A. V. xlv.) (supposing the date of Jehoiakim's reign therein erroneous,) might well come the remark which some post-Babylonian editor has placed at the end of chap. li.,

"Thus far are the words of Jeremiah."

---

the connexion in the writer's mind to have been with the Babylonian invasion. Hence we hardly go beyond presentiment. The absence in any secular historian of confirmatory mention of Nebuchadnezzar's conquest of Egypt made Scaliger suppose that Divine mercy had remitted

XLVIII.

Cн.
XLVIII.

[338] *The word which was to Jeremiah from the* ETERNAL, *saying, Thus saith the* ETERNAL, *God of Israel, saying, Write thee all the words which I spake unto thee, on a scroll: for behold days coming, is the* ETERNAL'S *saying, for me to restore the captivity of my people Israel and Judah, saith the* ETERNAL, *and I will bring them back to the land which I gave to their fathers, that they may inherit it.* [*And these are the words which the* ETERNAL *spake of Israel and of Judah.*] For thus saith the ETERNAL,

---

[338] The title, containing the Hebrew for *say, saying, speak, speech,* nine times, is evidently composite. The initial words of the piece, *For thus saith the Eternal,* are in their nature fragmentary. Whoever detached them from some whole now lost, prefixing them to our oracular poem, gave with them probably as a distinctive sign amidst MSS. the smaller title here bracketed, וְאֵלֶּה. *These too are words which Jehovah spake, &c.* The conjecture of a subsequent editor superadded the long paraphrastic title, which now ascribes the chapter, erroneously in its present form, to Jeremiah.

---

the penalty, as, he adds, in the case of Jonah and (less appropriately) of Nahum. Others have thought of the furious career of Cambyses, described in Herodot. ii. We should rather say that by him the pillars of Heliopolis were broken. (Comp. Rosenm. on xliii. 13.)

XLVIII. XLIX. (A. V.) XXX. XXXI. These two chapters, separated by a long title from the xxxviith (A. V. xxixth), by a shorter title from the xxxixth (A. V. xxxiind) and xlth (A. V. xxxiiird), and by subject, time, and treatment, from both, are sufficiently congenial to xxxii. and xxxiii. (A. V.) for an editor to have grouped them together early, and for most critics to retain the grouping. Closer examination shews (as in his treatise, Hamburg, 1837, Movers suggested), a very distinct character in these two chapters. No part of them is so early as the 10th year of Zedekiah's reign, when the city was yet besieged. Some parts may have followed close on the

Ch. .VIII.
1. A voice of trembling we heard:[339] terror *was*, and no peace.

A. V. xxx. 5.

2. Ask now, and behold, whether man is big with child: wherefore do I see every man with his hands on his loins, like a woman bearing child; and all faces are turned into paleness?

3. Alas! for that day is great, so that there is none

---

[339] *We heard.* So Heb. *Vulg.* audivimus, but LXX. ἀκούσεσθε.

---

capture, for Rachel's weeping in Ramah suits too well Nebuzaradan's probable treatment of his prisoners. So most of the verses here numbered 1, 2, 3, 8, 9, 10, 11, seem elegiac remembrances of the hour when princes were slain before the eyes of a father, soon to be blinded, and when fragments of the poor remnant of the people were spared by contempt. Other parts, such as the address to God's servant Jacob, and the picture of Jehovah's whirlwind going forth in fury, seem hardly in their natural place, and are found elsewhere. The general tone (most so in the 2nd chapter) is of the time when the exile was drawing to its end. Long suffering has been borne. Strangers have been lords. The old covenant has failed, through Israel's sin. God will strike a new one, more spiritual, of larger freedom. The sanctuary, long desolate, shall be restored. Such considerations have more force in such a book of fragments as we have before us, than in a compact whole; and ought, I think, to persuade us that the piece is a song of encouragement by some Baruch or later Isaiah, far on in the exile, who yet may have used relics of the older prophet (perhaps his master?) as key-notes, from which to start his strain. Probably he had chaps. xxxix. (A. V. xxxii.) xl. (A. V. xxxiii.) before him.

1—3. Perplexity and distress are described, out of which the writer hopes deliverance, (4) with breaking of

like it; and a time of distress it is for Jacob; yet out of it he shall be saved;

4. And it shall be in that day, is the saying of the ETERNAL of hosts, I will shiver his yoke from off thy neck, and burst thy bonds, and strangers shall make him serve no more;

5. But they shall serve the ETERNAL their God, and the David their king, whom I will raise up for them.[340]

6. [And thou fear not, my servant Jacob, is the ETERNAL's saying, and be not dismayed, Israel; for behold me saving thee from afar, and thy seed from the land of their captivity; so that Jacob return, and rest, and be tranquil, and there be none to affray *him*.

7. For I am with thee to save thee, is the ETERNAL's saying; for I will make an end with all the nations whither I have scattered thee; only with thee I will not make an end, but correct thee in measure, and not leave thee utterly unpunished.[341]]

8. Yea, thus saith the ETERNAL of thy wound, it is desperate, and thy stroke grievous.

---

[340] On v. 5, compare Hosea i. ii. iii. with the Notes upon those passages, and the Introduction to that prophet in my version. Possibly the *quasi*-definite article prefixed to the name David, may be understood as making it titular.

[341] Verses 6, 7, are wanting in the LXX., and suspiciously like the later Isaiah, chaps. xli.—iii.—iv., li., but also have been found above Jer. xxiv. 23, 24 (A. V. xlvi. 27-8), where also they have the air of an editor's addition, perhaps even more so than here.

---

stranger's yoke, and (5) restoration of king David's line to the throne.

6, 7. Such a hope throws in a promise, such as the later Isaiah in the exile's end lavishes on Jehovah's servant, ideal or prophetic Israel.

8. But at present the sickness is desperate, as in

'II. 9. None pleads thy plea for bondage; medicines of
VIII. healing thou hast none.

10. All thy lovers have forgotten thee, seek thee not out; since the stroke of an enemy I struck thee, the chastisement of a cruel one; for the multitude of thy iniquity, *wherewith* thy sins prevailed.³⁴²

11. Why criest thou over thy wound, *that* thy pain is desperate? for the multitude of thy iniquity, *wherewith* thy sins prevailed,³⁴² I wrought these things to thee.

12. Now then shall all thy devourers be devoured, and all thy enemies, the whole of them, go into captivity; and thy spoilers shall be a spoil, and all thy plunderers will I give to plunder.

13. For I will raise up healing for thee, and cure thee of thy wounds, is the ETERNAL's saying; though they have called thee Outcast, This Zion,³⁴³ whom no man seeks after.

14. Thus saith the ETERNAL, Behold me turning the captivity of the tents of Jacob, and pitying his dwelling-places; so that the city be built upon its mound, and the palace established in its rightful place;³⁴⁴

15. So that thanksgiving come forth from them, and the voice of mirth-makers; and I will multiply them, that they be not few, and glorify them, that they be not small.

---

³⁴² *Thy sins prevailed*, i.e. either were strong and overbearing in themselves; or were effectual for thy chastisement. *Vulg.* dura facta sunt. LXX. ἐπλήθυναν, and ἐπληθύνθησαν.

³⁴³ *This Zion, &c.*; or, Zion is outcast. *Vulg.* Hæc est quæ non habebat requirentem. LXX. ἐσπαρμένη ἐκλήθης, θήρευμα ὑμῶν ἐστιν. Philippsohn finds a verbal play in the word, as denoting *dryness* and desolation; rather a Rabbinising notion.

³⁴⁴ *Rightful place.* Heb. judgment, or custom.

Isaiah i. of Israel, (9) left to himself, and (10, 11) stricken of Heaven. 12, 13. One only can heal, and (14—16)

Ch. XLVIII.

16. Their children also shall be as aforetime, and their congregation shall be established before me, and I will punish all that oppress them.

17. And their lords shall be of themselves, and their rulers come forth from their midst; and I will draw[345] them that they come near to me; yea, whoso is the man that has pledged his heart, I draw to come near to me, is the ETERNAL'S saying; 18. so that you be to me a people, and I be to you God.[346]

[19. [347] Behold, JEHOVAH'S whirlwind is gone forth in fury; the tempest, gathering itself, whirls upon the head of the wicked.

20. The fury of JEHOVAH'S anger will not turn back, until he have finished, and until he have accomplished the intents of his heart; in the after-time of days you shall have understanding therein.]

21. In that time, is the ETERNAL'S saying, will I be to all the families of Israel God, and they shall be to me a people.

22. Thus saith the ETERNAL, the people of survivors

---

[345] *I draw.* Such an apodosis, suggested by the verb above, seems needful.
[346] Verse 17 is wanting in the LXX.
[347] Verses 19, 20, have already occurred Jer. xxii. (A. V. xxiii.) 19, 20, where, though little needed by the context, they disturb it less than here; but if we take them as a *locus poeticus*, an ornament added for energy's sake by an editor in both places, we see how easily the sentiment of vv. 18—21, expressed once by the prophet, might come in twice from an editor or confused transcriber. I owe the suggestion of this note in part to Hitzig.

---

will restore. This could only have been written after subjection to foreigners in exile.

17. Instead of strangers, Jehovah setting up their own race will make his people, (18—21) whoever vows the heart's allegiance to the eternal King; (19, 20) such deliverance coming about even with storm of vengeance.

21. As of old in the exit from Egypt and the wander-

of the sword has found grace in the wilderness; *as he went to give him rest,*[348] Israel, from afar, *he saith*, the ETERNAL appeared to me;[349]

23. Yea, with an everlasting love I loved thee; therefore I prolonged for thee mercy.

24. I will again build thee, that thou shalt be built, Virgin of Israel; again shalt be adorned with thy tabrets, and go forth in the dance of mirth-makers;

25. Again shalt thou plant vineyards on Samaria's heights, *saying*, Plant, planters, and eat freely;[350] 26. since there is a day for the watchers on Ephraim's mount to cry, Arise, and let us go up to Zion, to the ETERNAL, our God.

27. Since thus saith the ETERNAL, Sing out gladness for Jacob, and shout against the front of the nations,[351] proclaim, utter praise, and cry, Save, ETERNAL, thy people, the remnant of Israel.

28. Behold me bringing them from the land of the north, that I gather them from the ends of the earth; amongst them blind and lame,[352] pregnant, and child-

---

[348] *As he went to give him rest.* The Heb. infinitive is variously taken here, as a Divine resolve (let me go), or as an accompaniment; and again applied either to Jehovah, or to Israel; but comp. Psalm lxviii. 7.

[349] *Appeared to me.* So Heb. and Vulg. but the LXX. reading ὤφθη αὐτῷ is certainly far more probable.

[350] *Plant, planters, and eat freely;* or, planters, planted and ate freely, *lit.* desecrated, LXX. φυτεύσατε καὶ αἰνέσατε. Vulg. plantabunt plantantes, not so well.

[351] *Against the front of the nations.* Vulg. hinnite contra caput gentium. LXX. χρεμετίσατε ἐπὶ κεφαλὴν ἐθνῶν.

[352] *Amongst them blind and lame.* LXX. ἐν ἑορτῇ φασέκ, a most curious mistake; nor less, because arrived at by reading in the Hebrew, במועד פסח. Even this is not uninstructive as regards the nature of Heb. MSS. Jerome's own Text following the Greek: not so the Vulgate.

---

ing, God will draw his betrothed to him, (24) building not only Zion, but Samaria, (25) and restoring joy of vintage (26—29) in the day of universal restoration even from

Ch. XLVIII.
A. V. xxxi. 8

bearing woman together, a vast company shall return hither.

29. With weeping they come, and with supplications I lead them; I will make them walk along rivers of waters in a straight way, wherein they shall not stumble; for I am become a father to Israel, and Ephraim is my first born.

XLIX.

Ch. XLIX.
A. V. xxxi. 1

1. Hear, O Nations, the word of the ETERNAL, and proclaim in the isles afar off, and say, He that scattered Israel,[353] gathers him, and will guard him, as a shepherd his flock.

2. For the ETERNAL has redeemed Jacob, and ransomed him from the hand of one strong beyond him;

3. So that they come and sing in the height of Zion, and stream to the goodness of the ETERNAL, to corn, and to wine, and to oil, and to young of flock and of herd; and their soul is as a watered garden; and they sorrow again no more.

4. Then rejoices the virgin in the dance,[354] and young men and old men together, and I turn their mourning

---

[353] *He that scattered Israel.* So all versions and critics. But we may suspect that the subject of the verb is Jehovah, and the participle *he that scattered* should be pointed and translated as an infinitive; instead of scattering he gathers Israel.

[354] *The virgin in the dance, &c.* LXX. τότε χαρήσονται παρθένοι ἐν συναγωγῇ νεανίσκων.

---

afar. We have as it were the later Isaiah here. Here also Movers finds the special promise of the prophets during the rebuilding of the Temple, quoted by Zech. viii. 7, 8, 9.

1—5. Recalling Israel, instead of scattering him, Jehovah proclaims his will to the nations, and lavishes the

into gladness, and comfort them, and make them rejoice after their sorrow. A. V. xxxi. 13.

5. And I feed the souls of the priests full with fatness, and my people are satiated with my goodness, is the saying of the ETERNAL.

6. Thus saith the ETERNAL, *when* A voice was heard in Ramah,³⁵⁵ lamentation of weeping bitterly, Rachel weeping over her sons; refusing³⁵⁶ to be comforted for her sons, because they were no more;

7. Thus saith the ETERNAL, Refrain thy voice from weeping, and thine eyes from tears; for there is yet reward for thy labour, is the ETERNAL's saying, that they shall return from the enemy's land; 8. and there is yet hope for thy aftertime, is the ETERNAL's saying, that thy sons shall return to their border.

---

³⁵⁵ For *Ramah*, Jerome has in excelso, but understands the word, as a local name, of the townlet near Bethlehem. He points out, "nec juxta Hebraicum, nec juxta LXX. Matthæus sumpsit testimonium."

³⁵⁶ *Refusing*, etc. *Vulg.* fletus Rachel plorantis filios suos et nolentis consolari super eis quia non sunt. Heb. sing. because he is not; each is not.

---

bounties of earth on priests and people in the new-born commonwealth.

6, 7. The Prophet, seeing his countrymen bound at Ramah for exile by Nebuzaradan, imagines the wail of their ancestress, and bids her hope for the return in days to come. The imagination of infant Christendom, gathering into our first Gospel pictures of danger which threatened the mightier Deliverer's foreboded greatness, found here words easily applicable to Herod's rage at Bethlehem. Jewish interpreters, awakening between the 2nd and 4th centuries to a sense of strange wrong in having their own prophets wrested from them, but unable to acquiesce in the simple solution of Jeremiah's describing things before his eyes, contended for a prediction here of Vespasian's

Ch.
XLIX.

9. Surely I have heard Ephraim complaining, Thou hast chastened me, and I was chastened, like a young ox[357] untamed; turn thou me, that I may return, for thou, ETERNAL, *art* my God; 10. yea, after my turning I repented, and after my chastening I smote upon my thigh; I am ashamed, yea, even confounded, for I have borne the reproach of my youth.

A.
xxxi.

11. Is Ephraim a dear son to me? is he a darling child? that often as I reproach him, I earnestly remember him again; therefore my heartstrings are troubled for him; I pity him exceedingly, is the saying of the ETERNAL.

12. Set thee up way-marks, place for thyself columnar stones;[358] set thine heart upon the raised road, the way that thou wentest; return, virgin of Israel, return to these

---

[357] *A young ox.* A. V. bullock, in the provincial usage for the young of either sex, heifer, etc.

[358] *Set thee up waymarks, place for thyself columnar stones;* as it were palm-trees, pillars of palm-like shape. LXX. by an extraordinary blunder, Grecising instead of translating; στῆσον σεαυτὴν Σιών, ποίησον τιμωρίαν. Not much better, the Vulgate, after Jerome, has *amaritudines.*

---

sending Jewish captives by Gaza to Egypt, or of Hadrian's selling such in the slave market. *Dicant illi quod volunt,* says Jerome, vindicating our first Gospel's adaptation. In truth he and they were more guided by volition, than by obedience to the Prophet's text, or perception of his mind.

9—11. Tones savouring of Hosea suggest that the Divine tenderness will include the prodigal Ephraim as well as the more hopeful son Judah.

12, 13. The lost bride, wooed not in vain by Jehovah in the desert, but since gone astray after idolatrous pomp, shall now be brought back from exile, with her heart so renewed by miraculous grace, that instead of turning

thy cities. 13. How long wilt thou turn waywardly, thou refractory daughter? when the ETERNAL creates a new thing in the earth, that *the* bride shall court *her* lord.³⁵⁹

14. Thus saith the ETERNAL of hosts, the God of Israel, Again shall they utter this speech in Judah and in its cities, when I turn again their captivity: The ETERNAL bless thee, dwelling-place of righteousness, mount of the sanctuary; 15. And therein shall be established Judah and all her cities; husbandmen together, and *they that go forth with flocks;*³⁶⁰ 16. Since I feed full the weary soul, and satiate every soul that yearned.

17. Upon this I awoke, and beheld; and my sleep had been pleasant to me.

18. ³⁶¹ Behold days coming, is the ETERNAL'S saying, for me to sow the house of Israel and the house of Judah with the seed of man and with the seed of beast; 19. and it shall be, as I watched over them to uproot, and to shatter, and to ruin, and to destroy, and to afflict, So will

A. V.
xxxi. 22.

---

³⁵⁹ *The bride shall court;* or, shall protect; or shall turn round into a warrior. The novelty consists in Jehovah's spouse, so long refractory, turning round at his solicitation to seek whom she had forsaken. But many critics conceive safety, so that the very woman is protectress, to be intended. We can in no possible or tolerable way, gross or refined, extract any Messianic sense.

³⁶⁰ *And they that go forth with flocks;* or this clause may be co-ordinate with the former; i.e. and shall go forth, etc.

³⁶¹ 18, 19. Compare Hosea, chaps. i. and ii. which correspond with this part remarkably in style and sentiment,

---

away, she will turn to her heart's true lord, and cling to him. Comp. Hos. i. ii. iii.

14—16. Temple, home, and field, will attest God at peace with his people; (17) so pleasant the Prophet's vision.

18, 19. Entire restoration from ruin will (20) abolish

Ch. XLIX.

I watch over them to build, and to plant, is the saying of the Eternal.

20. [362] In those days they shall say no more, The fathers ate sour grapes, and the children's teeth are set on edge, 21. but each in his own iniquity shall die; every man that eats the sour grape, his teeth shall be set on edge.

22. [363] Behold days coming, is the saying of the Eternal, for me to strike with the house of Israel and with the house of Judah a New Covenant, 23. not like the Covenant which I struck with their fathers, in the day of my taking them by the hand to bring them forth from the land of Egypt, which my Covenant they made void, though I was their lord,[364] is the saying of the Eternal; 23. But this

---

[362] 20, 21. The proverbial saying of these verses is found in Ezekiel xviii. 2, and may be compared above with Jer. xviii. 8, and xxiii. 36—8.

[363] 22—24. With this passage, one of the most significant in the whole prophetic volume, should be compared Ep. Heb. viii. 7—13; but beware of adding to it, as is commonly done, e.g. by Alford and others, Ezek. xx. 25, 26; for the evil statutes and precepts there meant are not the Mosaic laws of Jehovah, but the abominable laws of Moloch, to which God's righteous reprobation gave over the undistinguishing minds of those who had dishonoured him. So sin is punished by sin repeating and scourging itself.

[364] *Though I was lord over them;* i.e. protector; but LXX. καὶ ἐγὼ ἠμέλησα αὐτῶν, whence some look out for a Hebrew term of reprobation. Barely might it mean, I became Baal to them.

---

temptation to repining proverbs, (21) the ways of God to man being justified. The perverseness of events, by which consequence oversteps desert, has often passed into human judgment of acts; the Prophet, seeing that this does not sway the Divine judgment, which is according to truth, hopes that events, in their power to make or mar man's happiness, may reflect the Divine equity.

22. Sounding the deepest mystery of religion, the Prophet predicts the New Testament, or rather, (23) seeing the weakness of outward instruments when treated as

is the Covenant, which I strike with the house of Israel after those days, is the saying of the ETERNAL; I put my law in their inner being, and write it in their heart; 24. So that I become to them God, and they become to me a people, and they teach no more each his neighbour, and each his brother, saying, Know the ETERNAL; for all of them shall know me, from little even to great, is the saying of the ETERNAL; because I forgive their iniquity, and remember their sin no more.

A. V.
xxxi. 33.

---

ends, (inasmuch as the unenlightened mind, not feeling their moral force, easily breaks from their forms,) he puts the conscience in place of Scripture, and makes the heart the page upon which the Spirit's writing must precede its transfer to outward document; (24) so that the congregation becomes both priesthood and temple; its reason is inspired, its voice oracular, its sense of God's pity in forgiving sin, creates it afresh into a life of humility and thankfulness beyond mere nature's grasp. This great word of God, employed by St. Paul, or as Saint Jerome well says, by whoever else wrote (sive quis alius scripsit) the Epistle to the Hebrews, (viii. 7—13,) is the Christian's warrant for a freedom of trust which takes up all truth into the faith of the Church. Hence no discovery can hurt Christianity, for whatever is true, is Christian, as St. Augustine often taught. But hence also St. Augustine is more right than St. Jerome, since the first makes every law of the letter, and of Old Testament literalism, abolished in Christ, while the second abolishes only the ceremonial law; all which Luther on the Galatians well shews. Hence all that the nobler mystics and more reasoning Quakers have said from St. Paul in 2 Cor. i. and iii. down to the purer neologians of our time, is justified; here is a charter which makes freedom of thought orthodox, so that without neology is no Christianity. Moreover, hence the Bible is the written voice of the con-

Ch. XLIX.

25. Thus saith the Eternal, who gives the sun for a light by day, the laws of the moon and stars for a light by night, who rouses[365] the sea that its billows roar, whose name is the Eternal of hosts; 26. If those laws can be removed from before me, is the saying of the Eternal, the seed of Israel also shall cease from being a nation before me days without end.

27. Thus saith the Eternal, If the heavens can be measured from above, and the foundations of the earth searched out to beneath, I also will reject the seed of Israel for all that they have done, is the saying of the Eternal.

28. Behold days coming, is Jehovah's saying, when the city shall be builded to Jehovah, from the tower of Hananeel[366] to the corner-gate; 29. and over against it shall go forth the measuring line upon the hill Gareb,[367] and

---

[365] *Who rouses* (or rebukes) *the sea, that its billows roar.* Vulg. not much amiss, qui turbat mare, et sonant fluctus ejus, but LXX. more confusedly, ὁ δοὺς . . . . . . κραυγὴν ἐν θαλάσσῃ, καὶ ἐβόμβησε τὰ κύματα αὐτῆς.

[366] *Hananeel*, the tower of, was N. E. of the city, near the fish-gate, Nehem. iii. 1—3, and xii. 39, Zech. xiv. 10.

[367] *Gareb*, the hill, whether meaning the rough place, or the lepers' abode, (like our St. Giles's quarter,) outside of the city, is placed by Schleusner N. (perhaps N. W.) and identified with "the fourth hill, called Bezetha," of Josephus, B. J. v. 4, 2.

---

gregation; *i.e.* the record of its experience, and the expression of its God-determined spirit. Not merely the canonisation of Scripture is from the Church, but through the Church also its inspiration: only the Church is made up of men.

25—27. Still the Prophet views such Divine freedom from a national, though not a strongly sacerdotal, point, and places its sphere chiefly in Israel; whereas Christ and St. Paul will place it in mankind.

28—30. The nobler utterances shrink to a contempla-

XLIX. reach round to Goah ;³⁶⁸ 30. and all the valley of the car-   A. V.
cases, and the ashes, and all the channels³⁶⁹ to the Kidron   XXXI. 40.
ravine, to the corner of the horse-gate from the east, *shall
be a sanctuary to* JEHOVAH; *it shall not be uprooted, nor
ruined, any more for ever.*

L.

u. L.   *The word which* JEHOVAH *spake against Babel.* [*Against*   A. V. L. l.
*the land of the Chaldees, by the hand of Jeremiah the pro-
phet.*]³⁷⁰

---

³⁶⁸ *Goah;* not the height, but the lowing-place, or cattle-pond, is vaguely guessed E. between the Temple and the Kidron, perhaps near the sheep-pond; though others infer it to have been in an opposite quarter to the horse-gate, described as East.

³⁶⁹ *The channels* (if so, with the Targum, we are to translate the unique word *Sheremoth,* for which the Masora conjectures *Shedemoth,* fields,) are mentioned in order to comprehend the area of the Temple, precinct, suburb; the sense being that the sanctuary should have the widest extent, and unfailing duration. The LXX. confess the obscurity of the word *Sheremoth* (channels?) by Grecising it, πάντες ἀσαρημώθ. Jerome's version here differs, I know not why, from the Roman Vulgate; he writes, "norma sive juxta Symmachum funiculus, mensuræ ejus contra eam super collem Gareb, et circuibit Goatha; sive juxta LXX. de electis lapidibus [Gr. ἐξ ἐκλεκτῶν λίθων]. Et omnem vallem ruinarum (pro quibus Theodotio ipsum verbum Hebraicum posuit *phagarim*) et cineres et omnem Assaremoth, quod melius legimus Shedemoth, (pro quo Aquila suburbana interpretatus est,) usque ad torrentem Cedron." But the Vulgate has omnem vallem cadaverum, et cineris, et universam regionem mortis (this is a subdivision of the Hebrew word into two inappropriate vocables,) usque ad torrentem C. Jerome's marginal comment countenances the variation.

³⁷⁰ The title in the Greek ends with the word Babel, or Babylon. The remainder is more likely to have been added by a Hebrew editor, than omitted by the LXX.

---

tion of the sanctuary restored to its full limits on Zion, much in the manner of Ezekiel, and of the close of Obadiah. The transition here corresponds with that in the closing verses of Psalm li.

As Jeremiah's mission had been to present the cup of

Ch. L.   1. Proclaim among the nations, and announce, and lift up banner; announce, keep not secret, cry, Babylon

---

Divine wrath to the reluctant lip of tyrants, and his original book, xxx. (A. V. xxxvi.) 2 had contained, in Jehoiakim's fourth year, the threats spoken by him, as specified in chap. xxiii. (A. V. xxv.) during the preceding twenty-three years, so we must believe that, about chap. xxiii. (A. V. xxv.) his original book contained utterances on the nations. So the Greek, more faithful than our existing Hebrew, to what must have been the original form of the book, still presents at xxv. 34, ἃ ἐπροφήτευσεν Ἰερεμίας ἐπὶ τὰ ἔθνη τὰ Ἀιλάμ, κ. τ. λ.

But even if Jeremiah, in adding to the restored book of Jehoiakim's fourth year his later utterances of Zedekiah's reign, or the account of his release by Nebuzaradan, and doings in Egypt, did not gather all his warnings against Judah together, and range them in priority to the utterances on the nations, the fitness of doing so might strike Baruch, as in Egypt he arranged all that belonged to his master; especially if he, or later editors, added things subsequent to the Prophet's death; such a fitness would commend itself strongly. Still more, when the Hebrew point of view of Babylon had changed at least once, or oftener, and Nebuchadnezzar became no longer God's servant, nor the exiles were any more to be exhorted to patience, but the Median horse and the Elamite bowstring were to sound deliverance in their ears, the Hebrew genius would have failed in its ready responsiveness to the touch of Divine Providence in events before its eyes, had it not broken out into some poetic interpretation of the time, which should sound as a judicial song. But as neither all times are equally fruitful, nor all seers equally creative, such a song might be little more than a recast of expressions become conventional, or join together bursts of passion with languid incoherence. Such is in

JEREMIAH.

L. is taken; abashed is Bel, dismayed[371] Merodach; con- A. V. L. 2.
founded are her idols, shattered[371] her images.
2. For against her is gone up a nation from the north,

---

[371] *Dismayed* and *shattered*. The same Hebrew word has both meanings.

---

effect the impression of these two chapters, if compared with the more splendid parallels which pass under the name of Isaiah, where superiority, whether due to a more creative or more artistic type of genius, is very apparent. Not the less, whoever compiled these chapters, at earliest in the time of Cyrus, and at latest perhaps in the reign of Darius Hystaspes, would associate them with the songs on the nations; and he, or whoever edited the whole after him, would feel the incongruousness of describing Babel's fall in the midst of Jeremiah's exhortations to accept her yoke and drink her cup; hence more than ever it became natural to re-arrange the book, and to group together all the songs on the nations at the end. I should have done the same, if I had not wished to mark my sense of the later time of these chapters. Nor would I now be understood, as if I claimed strongly a clear priority for all the pieces in chaps. xxiv.—xxvii. (A. V. xlvi.—xlix.) since they also, specially that on Elam, may have been retouched, and perhaps by the compiler of these two chapters. But I think, with some sanction from Eichhorn and Ewald (though not from Hitzig), that the signs of a date subsequent to Jeremiah are more manifest in l.—li. than in xlvi.—xlix. Those who think judgments of style (though this also guides me) must be arbitrary, may observe a more palpable proof in the Greek of chaps. xxv. and xxxii. (Gr.) since no mention is therein of the king of Babel (Sheshach) drinking last. Therefore some MSS. and important enough to guide the LXX, wanting the allusion to these chapters, probably wanted the chapters themselves.

The signs of long residence in Babylon are also evident

Ch. L. that will make her land a desolation, so that there be a no dweller therein: from man, even to beast, they are fled, they are gone.

3. In those days and in that time, is the ETERNAL's saying, the sons of Israel shall come, they and the sons of Judah together; weeping as they go, they shall come, and seek the ETERNAL their God.

4. They shall ask the way to Zion, with their faces hitherward, *saying*, Come, and be joined[372] to the ETERNAL, in an everlasting covenant, that shall not be forgotten.

5. My people has been a perishing flock: their shepherds led astray, turning them aside from the mountains;[373] they went from mountain to hill, forgot their resting-place.

---

[372] *Come, and be joined.* This change of punctuation, after Hitzig, preserves regularity of tense.

[373] *Turning them aside from the mountains.* So I divide the text; more commonly, turned them aside on the mountains; the margin slightly varies. The idea of rebellious mountains, as if idolatrous, is too refined here, and against the next clause.

---

here, vv. 31—33 (A. V. 33—35) as in Isa. xii. 23—35 (A. V. xiv. 2—17). On the whole, we can distinguish three phases in the prophetic sentiment towards Babel, (1) the practical exhortation to submit; (2) the moralising view of the conqueror as Jehovah's servant; the date of which seems to me dubitable; (3) the patriotic recoil of exultation, when the prison-house falls. I omit here the opposite side represented by Hananiah.

1, 2. The work of Cyrus (rather than Darius Hyst.) is done, in storming the city of which Bel was ancestral (unless taken as Baal?) and tutelary genius; Merodach the martial or lordly divinity; and stunning crash of images follows.

3—7. The Jew sees in Babel's fall only Jehovah's care for Judah: as things have many aspects; and only

L. 6. All that found them devoured them, and their A. V. L. 7. adversaries said, We are not guilty; since they have sinned against the ETERNAL, the habitation of righteousness, and the hope of their fathers [*the Eternal*].[374]

7. Flee out of the midst of Babel, and out of the land of the Chaldees let them go forth,[375] and be as he-goats in front of the flock.

8. For behold, I raise, and bring up against Babel, a company of mighty nations from the northern land; as they encamp against her, thence shall she be taken; their arrows *are* as *of* a triumphant warrior, that turns not back empty; 9. and Chaldæa becomes a spoil, all her spoilers are glutted, is the ETERNAL'S saying;

10. Since thou rejoicest,[376] since thou exultest, plun-

---

[374] *The Eternal.* The second Jehovah is omitted in the Greek, perhaps rightly.

[375] *Flee out of the midst . . . and let them go forth.* All the versions and critics make the first clause imperative; most follow the Masora in turning the future imperative יֵצְאוּ into the 2 p. imp. צְאוּ. My own inclination is to put the entire verse in the historical past, with a narrative triplet; and a suspicion haunts me throughout this chapter, that two-thirds of the imperatives, all those which commence couplets, were meant by the writer as narrative præterites.

[376] *Since thou rejoicest.* It is highly disputable whether the opening particle is causative, or only intensive, e.g. *yea, verily.* The LXX and *Vulg.* take it as above, and I think the sequence of thought favours. The Text mixes strangely singular and plural objects of address. The Masora turns all into the plural. I have retained in the singular all that I could, taking plunderess as a Chaldaising feminine participle. In any way, there is some abruptness; and I cannot think the text had so many singulars by miswriting. *Vulg.* Quoniam exultatis, et magna loquimini, diripientes hæreditatem meam; quoniam effusi estis sicut vituli super herbam, et mugistis sicut tauri.

---

an infinite Providence turns human ends into Divine means, and sees cause and effect, each in each, by itself, and for something else. The scattered sheep become leaders of released captives.

8—15. The siege is described, in the historical past,

Ch. L. deress of my inheritance; since thou art puffed fat as a A.V.L. l
heifer grazing, and neighest as the war-horses; confounded is your mother exceedingly, ashamed is she that gave you birth; 11. behold, the hindermost of the nations, a wilderness, a dry land, and a desert, because of the wrath of the ETERNAL, 12. she shall not be inhabited, but be a desolation altogether; every passer by Babel shall be amazed, and hiss, at all her wounds.

13. Stand[377] in array against Babel all around; all benders of the bow, shoot at her; spare not for arrow, since she has sinned against the ETERNAL.

14. Raise[377] the shout against her all around; she has rendered her hand; her foundations are fallen, her walls ruined; since *this* is JEHOVAH's vengeance, be avenged on her; as she has done, do unto her.

15. Cut off from Babel sower and handler of sickle in time of harvest; because of the sword of the oppressor let them turn, each to his people, and flee, each to his own land.[378]

16. Israel is a scattered flock, whom lions have driven away: the first devoured him [*the king of Assyria;*] and this the latter one crunched his bones [*Nebuchadnezzar king of Babel.*][379]

---

[377] Verses 13, 14. The opening imperatives in both verses might easily be treated as præterites.

[378] This verse resembles xxiii. (A. V. xxv. 38), more strikingly xxiv. 12, (A. V. xlvi. 16), from the latter perhaps this being imitated; and certainly the return of mercenary soldiers to their own lands seems more appropriate than that of sowers and reapers here. The Vulgate has *columbæ* for oppressor in each place.

[379] The versions (as e. g. *Vulg.* primus comedit eum rex Assur, iste

---

and in the supernatural injunction; with the pride of the lady of the nations.

16—19. Extending his view from the two tribes to

Ch. L. 17. Therefore thus saith the ETERNAL of hosts, the A.V. L. 18. God of Israel, Behold me visiting the king of Babel and his land, as I visited the king of Assur and his land; 18. and I will bring Israel again to his fold,[380] and he shall pasture Carmel and Bashan, and on the mount of Ephraim and Gilead shall his soul be satiated. 19. In those days, and at that time, is the ETERNAL's saying, shall the search be made for the iniquity of Israel, but there shall be none; and after the sins of Judah, but they shall not be found; because I pardon those whom I make remnant.

20. Against the land doubly-rebellious,[381] go up against her, and against the inhabitants of Visitation :[381] waste, and destroy utterly behind them, is the ETERNAL's saying, and do according to all that I have commanded thee.

---

novissimus exossavit eum Nabuchodonosor rex Babylonis) do not mark so distinctly as the Hebrew, the merely exegetical manner in which the name and the titles are appended. The LXX. have not the name Nebuchadnezzar.

[380] *Fold;* or, habitation, but with constant recurrence to the primitive pastoral sense.

[381] *Doubly-rebellious,* and *Visitation.* Instead of Mesopotamia (*Aram-Naharaim*), the land of the Euphrates is here called Medio-rebellious, or doubly-paramount, (if we remember the sense of *Mar*), whence Jerome's terra dominantium; while the Pactyan land, (see Herod. vii. on the Pactyan archers who wore goat-skins), supplies a play for visitation or vengeance. Comp. Ezek. xxiii. 23. We need not introduce Iranian etymologies. But the LXX. and *Vulg.* suggest, that we might take *Pekod* as a verb, visit them, and perhaps the verb *lay waste,* as the substantive *sword,* ἐκδίκησον μάχαιρᾳ. We should then read, *her* inhabitants. But we may also ask, whether the article can by Hebrew idiom stand with a noun in regimen ; and we may suspect that some cabalistic inversion of letters escapes us ; or perhaps, that the three first words are a titular prefix ; *e. g.* "Against the "land Medio-rebellious. Go up upon her, and visit her inhabitants, O "sword, and utterly destroy behind them, is the utterance of the ETERNAL," &c. We should then compare below vv. 34—36.

---

the twelve, the writer glances at Israel's past, and forecasts a quiet pastoral life for the restored nation.

20—26. On the side of its causation the havoc must

Ch. L. 21. A sound of battle in the land, and of great crash; A.V. L. 22. How is the hammer of the whole earth cut asunder, and broken! how is Babel become a desolation among the nations!

23. I laid snare for thee, Babel, and thou art also taken, though thou wast not aware; thou art found, yea, thou art caught, because thou hast striven against the ETERNAL.

24. The ETERNAL opened his armoury, and brought forth the weapons of his indignation; for the Lord, the ETERNAL of hosts, has a work in the land of the Chaldees; 25. [382] Come thereunto from a far end; open her storehouses, cast her up as heaps, and destroy her utterly; let her have no remnant.

26. Slay all her steers; let them go down to the slaughter; woe to them, because their day is come, the time of their visitation.

27. A sound of fleers and escapers out of Babel's land, to announce in Zion the vengeance of the ETERNAL our God, vengeance for his temple; 28. Summon against Babel archers;[383] all benders of the bow, encamp around against her; let her have no escape; requite her according to her earning; according to all that she has done, do to her; 29. since she has been haughty against the ETERNAL, against the Holy One of Israel, therefore let her choice youth fall in her streets, and all her men of war be cut off in that day, is the saying of the ETERNAL.

---

[382] *Vulg.* tollite de viâ lapides, et redigite acervos, et interficite cam—a rendering too Rabbinical not to have been derived by Jerome from his tutor.
[383] *Archers. Vulg.* plurimis. LXX. πολλοῖς.

---

be traced back to One who sends nations as doers of his work.

27—30. Exiles, not as yet restored by Cyrus, but

I. L.   30. Behold me against thee, Haughtiness, is the Lord, A.V. L. 31.
the ETERNAL of hosts's saying, since thy day, the time I
visit thee, is come ; and haughtiness stumbles and falls,
with none to lift it up, and I kindle fire in its cities, to
devour all its precincts.

31. Thus saith the ETERNAL of hosts, Oppressed are the
sons of Israel and the sons of Judah together, and all
their slave-holders have held them fast, refused to let them
go ; 32. their mighty redeemer, whose name is the ETERNAL
of hosts, will plead terribly their plea, in order that he
may rebuke the earth,[384] and astound the dwellers of
Babel. 33. A sword upon the Chaldees, is the ETERNAL'S
saying, and upon the dwellers of Babel, and upon princes,
and upon her counsellors ; 34. a sword upon the diviners,
that they may dote ; a sword upon her warriors, that they
may be dismayed; 35. a sword upon their horses and
upon their chariots, and upon all the mixed people that
are in her midst, that they may become as women ; 36.
a sword upon her treasuries, that they may be plundered ;
a sword upon her waters,[385] that they may become dry.

37. Since it is a land of graven images, and they are in-

---

[384] *That he may rebuke the earth, &c.* Vulg. ut exterreat terram, et
commoveat habitatores Babylonis. For the sense of the word rebuke, comp.
Job xxvi. 12; Jer. xlix. 25 (A. V. xxxi. 35); Isa. li. 4, 15. LXX. ὅλως
ἐξάρῃ τὴν γῆν καὶ παροξυνεῖ . . . μάχαιραν.

[385] *A sword upon her waters.* So apparently the writer; but the Masoretic points make it *drought*, with prosaic appropriateness to the waters. So
Vulg. siccitas super aquas ejus. The LXX. omit.

---

wending their way by stealth, may carry to fallen Zion,
and her Temple, tidings of a more ruinous fall.

31—35. Since the dynasty of Nebuchadnezzar would
not send its prisoners homewards, the God of battles and
of trampled nations opens the dungeon doors, and says
to the invader, Slay, or to the sword, Go forth. 37, 38.
Instead of being wholly covered with idols and images,

Ch. L. fatuated with idols; therefore let wild cats, with jackals,[386] A.V. be inhabitants, and the ostrich's daughters dwell therein; and let it not be inhabited again for ever, nor dwelt in, from generation to generation; 38. as in God's overthrowing of Sodom and Gomorrah, and the neighbouring towns thereof, is the ETERNAL's saying, Man shall not dwell there, neither son of man sojourn therein.

39. Behold a people coming from the north, and a nation vast; and mighty kings are roused from the ends of the earth; 40. they hold fast bow and lance; cruel are they, and have no pity; their voice roars like the sea, and they ride upon horses; arrayed against thee, daughter of Babel, man by man for the battle.[387] 41. Babel's king heard their rumour, and his hands fainted; distress took hold of him, as pangs are in childbirth.

42. [388] Behold, he comes up as a lion from the pride of

---

[386] *Wild cats and jackals.* Comp. note on Isa. xii. (A. V. xiii.), with Bochart, or Rosenm. The LXX. have ἐν ταῖς νήσοις, and θυγατέρες σειρήνων.

[387] That vv. 37—40, are reproduced here from Isa. xii. (A. V. xiii.) and 42, 43, from Jer. xxvii. 19, 20, (A.V. xlix. 19, 20), is evident enough; but the resemblance does not justify us in considering the verses out of place here, since the whole chapter is a cento, or half-coherent recast and amalgamation of older pieces.

[387] See on vv. 42, 43, note, above, or xxvii. 19.

---

let the city become a haunt of the wildest creatures. How far events led to some fulfilment but neither immediate, nor unnatural, nor utter, of this imprecation, see Note on Isa. xii.*

39—41. Language reflecting perhaps Jer. v. 13 (A.V. 15.), though there applied to the Scythian invaders of Palestine, is here employed to describe Mede, Kurd, Armenian, breaking in upon southern Babylon. Comp. Isa. xviii. 2—10 (A. V. xxi.)

42, 43. As the Chaldee formerly against Edom, Syria,

---

* Vol. i. p. 297.

L. Jordan to the perennial pasture, since in a moment, he A.V.L.44. saith, I will drive them from thereupon; and who is the champion I shall meet thereon? for who is like me? and who will challenge me? and what shepherd is he, who will stand before me?

43. Therefore hear the design of the ETERNAL, which he has designed against Babel, and the plans which he has planned against the land of the Chaldees: Surely he will rend even of the least of the flock; surely he will lay waste for them their pasture.

44. At the sound, Babel is taken, the earth trembled, and crying was heard among the nations.³⁸⁹

LI.

LI. 1. Thus saith the ETERNAL, Behold me raising up A.V. LI. 1. against Babel, and against the inhabitants of Chaldæa,³⁹⁰ a destroying wind; and I send unto Babel winnowers, to

---

³⁸⁹ From the description here, and in the next chapter, is suggested, and in some expressions imitated, though with great freshness, the vision of the Apocalypse, xviii. 2—10. 'Fallen, fallen, is Babylon,' &c., where imperial Paganism, with its representative city, drunk with the blood of martyrs, seems intended.

³⁹⁰ *Chaldæa.* LXX. τοὺς κατοικοῦντας Χαλδαίους. Heb. text. *Levkamai*, i.e. the heart of them that rise, or, as Jer. qui cor suum levaverunt, (so A. V.); but this is a case of the cabalistic inversion, which reading the alphabet backwards from its end, ח for א and ש for ב, (whence *Athbasch*,) expresses enigmatically the word Chaldæa, comp. v. 34 (A. V. 35.)

Arabia, so in turn the Medo-Persic host against Babel comes like a lion from Jordan's thickets on to a verdant pasture, rending even of the little ones of the flock. 44. Babel's fall supplies text and parable for tragedies which are the world's amazement.

1. In connexion so close, that the last verse of the preceding chapter might be well transferred here, Jeho-

Ch. LI. winnow her, and empty out her land; 2. For they press upon her all around, in the day of trouble; let the archer bend his bow against the bowman,[391] and against him that exalts himself in mail; and have no pity upon her warriors; 3. destroy utterly all her host, and let them fall wounded in the land of the Chaldees, and pierced through in her streets.

4. Surely, Israel and Judah are not bereaved of their God, of the ETERNAL of hosts; yea, their land was filled with sin[392] against the Holy One of Israel; 5. flee out of the midst of Babel, and deliver each man his life; be not cut off in her iniquity; since it is the time of the ETERNAL's vengeance; he is rendering to her recompence.

6. Babel was a golden cup in the ETERNAL's hand, making all the earth drunken; of her wine the nations drank, therefore the nations madden.

7. Suddenly Babel fell, and was shivered; wail over her, carry balm to her wound, *see* if she may be healed. 8. We healed Babel, but she has no health;[393] leave her,

---

[391] *Let the archer bend his bow against the bowman.* Misdirected by the Masora, most, or all, versions have omitted one of the verbs, which is here, I trust, satisfactorily rendered.

[392] *The land filled with iniquity*, is Babel's land, as the sequence of ideas throughout shews, unless we were to parenthesise the words (*though their land was filled with sin*) as I see Zunz before myself had conjectured; but this would be involved, as Philippsohn says; though any way the construction is harsh; *e.g.* אשם followed by ב.

[393] *We healed Babel, but she has no health.* Vulg. Curavimus Babylonem, et non est sanata; a sentence adapted hortatorily to incurable sinners.

---

vah summons a wind to scatter the chaff of winnowed Babel. 2. For her defenders, quivered or mailed, are overborne by greater weight of assault, (3) and slaughter ensues. The parallelism is not so perfect as in the higher poetry.

4—10. The fall of the overbearing city is a sign of

LI. and let us go each to his own land; since her judgment A.V. LI. 9. reaches to heaven, and mounts to the skies. 9. The ETERNAL has brought forth our justification;[394] come, and let us relate in Zion the work of the ETERNAL our God.

10. Make bright the arrows, fill the quivers:[395] the ETERNAL has roused the spirit of the Median kings; since his design is against Babel, to destroy it; yea, it is the ETERNAL's vengeance, vengeance for his temple. 11. On the walls of Babel lift up standard, strengthen the watch; set fast the guards, prepare the ambushes; for both designed has the ETERNAL, and performed, what he spake against the dwellers of Babel.

12. [396] Thou that dwellest on many waters, abounding in treasures; thine end is come, the limit of thy plundering; 13. the ETERNAL of hosts has sworn by his life,[397] Surely I fill thee with men, as with locusts, who shall echo over thee alarm-cry.[398]

14. [399] The Maker of the earth by his might, esta-

---

[394] *Our justification;* or, righteousness; but in a somewhat forensic sense, as in Psalm xxiv. 5, and St. Paul, Rom. iii. iv. v. *Vulg.* protulit Dominus justitias nostras; as it were acquittal, favourable verdict, forgiveness.

[395] *Fill the quivers;* or, set close the shields, as A. V. *Vulg.* implete pharetras.

[396] vv. 5—12. *Flee out of Babel,* and *thou that dwellest upon many waters.* Comp. as imitated from all this passage, Rev. xvii. 1, 15; xviii. 4, 5, 6. Hence perhaps in v. 8, here, the phrase *her judgment* should be understood as her sin, as many critics take it.

[397] *By his life,* or soul; but LXX. κατὰ τοῦ βραχίονος.

[398] Verse 24 here seems naturally to continue verse 13.

[399] 14—18. On these verses, which can only be admitted as genuine

---

God's fatherhood of Israel, and of his forgiveness of his people, comp. Isa. xii. 22—24 (A. V. xiv. 1, 2,) which is here vividly reproduced.

10—13. Echoes of the later Isaiah, and of Nahum, prolong the vengeful strain.

14—18. Five verses, repeated from chap. x., express

Ch. LI. blishing the world by his wisdom, and by his understanding he spread out the heavens, 15. at the voice of his utterance is a tumult of waters in the heavens, and he brings up mists from the end of the earth, makes lightnings for the rain, and brings forth wind[400] out of his treasures, 16. every man is imbruted out of knowledge— every founder is ashamed of graven image; for his molten image is a lie, and there is no breath in them. 17. Falsehood are they, a work of errors; in the time of their visitation shall they perish. 18. Not like them is Jacob's portion; for the framer of all is his inheritance,[401] the ETERNAL of hosts his name.

19. Thou art battleaxe to me, weapon of war, so that I break with thee nations, and destroy with thee kingdoms, 20. and break with thee horse and his rider, and break with thee chariot and his charioteer, 21. and break with thee man and woman, and break with thee old and young, and break with thee gallant and maiden, 22. and break with thee shepherd and his flock, and break with thee husbandman and his yoke, and break with thee pashas and prefects,[402] 23. and render to Babel and to all

---

here on supposition of the whole chapter being a cento, see x. 12—15, (A.V. 12—16), where they have been already found, and where they seem more coherent than here.

[400] *Brings forth wind*; the LXX. have ἐξήγαγε φῶς.

[401] *The framer of all things is his inheritance.* LXX. ὁ πλάσας τὰ πάντα αὐτός ἐστι κληρονομία αὐτοῦ. We find in the Hebrew שבט, *and the rod*, which some confusion of the transcribers has introduced, as with the addition of the word Israel in x. 12—16, where see note.

[402] *Pashas and prefects.* Heb. *Pashas and Sagans.* These two words, exotic in Hebrew, and hardly (though see 1 Kings x. and xx), appearing

---

the vivid contrast felt by the exiled Hebrews, between their living Dread, and Chaldæa's dead idols.

19—23. Another piece of five verses is so introduced

the dwellers of Chaldæa all their evil that they wrought in Zion before your eyes, is the saying of the ETERNAL.

24. Behold me against thee, mount of the destroyer, that destroyest all the earth, is the ETERNAL's saying, and I stretch forth my hand upon thee, and roll thee down from the rocks, and make thee a mount of conflagration; 25. so that they shall not take of thee a stone for a corner, or a stone for foundations, but thou shalt be perpetual desolations, is the saying of the ETERNAL.

26. Lift up standard in the land, sound trumpet among the nations; consecrate against her nations, summon against her the kingdoms of Ararat, *ar*-Menia, and Ashchenaz;[403] appoint (marechal)[404] against her; bring up horses as (rough) locusts.

A. V.
LI. 24.

---

before the Exile, are suggestive here of late compilation. They seem, from comparing Gesenius with Fürst, to be of Persian or Sanscrit origin, with the primary sense of friend, *i.e.* companion to the king, and deputy manager, *i.e.* satrap.

[403] *ar*-Menia. Heb. Minni, here, and perhaps in Psalm xlv. 9, more obviously it seems the Greek Minyas, and with the Hebrew for mountain or city, gives the name Ar-menia. The LXX. here funnily give Ararat as ἄραrε, and Minni as παρ' ἐμοῦ, Ashchenaz as 'Αχαναζίοις. The Hebrew Ashchenaz contains perhaps the root of the name Asia, and of the Phrygian Ascanius.

[404] On *marechal*, Heb. Tiphsar, see note on *taph-sarim* in Nahum, iii. 16, (A. V. 17;) here, perhaps, dense host.

---

here as to seem descriptive of Babel's power as Jehovah's instrument in the past; but in its inner character it seems to belong to the Median king, of verse 10, and was probably addressed (as by the later Isaiah), to Cyrus, to whom, notwithstanding the disorder of the context, we may best apply it here.

24—25. In these two verses, the threats addressed to Babel in vv. 12, 13, seem to be resumed, and, but for two inharmonious insertions, would be continued.

26—28. Resuming as it were the key-note of vv. 10,

Ch. I..   27. Consecrate against her nations, the kings of the Medes, the pashas thereof, and all the prefects[405] thereof, and all the land of his dominion; 28. and let the land tremble and be troubled, since established against Babel is the ETERNAL's design, to make the land of Babel a desolation, that it have no inhabitant.

29. The warriors of Babel forbore to fight, remained in their strongholds; their valour failed, they became as women; her habitations are burnt,[406] her bars shivered, 30. courier runs to meet courier, and messenger to meet messenger, to tell the king of Babel that his city is taken at the extremity; 31. that the bridges are seized, and the waterponds are burnt with fire, and the men of war confounded.

32. For thus saith the ETERNAL of hosts, the God of Israel, The daughter of Babel is as a garner in the season to thresh her out; yet a little while, and her time of harvest is at hand.

33. [407] Nebuchadrezzar, king of Babel, devoured us

---

[405] On *pashas* and *prefects*, see v. 22.

[406] *Habitations are burnt.* So LXX. ἐνεπυρίσθη, though Masora, *they* (*i.e.* the enemy) have burnt.

[407] Compare with the strong image of vv. 33, 43, Job xx; 15, Haggai ii. 7, 8, Daniel i. 2; and in a more prosaic form, the story of Bel and the Dragon. We may even ask, if that story may not bear to the image before us the same sort of relation as perhaps the fiery furnace of the Three Children to the imprecation on Ahab son of Kolaiah, in Jer. xxxvii. (A. V. xxix.) 22.

11, the poet expresses the Divine counsel against Babel under the lyrical image of summons to standard and trumpet. Exotic words mark the late origin of the poem.

29—31. Passing, in the manner of Nahum, from lyrical summons to dramatic narrative, the poet records the confusion, which his compatriots had seen in the

LI. crushed us, made us an empty vessel, swallowed us as a dragon: when he had filled his belly with my dainties, he vomited us forth: 34. my wrong and my flesh be upon Babel, saith the daughter of Zion, and my blood upon the dwellers of Chaldæa, saith Jerusalem.

35. Therefore thus saith the ETERNAL, Behold me championing thy cause, that I wreak thy vengeance, and dry up her sea, and parch her fountain; 36. until Babel becomes ruins, a haunt of jackals, a desolation, and a hissing,[408] without inhabitant.

37. *While* they roar as lions together, *while* they yell as lions' whelps, in their heat I set forth their banquet, and make them drink, that they may revel, and *then* sleep an everlasting sleep, and not awake, is the ETERNAL's saying; 38. I will bring them down as lambs to the slaughter, as rams with he-goats.

39. How is [*Sheshach*[409]] the praise of the whole earth

---

[408] *A hissing;* or, as Ewald suggests from the Arabic, a void: but the sibilant expression of taunt or amazement is very Jewish; and the word mostly by me translated desolation will equally bear the sense of stupor or astonishment.

[409] *Sheshach,* wanting in the LXX. and implying an enigmatic inversion of the alphabet, hardly practised in Jeremiah's time, is more possible in this

---

hour of storm and sack in Babel. Comp. Herod. i. 185, 6, —191; Arrian, Alex. vii. 17; Xen. Cyrop. vii. 5, 15; Curt. 5. 1. The details, as by an eye-witness in the past, seem true to history. Narrative is succeeded, (32) by reflexion on Jehovah's will, on (33) Israel's suffering, (34) her cry for vengeance, (35) the visitation, (36) the sentence.

37. Insolence is the infatuation with which God (38) prepares the way of ruin. Compare, in Nahum, the stories of Nineveh's capture.

39. The glory of Babel, dubiously entitled Sheshach,

Ch. LI. taken and seized! how is Babel become desolate among A. V. the nations! 40. the sea is come up upon Babel; she is covered with the swell of its billows.

41. Her cities are become a desolation, a dry land, and a wilderness, a land wherein no man dwells, neither son of man passes thereby. 42. Yea, I judge Bel in Babel, and disgorge out of his mouth his prey; neither shall nations flow thereunto any more;[410] [already[411] Babel's wall is fallen; 43. go forth from the midst of her, my people, and deliver each his life from the fierceness of the Eternal's anger, 44. and lest your heart faint, or you fear, at the rumour that is heard in the land, when comes by year the rumour, and afterwards by year the rumour, and violence in the land, ruler against ruler; 45. Therefore, behold days coming, for me to judge the graven images of Babel, and all her land shall be confounded, and all her slain fall in her midst; 46. but the heavens and the earth, and all that is therein shall rejoice over

---

late Babylonian chapter than the clause containing it was in xxiii. 25. (A. V. xxv. 26), but yet must be regarded of doubtful genuineness. The Text runs as well without it.

[410] The clause, "neither shall nations flow unto her any more," in v. 42, seems a remembrance by antithesis of Isa. ii. Micah iii. (A. V. iv.), but the following [bracketed] passage here is more like a paraphrase or Hebrew Targum upon the adjoining portion of our chapter. The style of it has a certain looseness of idiom.

[411] From the last clause of ver. 42, to the middle of ver. 47, (A. V. 44—49) the five bracketed verses are wanting in the LXX.; and there is something in their particularising style, as well as in the easier connexion of the passage without them, which suggests the amplifying hand of some Hebrew editor.

---

(40) sinks in the deluge of warriors. 41. In ruin, the Babylonian dragon, like the Assyrian lion erst, vomits forth his prey.

43—47. Four or five verses, dubious in genuineness or

LI. Babel, because from the north came against her the destroyer, is the ETERNAL's saying; 47. already Babel *has been* for the falling of the slain of Israel;] already to Babel are fallen the slain of the whole earth.

A. V. LI. 48

48. Go away, fugitives from the sword, stand not still; remember from afar the ETERNAL, and let Jerusalem come up to your mind.

49. We were ashamed, because we heard reproach: contempt covered our faces: because strangers came into the sanctuaries of the house of the ETERNAL.

50. Therefore, behold days coming, is the ETERNAL's saying, for me to judge her graven images; and in all her land the wounded shall groan.

51. Though Babel mount up to heaven, and though she fortify the height of her strength, from me shall come spoilers to her, is the ETERNAL's saying.

52. *There is* sound of crying from Babel, and a vast ruin from the land of the Chaldees; because the ETERNAL is storming Babel and destroying,[412] out of her *comes* a vast sound, and their billows roar like mighty waters; their cry is uttered destruction.

---

[412] The punctuators, and all their followers, make Jehovah destroy out of Babel the vast sound, or great voice, but the connexion of thought, and, I think, even of grammar, suggests in preference the version given above. For how could the destruction of voice be the explanation of a great sound coming, or the cause of the sea of nations roaring? Comp. Isaiah xv. 11. (A. V. xvii. 12.) Rev. xvii. 15; xix. 6.

---

in position, revert from the downfall to the deported exiles, who are advised to escape from the city which had defied Heaven, and (48) to remember the home of peace.

49. The past humiliation is merged (50) in a vision of judgment, and (51) the billowy sound of conflict, (52) brings in retribution.

x 2

Ch. LI.   53. For upon her, upon Babel, is come the destroyer, and her warriors are taken: broken each their bows: for the ETERNAL is a God of recompense; assuredly he will requite.

54. Yea, I make drunk her princes, and her counsellors, her pashas and her prefects,[413] and her warriors, that they sleep an everlasting sleep, and not awaken, is the saying of the King, whose name is the ETERNAL of hosts.

55. Thus saith the ETERNAL of hosts, The broad walls of Babel[414] are laid utterly bare, and her lofty gates burnt with fire; so that populations labour for nought, and nations in the very fire, and are weary [in vain.]

*** The word which Jeremiah the prophet commanded Seraiah the son of Neriah, the son of Maaseiah, when he went from Zedekiah[415] king of Judah, to Babel in the

---

[413] *Pashas and prefects*, see note v. 22 (A. V. 23).

[414] *The broad walls of Babel;* lit. Heb. the walls of Babel the wide (one): but the rhythm of lofty gates may justify the A. V. as above. The closing words of the verse, and of the poem, are a citation from Hab. ii. 8. (A. V. 12—14). Hence, natural as it may seem to take that passage as a Divine rebuke of conquered populations being made by violence to labour in the very fire, the more usual method of treating it as a taunt of the victorious nations who build their metropolis for nought, or for consuming fire, is justified in preference here.

[415] *When he went from Zedekiah.* Heb. went with Zedekiah. But LXX. ὅτε ἐπορεύετο παρὰ Σεδεκίου βασιλέως, κ. τ. λ. which some have followed: and since Zedekiah sent an embassy in his fourth year, as we saw in chap. xxxvii. (A. V. xxix.), but does not in any early history appear to have gone

---

54. Thereby, with wineless intoxication of frenzy is a prelude to the sleep of extinction, and (55) the fabric reared by the desolating king out of the toil of captive nations, becomes a thing of nought.

*** An epilogue, which may have once stood as prologue to this poem, suggests in the name of Seraiah, borne by a high priest, by a brother of Baruch, Jeremiah's

fourth year of his reign; then Seraiah was prince-chamberlain.[416] So Jeremiah wrote in a book all the evil that should come upon Babylon, *even* all these words that are written against Babylon. And Jeremiah said to Seraiah, When thou comest to Babylon, and shalt see, and shalt read all these words; then shalt thou say, O LORD, thou hast spoken against this place to cut it off, that none shall remain in it, neither man nor beast, but that it shall be desolate for ever. And it shall be, when thou hast made an end of reading this book, *that* thou shalt bind a stone to it, and cast it into the midst of Euphrates: and thou shalt say, Thus shall Babylon sink, and shall not rise from the evil that I will bring upon her: and they shall be weary.[417] Thus far *are* the words of Jeremiah.

A. V.
LI. 60.

---

himself, nor is he likely to have gone, as well as sent, nor if he did, would this chapter have been an appropriate accompaniment, nor consistent with Jeremiah's feeling and policy at that date, we must consider the Greek to be of the two statements the least inadmissible; as more self-consistent.

[416] *Prince chamberlain.* Heb. prince of resting-place; hence with some the king's quarter-master, or marshal in attendance; but better, head-chamberlain—certainly not 'quiet prince.'

[417] In the penultimate clause, the words "*And they shall be weary,*" seem to have dropt into this place out of the end of the 55th (A. V. 58th) verse. This might happen, if whoever appended this epilogue (whether he originated or perhaps only transferred it to this place from the beginning of chap. L. where it may have stood as prologue,) found the remark, *Thus far are the words of Jeremiah,* at the end of verse 55, and intending to transfer it to the end of the epilogue, unintentionally transferred with it the adjoining verb. Comp. Hitzig, after Movers, with Rosenm.

---

secretary, and by a leader amongst the returned exiles, (specially by Ezra's father,) a possible compiler of the collection of fragmentary pieces combined in this utterance on Babel. The Vulgate calls Seraiah *princeps prophetiæ*. It is easier to suppose an embassy from Zedekiah, than the king himself a suppliant in Babylon: comp. xxxvii. (A. V. xxix.) 3.

LII.

Ch. LII. 1. Zedekiah *was* one and twenty years old when he A.V. LII began to reign, and he reigned eleven years in Jerusalem. And his mother's name *was* Hamutal the daughter of Jeremiah of Libnah. 2. And he did *that which was* evil in the eyes of the LORD, according to all that Jehoiakim had done. 3. For through the anger of the LORD it came to pass in Jerusalem and Judah, till he had cast them out from his presence, that Zedekiah rebelled against the king of Babylon.

4. And it came to pass in the ninth year of his reign, in the the tenth month, in the tenth *day* of the month, *that* Nebuchadrezzar king of Babylon came, he and all his army, against Jerusalem, and pitched against it, and built forts against it round about. 5. So the city was besieged unto the eleventh year of king Zedekiah. 6. And in the fourth month, in the ninth *day* of the month, the famine was sore in the city, so that there was no bread for the people of the land. 7. Then the city was broken up, and all the men of war fled, and went forth out of the city by night by the way of the gate between the two walls, which *was* by the king's garden; (now the Chaldeans *were* by the city round about:) and they went by the way of the plain.

8. But the army of the Chaldeans pursued after the king, and overtook Zedekiah in the plains of Jericho; and all his army was scattered from him. 9. Then they took

---

LII. At a date, late enough for manifest work of editors in diverse places, (as chaps. x., xv., xvi., xxiii., (A. V. xxv.), xlviii. (A. V. xxx.), xlii. (A. V. xxxix.), li. to pass, as alleged, among words of Jeremiah, some one added as an historical appendix, the close of 2nd Kings; the greatest discrepancy being in the numerical summary

the king, and carried him up unto the king of Babylon to Riblah in the land of Hamath; where he gave judgment upon him. 10. And the king of Babylon slew the sons of Zedekiah before his eyes: he slew also all the princes of Judah in Riblah. 11. Then he put out the eyes of Zedekiah; and the king of Babylon bound him in chains, and carried him to Babylon, and put him in prison till the day of his death.

12. Now in the fifth month, in the tenth *day* of the month, which *was* the nineteenth year of Nebuchadrezzar king of Babylon, came Nebuzar-adan, captain of the guard, *which* served the king of Babylon, into Jerusalem, 13. and burned the house of the LORD, and the king's house; and all the houses of Jerusalem, and all the houses of the great *men*, burned he with fire: 14. And all the army of the Chaldeans, that *were* with the captain of the guard, brake down all the walls of Jerusalem round about. 15. Then Nebuzar-adan the captain of the guard carried away captive *certain* of the poor of the people, and the residue of the people that remained in the city, and those that fell away, that fell to the king of Babylon, and the rest of the multitude. 16. But Nebuzar-adan the captain of the guard left *certain* of the poor of the land for vinedressers and for husbandmen. 17. Also the pillars of brass that *were* in the house of the LORD, and the bases, and the brazen sea that *was* in the house of the LORD, the Chaldeans brake, and carried all the brass of them to Babylon. 18. The caldrons also, and the shovels, and the snuffers,

---

of vv. 28—30. Whereas the history made Jehoiachin's captivity embrace eighteen thousand, the summary here makes all the three captivities reach but four thousand six hundred. Jewish expositors, as Philippsohn, consider the larger number the truer. Others have guessed

Ch. LII. and the bowls, and the spoons, and all the vessels of brass wherewith they ministered, took they away. 19. And the basons, and the firepans, and the bowls, and the caldrons, and the candlesticks, and the spoons, and the cups; *that* which *was* of gold *in* gold, and *that* which *was* of silver *in* silver, took the captain of the guard away. 20. The two pillars, one sea, and twelve brazen bulls that *were* under the bases, which king Solomon had made in the house of the LORD: the brass of all these vessels was without weight. 21. And *concerning* the pillars, the height of one pillar *was* eighteen cubits; and a fillet of twelve cubits did compass it; and the thickness thereof *was* four fingers: *it was* hollow. 22. And a chapiter of brass *was* upon it; and the height of one chapiter *was* five cubits, with network and pomegranates upon the chapiters round about, all *of* brass. The second pillar also and the pomegranates *were* like unto these. 23. And there were ninety and six pomegranates on a side; *and* all the pomegranates on the network *were* an hundred round about.

24. And the captain of the guard took Seraiah the chief priest, and Zephaniah the second priest, and the three keepers of the door: 25. He took also out of the city an eunuch, which had the charge of the men of war; and seven men of them that were near the king's person, which were found in the city; and the principal scribe of the host, who mustered the people of the land; and threescore men of the people of the land, that were found in the

A. LII.

---

the reverse. A feature of more significant import is, that neither the history, nor the summary here, betrays any knowledge of a deportation earlier than Jehoiachin's, in 597. Hence the date ordinarily assumed for the Exile's commencement, some nine years earlier, from the third of

LII. midst of the city. 26. So Nebuzar-adan the captain of the guard took them, and brought them to the king of Babylon to Riblah. 27. And the king of Babylon smote them, and put them to death in Riblah in the land of Hamath. Thus Judah was carried away captive out of his own land. 28. This *is* the people whom Nebuchadrezzar carried away captive: in the seventh year three thousand Jews and three and twenty: 29. In the eighteenth year of Nebuchadrezzar he carried away captive from Jerusalem eight hundred thirty and two persons. 30. In the three and twentieth year of Nebuchadrezzar Nebuzar-adan the captain of the guard carried away captive of the Jews seven hundred forty and five persons: all the persons *were* four thousand and six hundred.

31. And it came to pass in the seven and thirtieth year of the captivity of Jehoiachin king of Judah, in the twelfth month, in the five and twentieth *day* of the month, *that* Evil-Merodach king of Babylon in the *first* year of his reign, lifted up the head of Jehoiachin king of Judah, and brought him forth out of prison, 32. And spake kindly unto him, and set his throne above the throne of the kings that *were* with him in Babylon. 33. And changed his prison garments: and he did continually eat bread before him all the days of his life. 34. And *for* his diet, there was a continual diet given him of the king of Babylon, every day a portion until the day of his death, all the days of his life.

Jehoiakim, rests exclusively on Daniel i. 1. It should be noticed in favour of the Greek version, that it is closer to the earlier Hebrew text of the book of Kings, than to the later text in this place.

LAMENTATIONS; OR, AYECHA.

PREFACE: SEPTUAGINT, AND VULGATE.

And it came to pass, after Israel was carried captive, and Jerusalem made desolate, Jeremiah sat down and wept, and lamented this lamentation over Jerusalem, and said: Vulg. et amaro animo suspirans, et ejulans dixit.

Assigned to Jeremiah by the above early tradition, which is naturally repeated by Josephus, and perhaps for this reason having no separate place in the catalogue of Melito, the following five chapters constitute an elegy, which in our Hebrew Bibles is placed among the Hagiographa, as not prophetic; but, in all the Versions which I have seen, is appended to the Prophet's works, whose name it bears.

We must not follow Josephus, Arch. x. 5, 1, in supposing it to represent the elegy over Josiah mentioned in 2 Chron. xxxv. 25. We may rather doubt, whether the highly artificial form, the frequency of Chaldaizing idioms, and the tone of mere indulgence in poetical melancholy, do not tell more against Jeremiah's personal authorship, than the tradition weighs in its favour. But this question is one on which the arguments, turning chiefly upon taste, do not suffice for certainty. There are not, as in some other cases, internal proofs, decisive against genuineness.

The alphabetical structure of verse, preserved strictly in the first chapter, more loosely in the 2nd, 3rd, 4th, and laid aside in the 5th, could hardly fail to act as a fetter upon the writer. Hence, amidst many outbursts of unsurpassed pathos and natural tenderness, and in the 1st, 2nd, and 4th chapters a sustained strain of beauty, the impression left by the whole includes a sense of weariness of the recurrence of the same burthen. When to the feeling of monotony, produced by repetition, we add the vindictive tone, not least towards the hated kinsmen of Edom, we are inclined to say, the book illustrates remarkably the richness and the narrowness of the Hebrew mind; the strength, and also the weakness, of its poetry.

[The alphabetical order followed by the author in the four first chapters is in strict accordance with that of the Hebrew text; following in c. i. the usual run of the Hebrew alphabet; but in ii. iii. iv. inverting the order as regards the letters P and Ayn.

The LXX throughout follow the present order of the Hebrew alphabet, and in the three last cited chapters mark with Ayn verses beginning with P, and *vice versâ*. Any transposition of verses must have been antecedent to the LXX translation.—W. W. H.]

LAMENTATIONS.

Ch. I.   A. ¹Ah! seated solitary, the City that abounded in A.V. 1. people! become as bereft, *she that was* mighty among nations! princess among provinces, become tributary!²

B. Bitterly she weeps at night, with her tears upon her cheeks; she has no comforter out of all her lovers; all her friends have betrayed her, become to her enemies.

G. Gone into exile is Judah, out of sorrow; and settled amidst the nations, from great servitude: she finds no rest, all her pursuers overtake her between the straits.

D. Darksome are Zion's paths, for lack of pilgrims to festival; all her gates are desolate, her priests sighing; her maidens are afflicted, herself, bitter her lot.

H. Haughty are become her adversaries, her enemies at ease; since JAHVEH afflicted her for the number of her transgressions; her children are gone into slavery before the adversary.

V. or F. Forth from Zion's daughter is gone all her beauty; her princes are become as deer that find no pasture; yea, are gone, helpless, before the pursuer.

Z. Zealous is Jerusalem, in the days of her affliction and her wanderings, for all her delights, which she had in the days of old; when her people fell into the adver-

---

¹ The rhythm of the verses mostly for three chapters, and here of the first verse, is decidedly that of a triad; though it has been disturbed by the Masoretic punctuation, in a servile quest of parallelism.

² Three Chaldaising terminations in the first verse, another in the fourth, give early intimation of the high moral probability, that our book should be regarded, in the language of Italian art, as belonging to the Jeremianic school, instead of as the Master's own work.

Ch. I. sary's hand, and she had no helper, adversaries gazed on her, mocked at her desolation. A. V. 1. 7.

CH. Exceedingly sinned Jerusalem, therefore she became an aversion; all her admirers count her vile, since they saw her nakedness; yea, she sighs, and turns away backwards.

Th. Trolled in filthiness her skirts, she regards not her trailing; yea, she is fallen wonderfully, has no comforter; behold, JAHVEH, my affliction, how the enemy has wrought mightily.

Y. Yawning *spread* the enemy his grasp, on all her treasures; yea she gazed, *as* the nations entered her sanctuary; whom thou forbadest to enter thy congregation.

K. Keep groaning all her folk, as they seek bread; they have given their treasures for food, to restore life; behold, JAHVEH, and observe, how I have become abject.

L. Look not from me, all passing wayfarers; gaze, and behold, is there any pain like my pain, which is wrought to me; wherewith JAHVEH afflicted me in the day of the fierceness of his anger.

M. Might of fire from the height he sent into my bones to shatter them; he spread a net for my feet, made me turn backwards; he made me desolate, sickly all the day.

N. Nay, fastened by his hand[3] is the yoke of my sins; they entangle themselves, go up over my neck; the LORD

---

[3] *Fastened by his hand.* Our Hebrew text, with designed inversion of metaphor, makes the thongs which should be fastened to the driver's hand, entangle themselves over the yoked heifer's neck. A simple, perhaps truer, reading, is suggested by the LXX. ἐγρηγορήθη ἐπὶ τὰ ἀσεβήματά μου, ἐν χερσί μου συνεπλάκησαν, ἀνέβησαν ἐπὶ τὸν τράχηλόν μου, ἠσθένησεν ἡ ἰσχύς μου, κ. τ. λ.

Ch. I. has made my strength stumble, set me from whence I shall A. V. not be able to rise.

S. Scattered all my warriors in my midst hath the LORD; proclaimed over me a season for shattering my choice youth; the winepress hath the LORD trodden of the maiden daughter of Judah.

Ayn. Aye, over these things I am weeping of eye, my eye runs down with water; since far from me is comforter to restore my life; desolate are my sons because the enemy has prevailed.

P. Parting with her hands stands Zion, she has no comforter; JAHVEH has summoned beleaguerers for Jacob his foes; Jerusalem in their midst has become an abhorrence.

Tz. Zealous is JAHVEH righteously, for I disobeyed his word; hearken, all you populations, I pray, and behold my pain; my maidens and my choice youth are gone into slavery.

Q. Quest of my lovers I cried, *even* they deceived me; my priests and my elders died fainting in the city; yea, while they sought them food, to restore their life.

R. *Rise*, JAHVEH, behold how I am distressed, my bowels are troubled; my heart within me is shaken, since I rebelled grievously; abroad bereaves the sword, at home [*sickness*[4]] as death.

Sh. Sighing as I am, they have heard, *yet* I have no comforter; all my enemies have heard of my calamity, rejoiced, because thou hast wrought it; bringest thou the day that thou hast summoned? So let them be as me.

T. *Time is* for all their wickedness to come before

---

[4] On the apparent ellipse of the word *sickness*, comp. Jer. xiv. 17, (A.V. 18), Ezek. vii. 15.

thee; and do thou to them, even as thou hast done to me A.V. 1. 22. for all my transgressions: for many are my sighs, and my heart sick.

II.

A. Ah! how the LORD in his anger overclouds the A.V. II. 1. daughter of Zion; casts down from heaven to earth the excellency of Israel; and remembers not the resting-place of his feet, in the day of his anger!

B. The LORD has swallowed, unpitying, all the dwelling-places of Jacob; ruined in his wrath the strongholds of Judah's daughter; dashed to the earth, defiled, kingdom and its princes.

G. He has hewn off in his fierce anger every horn of Israel; turned his right hand backwards before the enemy; and burnt against Jacob, as a flaming fire, that devours all around.

D. He bent his bow as an enemy, stood at his right hand as an adversary: yea, he slew all things pleasant to the eye in the tent of Zion's daughter; he poured out, like fire, his fury.

Heh. The LORD has been as an enemy, swallowing Israel; he hath swallowed all her palaces, destroyed their strongholds; and multiplied for Zion's daughter sighing and groaning.

V. or F. Yea, he rifled as a garden, his tent; destroyed his meeting-place: JAHVEH has made congregation and sabbath forgotten in Zion; and spurned in the disdain of his anger king and priest.

Z. The LORD has abhorred his altar, loathed his sanctuary; delivered into the enemy's hand the walls of her palaces; they uttered shout in JAHVEH's house, as on day of congregation.

Ch. JAHVEH has purposed to destroy the wall of the

Ch. II. daughter of Zion; he has stretched out line, not withdrawn his hand from swallowing; so made he rampart and wall to mourn; they are enfeebled altogether.

Th. Sunken in the earth are her gates; destroyed and broken [are] her bars; her king and her princes are among the nations; there is no law; her prophets also find no vision from JAHVEH.

Y. The elders of the daughter of Zion sit upon the ground, and keep silence; they have cast up dust upon their heads; the maidens of Jerusalem have girded on sackcloth, bowed their head to the ground.

C. Mine eyes fail with weeping, my bowels are troubled, my liver is poured upon the ground, for the ruin of the daughter of my people; because child and suckling faint in the streets of the city.

L. They say to their mothers, Where is corn and wine, when they faint, as wounded, in the streets of the city; when they pour out their life into their mother's bosom.

M. How shall I parable thee;[5] what shall I liken to thee, daughter of Jerusalem : what shall I compare to thee, that I may comfort thee, maiden daughter of Zion; for thy breach is vast as the sea, who can heal thee?

N. Thy prophets had visions for thee of falsehood and folly; and laid not bare thine iniquity, to turn back thy captivity; but saw for thee oracles of falsehood and beguilement.

S. All passers by the way clapped their hands over thee; hissed, and wagged their head over the daughter of Jerusalem; Is this the city, whereof[6] men say, Perfection of beauty, Joy of the whole earth?

---

[5] *Parable thee;* or, attest, as LXX. μαρτυρήσω, and so the Hebrew word; yet better *Vulg. cui comparabo*, making עוּד borrow as it were the sense of חוּד and חִידָה.

[6] *Whereof.* Heb. שׁ for אֲשֶׁר, an idiom supposed to belong to the earliest

CH. II. P. All thine enemies opened their mouth against thee; hissed, and gnashed *their* teeth, as they said, We have swallowed; yea, this is the day for which we looked, we have found, we have seen.

A.V. II. 16.

Ayn. JAHVEH has fulfilled what he designed, accomplished his speech, which he commanded from days of old; he has ruined, and not pitied; yea, he has gladdened over thee enemy, exalted horn of thine adversaries.

Tz. Their heart cried to the LORD; O wall of Zion's daughter, drop like a river tears day and night; give thyself no rest, let not the pupil of thine eye be still.

Q. Arise, cry out in the night at the beginning of the watches; pour out like water thy heart before the face of the LORD; lift up thy hands toward him for the life of thy children, that faint for hunger at the top of every street.

R. Regard, JAHVEH, and behold, to whom hast thou done thus—shall women eat their fruit, infants of the hand's span?[7] Shall priest and prophet be slain in the LORD's sanctuary?

Sh. Young man and aged lie along the ground in the streets; my maidens and my choice youth are fallen by the sword; thou hast slain in the day of thy wrath, slaughtered, not pitied.

T. Thou callest, as on a day of gathering my terrors[8]

---

stages of the language, and found in the book of Judges four times; yet not in the Pentateuch, and rare enough to be suspicious, until we reach the borders of Chaldaism. Still later, and more decidedly Chaldaising, almost Rabbinical, is the compound relative particle שׁל.

[7] *Of the hand's span*, or rather infants in arms, nurselings, as in v. T. LXX. νήπια θηλάζοντα μαστούς.

[8] *My terrors.* Better, my flight, or exiling. LXX. παροικίας, and so in Jer. xx. 3, 4, 6, Magor-missaviv.

Ch. II. round about; neither in the day of JAHVEH's wrath has been fugitive or survivor; what I nursed and made to grow, the enemy has consumed.

A. V. II. 22

III.

Ch. III. A.[9] I am the man that has seen affliction by the rod of his fury; me he led, and brought into darkness, and not light; yea against me he turns again and again his hand all the day.

A. V. III.

B. He has wasted my flesh and my skin, broken my bones; he has laid siege against me, and brought bitterness and sorrow around; in dark dungeons has he laid me, like the dead of old.[10]

G. He has fenced around me, lest I go forth, weighted my chain; yea, when I cry and shout, he encloses my prayer; he fences my ways with hewn stone, entangles my paths.

D. He is a bear lurking for me, a lion in coverts; my ways he watches,[11] to tear me in pieces; he has set me desolate; he has bent his bow, and made me as a mark for the arrow.

Heh. He has driven into my loins the offspring of his quiver; I became a mockery to all my people, their song all the day; he glutted me with bitterness, drunkened me with wormwood.

---

[9] Not only each triplet, but each clause of the triplets, in this chapter commences alphabetically. After A thrice, we have B thrice, and so on.

[10] The second verse has a clause, which, with Jerome's version, *sempiternos mortuos*, might be rather more tolerably quoted for eternal pain, than some of the usual testimonies.

[11] *He watches*, i. e. quasi סור vice שור exstaret scriptum. cf. Jer. v. 20 (A. V. 26), Hos. xii. 4 (A. V. xiii. 7) text. Mas., but the sense may be, he turns aside, makes me stray. *Vulg.* semitas meas subvertit. LXX. κατεδίωξεν.

Ch. III.   V. or F.   ¹² Yea, he ground my teeth with gravel, co-   A. V.
vered me with ashes; so that my soul turned loathing¹³   iii. 16.
from peace, I forgat prosperity; even I said, Perished my
strength,¹⁴ and my trust upon Jahveh.

Z. Remember my misery, and my wandering, the
wormwood and the gall; surely thou wilt remember, and
let my heart bend within me; this I recall to my mind,
therefore will I trust;

Ch. The mercies of Jahveh are surely not consumed,¹⁵
his compassions surely not come to an end; they are new
every morning, great is thy faithfulness: Jahveh is my
portion, saith my soul, therefore upon him will I trust.

Th. Good is Jahveh to them that wait for him, to the
soul that seeks him; good it is, that a man trust, and
wait quietly for Jahveh's salvation; good for a man, that
he bear the yoke in his youth.

Y. That he sit alone and be silent, because it is laid
upon him; that he humble his mouth to the dust, per-
adventure there is yet hope; that he give his cheek to
the smiter, be filled with reproach;

C. Since the Lord will not cast for ever; but though
he afflicts, yet he pities, according to the abundance of
his mercies; for he vexes not willingly, nor afflicts the
sons of man.

---

¹² On the first clause of this verse Jewish expositors (*e. g.* Jarchi in Phil.)
exemplify their painful literalism by inventing a story of the Jews in
Babylon being compelled to bake their bread in holes of the earth, and therefore to eat it be-gravelled!

¹³ *Turned loathing.* I prefer, with Philippsohn, the third person. So *Vulg.*
repulsa est a pace anima mea.

¹⁴ *My strength,* i. e. in effect, my existence, or life.

¹⁵ *Mercies are not consumed;* i.e. taking the verb, by a possibly Chaldaising usage, or from misreading, as a third instead of first person plural,
as the Chald. Targ. Jarchi, Ewald, and others, take it, and the sense per-
suades; though LXX. *Vulg.* Rosenm. Philipps. and others, with A. V. take
the first person, which is more regular. Jer. xlvii. 18 (A. V. xliv. 18.)

Y 2

Ch. III. L. To crush under one's feet all the prisoners of the earth; to pervert man's right before the most High; to entangle man in his cause, the LORD does not approve.

A. V.
III. 34.

M. Who is it that speaks, and it comes to pass, *if* the LORD has not commanded? Come not evil and good out of the mouth of the most High? wherefore murmurs living man, mortal for his own fault?

N. Let us search and try our ways, and return again to JAHVEH; let us lift up our heart with both hands to God in heaven; we have transgressed and rebelled, Thou hast not pardoned.

S. Thou hast covered with anger, and pursued us; thou hast slain, hast not pitied; thou hast made a covering for thyself with cloud, lest prayer pass through; thou makest us offscouring and refuse in the midst of the populations.

P. Opened against us their mouths have all our enemies; terror and snare is come upon us, desolation and ruin; mine eye runs down with rivers of water, for the ruin of the daughter of my people.

Ayn. Mine eye trickles down, and ceases not, without intermission; until JAHVEH regard, and look from heaven; mine eye troubles my soul, for all the daughters of my city.

Tz. They that hate me without a cause, chaced me with chace as a bird; they hemmed round my life in the dungeon, and cast stone upon me; the waters spread over me; I said, I am cut off.

Q. I called on thy name, JAHVEH, out of the lowest pit; thou heardest[16] my voice, hide not thy ear at my groaning, my crying; thou drewest nigh in the day that I called, thou saidest,[16] Fear not.

---

[16] The preterites of the second person, *thou heardest, saidest, pleadest, &c.*, are treated by some critics as imperatives, and perhaps rightly so.

Сн. III.   R. Lord, thou hast pleaded[16] the causes of my soul, thou hast redeemed my life: thou hast seen, JAHVEH, my wrong; judge thou my cause; thou hast seen all their vengeance, all their devices against me.

Sh. Thou hast heard, JAHVEH, their reproach, all their devices against me; whisperings of risers against me, and their murmuring against me all the day; in their sitting down, and their rising up, I am their jest-song.

T. Render to them requital, JAHVEH, after the work of their hands; give them heart's abandonment,[17] thy curse to them; pursue in anger, till thou destroy them from under JAHVEH'S heavens.

A. V.
III. 58.

IV.

Сн. IV.   A. How is darkened the gold! changed the fine gold! poured out the stones of the sanctuary at the head of every street!

B. The sons of Zion, that were precious, balanced with fine gold, how are they esteemed as earthenware pots, the work of the potter's hands!

G. Even the jackals loosen the breast, suckle their whelps; the daughter of my people is become cruel, as the ostriches in the desert.

D. The tongue of the suckling cleaves to his palate for thirst; the infants ask for bread; there is none to break it to them.

Heh. The feeders on dainties are desolated in the streets; they that were nursed in purple[18] embrace dung-hills.

A. V.
IV. 1.

---

[17] *Heart's abandonment;* a conjectural rendering, for the more authorized *heart's blindness*. The *shield* of LXX. and *Vulg.* is hopelessly wrong; the *covering* of Kimchi, though with no reference to the Mosaic veil of St. Paul, may be accepted. Instead of גנן, I have derived from מגן in the sense of מגר, but not without a wistful glance at the מכנינה of the previous verse.

[18] *Nursed in purple,* here of the Tyrian scarlet dye, so famous in poetical

Ch. IV. V. or F. Yea, the guilt of the daughter of my people has been greater than the sin of Sodom that was overthrown as in a moment, and no hands dealt stroke upon her.

A. V. iv. 6.

Z. Her nobles[19] were fairer than snow, whiter than milk; they were more ruddy in body than coral,[20] their figure of sapphire.

Ch. Blacker than coal is their visage; they are not known in the streets; their skin cleaves to their bones; it is withered, become as wood.

Th. Happy are the slain with the sword, more than those slain with famine; since these pine away pierced, for lack of fruits of the field.

Y. The hands of the pitiful women have boiled their own children; they became food for them in the ruin of the daughter of my people.

C. JAHVEH has accomplished his fury, poured out the fierceness of his anger; yea, kindled in Zion a fire, that devoured her foundations.

L. Little trusted[21] the kings of the earth, and all the inhabitants of the world, that adversary should enter, and enemy, the gates of Jerusalem.

M. Because of her prophets' sins, her priests' iniquities; that shed in her midst the blood of righteous men.[22]

---

illustrations, permitted in stripes to knights and senators, but restricted in full-length robe to the emperor only. But the Byzantine term, Porphyrogenetes, is explained to mean, born in a chamber of porphyry.

[19] *Her nobles.* Heb. Nazarites; *i.e.* her crowned ones; and so perhaps in Gen. xlix. 26, of Joseph, as crowned among his brethren. See my preface to Nahum, on *Minnezarim.**

[20] *More ruddy than coral;* or, brighter than pearls, the more usual sense of *Peninnah,* the rendering of which is here biassed by the verb *to redden.*

[21] *Little trusted;* or, affirmed. Comp. Isaiah vii. 8 (A.V. 9), Habak. ii. 3 (A.V. 4).

[22] In illustration of this verse, note our Lord's sorrowful cry, Luke xiii. 34.

* Vol. I. p. 432.

Cн. IV.   N.   They wandered blinded in the streets, they were defiled with blood; so that they could not, who would touch their garments:

S.   Away, unclean, *men* cried to them; away, depart, touch *us* not; though they migrate, yet they wander; *men* said among the nations, they shall be dwellers no more.

P.   JAHVEH's face *was* their portion;[23] he will no more gaze upon them; they regarded not face of priests, had no pity upon elders.

Ayn.   While we wait, our eyes fail, for our help, in vain; while we looked earnestly to a nation that would not save.

Tz.   They have tracked our steps, that we cannot walk in our streets; our end is near, our days are fulfilled; yea, our end is at hand.

Q.   Swift were our pursuers, above the eagles of heaven: on the mountains they followed us, in the desert laid wait for us.

R.   The breath of our nostrils, the Anointed of JAHVEH,[24] is taken in their snares; of whom we said, Under his shadow we shall live among the nations.

Sh.   Rejoice, and be glad, daughter of Edom, inhabitress in the land of Uz; yet over thee shall pass the cup; thou shalt drink thyself drunk,[25] and strip thyself bare.

T.   Daughter of Zion, thy guilt is ended; thou shalt no more be led captive: visited is thy guilt, daughter of Edom; the veil taken off thy sins.

---

[23] *Jahveh's face was their portion.* LXX. πρόσωπον Κυρίου μερὶς αὐτῶν· οὐ προσθήσει ἐπιβλέψαι αὐτοῖς.

[24] *Anointed of Jahveh;* or, Messiah; the person meant is Zedekiah, as his fate is described, 2 Kings xxv. 5. Hence may be suggested the speech, St. Luke xxiv. 21.

[25] *Drink thyself drunk,* i.e. the cup of wrath and conquest, as in Obad. ver. 16., Hab. ii. 9, (A.V. 15, 16, 17).

A. V. iv. 14.

V.

(Vulg. Oratio Jeremiæ prophetæ.)

Ch. V. 1. Remember, JAHVEH, what is come upon us; re- A. V. v. gard, and behold our reproach; our inheritance is turned to aliens, our houses to strangers.

2. Orphans are we and fatherless; our mothers as widows: our water we drink for money; our wood comes to us at a price.

3. Upon our necks we are driven with yoke; we toil, no rest is granted us; we stretch hand to Egypt; to Assyria, to be satisfied with bread.

4. Our fathers sinned; they are no more: we bear their iniquities: slaves rule over us: deliverer is none out of their hand.

5. For our lives fetch we our bread, from out the drought[26] of the desert; our skin, like the furnace, is parched, because of the scorchings of hunger.

6. Matrons in Zion are shamed, maidens in the cities of Judah; princes are hung up by their hand; the face of elders disregarded.

7. Warriors bear the mill-stone, and young men stumble in the stocks: elders cease from the gate, warriors from their song.[27]

8. Ceased the joy of our heart, turned into mourning our dance, fallen the garland from our head; ah! woe for us, that we have sinned.

9. For this has grown faint our heart; for these things bedimmed our eyes; for Zion's mount, which is desolate, that foxes stray upon it.

---

[26] *Drought;* or, sword, as all the Versions; but not so well.

[27] *From their song;* or, better, are their jest-song; as in the penultimate verse, S. of ch. iii.

V. 10. Thou, JAHVEH, abidest for ever; thy throne from A.V. v.19. generation to generation; wherefore dost thou forget us eternally? forsake us, for length of days?

11. Turn us again, JAHVEH, to thyself, that we may return; renew our days, as of old; nay, if thou hast utterly rejected us,[28] thou art wroth over us exceedingly.

---

[28] *Nay, if thou hast utterly rejected us;* or, disjunctively and interrogatively, hast thou made us reprobate? art thou so exceedingly wroth? The word is *Ma'as*, whence Calvin's "horribile decretum." But the eternity of God is, in a manner which might be strangely applicable to a modern and different question, here made a ground of faith in disbelieving the perpetual reprobation of Zion.

EZEKIEL.

Ch. I. 1. It was in the thirtieth year, in the fourth *month*, A. V. 1. the fifth of the month, as I was in the midst of the exile on the river Chobar,[1] that the heavens were opened, and I beheld visions of God;* 4. and as I looked, behold a stormy wind coming out of the north, a vast cloud, and a fire enfolding itself, with brightness about it, and out of its midst the colour of bright bronze, out of the midst of the fire; 5. and out of its midst the likeness of four living creatures; and this was their appearance; they had the likeness of a man; 6. and every one had four faces, and every one had four wings; 7. and their feet were straight feet; and the sole of their feet *was* like the sole of a calf's foot: and they sparkled like the colour of burnished brass. 8.

---

[1] *Chobar.* So Vulg. and LXX. "*Chobar* aut nomen est fluminis, aut . . . . Tigrim significat et Euphratem, et omnia magna et gravissima flumina, quæ in terrâ Chaldæorum."—*Hier.* He fancied the word meant *weighty.* "Est autem Chobar flumen Mesopot. quod oritur super Rasænam in montibus "Masiis, et prope Circesium Euphrati illabitur, Ptolemæo *Chaboras* dictum." —*Rosenm.* One of Mr. Rawlinson's fanciful reconstructions would place it farther south.

* [2. In the fifth *day* of the month, which *was* the fifth year of king Jehoiachin's captivity. 3. The word of the Lord came expressly unto Ezekiel the priest, the son of Buzi, in the land of the Chaldeans by the river Chobar; and the hand of the Lord was there upon him.]

1—16. In the thirtieth year of his age, as priest, or from Josiah's restoration of the law, or more probably from the Chaldæan era of Nabopolassar, 625, therefore in the year 595, Ezekiel, deported under Jehoiachin, has a vision of the Divine majesty, suggested by the sculptured para-

Ch. I. And *they had* the hands of a man under their wings on A. V. 1. 8. their four sides; and they four had their faces and their wings. 9. Their wings *were* joined one to another; they turned not when they went; they went every one straight forward. 10. As for the likeness of their faces, they four had the face of a man, and the face of a lion, on the right side: and they four had the face of an ox on the left side; they four also had the face of an eagle. 11. Thus *were* their faces: and their wings *were* stretched upward; two *wings* of every one *were* joined one to another, and two covered their bodies. 12. And they went every one straight forward: whither the spirit[2] was to go, they went; *and* they turned not when they went. 13. As for the likeness of the living creatures, their appearance *was* like burning coals of fire, *and* like the appearance of torches: it went up and down among the living creatures; and the fire was bright, and out of the fire went forth lightning. 14. And the living creatures ran and returned as the appearance of a flash of lightning.

15. Now as I beheld the living creatures, behold one wheel upon the earth by the living creatures, with his four faces. 16. The appearance of the wheels and their work *was* like the colour of chrysolith: and they four had one like-

---

[2] vv. 12 and 20. *The spirit;* so best; or else, the inclination of the creatures. Strangely the LXX. introduce ἡ νεφίλη, from some misunderstanding.

---

bles in stone of the land in which he sojourned, yet tinged by reminiscence of the bases of the gigantic lavers in Solomon's temple, 1 Kings vii. 29. Forest, field, air, with lion, ox, eagle, add awe, strength, swiftness as attributes to the human figure, which disputes, or combines, with the ox (chap. x. 14), the attributes of cherub, or griffin, the Asiatic symbol of heavenly ministration. 17—28. All

ness: and their appearance and their work *was* as it were a wheel in the middle of a wheel. 17. When they went, they went upon their four sides: *and* they turned not when they went. 18. As for their tires,[3] they were so high that they were dreadful; and their tires, *were* full of eyes round about them four. 19. And when the living creatures went, the wheels went by them: and when the living creatures were lifted up from the earth, the wheels were lifted up. 20. Whithersoever the spirit[3] was to go, they went, thither *was their* spirit to go; and the wheels were lifted up over against them: for the spirit of the living creatures *was* in the wheels. 21. When those went, *these* went; and when those stood, *these* stood; and when those were lifted up from the earth, the wheels were lifted up over against them: for the spirit of the living creatures *was* in the wheels. 22. And the likeness of the firmament[4] upon the heads of the living creatures *was* as the colour of the awful crystal,[5] stretched forth over their heads above. 23. And under the firmament *were* their wings straight, the one toward the other: every one had two, which covered on this side, and every one had two, which covered on that side, their bodies. 24. And when they went, I heard the noise of their wings, like the noise of great waters, as the voice of the Almighty, the voice of speech, as the noise of an host: when they stood, they let down their wings. 25. And there was a voice from the firmament

---

[3] *Tires;* or, felloes, i.e. wheelbands=wheels.
[4] *Firmament.* Heb. *rakia,* Gr. στερίωμα. Lat. firmamentum, whether solidity, or only expansion were the idea of the Hebrew term.
[5] *The awful crystal;* like the sacred sky, the awe-inspiring, and infinite æther, of Homer.

---

directions of space are simultaneously open to the movement, of that which the Providence of the living God ani-

Ch. I. that *was* over their heads, when they stood, *and* had let A.V. 1.25.
down their wings.

26 And above the firmament that *was* over their heads *was* the likeness of a throne, as the appearance of a sapphire stone: and upon the likeness of the throne *was* the likeness as the appearance of a man above upon it.

27. And I saw as the colour of bright bronze, as the appearance of fire round about within it, from the appearance of his loins even upward, and from the appearance of his loins even downward, I saw as it were the appearance of fire, and it had brightness round about. 28. As the appearance of the bow that is in the cloud in the day of rain, so *was* the appearance of the brightness round about. This *was* the appearance of the likeness of the glory of the LORD. And when I saw *it*, I fell upon my face, and I heard a voice of one that spake.

II.

Ch. II. 1. And he said unto me, Son of man, stand upon thy A.V. II, 1.
feet, and I will speak unto thee. 2. And the spirit entered into me when he spake unto me, and set me upon my feet, that I heard him that spake unto me. 3. And he said unto me, Son of man, I send thee to the children of Israel, to a rebellious nation that hath rebelled against me: they and their fathers have transgressed against me, *even* unto this very day. 4. For *they are* men hard of face and stubborn of heart. I send thee to them; and

---

mates with one life. Hence St. John's imagery in the Apocalypse, iv. 6—8. The chrysolith is our topaz, called here Tarshish, as coming from the Guadalquiver in Spain.

II. 1.—III. 3. Lifted symbolically on to his feet, really into the full enjoyment of his powers, by the quickening influence of God's spirit, that is, of God Himself, the pro-

Ch. II. thou shalt say to them, Thus saith the Lord God. 5. A.V. ii. And they, whether they will hear, or whether they will forbear, (for they *are* a rebellious house,) yet shall know that there hath been a prophet among them.

6. And thou, son of man, be not afraid of them, neither be afraid of their words, though briers and thorns *be* with thee,[6] and thou dost dwell among scorpions: be not afraid of their words, nor be dismayed at their looks, though they *be* a rebellious house.

7. And thou shalt speak my words unto them, whether they will hear, or whether they will forbear: for they *are* most rebellious. 8. But thou, son of man, hear what I say unto thee; Be not thou rebellious like that rebellious house: open thy mouth, and eat that I give thee.

9. And when I looked, behold, an hand put forth to me; and, lo, a roll of a book therein; 10. and he spread it before me; and it *was* written within and without: and *there was* written therein lamentations, and mourning, and woe.

---

[6] *Though briers and thorns be with thee;* or, better, nettles and thorns; yet both words may signify merely rebellious and hostile. So *Vulg.* increduli et subversores sunt tecum. So nearly the Chald. Targ. LXX. παροιστρήσουσι καὶ ἐπισυστήσονται ἐπὶ σὲ κύκλῳ. *Burning* and *elevation* seem the sense of the roots. The word scorpions has also been taken metaphorically for scourges, as in 1 Kings xii. 11, and it seems proverbial. The phrase *Son of Man*, vv. 1—8, if taken merely as man, as the sons of Israel are Israelites, is partly a sign of the Aramaising stage of the language in Ezek. and Dan., but also has a propriety here in contradistinction to the Eternal God. So again in the New Testament we may contrast the phrase with Judaism, as denoting our Lord's large humanity; but also with Deity, in that his great humility took upon him the form of a servant: for thus the Infinite expressed itself in the finite.

---

phet conceives of his mission to a refractory and rebellious nation, as requiring the strength which comes of obedience and truth. Yet is he not to fear. His message, most anthropomorphically bodied forth, but to be conceived by

Ch. II. 11. Moreover he said unto me, Son of man, eat that A.V. III. 1.
thou findest; eat this roll, and go speak unto the house
of Israel. 12. So I opened my mouth, and he caused me
to eat that roll. 13. And he said unto me, Son of man,
cause thy belly to eat, and fill thy bowels with this roll
that I give thee. Then I ate *it*; and it was in my mouth
as honey for sweetness.

III.

Ch. III. 1. And he said unto me, Son of man, go, get thee unto A.V. III. 4.
the house of Israel, and speak with my words unto them.
2. For thou *art* not sent to a people deep of lip, and
heavy of tongue, *but* to the house of Israel; 3. Not to
many populations deep of lip, and heavy of language,
whose words thou canst not understand. Surely had I
sent thee to them, they would have hearkened unto thee.
4. But the house of Israel will not hearken unto thee; for
they will not hearken unto me: for all the house of Israel
are stern of brow, and hard of heart. 5. Behold, I have
made thy face strong against their faces, and thy brow
strong against their brows. 6. As a diamond harder than
rock have I made thy forehead: fear them not, neither be
dismayed at their looks, though they *be* a rebellious house.
7. Moreover he said unto me, Son of man, all my words
that I shall speak unto thee receive in thine heart, and
hear with thine ears. 8. And go, get thee to them of the
captivity, unto the children of thy people, and speak unto

---

us spiritually, is of dirge or funeral songs, sighing, and
cries of woe. Yet, as in the beginnings of religious life
comfort or sweetness comes with faith, so the Divine messages though tragical, taste sweet as honey.

III. 4—11. As Capernaum worse than Tyre, so the
familiar friends in Israel will be harder to persuade, than

them, and tell them, Thus saith the Lord GOD; whether they will hear, or whether they will forbear. 9. Then the spirit took me up, and I heard behind me a voice of a great rushing, *saying,* Blessed be the glory of the LORD from his place. 10. *I heard* also the noise of the wings of the living creatures that touched one another, and the noise of the wheels over against them, and a noise of a great rushing. 11. So the spirit lifted me up, and took me away, and I went in bitterness, in the heat of my spirit; but the hand of the LORD was strong upon me.

12. Then I came to them of the captivity at Tel-abib,[7] that dwelt by the river Chabor, and where they sat I sat,[8] and remained there astonished among them seven days.

13. And it came to pass at the end of seven days, that the word of the LORD came unto me, saying, 14. Son of man, I have made thee a watchman unto the house of Israel: therefore hear the word at my mouth, and give them warning from me. 15. When I say unto the wicked, Thou shalt surely die; and thou givest him not warning, nor speakest to warn the wicked from his wicked way, to

---

[7] *Tel-abib*, the hill of corn. Vulg. acervum novarum frugum. An Aramaically named place, near the Chabor, whether in Mesopotamia, or Chaldæa proper. Jerome, in his way, allegorises the word Tel-abib. "Sementem Judaici populi promittebat."

[8] *And where they sat, there I sat.* Vulg. sedi, ubi illi sedebant. But LXX. τοὺς ὄντας ἐκεῖ. The Masora, turning אשר into אשב, is not to be followed textually, though right in meaning.

---

men of strange speech. Therefore the consciousness of his message must make firm the prophet's brow. 12—14. When his resolve is taken, the Divine vision fades away, with rushing awe. 14, 15. Unwillingly, yet impelled by the burden of thought, he goes to those who sat by Chabor's stream, and sits with them in stupor, as Job and his

III. save his life; the same wicked *man* shall die in his iniquity; but his blood will I require at thine hand. 16. Yet if thou warn the wicked, and he turn not from his wickedness, nor from his wicked way, he shall die in his iniquity; but thou hast delivered thy soul. 17. Again, When a righteous *man* doth turn from his righteousness, and commit iniquity, and I lay a stumblingblock before him, he shall die: because thou hast not given him warning, he shall die in his sin, and his righteousness which he hath done shall not be remembered; but his blood will I require at thine hand. 18. Nevertheless if thou warn the righteous *man*, that the righteous sin not, and he doth not sin, he shall surely live, because he is warned; also thou hast delivered thy soul.

A. V.
III. 18.

19. And the hand of the LORD was there upon me; and he said unto me, Arise, go forth into the plain, and I will there talk with thee. 20. Then I arose, and went forth into the plain: and, behold, the glory of the LORD stood there, as the glory which I saw by the river Chabor: and I fell on my face. 21. Then the spirit entered into me, and set me upon my feet, and spake with me, and said unto me, Go, shut thyself within thine house. 22. But thou, O son of man, behold, they shall put bands upon thee, and shall bind thee with them, and thou shalt not go out among them: 23. And I will make thy tongue cleave to the roof of thy mouth, that thou shalt be dumb, and shalt not be to them a reprover: for they *are* a rebellious house. 24. But when I speak with thee, I will open thy mouth, and

---

friends for seven days. 16—21. When the period, symbolizing difficulty, is complete, the nature of the preacher's mission becomes known to him. 22—27. Retiring into solitude for clearer reflexion, he feels all the weight of the

Ch. III. thou shalt say unto them, Thus saith the Lord God; He that heareth,[9] let him hear; and he that forbeareth, let him forbear: for they *are* a rebellious house.

A. V. III. 27.

IV.

Ch. IV. 1. Thou also, son of man, take thee a tile, and lay it before thee, and pourtray upon it the city, *even* Jerusalem: 2. And lay siege against it, and build a fort against it, and cast a mount against it; set the camp also against it, and set *battering* rams[10] against it round about. 3. Moreover take thou unto thee an iron pan, and set it *for* a wall of iron between thee and the city: and set thy face against it, and it shall be besieged, and thou shalt lay siege against it. This *shall be* a sign to the house of Israel. 4. Lie thou also upon thy left side, and lay the iniquity of the house of Israel upon it: *according* to the number of the days that thou shalt lie upon it thou shalt bear their iniquity. 5. For I have laid upon thee the years of their iniquity, according to the number of the days, three hundred and ninety days: so shalt thou bear the iniquity of the house of Israel. 6. And when thou hast accomplished them, lie again on thy right side, and thou shalt bear the iniquity of the house of Judah forty days: I have appointed thee each day for a year. Therefore thou shalt

A.V. IV.

---

[9] *He that heareth, &c.* Rev. xxii. 11.
[10] *Battering rams;* or, chieftains.

Divine hand, yet the impediments which will be as bonds on lip and limb. But there is One that can loose him.

IV. 1—8. In a country, where bricks are monumental records, a tile serves to portray in symbolical map, Jerusalem's siege under Jehoiachin or Zedekiah, with circumvallation and famine. As the Egyptian bondage had

Ch. IV. set thy face toward the siege of Jerusalem, and thine arm *shall be* uncovered, and thou shalt prophesy against it. 8. And, behold, I will lay bands upon thee, and thou shalt not turn thee from one side to another, till thou hast ended the days of thy siege.

A.V. iv. 7.

---

been traditionally 430 years, a like period is here assumed in imagery, with the larger part, 390 years, assigned to Samaria on the left, or north, (4) and a shorter period of 40, but still indefinite, augured for Judah.

FRAGMENTARY VERSION OF ISAIAH LIII.

Ch. LII. 1. Behold *then* my Servant shall be *counted* wise, he shall be exalted and extolled, and be very high.   A. V. LII. 13.

2. Even as many abhorred thee; so marred was his visage more than man, and his form more than the sons of men.

3. So shall he cause to start many nations; the kings shall shut their mouths at him: since what had not been told them they have seen; and what they had not heard they have experienced.

4. But who had believed our message: and to whom was the ARM OF THE ETERNAL revealed?   A. V. LIII. 1.

5. For he grew up before him as a tender plant, and as a root out of a dry ground: he had no form nor comeliness that we should look upon him; and no beauty that we should desire him.

6. He was despised and rejected of men; a man of sorrows, and acquainted with grief: and as one that hideth his face from us, he was despised and we esteemed him not.

7. Surely he bare our griefs, and carried our sorrows; yet we esteemed him stricken, smitten of God and afflicted.

8. But he *was* wounded for our transgressions, *he was* bruised for our iniquities; the chastisement of our peace *was* upon him; and with his sores we were healed.

9. All we like sheep had gone astray: we turned every one his own way: and the Lord laid on him the iniquity of us all.

10. When he was oppressed, then he humbled himself,

Ch. LII. and opened not his mouth: as a lamb is brought to the slaughter,[1] and as a sheep before her shearers is dumb, so he opened not his mouth.

A.V. LIII. 7.

11. By distress and condemnation he was taken away; and who would recount his posterity? for it was cut off from the land of the living: for the transgression of my people was the stroke upon them.

12. [2]Men assigned his grave with the wicked, and his tomb with the oppressor; though he had done no violence, neither *was there* guile in his mouth.

13. Yet it pleased the LORD to bruise him; he hath put *him* to grief: when his soul shall make an offering for sin,[3] he shall see a seed, that shall prolong his days, and the pleasure of the LORD shall prosper in its hand.

14. After the travail of his soul, he shall see and be satisfied: by his knowledge, since my servant is righteous, he shall justify many: for he bore their iniquities.

15. Therefore will I divide him *a portion* with the great, and he shall divide the spoil with the strong: because he hath poured out his soul unto death: though he was numbered with the transgressors; and he bare the sin of many, so that he had place among the transgressors.

---

[1] Jer. xi. 18 (A.V. 19).

[2] Ewald beautifully reads עָשִׁיק (an oppressor): but if we retain עָשִׁיר the sense is the same, as the parallel רָשָׁע clearly shows. So Luther: so Calvin. The wealthy — the proud. Also for בְּמֹתָיו Ewald reads בָּמוֹרְתָיו hillocks, or grave; possibly: but needlessly.

[3] Proverbs xxi. 18.

THE END.

www.ingramcontent.com/pod-product-compliance
Lightning Source LLC
Chambersburg PA
CBHW032351230426
43672CB00007B/668